THE Care AND Maintenance OF A New England Home

250+ Home Upkeep Items That EVERY
New England Homeowner Should Be Aware Of!

TOM LOPATOSKY

*This book is dedicated to my Mother – Lucy Lopatosky –
whose incredible work ethic, gritty perseverance, and caring
nature set a bar astronomically high for any human being,
but one that I enjoy chasing on a daily basis.*

Contents

Foreword
by Tom Reber

When Tom Lopatosky asked me to write the Foreword to "The Care And Maintenance Of A New England Home," I was both surprised and honored. Having known Tom for several years and working in the Home Improvement industry myself as a contractor and coach, I've seen firsthand the myriad of questions that contractors face when it comes to home care. This book took me by surprise on several levels.

Firstly, it's an exceptional resource for homeowners. With over 250 tips and bits of advice, this book educates and assists you in taking care of your home. From understanding "what is a flue" to knowing "when you need to use a primer" to "what you should do in the Springtime to care for your home," this book is packed with money-saving tips and preventative measures. These tips ensure that the seemingly minor issues that pop up don't escalate into major problems costing you tens or even hundreds of thousands of dollars. This book is essentially a cheat code for educating yourself so you can handle things on your own or prepare for conversations with Home Improvement contractors.

Speaking of contractors, this book is also a fantastic resource to refresh the knowledge you already have. Yes, you've worked on hundreds, maybe even thousands of homes. But how often do you encounter an uncommon issue or situation and need a quick refresher to ensure you're doing things correctly? I know I frequently need that in my own business. While the subtitle reads "250+ Home Upkeep Items That EVERY New England Homeowner Should Be Aware Of!," I believe this book also doubles as a handy field guide for contractors on the go.

One aspect that didn't surprise me when I received an advanced copy of the book was the depth of Tom's educational approach. I've always known Tom to be an overachiever who tackles everything with intense focus, attention to detail, and passion. He brings all of this to the book, resulting in OVER 500 pages of in-depth knowledge and practical advice.

Whether you're a homeowner wanting to handle some tasks yourself or properly vet your contractor, or a home improvement contractor aiming to expand your knowledge base, you will find immense value in every item covered in this book.

Thank you, Tom, for writing this book. Thank you for sharing your wisdom with the world. Thank you for your efforts to restore respect and dignity to the trades.

Tom Reber

Contractor, Entrepreneur, & HGTV Host

Introduction

Living in New England is super fun and I think at times taken for granted by many of us who are fortunate enough to call it home.

Though we do not typically have to work through some of the most severe elements of weather which the majority of folks in other parts of the country are exposed to (earthquakes, tornadoes, hurricanes, and the like – although we do get a taste of each of these on occasion!), we certainly get a good dose of our own weather challenges!

We are located in an area of the country that gets above average rainfall and our exposure to ocean-related weather items (wind, salt, etc.) definitely adds their own spice to the mix.

Our unique weather patterns test our homes in ways that other areas of the country simply do not have to navigate through.

Between bitterly cold Winters, damp Springs, super-hot Summers, and a bag of tricks weatherwise in Fall, our homes are no stranger to being tested with weather that runs the gamut.

On top of all this, there is an old saying that if you do not like the weather in New England, just wait 5 minutes as it most likely will change.

Over the years I have found this to be VERY true!!

As one can imagine, these severe fluctuations in both types of weather and the pace at which they can sometimes occur, leads to the constant expansion and contraction of our homes.

Whether on the exterior or the interior (or in-between!), the constant pulling and tugging which naturally happens, leads to a whole host of maintenance issues that should really be addressed as they pop up.

Many may think that having Central Air Conditioning in their homes or more contemporary climate control systems helps alleviate this to some degree, and to some degree it does.

However, the innards of the walls in our homes - i.e. where the (wood) framing is located – is not shielded from the dimension-bending properties which are triggered by variations in humidity and moisture; this leads to things on the interior which often may need to be tended to.

When I was coming up with the design for the cover on this book, a number of people reached out to me and, in knowing the title, questioned, "Why a lighthouse?"

After all, although synonymous with New England, a lighthouse isn't really what most folks live in, whether in New England or anywhere else!

The answer to this is twofold.

The lighthouse in the picture is the Portland Head Light Lighthouse in Cape Elizabeth, Maine, and if the main living quarters are focused on, vs. the lighthouse itself, one will notice that the house is VERY much in-line with what one might envision when thinking about the look of a New England home, particularly one on the water.

The lighthouse comes into play when coupled with this beautiful home as my Mother LOVED lighthouses.

My Mother was my best friend (and perhaps biggest inspiration) and passed away at the early age of 50 on January 16, 1997, from Creutzfeldt-Jakob disease (an extremely rare fatal degenerative brain disorder of which very little is known).

I often wonder what her thoughts would be if she happened to still be alive and listening to my weekly home improvement radio show, reading one of the home improvement articles I had written that are published in various magazine and newspaper publications each month, or perhaps even settling down and reading this book while on the beach on a warm Summer day as she used to enjoy doing as an escape from a busy life in the city.

While I am certainly far from Ernest Hemingway (one of my Mom's favorite authors, who I, ironically, years ago had the chance to climb up the lighthouse in the park directly across the street from his home/museum in Key West, FL), I sense that she would enjoy the book, though knowing her I am sure she would have had plenty of questions while reading through it!

Curiosity answering questions such as those my Mom may have had as they relate to home improvement is definitely what has led me to what you are going to find as the backbone in the following pages when reading further and further into the book.

There are no shortages of home improvement items which need tending to, and there are a number of ways in which to tackle them.

From peeling paint to questions about rotting wood and leaking roofs, while on the surface many of these subjects may seem to be universal, I assure you that pretty much each item in this book can have a spin on it that is uniquely New England.

There are features of homes in New England which although very common there, are just not found as prevalently anywhere else.

One example of this is plaster.

Where plaster is used throughout residential construction in New England, in many areas of the country you would be hard-pressed to find a single plasterer, never mind be able to choose amongst a number of them to see who would be the best fit to help your specific project (other areas of the country are more apt to use wallboard, taping, and compounding).

Another great example is the type of wooden housing stock which is often thought about when thinking of a New England Home – think naturally weathering wood shingle siding with white trim as one example.

Knowing the ins and outs of how wood siding should be maintained is critical for a good number of New England homeowners.

Whereas stucco and masonry siding may be the way to go in many Southern and Southwest areas of the United States, our wood sided homes – even those converted to vinyl siding on their exteriors – simply function differently than those in other regions of the country.

Understanding what to look out for, different tips and guidance as to how to really go about caring for your home, and how to approach some of the larger home improvement items you may come across could be tremendously beneficial.

My aim is that this book, though nowhere near touching on every single imaginable item of what to be mindful of, might at the very least provide solid direction, and serve to be as comprehensive a guide as possible, in setting a firm foundation of basic home improvement knowledge that hopefully any New England homeowner may find solid value in.

The Care and Maintenance
of a New England Home

What is a Flue?

A while back, I messaged one of our masons that we had a client who needed to have a flute on their chimney fixed.

Thankfully, although it would have been the perfect opportunity to do a deep dive into chop-busting, our mason chose otherwise and was relatively tame with the snarky remarks that ensued, which I very much deserved.

"A flute? LOL, you mean a flue?"

Yikes! I immediately felt like an idiot.

So, what exactly is a flue (or, in my case, in this instance, a 'flute'!)?

A flue is an integral component of a chimney system and plays a crucial role in safely expelling combustion gases from a home's heating appliance, such as a fireplace, wood stove, or furnace, to the outside atmosphere. Consisting of a passage or duct that runs through the chimney, the flue serves as a conduit for the removal of smoke, gases, and other byproducts generated during this combustion process.

Structurally, the flue is typically constructed of fire-resistant materials, such as clay tile, metal, or concrete, and is designed to withstand high temperatures and corrosive elements. It is strategically positioned within the chimney to ensure efficient ventilation and prevent the buildup of dangerous gases, such as carbon monoxide, inside the home.

In New England, the flues we run into most often on the residential side are made out of clay tile.

One of the primary functions of the flue is to create a draft, or upward flow of air, which pulls combustion gases out of the heating appliance and directs them safely outside. This draft is generated by the temperature differential between the air inside the flue and the cooler air outside, as well as by the buoyancy effect of hot gases rising. Proper drafting is essential for the efficient operation of the heating appliance and for minimizing the risk of backdrafting, which occurs when combustion gases are forced back into the home.

The flue must be properly sized and maintained to create an effective draft and prevent obstruction. The size of the flue is determined by factors such as the type and size of the heating appliance, the height and diameter of the chimney, and the local building codes and regulations. A flue that is too small can impede airflow and lead to poor combustion, while one that is too large may result in excessive cooling of the gases and reduced draft efficiency.

Regular maintenance of the flue is essential to ensure ongoing functionality and safety. Over time, creosote, a highly flammable substance formed by the condensation of combustion byproducts, can accumulate on the walls of the flue. If not removed through chimney sweeping, creosote buildup can pose a serious fire hazard and impair draft performance. Additionally, debris such as leaves, bird nests, and other obstructions may block the flue, further hindering airflow and increasing the risk of carbon monoxide poisoning—hence the value of the stainless-steel chimney caps that we often see protecting the flues above the chimneys in many homes.

In addition to facilitating ventilation, the flue also serves as a barrier to prevent heat transfer and protect the surrounding structure from fire damage. By containing the intense heat and flames produced by the heating appliance, the flue helps to prevent the ignition of combustible materials within the chimney and adjacent walls.

A flue—not 'flute'!—is a critical component of a chimney system that functions to safely expel combustion gases from a home's heating appliance to the outside atmosphere. By facilitating efficient draft, preventing obstruction, and protecting against fire hazards, the flue plays a vital role in ensuring the safe and effective operation of the heating system. Regular inspection, maintenance, and cleaning of the flue are essential to its continued functionality and the safety of the occupants.

Quick and Easy Interior Do-It-Yourself Projects

During the colder months of the year, particularly during the homestretch of winter, it is understandably easy to get a bit antsy; however, wanting to do "something" productive around the home, especially a project outside, may not be the best option given the weather.

Keeping in mind that everyone's home situation, age of home, style of home, etc., can be quite different, here are some ideas for interior 'Do-It-Yourself' (DIY) projects around the home that can be considered 'quick and easy' and can refresh your space without requiring extensive time or resources:

Paint an Accent Wall: Choose a bold color and paint one wall in a room to serve as a focal point. This can add visual interest and personality to the space without painting the entire room.

Create a Gallery Wall: Gather a collection of your favorite photos, prints, or artwork and arrange them on a wall to create a gallery-style display. Mix and match frame styles and sizes for an eclectic look.

Install Removable Wallpaper: Use removable wallpaper to add pattern and color to a room without the commitment of traditional wallpaper. It's easy to apply and remove, making it perfect for those who like to change up their decor on occasion.

Create Custom Shelving: Install floating shelves in any room to add storage and display space. Customize the size and placement of the shelves to suit your needs and style.

Upgrade Cabinet Hardware: Replace outdated cabinet knobs and pulls with new hardware to give kitchen or bathroom cabinets a fresh look. This simple update can make a big difference in the overall appearance of the room.

Hang Statement Curtains: Choose curtains with a bold pattern or vibrant color to add personality to a room. Hang them high and wide to create the illusion of larger windows and make the room feel more spacious.

Create a Fabric Headboard: Make a DIY headboard using plywood, foam padding, and fabric. Simply upholster the plywood with the fabric of your choice and attach it to the wall behind your bed for an instant style upgrade.

Make Decorative Throw Pillows: Sew or non-sew your own decorative throw pillows using fabric remnants or old clothing. Mix and match patterns and textures to add visual interest to your sofa or bed.

Create a Cork Memo Board: Turn a plain corkboard into a stylish memo board by covering it with fabric or wrapping paper and framing it with molding. This provides a functional yet decorative way to display notes, photos, and reminders.

Install Under-Cabinet Lighting: Add LED strip lights underneath kitchen cabinets or bathroom vanities for extra task lighting. This not only improves visibility but also adds a modern touch to the space.

These quick and easy DIY projects are perfect for adding style and personality to your home without major time or financial investments. Plus, they're a fun way to unleash your creativity and make your space truly your own at a time of year when outside projects simply may not be feasible.

Can Vinyl Siding Be Painted?

_____

With a question that seems almost counterintuitive on the surface, we receive numerous calls every year asking if vinyl siding can be painted.

If vinyl siding in one's home is meant to eliminate (or at least dramatically reduce) maintenance, then why would someone want to entertain painting it?

There are actually many reasons why.

One reason is that perhaps the person whose home it is inherited the vinyl siding and never liked the color but did not think that it could be painted.

Another reason is that someone falls in love with the home during the buying process, loves everything except the color, and is bummed because the siding is vinyl, but they are not sure if it can be painted.

Yet still another reason is if someone had lived in their home for decades and the vinyl siding is a bit faded (which is wholly conceivable if the home was vinyl-sided well before the much more color-retentive vinyl siding products of today!).

Regardless of the reasoning, the answer is a simple 'Yes!' The challenge, however, is painting it correctly so that there are no problems down the line.

When deciding to paint vinyl siding, the most critical component of any paint system applied is the prep process.

Certainly, the vinyl siding should be properly cleaned.

After cleaning, the surface should be dry and free from as much "chalking" as possible.

Once these conditions are satisfied, the next step is to make sure the correct 'bonding primer' is applied.

If this step is not done properly, subsequent coatings could start to peel in "sheets" if the correct bond does not exist between the finish coat system that is applied and the vinyl surface that is being painted.

Upon successful application of the bonding primer, the finish coat can now be applied.

A 'vinyl-safe' finish coat should be utilized. If there are any questions about whether a product or specific color is okay to use on vinyl siding, the best bet would be to consult with thel paint supplier from whom the product is being purchased to confirm that everything is ok to use.

Both the bonding primer and finish coat should be applied using a 'sprayed application,' preferably with an airless paint sprayer (utilizing a brush to 'cut in' where necessary and obviously making sure that all surrounding surfaces are properly protected).

Because of the variety of nuances involved, painting vinyl siding is super tricky, and the best results are accomplished when done by an experienced professional.

An important note is to make sure that after all products have been applied and given a chance to thoroughly dry, someone goes around the home and ensures that each and every seam where the vinyl comes together is "freed up" and makes sure that there are no paint-oriented products which could prevent the natural expansion and contraction of the vinyl siding itself.

Painted vinyl siding, if done properly, should have an almost infinite time period associated with it in terms of when it will need to be done again, as paint products on vinyl are not nearly as susceptible to peeling as they are on wood products, and the color retention of paint products on vinyl today vastly supersedes that of those previously available on the marketplace.

If you are contemplating having your vinyl-sided home painted, I would not let the naysayers influence you.

If done properly, the results may be more beautiful and long-lasting than many folks would ever imagine possible!

How I Prevent Mold on Bathroom Ceilings

The list of items that I have found of 'things that get people concerned around the home' reads almost like a frightful scroll of 'heart-dropping-into-stomach' moments…

- The discovery of peeling paint

- The discovery of an annoying leak which subsequently cannot seem to be properly sourced

- The discovery of a broken pane of glass on a window or a window that will not properly open/close/lock

- I can go on and on.

One of the items highest on the list is the discovery of some type of mold. While certainly there can be 'one-offs' like a random patch of mold that is simply related to a recent leak—and there are definitely grave causes of concern, such as the spread of a deep case of toxic black mold that goes unnoticed in someone's basement for years—perhaps one of the more frustrating examples of mold is the mold that is found on someone's bathroom ceiling that no matter what they do, they simply cannot get rid of.

Fortunately, I have worked through countless examples of this specific situation and have been able to come up with a process to help even the most discouraged of homeowners work through this type of scenario.

There are a number of tactics I would initially steer folks toward in eliminating the mold.

Here is my checklist:

- Make sure there is a bathroom ceiling fan (especially in bathrooms with a shower/bathtub)

- Ensure the ceiling fan is functioning properly (toilet paper test)

- Make sure the ceiling fan is correctly vented to the outside of the house (preferably through the roof if possible)

- Clean all of the existing mold (prior to doing so, if there is a concern that the mold is of the harmful variety, have the mold tested by a professional testing company and then have the mold cleaned by a professional remediation company)

- Ensure the surface is well-prepped

- Apply a mold-killing primer to the entire ceiling

- Properly apply a mold-resistant finish coat

Adhering to these steps should get you where you need to be in terms of stopping the mold once and for all.

If, for some reason, this develops into one of those extremely rare instances where the mold returns, a more drastic approach would be recommended as there may somehow be mold trapped deeper into the building material of the ceiling, and at that point, the recommendation would be to take down and dispose of the existing ceiling, hang a new ceiling (I prefer blue board and plaster), and repeat the painting process recommended above from there.

Though there are many occurrences around the home can be very disheartening, having mold return on a bathroom ceiling after seemingly countless attempts to eliminate it can be top of the list of irritating dilemmas.

As maddening as these situations may be, there is a path to work through them—as there almost always is—just be sure that your approach is methodical and in line with what is recommended, and rest assured that this will be one more thing that can be crossed off the 'things that bother me about my house' list.

Put Your Pride Aside—Fix the Leak!!!

Often, I am called upon to help a homeowner figure out why something in their home is leaking and what can be done to fix it properly.

I have been fortunate to build a career out of being somewhat of a 'leak whisperer' and be able to pinpoint an issue homeowners near and far have battled with over the course of history—where is that leak coming from and how can we stop it before things get worse?

Any veteran homeowner will tell you that having a leak can often be a course of frustration to the point that every time they hear that there is rain in the forecast, they cringe internally, their heart starts quickly palpitating, or perhaps feels as though it drops right into their stomach.

Leaks can be annoyingly challenging to diagnose, particularly if you are not accustomed to looking for the source.

This predicament becomes even more pronounced if the leak is coming from some type of flashing nuance around windows, doors, roofs, chimneys, dormers, etc., where the average homeowner may not even begin to know where to start to look.

If the source of the leak is found, it should obviously be important to address it as fast as you can!

However, I have had quite a number of instances recently where, as crazy as it may sound, I literally have shown the homeowner who had called me in to help find the leak where the leak was EXACTLY coming from, and the homeowner then thanked me and turned to say that they were going to "go after the roofer who didn't flash something correctly" or "make the window company come back and fix the missing drip cap areas around their window install."

Open palm, insert face.

This is all fine and dandy, but this challenge is certainly twofold.

First, if things were not done correctly and have risen to the point where outside experts are being called in to help find the leak, what makes you think it is going to be easy to get the initial company back to correct things properly and that if they do come back, that they will actually properly fix things?

Secondly, the longer this process drags on, the more water you are likely to take on, which increases the likelihood that you will have to work through some type of rotted wood or even mold challenge when things finally get fixed.

If at all possible, once the leak's source is recognized, the leak should be neutralized as fast as possible!

While "going after" an erring tradesperson or making someone come back to fix something that was not done properly in the first place may feel like the right thing to do, rot, mold, and things getting damaged by continually leaking water could care less about your pride and will continue to wreak havoc until they are properly fixed.

Leaks are not something that should be played around with.

The mere action of the leak is annoying enough.

Chasing leaks with empty cooking pots every time it rains is not fun, and continuing to do so because you want to make another person/entity "pay" in some way, shape, or form for their actions may very well be an exercise in futility, while time your home is possibly becoming more damaged and the cost to correct things will undoubtedly continue to rise in the process.

Stop playing around.

Find where the leak is coming from and get it fixed ASAP.

Your home (and bank account) will thank you for it as the sooner it is fixed, ultimately, the less damage there will be to pay to fix in the long run.

What are the Advantages of a Slider Window, and How Do You Properly Install One?

Slider windows—also known as sliding windows or gliding windows—offer several advantages that make them a popular choice for many homeowners. Here are some of the reasons why:

Ease of Operation: Slider windows are easy to open and close. They operate on a horizontal track, allowing you to simply slide one pane over the other to open or close the window. This ease of operation makes them a convenient choice for areas where reaching or operating a crank handle might be challenging.

Space-Saving Design: Since slider windows don't protrude outward, they are a space-saving option, making them suitable for areas with limited clearance This can be particularly advantageous in smaller rooms or where external features like walkways or landscaping limit the space available.

Contemporary Look: Slider windows often have a sleek and modern appearance, making them a popular choice for homeowners who prefer a contemporary aesthetic. They can contribute to a clean and uncluttered look in both residential and commercial settings.

Ventilation: Slider windows provide excellent ventilation. You can open one side or both sides of the window to allow fresh air to flow into the room. This can be especially beneficial in areas where cross-ventilation is desired.

Cost-Effective: Slider windows are often more cost-effective than some other window types, such as casement windows or double-hung windows. This can make them an attractive option for budget-conscious homeowners.

Unobstructed Views: The design of slider windows typically includes larger glass panes and narrower frames, providing unobstructed views of the outdoors. This feature is especially appealing if you have a scenic view that you want to enjoy from inside your home.

Low Maintenance: Slider windows are relatively low-maintenance. With fewer moving parts compared to some other window types, there are fewer components that might require regular upkeep or repairs.

Versatility: Slider windows come in various sizes and configurations, making them versatile for different architectural styles and room layouts. They can be customized to fit specific design requirements.

Despite these advantages, it's important to note that no window type is universally ideal. The choice of window style depends on factors such as personal preferences, the architectural style of the home, climate considerations, and budget constraints.

From an installation standpoint, installing a slider window is a task that requires careful attention to detail to ensure proper fit, insulation, and functionality. Here's a general guide on how to install a slider window. Please note that this is a simplified overview, and you should always follow the specific instructions provided by the window manufacturer:

Materials and Tools Needed

- Slider window
- Flashing tape
- Shims
- Caulk

- Screws
- Screwdriver/drill
- Level
- Measuring tape
- Pry bar
- Insulation

Procedure

Measure and Prepare: Measure the opening where the slider window will be installed to ensure that the window fits properly. Remove any existing window or debris from the opening. Check the sill for levelness. If it's not level, you may need to make adjustments.

Apply Flashing Tape: Apply self-adhesive flashing tape to the sill. This helps prevent water infiltration. Extend the tape up the sides of the opening, ensuring a proper seal.

Place the Window: With the help of at least one other person, lift the slider window into the opening. Rest it on the sill and center it.

Check for Level and Plumb: Use a level to ensure that the window is both level and plumb. Shim as necessary to achieve the correct alignment.

Secure the Window: Once the window is level and plumb, secure it in place by screwing it into the frame. Follow the manufacturer's guidelines for screw placement.

Insulate the Gaps: If there are any gaps around the window frame, use insulation to fill them. This helps with energy efficiency and prevents drafts.

Apply Exterior Sealant: Apply exterior-grade caulk around the perimeter of the window, sealing the joint between the window frame and the opening.

Install Interior Trim: Install interior trim around the window to cover any gaps between the window frame and the wall. Use finishing nails to secure the trim.

Check Operation: Test the sliding mechanism of the window to ensure it operates smoothly. Make any adjustments as needed.

Apply Finishing Touches: Clean any excess caulk or debris from the window and surrounding areas. If the window comes with a nailing flange, make sure it is properly integrated into the exterior siding.

Always refer to the installation instructions provided by the window manufacturer, as they may have unique requirements or recommendations. If you're unsure or uncomfortable with any part of the installation process, it's advisable to seek professional help. Proper installation is crucial for the window's performance and energy efficiency.

How to Pick the Correct Paint Sheen

Certainly, one of the more asked questions that I receive when I am having conversations about painting, whether interior or exterior, is what sheen of paint should be used when painting the surfaces that are being coated.

While the decision really is situational depending on who is viewing the freshly painted surface, both right afterward and in the future, certain common themes should be considered when determining what sheen makes the most sense for you individually.

Terminology can vary from one paint manufacturer to another, but as a general rule of thumb, here is list of paint sheen terms, listed from lowest to highest sheen, that you may run into most often:

- Flat
- Matte
- Low Lustre
- Satin
- Semi (or Soft) Gloss
- Gloss
- High Gloss

There are some universally accepted truths that should be considered while evaluating which sheen to choose for your project:

- The higher the sheen, the easier the surface will be to clean.
- The higher the sheen, the easier any defects in the surface that is painted will be able to be seen.
- In terms of the exterior, the higher the sheen, the more natural resistance against the sun's ultraviolet rays, and therefore the more fade resistance.

Some sheens are looked to as the 'go-to' sheens for specific surfaces, almost regardless of the situation.

Take ceilings as an example. North of 97% of the ceilings we paint are done in a 'Flat' sheen.

The few exceptions I have seen to this are in cases in which someone has an historic home where the ceiling has a super high sheen to it, and the owners are working to maintain this look.

This is generally because many times, 'back in the day,' the mindset was a bit opposite of what it is today, and it was much more commonplace to see a higher sheened ceiling.

The one other exception I have run into was where someone was aiming for a specific type of decorative look to their ceiling, either to mimic that of one of these historic ceilings or because it is their personal preference for a highersheened ceiling.

On the opposite end of the spectrum would be the exterior-facing side of entry doors—particularly front ones!

In these cases, a higher sheen is preferred, more so for aesthetic purposes than anything else (these higher glosses also tend to be SUPER easy to clean!).

While it is not always necessarily a 'High Gloss' (though in many cases a 'High Gloss' is definitely desired!!), doors in general are painted a higher gloss than one might utilize on other areas of their exterior.

Keep in mind that whether it is the rare instance of it being used on a ceiling, in the application of the exterior side of an entry door, or any other substrate that the finish may be being applied to, the higher the gloss, the trickier the finish will be to work with and the less forgiving any stray brush or application marks will be.

Regardless of the surface that is being painted, ease of application may be a short-term idea that you balance with the benefit of your utopic finish for the surface to which you are applying the paint.

Whether you naturally lean toward liking higher sheens, lower sheens, or somewhere in between, doing a small sample test before you paint is the best way to get an idea of what the sheen will ultimately look like when used on a larger scale.

Who knows?

You may even surprise yourself, and by testing in this manner, you might discover that a sheen you thought you would like, you do not actually like, and instead be led down a path where you choose a sheen you may have never thought of if you never tried testing!

How I Remove Ice From Walkways

Sometimes, no matter how advanced technology gets, the best methods of approaching a particular task may never be improved beyond the point they are currently.

A great example of this is a story my brother-in-law shared with me a while back.

He is now retired Navy, but during his career, he was an engineer within the armed forces who most of what he did he could never talk about—the Top Secret stuff—but I do remember an interesting tidbit that stuck in my mind when he was sharing of a recent trip he had taken.

Part of his job was to travel around the country to make sure that factories manufacturing military equipment components that were operating as optimally as possible.

From the teeny tiny to the humongous, I can only imagine how cool it must have been to see all of these things being made and also being entrusted by our government to make suggestions for not only the products themselves but also the ways that they were being produced.

The particular item that stands out in my head was made at—literally—an ancient factory in Pennsylvania where the tools they use today to make this one specific "widget" are the same tools that have been used for decades.

Not only have these tools remained the same for eons, but so have the specifications of the widget itself.

I quizzed my brother-in-law on this, and even when being pressed, he confidently relayed that for what the widget is called upon to do, it has maxed out in any other way it can be perfected, and the system that is used to create the widget also is maxed out in productive efficiency.

This widget cannot be improved further, and it is a good example of items around us under this same umbrella.

During the winters in New England, it is not uncommon for us to be faced with areas around our homes and businesses that become sheets of ice.

While there are all kinds of approaches to remove these annoying patches of ice, I tend to default to one which cannot be done any better than the way it is done already.

I am sure some folks would suggest to:

- Use some type of salt/ice melt; while this will work, there is the idea of what some folks will get concerned about the damage the product may cause to the areas around it

- Use heavier machinery; while this will work, not everyone has easy access to more robust equipment

- Use hot water; while this will work, there is a good chance—depending on the temperatures—that things will freeze again to some degree afterward.

So then, what do I suggest using?

An 'ice chopper.'

This is a long-handled tool that may even be multi-purposed to serve as a lawn edger during warmer times of the year.

The head of the ice chopper is made out of steel and looks almost like a tiny, uncurved dustpan.

An ice chopper is super effective, though it certainly does take a bit of elbow grease to use.

To use it, all you do is (a little bit at a time) hold the handle and strike the ice repeatedly in an up-and-down fashion.

As you do this, you will get more and more used to it and develop techniques to increase your efficiency.

Though there may be an extended time element involved, this will definitely work and help free the walkway of dangerous ice.

My guess is this is the same tool that folks used a hundred years ago and one that will still be relevant a hundred years from now.

Similar to the military widget, the ice chopper is a highly effective product that works as wonderfully today as it did decades ago and has very much maxed out all areas around it for improvement.

These examples are perhaps the perfect combination of the age-old sayings:

"If it ain't broke, don't fix it."

and

"The more things change, the more they stay the same."

Why Snow is Fool's Gold

When I was growing up (by the way, I hate to sound like "that guy"...), like many folks, our household was quite busy.

Between multiple siblings, school, activities, work, etc., the day-in and day-out house environment was quite "lived-in."

With exhaustive schedules the tidiness of the home was something that seemed like we were all 'fighting the tide' with.

So much so that when we had family get-togethers at the house (birthday parties and things along those lines), cleaning the house often looked like shoving items "temporarily" into places that they really did not belong out of the convenience of necessity.

Think of bedroom belongings shoved into closets and under beds, dirty pots and pans stashed in the oven, and numerous other examples of these types of things.

Though the house may look clean at first glance to someone visiting, the pristine appearance was nothing more than 'Fool's Gold.'

Similarly, when we receive a blanket of snow across our region, it often hides, and unfortunately delays, the inevitable.

Many folks enjoy the appearance of new-fallen snow—particularly the first snow of the season—and the way it seems to provide a serene appearance to the chaotic environment in which we all seem to operate on a daily basis.

The challenge, of course, is that although the snow may seem to provide a picturesque scene utilizing the Earth as its canvas, it is hiding (and possibly delaying from being addressed) items that really need attention.

While many of the repairs we conduct we are able to do year-round (roofing, carpentry, and the like), snow often briefly sets back thought processes of getting needed repairs either done or scheduled to be done.

Recognizing this, this is actually a tremendous opportunity to speak with folks in the home improvement industry and work toward getting on their calendars.

Whether they are exterior repairs such as a roof, a leak needing correcting, or a series of rotted wood, interior repairs such as a kitchen or bathroom update, windows needing to be replaced, or a room in need of painting, because so many put off thinking about addressing these types of things in the middle of winter, times when the "snow falls" are actually the PERFECT opportunity to have the conversation about getting on someone's schedule.

This has been a repetitive cycle, which I certainly have observed since we opened up shop in 1995.

Those who have planned properly have the best shot of getting their project scheduled at the most ideal time.

February is certainly far too late if you would like a project to be guaranteed to be done in the "Spring."

March is almost impossible to make this happen.

While it is absolutely conceivable that people reaching out to folks in those months could connect with a viable contractor and somehow arrange for their project to be done by the spring, January is actually the key to really ensuring that those wanting projects done by or in the spring are able to most likely lock in their ideal timeslots.

There is no doubt that snow can be breathtakingly pretty, but if you are someone who has a budding home improvement project that you are planning on doing in the near future, DO NOT fall victim to the Fool's Gold that encourages procrastination.

Instead, I very much implore you to take advantage of the downtime and work through the discipline of figuring things out and scheduling NOW before you miss out on YOUR most ideal time to have your project completed.

Why Chimney Maintenance is SO Important

When it comes to the holiday season, it should be obvious why chimney maintenance is so important.

After all, if you have a heavier-set gentleman in an enormous red and white suit, toting around large packages in a sack behind him, who—by any means necessary—is laser-focused on squeezing down your chimney, it is safe to say that your chimney had better be in good shape!

If your chimney is not in the best condition, one wrong move by the jolly guy and things could all come tumbling down and become quite messy quite quickly.

Because chimneys are typically situated far up high, thinking about keeping an eye on your chimney is probably not at the top of your mind on a daily basis.

Nor does it necessarily need to be.

However, every once in a while—ideally, at least annually—an inspection of the chimney should be conducted either by yourself (assuming you are able and know what to look for) or by a qualified party who is accustomed to checking out chimneys.

Though there are a variety of items that should be keyed in on, here are some of the ones that I tend to pay attention to when making sure that the portal for our friend from North is in as tip-top shape as possible:

- Chimney flashing: Is the condition of the chimney flashing satisfactory enough to do its job? Is the flashing performing as it should to not allow leaks? Is the lead used as flashing chewed up by squirrels with a beckoning leak waiting to happen?

- Chimney cap: Is the chimney capped properly? Does the chimney have a stainless steel cap, properly anchored, to help in guarding against allowing moisture in and/or protection from birds, squirrels, etc. (one of life's big mysteries is how these chimney caps do not allow birds and squirrels in, but they allow larger than normal sized humans with big furry coats to seemingly get in with ease...)? Is the cement cap swaddling the steel cap attached to the flue in good condition?

- Mortar joints: are the mortar joints of your chimney in good condition? Are they at the point (no pun intended) where they need to be cut and repointed?

- Flue/Liner situation: Does your chimney have a flue and/ or a liner? If so, are they in suitable shape?

- Sealant: When was the last time the brick on the exterior was properly sealed? Every natural brick chimney should be weather-sealed every few years to help extend the life of its brick and guard against premature deterioration.

There certainly are a number of items to be conscious of when doing the best you can to take care of your chimney.

Not only will being mindful of your chimney's maintenance help protect against significant one-time costs heading through the future, but it will also help ensure that on December 24th of each year, when perhaps the most unorthodox entrance into our homes by any welcome guest occurs, is able to safely continue year after year, just as it has since the early 1800s.

Diagnosing Leaks—the Last Resort!

Attempting to figure out where a leak is coming from can often be the ultimate exercise in frustration.

Whether the leak is coming from the interior, the exterior, or someplace in between, correctly figuring out where a leak is stemming from is enough to drive even the coolest, calmest, and most collected of us entirely batty!

Sometimes, you believe you have found "it" and corrected the problem only to hear the dreaded "Drip...Drip...Drip..." at some point after.

Totally NOT fun!

What convolutes these types of things even further is that sometimes the leak comes from multiple sources, some easier to diagnose than others.

So, what is one to do?

If you have a situation where you have tried to figure out a leak again and again, and it just does not seem to be stopping, what is now the next step?

While I am totally a fan of cerebrally eliminating possibilities and coming up with the correct answer (believe it or not), there are moments when I myself become stuck and begin to scratch my head.

When things reach this level, there is simply one logical thing that can be done to truly get a handle on the leak.

Begin to open up ceiling and wall areas from the inside out.

Though some folks may be more of fans of doing this from the outset, I prefer the process of elimination and 'when all else fails' then turn to open up the ceiling, or the wall, or whatever else makes sense to open up to more aggressively track the leak.

There is absolutely something to be said for doing this from the very beginning with the idea of ripping the proverbial band-aid off and getting to the root of the problem as fast as possible, and many times, this approach from the very beginning is actually quite necessary.

The challenge that I have with going right to this tactic immediately is that the solution to the leak could be quite simple if you are experienced enough to know what to look for.

My preference is to save ripping into the ceiling and wall areas until all other "kinder/gentler" avenues are exhausted.

I also believe that sometimes you simply do not have a choice, and it absolutely makes sense to begin opening things up to explore from the inside right from the very start of the leak discovery process.

This type of situation probably occurs about 20% of the time.

80% of the time, if you methodically work to analyze component by component where the leak most sensibly can be coming from, then you should be able to figure out how to neutralize the leaking without causing a bunch of collateral damage.

For times, however, when the mystery cannot be solved, strategically opening things up from the inside out and paying VERY close attention to any paths that the moisture may have created over time—so that the leak can be properly fixed—is an approach that is not only the obvious next step but also what I tend to view as the last resort for an accurate diagnosis and subsequent correction.

Powderpost Beetle Damage

If you have ever ventured into your basement and noticed a number of holes in its wooden components, you may have come across Powderpost beetle damage.

These holes typically are numerous in nature and are about the size of pencil lead or slightly larger.

Any bumping (even lightly) of the affected wood and a fine, flour-like powder will come flying out of these holes.

Scientifically speaking, Powderpost beetles are a group of dozens of species of woodboring beetles listed in the insect subfamily 'Lyctinae.'

As gross as it sounds, the larvae of Powderpost beetles can spend two to five years growing up in the wood components of your home.

This is because they hatch from eggs that are laid by the adults, and as the larvae grow into pupae and eventually their own adulthoods, they are constantly feeding on the wood, burrowing through the wood until fully grown and tunneling all the way out of the wood, leaving behind their exit holes in the process.

Utopically, wood arriving at the manufacturer is carefully examined to see if it has any signs of potential Powderpost beetle damage prior to being processed and ultimately shipped to market. It is not used if any damage is discovered or if the wood seems suspect.

Because Powderpost beetles lay their eggs in only wood that is unfinished, sealing the wood (via stain, varnish, or paint) will guard against Powderpost beetles being tempted to bore their way into it and do their thing, but if the Powderpost beetle is already in the wood, sealing the wood at that point clearly would be moot as it relates to that specific beetle.

There are quite a number of treatments available to help rid Powderpost beetles.

Though many are do-it-yourself-oriented, my best guidance is to hire a reputable pest control company, preferably one with some type of warranty, to most readily assure that the Powderpost beetles are properly gotten rid of.

Once Powderpost damage is recognized and treated, then the damage should be evaluated to determine what should be done from there.

We receive many calls on a yearly basis asking for help with regard to how to approach the damage that Powderpost beetles have caused.

Although often the damage is confined to certain areas, sometimes it can be quite significant.

Of greater concern, particularly in older homes, is when the Powderpost beetle damage is done to the structural components that are bracing the actual home itself and have developed into something that is now quite costly to fix.

Whenever possible, we prefer to shore up the wood members that have been affected. This has to be done very carefully and requires tradespeople with proper structural knowledge in order to execute this strategy correctly.

If the wood member is too far gone, surgically replacing—again, with someone who is quite knowledgeable with structural wood construction—should be utilized in addressing this type of repair.

While rotted wood, in general, can be overwhelming to deal with, having to work through situations where wood-boring pests are involved can be even more frustrating to a degree, as before repairs can even begin, the wood-boring pests have to be eradicated.

Powderpost beetles are at the top of the list of these types of insects as even though they do essentially the same thing as termites, they do so in a manner that is faster, on a larger scale, and once they are in the home, are more challenging to get rid of.

Certainly, working through a Powderpost beetle situation is not fun, but as with anything, the sooner that it is discovered and addressed, the easier and less costly it will be to work through.

How to Remove Oil Stains from Your Basement Floor

In New England, one of the things that is different about our homes in comparison to a lot of the other parts of the country is that we have basements.

With the absence of a basement, many other regions have their homes built on concrete slabs.

The pros and cons of having a home with a traditional basement vs. one built on a slab can certainly be listed and used to debate which overall is the "better" to have.

One of the items that come with the territory when one has a basement, particularly one that currently has or at some point has had an oil tank in the basement for its heating system, is the possibility that oil spillage—even in small amounts—can be a bit of a challenge to clean up.

If you have a basement floor with some type of coating on it, cleaning up any spilled oil will be MUCH easier than if the oil has penetrated a bare concrete floor and has had a chance to soak into its porous surface.

When the spill occurs on a basement floor that has a protective coating on it, simply dab any excess oil as best you can with some clean rags and then clean the area with a mixture of hot water and Dawn (my personal favorite because of its degreasing properties).

This method may have to be repeated a few times until the oil has been satisfactorily cleaned, but it will get you there!

Instances where the concrete floor is bare, and the oil has had a chance to REALLY soak in—perhaps over a period of 'years'!—are a bit more involved.

If the oil stain is "newer," my first plan of attack would be to soak up any excess oil with clean rags, then pour some traditional clay kitty litter on the stain and let it sit overnight.

The next step would be to sweep up the kitty litter the next day and then put some baking soda on the area where the oil had stained.

If you have older oil stains, the process would begin with the baking soda step.

Once the baking soda is in the area, let this sit for an overnight period of time.

The next day, clean up the baking soda and fire up the concoction of hot water and Dawn.

Now, with a stiff scrub brush, begin to work the stained area with the solution and the scrub brush.

The cleaning portion with the hot water, Dawn, and scrub brush may have to be repeated, maybe even a number of times, in order to truly get the area clean to the point where you are satisfied with the results.

As you work through the whole process, please remember to properly dispose of the cleaning materials that are used (the suggested way to do this may vary from community to community).

When all is said and done and dried out, you should have a clean surface that is free from the oil staining.

Once it is clean, it may be worth looking into some type of appropriate concrete coating that, once applied, may make the cleaning procedure much simpler (as discussed earlier) if oil were to get on the floor in the future.

Help! My Door Will NOT Close... Or Will It?...

One of the more challenging items around the home that, if you have been around long enough, you have surely had to navigate through at one point or another, is a door that just will not seem to close.

Even more perplexing are situations where the door seems to not close, and then all of a sudden, it seems to close ok.

How the heck does one deal with situations like this?

In fact, many times (though not always!), the older the home, the more likely these types of situations are to occur more frequently.

When this happens, what is happening, why is it happening, and how can it be better prevented?

The majority of the time, when a door does not seem to want to close, the door has expanded due to humidity or an excess of moisture in the air.

In the summer, when the air is more humid, doors are more likely to experience these types of issues, whereas during the times of the year when the air is "drier," the doors can contract a bit, and what may be a difficult door to open at one time of the year, can strangely be quite functional at another time of the year.

"But my doors are painted. How is the moisture causing them to expand?"

While your doors may indeed be painted, most commonly, folks neglect to paint/seal the top and bottom edges of the door, either at the time when they are initially installed or when maintenance is done to them at some point down the line.

To prevent this from happening or to correct this from occurring in the future, I have found that there are only two choices:

1) Wait until a time of the year when the door seems to be closing properly, take the door off its hinges, and properly seal its edges (prime and paint, seal with stain/polyurethane, etc.), correctly re-hang the door when its edges are dry.

2) If you cannot wait until a time of year when the door naturally becomes easier to operate, or the door has reached its point of no return and no matter what time of year, the door always seems "stuck," your best bet is to get a carpenter involved who knows and is comfortable with adjusting the door through a methodology of surgical planing and door and door jamb adjustments. When this is done, and the door seems to perform as it should, then apply the steps laid out in #1 above.

If either of these is enacted, your door should be at its optimum functionality from this point moving forward.

It certainly can be frustrating when a door, very literally, seems to be impossible to close at one moment in time, and then a very short time later seems to work just fine.

Fortunately, there are very simple reasons why these types of things tend to take place, and even more fortunately, they are nowhere near impossible to fix once you realize what is happening.

Do You Have Trees Growing out of Your Gutters?

_____

It is not unusual for me to be walking around someone's property with them and for us to notice something occurring that the client was completely unaware of prior to doing so.

This can range from a water stain that had gone unnoticed, rotted wood, to a coyote living in their back shed (true story!)...you name it!

Besides opening the door to your shed in the process of checking something out and instead finding a coyote peacefully sleeping, there are other items that are often discovered that are also unnerving.

One such discovery that falls into this category is when a tree (or a plant in general) is found to be growing in someone's gutter system.

Though I am not a plant expert, it does not take a botanist to know that if a tree or plant is growing in someone's gutter, the conditions obviously have to be ripe for it to be doing so.

One recent pre-Thanksgiving Day morning, I was conducting a walk-through around someone's home with them, and we both were a bit astonished to find a Christmas Tree (yes, literally a Christmas Tree!) growing out of the gutter system in the rear of their home.

While not necessarily the most cherished memory associated with the holidays that the client may wish to remember, and although not exactly what the client wanted to see during our walk, it clearly was also a blessing in disguise.

The tree called our attention to look deeper into an area of the home that was in severe disrepair.

If the tree had not been seen, we may not have discovered how gravely damaged the entire area encompassing the tree had become.

On my end, it allowed me to provide initial pricing to the client, which was more in line with what the cost of the project would ultimately end up being vs. discovering this great amount of damage after the project had already begun and then having to break the news to the client at that time.

On the client's end, although extraordinarily disheartening, at least this finding provided better insight in terms of what they were truly going to be up against as the project was delved into.

Certainly, this is a dramatic example of coming across things you may not normally do on a day-in and day-out basis, but nonetheless, it is a real-world sample of what may indeed be found when doing an inspection around your home and honing in on potential problematic key areas.

Not every time someone finds a tree or plant growing out of their gutter will lead to such a significant undertaking as this situation ended up being.

Many times, trees and plants seen growing out of someone's gutter system simply stem from a small pile of decaying matter in the gutter and are easily cleaned out.

Other times, they may call attention to a gutter system that is clogged and needs some cleaning and flushing in order to free itself of debris and become properly functioning again.

Whatever the case, my suggestion is to not get discouraged by seeing a tree (or plant) growing out of your gutter system and automatically assume that you have a real problem on your hands.

While this may end up being true, it may only be a call for some type of routine maintenance that needs to occur.

I believe this should actually be looked at as a positive, kind of like your gutter system raising its hand and saying, "Yoohoo, over here! We have an issue that needs to be looked at. Please help!!"

Just be sure to listen because ignoring this, once seen, truly could lead to bigger problems down the line, which could have been avoided if the opportunity to look further into things was done once awareness was raised that something funky may be going on.

Scared of the Dark?

Every year, when the length of daylight hours slowly shrinks as we head toward fall, the time of day that requires daylight to get things done naturally shrinks as well.

There are some tasks, though, that one would normally think you need daylight for, which may actually be more productively done in the dark.

As a parallel example, sometimes I am called to review an exterior project on a day when the rain is coming down like cats and dogs.

While certainly not fun, and while on the surface, this may seem like an absolutely horrible time to review the outside of someone's home, it is actually one of the best times.

The reason for this is when I look at someone's home when it is pouring out, it is much easier to recognize problematic areas that do not show their faces when the weather is much nicer.

An example of this is a gutter system that is not functioning the way it should be, a porch roof that is leaking, or any of a wide variety of items that may only be able to be observed during a period when rain is falling and, in some cases, the more rain, the better!

Perhaps equally counterintuitive is the exterior inspection of someone's home in the dark.

If it is thought that reviewing the exterior of a property in the rain is not ideal, what could possibly be the advantage of looking at someone's home in the dark???

Recently, I looked at two jobs, one in Barrington, RI, and the other in Glendale, RI, at a time of day (around 6 pm) that in other periods of the year might be full of daylight.

However, at the time of year when these particular site inspections were conducted, it was as if these took place in the middle of the night.

How can this possibly be a fruitful venture for anyone??

Quite easily, actually.

By working through the exterior of both of these projects in a period of literal complete darkness, this scenario forced me to use special lighting and focus even more intently on potential problem areas!

With the conditions being what they were, I was easily able to decipher complicated areas of rot that, in daylight, may not have been able to be as easily exposed.

I am only half-joking when I say the only better situation would have been if the skies had opened up and it started to pour on me during these inspections!!

There is an old saying, "One person's trash is another one's treasure."

While the majority of those in the industry may frown and push off to the side a chance to inspect a home on a dark (and/or rainy!) night, I cherish it!

For in thoroughly investigating something after night has set in (or rain begins to fall...), I believe one has the rare opportunity to, with focus, discover serious challenges that may exist on the outside of our properties, which may otherwise go undetected.

Protect Your Butts!

Recently, I was asked to testify in a court case that involved a bit of a messy situation between a contractor and a client.

In this particular situation, the contractor that was hired to do the work was confident that they were done with the project, less a minor punch list that would take a crew less than a day to complete.

The homeowner, on the other hand, was quite upset as they had hired the contractor to paint the exterior of their home, and there was actually a multitude of items that needing doing, so far beyond a punch list that there was almost more work to do now that the home is painted than there was before the project started.

I was asked to come in to provide testimony as to what my observations were on a day that the client had arranged for me to come out to take a look at things and review what I believed it would now take to fix what I saw.

Although there were a plethora of items that need correction, there was one specific item that would potentially take much more than a day to properly fix.

The home at the center of things is a cedar shingle home, with a mixture of decades-old shingles and shingles that are much newer.

Perhaps one of the bigger pet peeves of knowledgeable homeowners and experienced painters alike, the butts on the shingles were not properly done.

In this case, literally, like completely ignored.

This was an issue that I had on my list of items needing to be addressed, and it was one that would be glaringly obvious to anyone in the know looking at the home—very much sticking out like a sore thumb.

One of the representatives of the company referred to them as purely needing to be touched up.

Keep in mind many of these shingles were weathered to some degree, and butts, by nature, are the most porous part of the shingle.

These butts are now going to be a pain in the b**t to fix.

Not only do the butts themselves need to be methodologically doused in product, but while this is being done to make sure the butts are truly protected, it will be nearly impossible to avoid getting product on the faces of the shingles.

With the finish being utilized being a solid stain, this process will require tactfully facing off each shingle on the home in order to avoid lap marks and/ or flashing issues.

Please note that there is a distinguished difference between sealing the butt of the shingle itself and sealing the bottom of the shingle by caulking it into place.

The bottom of shingles (or clapboard, for that matter) should NEVER be caulked, no matter how much one may be tempted to do so for cosmetic purposes.

Caulking the butts of the shingle will prevent them from naturally being able to expand and contract and may result in some significant issues down the line.

Correctly sealing the actual butts, though, with a viable paint/stain system is an absolute necessity as because they are so porous, the butts of the shingles will be the entry point for any moisture that comes their way and will soak it up like a sponge if this is not properly prevented!

Unsealed butts could be as problematic, though in a different fashion, as caulking the butts.

When you come across an entire home that needs its shingle butts protected, this can certainly be a bit troublesome...particularly if the home was recently painted and the one responsible for the job is working to pass off a task such as the now correction of the issue as a mere punch list item.

How to Get Tape (and Other Adhesives) Off a Wall

Many of those who know me are aware that I am a bit of an earlybird.

So much so that my haircut each Saturday morning typically occurs around 5 am or so.

Sometimes a little later, sometimes a bit earlier, but on average, 5 am would be a safe bet as to where to find me on a Saturday morning, having my weekly trimming (yes, because I have SO MUCH hair to begin with!).

A RI State Trooper buddy of mine is usually next up as he prepares for his day as well.

Even in these early hours, typical barbershop banter occurs while the majority of those in our neck of the woods are still fast asleep.

Recently, I was in the barber chair at the tail end of my haircut. My friend walked in and, after a short time of sitting down, blurted out (paraphrasing), "Hey, I have this super strong double-sided sticky tape that just will not come off the wall no matter what I seem to try. What do you recommend doing that causes the least damage to the wall?"

As you may have guessed, I love it when folks ask me questions like this [hence the creation of the weekly radio show! (PROTalk Home Improvement Radio, every Saturday @ 2 pm on WPRO 630 AM and 99.7 FM in RI)].

With little hesitation after a few clarifying questions, I relayed a procedure I thought would not only be able to help remove the tape and its accompanying adhesive but did so in a fashion that would create minimal collateral damage to the wall it was attached to and the areas around it.

There is a product known as 'GOOF OFF' that can be bought at pretty much any hardware, paint, or big box store.

There are definitely other products that may do the trick, but the ones I am most aware of are much less aggressive and more suitable for helping in similar situations where a heavier hand may not be as necessary (an example would be the removal of regular Scotch tape and its associated adhesive or something along those lines).

For situations where a more robust approach must be taken (such as in the case of my friend where the product remaining on the wall was used to hang a baby monitor), after years of trying different methods, I believe GOOF OFF is the best bet.

Please keep in mind that there is a bit of an odor that comes along with using GOOF OFF, and you should definitely keep this in mind as you go about its use.

The method that I recommended to my friend is one that could help in a variety of similar dilemmas:

- Saturate (though not to the point where it is dripping!) the area that you are trying to remove the tape and its adhesive

- Wait five minutes

- Use a stiff putty knife to remove the adhesive

- Repeat until the adhesive is off

- Clean the area with warm water and Dawn (my brand preference) dish detergent (this serves as a degreaser)

- Rinse the area with a warm cloth to make sure the soap residue is removed

- After things have dried out, evaluate the wall to see if any minor surface/paint correction needs to take place, and if so, proceed appropriately to do so

If you find yourself in a similar situation, you will be surprised at how easily the area is cleaned up using this process.

Although being at the barbershop prior to the crack of dawn on a Saturday morning may not necessarily be the ideal time for folks to get their haircut, there certainly are bonuses in doing so, such as helping each other in navigating annoyingly frustrating situations such as a stubborn piece of thick tape that purely does not want to budge off a wall!

How to Clean Old Paint from Paintbrushes

A good paintbrush has always been a decent investment.

Yes, of course, you can buy what we in the industry refer to as a "throw-away" brush, but unless the project you are doing is literally a 'one-time' event, there certainly is value in learning to maintain this seemingly small investment.

If you want to know how to clean old paint from paintbrushes, it's not too hard!

Paintbrushes can get messy when we use them, but we can absolutely clean them up and use them again.

Here's how to do it...

Materials you'll need:

- Sheet or Dropcloth
- Old Paintbrushes
- Brush Cleaner
- Brush Comb or Wire Brush
- Water
- An Empty Bucket
- Mild Dish Soap
- A Soft Cloth

Step 1: Gather Your Brushes

First, gather all the old paintbrushes you want to clean. Make sure you have a safe place to work, like a table covered with a sheet or dropcloth to catch any drips.

Step 2: Rinse with Water

Take a brush and run it under warm water. This will get rid of some of the old paint. Be gentle when you do this so you don't damage the bristles (the hairs on the brush). Try to remove as much paint as possible by rinsing.

Step 3: Utilize 'Brush Cleaner'

This is a product that can be bought from a variety of places (box stores, hardware stores, online, etc.). Follow the instructions on the label.

Step 4: Soak in Soapy Water

Next, fill an empty bucket with warm water and add a little bit of mild dish soap (I prefer 'Dawn'). Gently put the paintbrushes into the soapy water. Let them soak for about 10-15 minutes. This will help to soften the old paint.

Step 5: Scrub Gently

After soaking, take a brush out of the soapy water. Use a 'brush comb' and/or a 'wire brush' (both available, again, at box stores, hardware stores, online, etc.) to gently work the bristles of the brush and get as much of the remaining paint off as possible. Follow this by using a soft cloth to softly work away any remaining paint. Be careful not to scrub too hard so you don't damage the bristles.

Step 6: Rinse Again

Once you've scrubbed away most of the old paint, rinse the brush under warm water again. Keep rinsing until the water runs clear and there is no more paint residue coming off the brush.

Step 7: Dry the Brushes

After cleaning, shake off any excess water from the brush. You can gently reshape the bristles with your fingers if needed. Then, lay the brushes flat on a clean, dry surface to let them air dry. Make sure they are not touching each other (there is also a manual device called a 'brush spinner,' which, with the aid of an empty five-gallon bucket, can be used to help accelerate the drying process).

Step 8: Store Your Clean Brushes

Once your brushes are completely dry, you can put them away for the next time you want to paint. The next time you have a project, they will work much better without old paint on them.

If you have trouble getting all the paint off in the first run-through, you can always repeat the actions that were laid out for better results.

Cleaning old paint from paintbrushes is a terrific way to take care of your brushes and save money by being able to use the same brushes again and again.

An even more solid tip, however, may be to remember to thoroughly clean your brushes after each use, which lessens the chance of a more difficult cleaning being needed in the future.

Can You Paint Pressure-Treated Wood?

_____

There is no shortage of old wives' tales in the field of home improvement.

As in many other aspects of life, there is guidance and methods of suggested approaches regarding different aspects of enhancing your home that not only couldn't be further from correct but also may unintentionally cause pain in the long run when they are followed.

Similar to how it does NOT actually take seven years for a piece of swallowed gum to digest in your stomach (as within a week, the indigestible synthetic portion of the gum should be passed through your system), pressure-treated wood CAN be painted…but not necessarily in line with the recommended methodologies that are out there.

Often, I hear clients relay that they recently had a pressure deck built and that the folks who built it said that they should wait six months to a year for it to weather before staining or painting it.

While I appreciate the thought process, this is certainly not true, particularly if you would like a fighting chance of having the coating applied last for any decent length of time (vs. peeling dramatically a short period of time after it is completed).

Simply letting pressure-treated wood "weather" for six to twelve months will not allow the pores of the wood to "open" themselves to the point where they will allow stain or paint coatings to come anywhere near adequately penetrating.

Pressure-treated wood really does not need to be "treated"—period.

The whole reason why it is manufactured the way it is is to have wood that will last without having to treat it after it is installed.

In other words, staining or painting it at any point (although possible) is counterintuitive to the intent behind the process that makes pressure-treated wood the product that it is in the first place.

Uncoated, pressure-treated wood can last for decades without beginning to rot.

However, some people enjoy the idea of a stained or painted deck and would really like to coat the pressure-treated wood if possible.

Although this can be done, letting it weather for six to twelve months after it is installed is not enough to, in good conscience, give the coatings that are applied any shot at lasting any reasonable amount of time.

The only REAL way to prepare pressure-treated wood (no matter the length of time that is waited in between the time it is installed and the time someone would want to coat it) is to properly "etch" it through a process such as media blasting (NOT traditional "sanding," sanding alone will not suffice in the context of this conversation).

Etching—via a method like media blasting—pressure-treated wood is similar to processes used in etching concrete garage floors prior to applying epoxy systems to them.

Once the pressure-treated wood is "etched" by the media blasting or like process, the pores of the pressure-treated wood will be "opened up" to a point where they are able to most comfortably accept the proper coating system (solid stain, porch, and floor enamel, etc.) that one would like to see in place.

Please keep in mind that any time a horizontal surface (think: deck floor, deck stairs, top of deck hand rail system) is coated, it is not a coating that should be guaranteed for any length of time due to a number of variables (snow/moisture resting directly on it for long periods of time, furniture being moved across the surface in many cases, people walking on them).

This being said, by correctly etching the pressure-treated wood, a chance is at least provided so that the product being applied has as great a chance as possible of soaking into the wood.

So, can you paint pressure-treated wood?

The short answer is "Yes" if approaching the preparation of its surfaces quite thoroughly.

Should you paint pressure-treated wood?

That is a whole different answer... From a structural standpoint, it is not really necessary to do so, but from a cosmetic standpoint, the inner designer in you may believe it is important and, in those situations, hopefully, there is some comfort in knowing that it can be done, though perhaps not necessarily with the approach that is most commonly thought about.

The Purpose of an Astragal

Imagine a big door, like the one you use to enter a school or a store. Sometimes, these doors are extra big and have two parts that swing open in the middle. These are called 'double doors.'

Now, imagine that the two parts of the door meet in the middle. There's a little space where they touch. This is where an astragal comes into play.

An astragal is a special thing used in construction to make sure those double doors work well and keep things inside safe and cozy. It's like a guardian for the doors.

How it does this:

Guarding the Gap: When you have double doors, they need to meet in the middle to close properly. But there's a small gap between them, like the space between your two front teeth. This gap can let in cold air, rain, or even bugs. An astragal is like a superhero cape that covers this gap. It seals the space and keeps the outside things from coming inside.

Keeping Warm and Dry: During winter, you want your home or commercial property to stay warm. The astragal helps with that. It keeps the cold air outside and the warm air inside. It's like wearing a warm coat on a chilly day. In the rain, it's like an umbrella for the doors. It stops the raindrops from getting in and making the floor wet.

Security Buddy: Astragals are also great at security. They make it harder for folks who do not have the best of intentions to try and push the doors open. It's like having a secret lock that only the people who should be inside can open. So, it helps keep everyone safe.

Now, you might wonder what an astragal looks like. It's not very big or complicated. Imagine a long, thin strip, like a ruler, but not for measuring. It's usually made of tough materials like wood, metal, or rubber. This strip gets attached to one of the doors, and when the doors close, it covers the gap, just like how your fingers come together when you clap your hands.

Astragals, particularly those made out of wood, can also be decorative with a design woven into their makeup.

Here are some common types of doors where you would find an astragal:

French Doors: French doors are a classic example of double doors, often used for patios, balconies, or interior room dividers. They have two doors that meet in the middle, and an astragal can be applied to one of them.

Exterior Entry Doors: Many homes and commercial buildings have double doors at the main entrance. These exterior entry doors often use astragals to create a good seal, especially to keep out cold drafts and precipitation.

Closet Doors: In some cases, closet doors are designed as double doors that open from the center. An astragal can be used to improve the appearance and function of these doors.

Astragals can be very useful.

Although pretty much operating in an unnoticeable fashion—which, if they are designed properly, should indeed be the case—they can be tremendously helpful in a variety of capacities.

What is a Cupola?

Falling under the category of features on your home that people often call one thing when they actually mean another would be the 'cupola.'

Perhaps my biggest pet peeve with these types of items is when someone refers to a 'downspout' on their home as a 'gutter.'

In the same realm, I see the term 'cupola' thrown all over the place.

Recently, I was out to breakfast with a good friend of mine who was discussing the concept of a 'widow's walk' but was referring to it as a 'cupola.'

If you are familiar with the concept of a 'monitor' or a 'dormer,' I have seen these items being called 'cupolas' in the past as well.

What exactly, then, is a 'cupola'?

The easiest way to describe it is a cupola on someone's home, which is like a tiny house on top of their big house. It's like a little hat for the house! It's not for people to live in, but it makes the house look special and helps with some important things.

Imagine you have a big, tall house, like a farmhouse or a fancy mansion. On top of this house, there's a small, cute building that looks like a little tower with windows (typically glass or vented with louvers).

That's the 'cupola'!

It's usually made of wood or metal and can be shaped like a dome or a small house with a pointy roof.

Now, you might wonder why someone would put a cupola on their house. Well, there are a few good reasons:

Letting in Light: One important job of a cupola is to let sunlight into the house. It has windows on all sides, so when the sun shines through, it brightens up the inside of the house. That way, people inside don't need to use as many lights during the day.

Ventilation: The cupola also helps with air. It's like a chimney on top of your house, but instead of smoke, it lets out hot air and helps fresh air come in. This keeps the inside of the house from getting too hot in the summer.

Looks Pretty: Besides being useful, cupolas make a house look charming and unique. They come in all kinds of shapes and sizes, and people often decorate them with fun things like weathervanes or fancy decorations. It's like dressing up your house!

These days, particularly in newer homes, cupolas tend to be more decorative than functional, and the majority of the time, they are securely fastened (in a water-tight manner) somewhere on a roof instead of being integrated with the actual structure itself.

Many times, you will notice cupolas being stationed on a garage roof, especially on newer homes in New England.

A cupola is a cute little addition to a house. It's like a tiny tower that helps with things such as bringing in light, keeping the air fresh, and making the house look unique and charming.

If you ever see a house with a little house on top, you'll know it's called a cupola, and it's doing something important if nothing more than enhancing the beauty of the home.

How to NOT Damage Your Gutters When Working in and Around Them

---

I am an admitted Obsessive Compulsive.

Although there are varying degrees of 'OCD' (Obsessive Compulsive Disorder), outside of the normal items that you may see related to this way of life with a quick Google search, there are certain things that attract my eye like a magnet, which may not normally bother anyone else.

As an example, I could be in one of our offices in a Production Meeting, and my eye may catch a smudge on the large glass windows outside the office doors.

Once noticing this, I would be internally irked until the smudge was cleaned off.

Though this may not seem quite odd in and of itself, the entire shop could be a disaster area, and my eye would still be focused on that one smudge on the glass.

Over the years, this has carried itself over to the field, where one of the things that drives me insane is seeing a 'ding' on someone's gutter.

I am not referring to a 200-year-old trough gutter system that has seen its share of battles over time, but the random ding that may be seen on a more modern aluminum gutter system whose surfaces would be perfect if it were not for this one blemish, often caused by someone knocking the gutter with a ladder.

Many homeowners—and even contractors—approach working in and around gutters the same way.

They lean their ladder directly on the gutter in order to access the inside of the gutter or a point above it.

While one may argue that if the ladder is leaned up on the gutter softly enough, the gutter should be OK, my counterargument to that would be that even if the eye-catching tiny dent is avoided by the gentleness of the "lean," there would nevertheless most likely be some type of mark where the ladder leaned up against the gutter and rubbed a tiny bit of its finish off.

Well then, if leaning a ladder on a gutter will create some type of a mark, whether it is a small dent or a paint blemish, how does one do what they need to around the gutter without placing the ladder on the gutter itself in cases where that is seemingly their only option?

Enter the 'Ladder-Max Standoff.'

This product is phenomenal in aiding to avoid these types of dings, dents, and marks, which can so easily happen when a ladder is placed directly on the gutter itself.

The way the Ladder-Max Standoffs function is they attach to the ladder by being placed over two of its rungs with two safety clips and then being put into place.

Once the Ladder-Max Standoff is properly attached to the ladder, the ladder can be erected and placed in an area around the gutter, as you normally would, but the Ladder-Max Standoff prevents you from actually touching the gutter with your ladder as you proceed to do your work.

The Ladder-Max Standoff will have the bumpers on each of its arms touch the area above the gutter—typically the roof—and you will be able to comfortably navigate in and around the gutter without the worry of impacting the gutter in any way.

The Ladder-Max Standoff is available from a number of places online, and we quite simply find it to be an invaluable resource that we utilize in the process of working on the exterior of people's homes.

Whether you have tendencies like me, such as having your eye drawn to the tiniest details and having small markings drive you batty to no end, or you just want to make sure that you are able to work around your gutters and minimize the chances of you causing any type of damage to them in the process, the Ladder-Max Standoff is a tremendous product that when used properly hyper-minimizes all of these kinds of concerns.

The Widow's Walk

It was DEFINITELY NOT intended to be creepy.

And I have no idea what makes my mind go to the dark side of things when I hear them being spoken of.

But ever since I heard the term 'Widow's Walk' years ago, my thoughts always have traveled to this vision of a ghostly figure of a woman (a Widow), dressed in black garb from the 1800s, alone, and pacing back and forth on this thing called a 'Widow's Walk,' until she is ultimately called home to the afterlife and reunited with her long-departed husband.

I have no idea why I think this way.

Maybe it is my moderate interest in the paranormal intertwined with my good fortune of being involved with tons of historical architectural projects, stirred together with whatever connotation the concoction of these realities mixed with the subconscious triggers of the sound of those words when they hit my brain all have with each other.

Who knows?

Reviewing how Widow's Walks came to be known, however, it seems that I am not TOO far off when I think this way...

A Widow's Walk is a special kind of platform, often found on the roofs of old houses near the sea (though I have also seen them deep in the woods!). It looks like a little balcony that sticks out from the roof. People used it a long time ago to watch ships coming in from the ocean.

So then, just why is it called a 'Widow's Walk'? Well, back in the olden days, many people relied on the sea for their jobs. Husbands, fathers, and sons would go out on ships to catch fish, trade goods, or explore new lands. But the sea could be dangerous, and sometimes the ships didn't come back when they were supposed to.

When families were waiting for their loved ones to return, the wives or mothers would often go up to the Widow's Walk and look out at the horizon. They would scan the waters with binoculars or telescopes, hoping to see the familiar sails of their family's ship. They would wait and watch, hoping and praying that their loved ones would come back safely.

Sometimes, though, the ships didn't return. They might have been caught in storms or lost at sea. When this happened, the families would be very sad. The wives would become 'Widows' (meaning that their husbands had passed away). The Widow's Walk got its name because it was a place where these women would stand, looking out to sea, waiting for their husbands to come back. Sadly, sometimes, they never did.

Today, Widow's Walks are not used in the same way as before. We obviously have much better ways to communicate with ships—like radios and phones—so we have a much clearer understanding of where they may be at any given time. But these old platforms are still there in many homes, reminding us of the past. They provide a glimpse into the history of coastal towns and the brave people who faced the challenges of the sea.

The next time you see a house with a little balcony on its roof, remember that it might have been a place where someone stood, looking out at the sea with hope and worry in their heart. It's a connection to the past and a reminder of the strength of families who waited and watched, even when times were tough.

One of my favorite Widow's Walks is on a building we worked on a while back in New Bedford, MA, right across from the New Bedford Whaling Museum.

Although my particular thoughts that are conjured up upon hearing the mention of the term 'Widow's Walk' are more imaginary in nature, this particular Widow's Walk is as much in line with what they were truly utilized for as one can think, and its positioning along the sea gels entirely with that.

Though my mind may always go to the place it does when hearing the phrase, it is also cool to recognize the true significance of this particular portion of many homes and think about how truly appreciative those who used them back in the day must have been (even if only subconsciously) as they anxiously awaited the return home of their loved ones from a long trip at sea.

Baker Staging

Unique names that are synonymous with the contracting trades are always fun things for me to delve into the origins of.

'Baker Staging' is no exception to this.

Years ago, seemingly every time we utilized it, I attempted to piece together in my mind why this particular type of apparatus was called 'Baker Staging.'

Have you ever seen a big house being built or repaired? A cool piece of equipment that helps workers work on these houses, especially up high, is called 'Baker Staging,' and even though it might sound like it's about baking, it's actually about working on houses!

But why is it called 'Baker Staging'? To find out, let's proceed to dive into the story of how this helpful tool got its name.

A long time ago, there was a clever builder named Baker. He was VERY good at building things, and he wanted to make it easier for folks to work on tall parts of homes. When homes are being built, obviously, the walls can go up pretty high, and builders need a safe and steady platform to stand on while they do their work.

Baker had a bright idea. He designed a special platform made of strong materials such as wood and metal. This platform could be attached to the side of the house. It gave builders a safe place to stand, almost like a stage for them to do their building "performance."

When other builders saw what Baker had made, they thought it was fantastic. They wanted to give credit to the smart builder who came up with this helpful idea. So, they decided to call it 'Baker Staging' to remember him and his brilliant invention.

Now, let's picture a house being built or repaired in general. The walls are going up, and the workers need to access certain parts, which may be a bit tricky to get to. That's when Baker Staging comes into play. It's like a strong ladder that goes up the side of a house. On this ladder, the builders attach the platform that Baker designed. This platform becomes their safe and solid spot to stand while they do their magic.

If builders and tradespeople didn't have Baker Staging, they may have a much harder time reaching the higher parts of the house. They might have to balance on wobbly ladders or find other tricky ways to do their work. However, with Baker Staging, they can work comfortably and safely, just like being on a stage.

Baker Staging's diversity as a tool is exemplified as it can be used both when houses are originally being built and when they need fixing or painting during the course of their lives thereafter. Imagine needing to paint the second-story windows of the inside front foyer of a house. Baker Staging allows painters to stand on the platform and reach these high spots without any trouble.

With the integration of self-locking casters, outriggers, and stabilizers, Baker Staging increases its usefulness by allowing workers to safely reach higher areas in the middle of a room vs. only utilizing it when working along walls.

The next time you see a big house being built and notice a platform attached to the side of it or happen to come across an erected piece of staging sitting in the middle of a high-ceilinged room, remember that it might very well be Baker Staging! Named after a bright builder named Baker, this invention helps workers work high up in the air while staying safe and steady.

Hitching Posts

Chances are you have passed by one numerous times over the course of your life.

Most likely, you have never given much thought as to what it was (assuming you even noticed it!), nor have you ever needed to.

However, if this were "back in the day," prior to the advent of the automobile, this object may have been super important to you.

These days, particularly those made out of granite, hitching posts are super cool features around one's property.

Hitching posts essentially look like stone columns rising up out of the ground, guesstimating about three and a half feet high or so, often with an iron ring firmly anchored into the granite.

When horses ruled the way, after dismounting, you would tie the horse to the hitching post so that you could go about your business.

While this particular action is from a long time ago, granite hitching posts are quite commonly seen in certain areas of the country and not only serve as extraordinarily interesting features but also have a certain historical significance.

Horse-hitching posts are "super cool"—on many levels! The granite they are frequently made out of is quite a tough rock that feels cool to the touch and can last a REALLY long time.

These posts may often have designs carved on them that look fancy and show how skilled people were back when they were made.

Hitching posts are like a window into the past, helping us imagine what life was like back when hitching posts were much more commonplace.

They are like a piece of living history that we can see and touch. The designs might be different, but the idea was always the same—to help keep horses safe.

Imagine a granite horse hitching post as a blend of art, history, and durability. The smooth and cool touch of the granite, the intricate carvings that tell stories of the past, and the strong nature of the material—all of these come together to make these posts something truly unique and special.

Regardless of whether you are a horse lover, an art enthusiast, or just someone who likes fascinating historical things, granite hitching posts have a bit of everything. They're a connection between the old days and today, and they serve as examples of both beauty and practicality.

Sometimes, I run into them in places I least expect them.

Recently, I came across one while visiting a potential client's house in an area of Rhode Island where I would not normally believe I would see one, and it actually took me by surprise!

I laughed to myself as I saw it nestled nicely right next to the mailbox post at this particular home. I could not help but wonder if the homeowner knew what it was or if they simply kept it around because they thought it was neat to look at.

Because I noticed it on my way out, I have not had a chance to interrogate the client about it yet (though I am chomping at the bit to give them a call and ask them if they know what they have in their front yard!).

Whether buried deep at someone's property in the middle of the woods or scattered about a more well-defined historic district, granite horse hitching posts carry a piece of history from long ago that many can't help but pause for a minute and wonder about life "back then" upon running into one, or for that matter, the innocent homeowner who suddenly discovers the significance of this object that they knew was pretty fabulous when they first saw it but had no idea what they had on their hands until the awesomeness of this item was somehow revealed to them!

Mad Dog

In my younger years, in certain friend groups, if you happened to mention the words 'Mad Dog' in conversation, imagery in the group's mind would often jump to thoughts of an extremely popular (in various circles) alcoholic beverage at the time called 'Mad Dog 20/20' (these days I have no idea if this is even still around or if so, exactly how popular it is!).

This same train of thought still rears its head from time to time when I bring up the term 'Mad Dog' in conversations, and it may trigger a memory from years ago with the client I happen to be speaking with.

While I am sure hearing the term 'Mad Dog' in talking with someone may lead to thinking of a night out on the town from decades ago or, literally, a 'mad dog,' it can often generate an inquisitive look from the person I am speaking with when reviewing how Mad Dog products have been instrumental to our company being able to warranty our work for as long as we do (five years).

Although they have a variety of products that we find VERY useful, Mad Dog's flagship product—their exterior primer—the glue (no pun intended) that has been holding our exterior paint jobs and procedures together for many years.

As part of our prep process, specifically in older homes that have a bit of peeling associated with them, after the surface has been brought to the point where we would consider it to be sound, we apply Mad Dog's exterior product.

The way we position it with our clients when explaining how it works is that Mad Dog is almost like a glue that, when touched, even days after it is applied, never seems to fully dry and has a certain "tack" to it—which is AWESOME because of the way that the Mad Dog product not only seems to suck in and stabilize the surface it is being applied to, but it also is super "grippy" for the subsequent products which follow in the application process.

Although there are a number of products on the market that claim to perform in the same manner that Mad Dog does, our preference is the Mad Dog product because not only does it have tremendous bond-enhancing qualities, but it also neutralizes tannin bleed—a characteristic these other products simply do not exhibit.

After the Mad Dog is applied, our next step is to coat the areas where the Mad Dog primer was placed with a coat of a latex primer (for a very long time, our preference in this step has been utilizing Benjamin Moore's Latex Fresh Start Primer).

Upon the latex primer completely drying, the finish coat process starts from there, and when that is completed, the paint job will be well on its way to lasting for years to come.

Over the years, I have seen dozens of specialty products and systems that guarantee in one fashion or another that their product or way of doing things is your best bet for maximizing the longevity of your exterior paint job. However, barring rare types of paint failures, the ultimate approach towards truly getting as long life as possible out of your exterior paint job could quite possibly rely on this Mad Dog primer, which has been the backbone of our exterior paint systems for many years, and one we do not plan on deviating from at any point in the foreseeable future!

How Do I Keep Birds from Hanging Around My Home?

Many years ago, I was approached by a client with a bit of a dilemma.

They had a number of birds that seemed to like to hang around their property.

While they may have been pleasant to look at and sweet to hear their voices, the stuff that they left behind was not as pleasant to look at and certainly was not sweet smelling.

Short of doing something detrimental to the birds, the client was a bit stumped as to what they could do to keep the birds away, but in a manner that was not harmful to them.

Enter 'Birdguard.'

We had the perfect solution for our client stemming from a company that makes this product.

'Birdguard' is metal strips of spikes that you strategically attach to whatever property you are attempting to keep birds away from.

Because of the height that is involved in the process of installing the Birdguard product, as well as the fact that the edges of the spikes are razor sharp, the average homeowner should probably not venture out to begin to attach them to their home.

Instead, a qualified contractor who is experienced in working with heights as well as (ideally) the Birdguard product itself may be the more preferred approach.

Once the strips are properly anchored in place and the spikes are set up, no bird in their right mind would aim to return to the area where they are placed and sit on the spikes.

One of the challenges is setting up the spikes in such a way that there is no room for the birds to sneak behind them (in areas that may be susceptible to allowing these types of open spaces) and continue to hang out.

While Birdguard may look archaic or perhaps even barbaric, it is extraordinarily effective and actually quite humane.

The metal strips themselves are made of stainless steel, so they will not rust, corrode, etc.

They are typically not visible (unless, of course, you are intentionally trying to see if you can see them).

The best part about them is the innate savviness of the birds, who generally want nothing to do with these spikes.

In fact, after one install, I happened to glance up and just happen to catch a glimpse of a bird that normally would land in the place where the Birdguard had recently been fastened to, and I watched in amazement as the bird, literally, slammed on the brakes in mid-air (flapping its wings really quickly to do so) and flew off to someplace else.

There are few things more frustrating to a property owner who takes pride in their property than having to deal with bomb-dropping birds congregating on and around their home on a daily basis as if it were the most popular watering hole in town.

Fortunately, for these types of annoying circumstances, there are solutions that are long-lasting, aesthetically non-intrusive, and super successful with their intent!

What is a 'Mansard'?

The mansard roof, also known as a French roof or curb roof, is a distinctive architectural feature with a unique design that has left a lasting impact on various structures worldwide. Its origins can be traced back to 17th-century France, where it was popularized and named after the renowned French architect François Mansart (1598-1666). The mansard roof has since been adopted and adapted in different regions and periods, making it an enduring and versatile roofing style.

The fundamental characteristic of a mansard roof is its dual-slope design. It consists of four sides with two distinct slopes: a steeper lower slope and a shallower upper slope. The lower slope is almost vertical or slightly slanted, while the upper slope is generally close to horizontal. This configuration creates additional usable space within the attic or top floor of a building, making the mansard roof an excellent choice for increasing living or storage areas.

One of the primary advantages of the mansard roof is its efficiency in maximizing space. By providing more headroom on the top floor, the mansard roof allows for better utilization of the available area and potentially increases the property's overall value. The design's popularity surged during the 19th century as it became a prominent feature in the Second French Empire architectural style, which also spread to other countries during the period of architectural eclecticism.

Moreover, the mansard roof's adaptability to various architectural styles and building types further contributed to its widespread usage. It complements buildings with different aesthetics, ranging from classic to contemporary designs, and has found applications in residential, commercial, and institutional structures.

A notable example of mansard roof application is in the Haussmannian architecture of Paris. Under the leadership of Baron Georges-Eugène Haussmann, Paris underwent a massive urban renewal project during the mid-19th century. Mansard roofs became a key element of this transformation, defining the city's iconic skyline and preserving its uniformity.

In addition to its aesthetic and practical benefits, the mansard roof also offers functional advantages. The double-sloped design enhances water drainage, which is particularly beneficial in regions with heavy rainfall or snowfall. The relatively flat upper slope allows for efficient installation of gutters and downspouts, directing water away from the building effectively.

Despite its many advantages, the mansard roof does have some limitations. Its complex design may increase construction costs compared to simpler roofing styles. Moreover, the increased living space created by the mansard roof might lead to higher heating and cooling expenses due to the larger interior volume. Additionally, maintenance and repair of mansard roofs can be more challenging due to their intricate structure.

In contemporary architecture, the use of mansard roofs has evolved, with architects and designers incorporating modern materials and construction techniques. This evolution ensures that the timeless appeal and functional benefits of the mansard roof continue to be relevant in today's construction industry.

The mansard roof is a remarkable architectural feature that has stood the test of time since its inception in 17th-century France. Its dual-sloped design provides additional living or storage space while contributing to the visual character of the building. With its adaptability to various architectural styles and practical advantages, the mansard roof remains a beloved and enduring roofing option in both historical and modern contexts. As architecture continues to evolve, the mansard roof will undoubtedly continue to influence and inspire future generations of builders and designers.

What is a 'Brake'?

If you have ever seen a home that is vinyl-sided (perhaps even the one you live in), you may have noticed that the trim is covered ("capped") in aluminum.

The contour of the aluminum as it fits around the trim is not magically made this way.

In order to get to the point where it fits around the areas of trim (window and door trim, fascia, etc.) in the most cosmetically pleasing way possible, it takes a skilled metalworker to "bend" the aluminum to get to this point.

When this process is being done, it is done so with the help of a tool called a "brake."

The use of a brake in bending aluminum for trimming out a vinyl-sided home is a common practice in the construction industry.

A brake is a specialized tool that allows precise bending and shaping of metal sheets, such as the aluminum used in this application, to create custom trim pieces for various applications.

In the context of a vinyl-sided home, the brake is utilized to fabricate aluminum trim pieces that complement the aesthetics and functionality of the vinyl siding.

The process begins with selecting the appropriate gauge and size of aluminum sheet/coil stock.

The chosen aluminum is then measured and marked according to the required dimensions for the specific trim piece. Accurate measurements are crucial to ensure a proper fit and seamless integration with the vinyl siding.

Once the measurements are marked on the aluminum sheet, the next step is to set up the brake.

The brake consists of a flat bed with an adjustable clamping system and a hinged bending leaf. The bending leaf is positioned at a specific angle, depending on the desired bend radius and the shape of the trim piece. Typically, the bending angle ranges from 90 to 180 degrees, depending on the application.

The aluminum sheet is carefully aligned with the marked measurements on the bed of the brake, ensuring that the desired bend line matches the position of the bending leaf. The clamping system is then engaged to secure the sheet in place, preventing any unwanted movement during the bending process.

With the aluminum sheet securely clamped, the operator exerts pressure on the bending leaf, using a lever or foot pedal, to gradually bend the metal along the predetermined bend line. The brake's design enables precise control over the bending process, allowing the operator to achieve accurate angles and smooth curves in the aluminum trim pieces.

After the initial bend is made, the aluminum sheet may need to be repositioned to complete the desired shape. This involves releasing the clamping system, adjusting the position of the sheet, and re-engaging the clamps before continuing the bending process. This iterative approach is often required for complex trim pieces that involve multiple bends or intricate shapes.

Once the aluminum has been fully bent and shaped, it is carefully removed from the brake, and any sharp edges or burrs resulting from the bending process are smoothed out using appropriate tools. The finished trim piece is then ready for installation.

A brake is an indispensable tool used to bend and shape aluminum for trimming out a vinyl-sided home. The precise bending capabilities of the brake enable the fabrication of custom trim pieces that enhance the overall beauty and protective characteristics of the vinyl siding, ensuring a professional and polished look for the home's exterior.

As terrific and helpful a tool as a brake is, any tool is often only as useful as the individual using it.

When combined with the skills of a well-seasoned metalworker, the results of the work stemming from what is done on a brake can truly be remarkable!

'House Leak' vs. 'Groundwater Leak'

One of the things that I have found helpful in my professional career over the years is discovering what I am really good at and going 'all in' on those items, and discovering what I am not so good at and learning to comfortably acquiesce to others whose acumen may be a bit more developed.

The PERFECT example of this would be water leaking THROUGH someone's home because of some type of above-ground issue with the actual house vs. water leaking INTO someone's home because of something having to do with some type of groundwater issue.

I have come to the realization that if someone has some type of mysterious roof leak or water staining on a ceiling or something of that nature—I AM YOUR GUY!!!

On the other hand, if someone has water leaking into their basement from someplace around the home or due to a high water table, etc., I am probably NOT your guy.

Unless it is something that I can quickly recognize (i.e., a dysfunctional gutter system or something along those lines), groundwater challenges could have something to do with the grading around the home, water coming into the property from a neighbor's property, or the like.

Water that is infiltrating your home from a ground source can be particularly tricky to formulate a diagnosis for and an accompanying solution to.

As with other areas of the home, sometimes water that is making its way into your home from the ground can stem from one central issue or a combination of issues.

For some reason, groundwater coming into basements and the like has been a condition that is overly challenging for me personally to help solve.

If it is a leaking bulkhead, no problem. However, a situation where water is coming right through someone's foundation floor is much more difficult for me.

Although these scenarios are ones that I myself may not have the exact cure for, I am fairly proficient at being able to refer the correct folks to help solve these specific types of mysteries.

I am extraordinarily fortunate that the network of experts I have surrounded myself with over the years is quite deep, and there are a variety of professionals that I can lean on in situations like these.

These professionals are very knowledgeable about groundwater and how it makes its way into the home.

Whereas I may be a good referral for someone whose chimney flashing appears to be leaking, these types of tradespeople are invaluable in the way that groundwater tends to travel and come to show its face on the inside of one's property.

While I love working through dilemmas that are centralized from a leaking flashing, roof, or pipe issue, I get queasy when performing an investigation where I surmise that the moisture culprit is stemming from these issues, which I admittedly have much less knowledge about.

Fortunately, the connections I have been blessed to have over the years within the industry have helped a large number of people solve some seemingly very mysterious problems, even if I have not directly been able to resolve them myself!

Proper Decommissioning of the American Flag

There are certain things that I often wonder about, which when I find out the answer to, I think to myself, "Well, that makes sense!"

One of these such situations came about recently when I started to notice all of the new flags going up around municipalities and people's homes in preparation for the 4th of July.

For those with at least somewhat of a patriotic pulse among us, this is certainly refreshing to see, but in noticing Old Glory being hung in such admirable fashion, I could not help but think, "What happens to the old flag that is being replaced?"

Whether at a school or as a tribute hung outside someone's home, when the flag is taken down, there has got to be a proper way to dispose of it (though I hate even describing it like that), but what is it???

Enter my good buddy John Loughlin.

John is a decorated military vet who has a radio show on before my home improvement show each Saturday afternoon (WPRO; 630 AM; 99.7 FM).

On a recent Saturday, I ran the question by John and asked if he would mind staying an extra few minutes after his show to discuss the topic on my show.

He graciously obliged, and not only was John able to provide some stellar insight, but I believe he also inspired a number of callers to call in and do the same.

It turns out there are a number of ways to funnel an old flag towards its proper decommissioning.

The majority of municipalities have collection boxes for old flags on the premises of their town hall. You would simply need to call and verify if they do indeed have one and, if so, where you can find it.

If you have a Boy Scout Troop that you are familiar with, putting it in the hands of the Troop can also be a valuable way to ensure that this procedure is done correctly, as many Troops take part in decommissioning ceremonies at least at one point during the year.

Another avenue would be to drop the flag off at a local American Legion

Post/VFW (Veterans of Foreign Affairs) Hall, where they, too, may be able to steer the flag towards correct decommissioning (again, call in advance to confirm).

Decommissioning ceremonies are solemn events in which the flag is destroyed in a dignified manner.

Burning the flag is the preferred way to destroy the flag during these ceremonies and may even be combined with some type of passage reading during the event.

The 'Flag Code' does not provide specifics as to how to destroy the flag, though there are a number of guidelines as to proper protocol for these types of ceremonies and can be found at a link on the US Department of Homeland Security's website:

https://wow.uscgaux.info/content.php?unit=070-08-01&category=us-flag-retirement#:~:text=The%20United%20States%20Flag%20Code,how%20to%20destroy%20the%20flag.

Proper decommissioning of the American flag is not just a "thing." It is an actual process with a bit involved in it in order to ensure that it is done in the most respectful way possible.

Even if you do not have the time to perhaps see your old flag through to its end, knowing that there are folks out there who can help make sure that your flag is disposed of properly is certainly reassuring.

What is a 'Monitor'?

Many homes have really cool features to them.

So many cool features, in fact, that even after almost thirty years of working in and around them, at times, I forget what they are called.

Although I believe I hold my own, I am far from an expert in architecture. This is quite evident when these terms happen to elude me from time to time, perhaps even while being on the very tip of my tongue!

One really unique item that is found in many homes is the 'monitor.'

Far from a 'monitor' that is used in conjunction with your computer, a 'monitor' on a home refers to a specific architectural feature designed to provide light, ventilation, or both to the interior spaces of a building.

Monitors are commonly found in older or traditional homes, particularly those with steep-pitched roofs. The purpose of a monitor is to introduce natural light, improve air circulation, and enhance the overall aesthetics of the structure.

A monitor typically consists of a raised structure, often rectangular or square in shape, positioned along the ridge line of the roof. It protrudes above the main roof surface and contains windows or openings on multiple sides. The design and size of the monitor can vary depending on the architectural style of the home and the specific functional requirements.

One of the primary functions of a monitor is to bring natural light into the interior spaces. The windows or openings on the sides of the monitor allow sunlight to enter the building, illuminating the rooms below. This can help reduce the reliance on artificial lighting during the day, leading to energy savings and a more sustainable living environment. The natural light that filters through a monitor can create a warm and inviting ambiance, enhancing the overall comfort and visual appeal of the home.

In addition to providing natural light, a monitor also serves as a means of ventilation. The windows or openings in the monitor allow fresh air to circulate within the building, helping to regulate temperature and improve indoor air quality. As warm air rises, it can escape through the monitor's openings, while cooler air enters through lower windows or vents. This natural airflow can help create a more comfortable living environment, especially during hot summer months or in spaces with limited access to traditional ventilation systems.

Monitors can be particularly beneficial in homes with high ceilings or rooms located on the upper levels. These spaces often suffer from poor natural lighting and limited airflow, making them feel dark, stuffy, or claustrophobic. The addition of a monitor can transform these areas, making them brighter, airier, and more pleasant to inhabit. A monitor can provide a sense of openness and connection to the outdoors, as occupants can enjoy views of the sky and surrounding landscape.

Monitors also contribute to the architectural character and aesthetic appeal of a home. They add visual interest and create a unique focal point on the roofline, breaking up the monotony of a large expanse of roofing material. Monitors come in various styles—ranging from simple and understated designs to elaborate and ornamental structures—reflecting the architectural period or regional influences. I find homeowners often appreciate the charm and character that a monitor brings to their property, making it a distinctive feature that sets their home apart from others.

While monitors offer numerous advantages, it's important to note that they require proper design, construction, and maintenance to ensure their functionality and durability. Proper waterproofing measures must be implemented to prevent leaks or water infiltration during rainstorms or snowmelt. Regular inspection and cleaning of the windows or openings are necessary to keep them clear and functional.

Monitors definitely seem to enhance the overall living experience, providing a bright, airy environment while adding a unique touch to the building's design.

Whether it's a traditional-style home or a contemporary dwelling, a monitor can significantly enhance the functionality and aesthetics of a property—whether or not you are able to remember what they are called when you are attempting to describe it!

What is 'Homasote'?

Just as people searching for facial tissue often say they are looking for a "Kleen-ex," within the home improvement industry, there are a number of items whose names being referenced are the actual names of a leading company in the production of that particular product.

One such example of this is 'Homasote.'

Most notably manufactured by the West Trenton, NJ-based 'Homasote Company,' which prides itself (as referenced on their website) as the na-tion's oldest (founded in 1909) and leading manufacturer of environmental-ly-friendly and recycled building products, Homasote is a brand name for a type of building material which has been widely used in construction and other applications for over a century.

Homasote is a fiberboard product made from recycled paper, which is compressed and bonded together with a non-toxic adhesive. The resulting material is dense, durable, and possesses excellent soundproofing and insu-lation properties.

Similar to Kleenex, when someone is talking about using Homasote in construction, it may or may not be an actual product of the Homasote Compa-ny, but in line with someone asking for a Kleenex, the "Homasote" the person may be referring to is a similar product which may be a prominent piece of Homasote's product line, but in fact, made by an alternate manufacturer.

One of the key characteristics of Homasote is its environmentally friend-ly nature. It is composed of 98% recycled materials, primarily waste paper. The manufacturing process involves shredding the paper into fibers, mixing it with the adhesive, and then pressing it into large sheets. This sustainable ap-proach to production has made Homasote a popular choice for those seeking eco-friendly building materials.

Homasote boards come in various thicknesses, typically ranging from 1/2 inch to 1 inch. They have a unique texture that resembles cardboard, with a rough, fibrous surface. The material is easy to work with and can be cut, drilled, and shaped using standard woodworking tools. It is also compatible with a wide range of finishes, including paint, wallpaper, and fabric coverings, allowing for customization to suit different design aesthetics.

One of the primary applications of Homasote is as an acoustic panel. Its dense composition and sound-absorbing properties make it ideal for reducing noise transmission within buildings. It is commonly used as a wall covering in recording studios, theaters, and other spaces where sound control is critical. The material's ability to dampen vibrations and absorb sound waves helps to create quieter environments and improve overall acoustic performance.

Homasote also has insulation properties, making it an effective thermal barrier. It can help regulate temperature and reduce energy loss in buildings. The material's insulating qualities are particularly beneficial when used as an underlayment for flooring or as sheathing in walls. It provides an additional layer of insulation that contributes to energy efficiency and comfort.

Furthermore, Homasote exhibits fire-resistant properties, adding to its appeal as a building material. The paper fibers are treated with fire-retardant chemicals during the manufacturing process, making the boards resistant to ignition and minimizing the spread of flames.

Homasote is sometimes used in exterior construction as a protective sheathing or backing board. It can be applied under siding materials such as stucco or brick veneer to provide additional insulation and moisture protection. The dense composition of Homasote helps to reduce thermal bridging and improve energy efficiency. However, it is important to note that for exterior use, Homasote must be adequately protected from direct exposure to moisture by using appropriate weather barriers and coatings.

One of the more popular exterior uses that I have come across for Homasote over the years has been as the material used to close things in on the underside of a soffit. If protected from consistent moisture exposure (which, being on the underside of a soffit, it would most naturally tend to be) and covered by an appropriate coating system (think 'paint'), Homasote can work quite well in this application.

Homasote is a versatile building material that is diverse in its uses and, with its fire resistance and green-oriented nature of how it is made, is certainly an attractive option for its variety of possible applications within the home improvement industry, particularly in today's hyper-environmentally conscious world.

Stopping the Paint from Peeling Along the Edge of a Freshly Painted Door

Recently, I received a call from a client regarding a concern of theirs that a door we had painted kept having the paint along its edges lift up each time one of our techs had gone to correct it.

This was a frustrating endeavor because each side involved had thought the door had dried thoroughly enough so that it would be able to be closed without an issue.

After a few attempts at going through the same experience—paint door, believe the door is dry, close door, open door at a later point in time, beat head on the wall because the edge paint had peeled (again!)—the client reached out to me directly, and I realized what was occurring.

Fortunately, this is a challenge that has probably been around since doors started to be painted, and years ago, I learned a wise old trick (that I have apparently not been teaching as diligently as I should be lately!) to prevent this annoyance from occurring.

Using 'Vaseline' to prevent a newly painted door from peeling along the edge is a simple and effective trick that many DIY (Do It Yourself) enthusiasts and professional painters employ.

The application of Vaseline, a brand of petroleum jelly, creates a protective barrier that prevents the paint from adhering to unwanted areas and reduces the risk of peeling or chipping along the door's edges.

While it may sound unconventional, this method is tried and tested, offering a cost-effective solution to achieve clean and professional-looking results.

In a nutshell, here is a step-by-step process of using Vaseline to protect a newly painted door:

Step 1: Gather the necessary materials before starting the painting process

These include Vaseline, a small paintbrush or cotton swabs, painter's tape, paint, a paint tray, and a paint roller or brush.

Step 2: Prepare the door for painting

Proper preparation is crucial for achieving the best results. Begin by removing any existing paint or debris from the door surface. Clean the door thoroughly using a mild detergent and water. Allow the door to dry completely before moving on to the next step.

Step 3: Apply painter's tape

To ensure clean and crisp edges, apply painter's tape along the areas you want to protect from paint. This includes the doorframe, hinges, handles, and any other adjacent surfaces. Make sure the tape is securely adhered to and pressed down to prevent paint from seeping underneath.

Step 4: Apply Vaseline

Dip a small paintbrush or a cotton swab into the Vaseline. Apply a thin, even layer of Vaseline along the edge of the door where you want to prevent peeling. Pay close attention to the junction between the door and the doorframe, as this is where peeling is most likely to occur. Be careful not to apply too much Vaseline, as it can affect the paint's adhesion.

Step 5: Start painting

Once the Vaseline has been applied, it's time to start painting the door. Pour the desired paint color into a paint tray and load the paint roller or brush. Begin painting the door, starting from the top and working your way down. Apply the paint evenly, using smooth and consistent strokes. Take care not to overload the roller or brush with paint, as this can lead to drips and uneven coverage.

Step 6: Allow the paint to dry

After you've finished painting the door, allow the paint to dry completely according to the manufacturer's instructions. It's important to resist the temptation to touch or disturb the paint during this time, as it may lead to smudges or imperfections.

Step 7: Remove painter's tape and Vaseline

Once the paint is fully dried, carefully remove the painter's tape from the door. Take your time to ensure clean edges. As you remove the tape, the Vaseline will come off along with it, leaving behind a clean line where the paint won't adhere.

Step 8: Clean up and admire the results

Dispose of the painter's tape and clean your tools and workspace. Stand back and admire your newly painted door, free from peeling along the edges!

Bonus Step:

As a safety net, I often recommend applying a thin layer of Vaseline along the edge of the door's jamb. This should be a VERY small amount, just enough to provide the additional assurance that the paint will not stick to the edge of the jamb.

Using Vaseline as a protective barrier when painting a door can be a relatively unknown yet helpful way to prevent peeling along its edges during the painting process.

By following the steps outlined above, you can achieve professional-looking results with clean and crisp lines. Remember, proper preparation and application are key to ensuring success!

Why is it a Bad Idea to Caulk the Gaps in Between Shingle Siding?

Recently, I had a client message me with concerns about there being gaps in between the shingle siding on his family's home after we had conducted our prep and were well on our way through applying the finish coat.

While he was SUPER complimentary of how hard the crew had worked on things, he was not quite sure if they had properly caulked items that should have been caulked due to the noticeable gaps in between the shingles on the home's siding.

Caulking the gaps in between shingle siding may seem like a quick and easy solution to improve the appearance and weatherproofing of your home. However, there are several reasons why it is actually considered a bad idea:

Impaired Ventilation: Shingle siding is designed to allow for proper ventilation, allowing moisture to escape and preventing the buildup of condensation. By caulking the gaps, you disrupt this natural airflow, leading to potential moisture problems such as rot, mold, and mildew. These issues can compromise the structural integrity of your home and even pose health risks.

Trapped Moisture: Shingle siding is designed to shed water and allow it to flow downward. However, if you caulk the gaps, water can become trapped behind the shingles, leading to moisture infiltration. This trapped moisture can cause the shingles to deteriorate prematurely and result in costly repairs or replacements.

Decreased Durability: Shingle siding is intended to expand and contract with temperature changes. By caulking the gaps, you restrict this natural movement, which can lead to warping, buckling, and cracking of the shingles. Ultimately, this compromises the durability and lifespan of your siding, necessitating premature repairs or replacements.

Aesthetic Issues: Caulking the gaps in between shingle siding can create an unnatural and unsightly appearance. Shingles are designed to overlap and create a visually appealing pattern.

Applying caulk disrupts this pattern and can make your siding appear disjointed and unattractive. Furthermore, caulk may change color over time, leading to an even more noticeable and unappealing appearance.

Maintenance Challenges: Shingle siding requires periodic maintenance, such as repainting or re-staining. When you caulk the gaps, you create additional obstacles for future maintenance tasks. Removing and reapplying caulk can be time-consuming and difficult, and it may damage the shingles in the process. This can make future maintenance tasks more complicated and costly.

Potential Damage: When it comes time to replace or repair your shingle siding, caulking can cause significant damage and increase the complexity of the project. Removing caulk from between the shingles can be challenging, and it may require the use of harsh chemicals or scraping tools. This process can scratch or gouge the shingles, leading to additional repairs or the need for complete siding replacement.

Caulking the gaps in between shingle siding is generally considered a bad idea due to the negative consequences it can have on ventilation, moisture management, durability, aesthetics, maintenance, and potential damage.

While it may seem like a simple solution, it can result in significant issues and expenses—both short- and long-term!

If coming across a situation such as this, it is always advisable to consult with a professional who is able to provide expert advice on the best course of action for your specific situation as it relates to shingle siding.

How to Make Old Windows Easier to Open and Close

Old windows can be difficult to open and close, especially if they have not been maintained over the years as well as they could have been.

One way to make sure they function as best as possible is by using beeswax. Beeswax is a natural, non-toxic substance that can be used to lubricate and protect the moving parts of old windows, making them easier to operate.

Here are some steps you can follow to use beeswax to help old windows open and close more easily:

Clean the windows: Before applying beeswax, it's important to clean the windows thoroughly. Use a soft brush or cloth to remove any dirt or debris from the tracks and frames. You may also want to use a vacuum cleaner to remove any loose debris.

Apply the beeswax: Once the windows are clean, you can begin applying the beeswax. You can use a solid block of beeswax or a mixture of beeswax and other natural ingredients, such as coconut oil or olive oil. Simply rub the wax onto the tracks and frames of the window, making sure to cover all the moving parts.

Work the wax into the tracks: After applying the beeswax, you'll need to work it into the tracks of the window. You can do this by sliding the window back and forth a few times or by using a small brush or cloth to work the wax into the grooves. Make sure to apply enough wax to lubricate the tracks, but not so much that it will attract dirt and debris.

Clean up any excess wax: After working the wax into the tracks, you may notice some excess wax on the window frames.

Use a clean cloth to wipe away any excess wax, making sure to leave a thin layer on the tracks.

Test the window: Finally, test the window to see if it's operating smoothly. If it's still difficult to open or close, you may need to apply more wax or use a different lubricant. You may also need to make some repairs to the window, such as replacing broken hardware or adjusting the alignment of the sashes.

Here are some additional tips to keep in mind when using beeswax to help old windows open and close:

- Beeswax is a natural substance that can be used safely on most types of windows, including wood, vinyl, and metal. However, you should test a small area first to make sure there are no adverse reactions.

- If you're using a mixture of beeswax and other natural ingredients, make sure to use high-quality beeswax that is free from additives or contaminants.

- Beeswax can attract dust and debris over time, so it's important to clean the windows regularly to prevent buildup.

- If you're applying wax to a window that has been painted, be careful not to get any wax on the paint. It can be difficult to remove and may damage the finish.

- If you're unsure about how to properly maintain your old windows, it's always best to consult with a professional. They can offer advice on the best methods and materials to use, as well as provide repairs and maintenance services if needed.

Beeswax can be a simple and effective way to help old windows open and close more easily. By following these steps and taking the proper precautions, you can ensure that your windows will function properly for years to come.

What is a Pork Chop?

When it comes to home renovation, one potentially confusing term that you may come across when discussing the exterior trim on your home is "pork chop." What exactly is a pork chop as it relates to the trim on the outside of a home? In short, a pork chop refers to a type of trim that is commonly used on the eaves of a house.

The eaves of a house are the edges of the roof that overhang the walls. They are an essential part of any home's design as they protect the walls from rain and other elements. The eaves also play a vital role in the aesthetics of the house. They can be decorated with various types of trim to add character and style.

One of the most common types of trim used on eaves is called a pork chop. A pork chop is a decorative element that is typically made from wood or vinyl. It is designed to be placed at the bottom of the eave and is shaped like a pork chop (hence the name). The trim piece is wider at the bottom than it is at the top, providing its unique shape.

Pork chops are often used to add visual interest to a home's exterior. They can be painted to match the color of the house or painted a contrasting color to create a pop of color. Some homeowners choose to use multiple colors to create a unique look.

While pork chops are primarily used on eaves, they can also be used in other areas of a home's exterior. For example, they can be used on the trim around windows and doors. They can also be used to create decorative accents on gables and dormers.

Wooden pork chops are best made from cedar or redwood, which are both durable and weather-resistant.

Vinyl pork chops are most often made from PVC or another type of composite and are also durable and weather-resistant. Vinyl pork chops are more cost-efficient than installing wood pork chops and require less maintenance.

If you are considering adding pork chops to your home's exterior, there are a few things to keep in mind. First, it's important to choose the right material. Wood pork chops are more expensive than vinyl pork chops but may be a better choice if you prefer a more natural look (whereas vinyl-oriented pork chops may be a less expensive endeavor and require less maintenance).

It's also important to choose the right size pork chop for your eaves. Pork chops come in various sizes, so you will need to measure your eaves to determine the correct size. If you are unsure about what size pork chop to use, you can consult with a contractor or home improvement expert, perhaps even someone from a reputable local lumberyard.

Pork chops are a great way to add style and character to your home's exterior. Whether you choose wood or vinyl, their durable and weather-resistant feature can help your home withstand the elements.

With the flexibility of a variety of colors and sizes, pork chops can aid in creating a unique look that truly complements your home's architecture and style!

What is a Public Adjuster?

One of the more frustrating experiences that one can work through is dealing with a homeowners insurance claim.

The ironic part about this, of course, is the endless array of commercials that one sees from the various insurance companies touting their wares through creative marketing, celebrity appearances, and a whole lotta superfluous exaggeration as to how well taken care of their clients are.

I can only assume that the marketing departments of these companies unintentionally promote product benefits—other than the cost savings that may be realized in choosing one company over another—that simply do not exist.

This plays itself out in real-world scenarios on a daily basis, particularly in the home improvement industry.

When someone experiences a loss that is covered by their homeowner's insurance policy, whether it be due to a broken pipe, a tree falling on the house, etc., many times, it is assumed that their insurance company will simply "take care of them."

Even for those folks who realize there may be some initial 'hoop jumping' when filing a claim, there is still often the assumptive approach that the insured has nothing to worry about.

Unfortunately, this utopic mindset seldom truly plays itself out in reality.

The majority of homeowners really do not have experience filing a homeowners insurance claim.

For many, taking the insurance company's word and following its verbatim guidance could very well leave the insured in a quite compromised position.

In fact, in almost thirty years of working directly with insurance companies, I can say with absolute certainty that the truth of these types of situations is that as the public adjuster assigned by the insurance company works through the claim, 50% of the time they are reasonable to deal and work with.

For the other 50%, the public adjuster is out of their mind (please excuse the crass descriptor).

Literally, it is black and white.

50% of the time, a reasonable situation (all things considered), and 50% of the time, a situation in which the homeowner could really get raked over the coals for the simple reason of just not knowing any better.

Enter the Public Adjuster (the 'PA').

A Public Adjuster is an adjuster who does not work for an individual insurance company and works entirely on their own.

While they may at times be hired by the insurance companies themselves to adjust claims, many PAs work strictly with insureds as advocates for them to make sure that anything the insured is entitled to under their homeowner's policy is properly compensated for by their homeowner's insurance company.

Many PAs are former Public Adjusters who have been employed in the past by an insurance company, and hence the reason why they are often so much better at what they do than the potential junior adjuster that the insurance company happens to assign to any given case.

It is important that the PA has a copy of your policy (it is wise to keep a physical copy of it in a safe place, as well as an electronic version) as they will utilize the policy to aid in making a case for the amount the insurance company should ultimately be paying out on the claim.

PAs usually get paid 10% of whatever the total value of the claim is.

Considering how far off insurance companies' initial analyses can often be, this is very much worth it.

If you are in a pinch and can connect with a really good PA, after reviewing your particular case, they will be honest with you and let you know whether they will be able to help you out or not.

Although involving a PA can potentially drag a case out much longer than if the insurance company properly ponied up the money related to the claim right from the very beginning, in those instances where I evaluate a situation and recommend a PA become involved, I believe that the wait will be well worth it.

Having to deal with some type of insurance loss at your home can be painful enough. Having to deal with an insurance company that is intentionally or unintentionally not working in the best interest of their insureds is an additional excruciation that no homeowner should have to experience.

Fortunately, aligning yourself with a professionally competent PA can be as relieving as having Batman arrive on the scene when any downtrodden damsel finds themself in distress.

Media Blasting

"Back in the day" (really, only about ten years or so prior to me getting involved in the coatings industry), there was a process for removing paint that, although effective, was a bit brutal.

This process, known as 'sandblasting,' definitely did the job, but when its methodology was utilized on residential housing stock, its face was often shown in a fashion where pitted walls rivaling that of the worst case of acne imaginable were commonplace.

I can envision paint company owners who wanted to do a good job must have been torn at the time as they knew, from a surface preparation standpoint, that sandblasting was the way to go. The biggest challenge, however, was that after this process had taken place, the amount of follow-up surface prep necessary to make the sandblasted surfaces look even somewhat respectable was an endeavor in nothing short of monumental proportions.

Enter 'media blasting' or, as I like to refer to it, 'sandblasting's kinder, gentler cousin.'

Though similar to sandblasting in its intent, the end results that media blasting lends itself toward could not be further apart on the 'aesthetically pleasing' spectrum.

If utilized properly, media blasting can be incorporated into one's surface preparation tool arsenal as an unparalleled approach in aiding in some of the most thorough surface prep that one may look for.

Media blasting is referred to as 'media blasting' because of its utilization of a variety of media types—crushed glass, corn, walnut, garnet, etc.—all meant to either remove existing coatings or "coax" a surface into being highly receptive to a desired coatings system for providing its best long-term chance at success.

The variety of different types of media allows for truly the best route to be chosen when preparing a surface.

Where, once upon a time, sandblasting ruled the roost, media blasting permits greater flexibility toward the manner in which a surface is prepared.

Without going into a techy deep dive, these various forms of media are essentially "blasted" out of a contraption powered by a generator and other machinery, all aimed at most efficiently providing a means of achieving the surface preparation result one desires.

For us, we use media blasting in different capacities, but the two main areas are in prepping concrete surfaces (garage floors, for example) and helping to correct a surface (due to mill glaze, being pressure treated, etc.) of its inability to hold a paint or stain coating long-term.

Media blasting is an absolutely wonderful method in preparing concrete to receive a protective coating as it does a terrific job of opening pores in the concrete and providing a surface for whatever the system of choice may be to most properly "bite."

Equally useful are media blasting's benefits with helping to cure unique wood substrates challenges such as mill glaze and pressure-treated wood's inability to hold a coating for an extended period of time.

In these instances, media blasting will not only remove any previous coatings that need to come off in order to more adeptly access the surface you are preparing, but it also prepares the surface in the same fell swoop as—similar to the concrete example—it etches the surface of these wood products and makes them SUPER receptive to whatever coating system you are applying.

Media blasting's superpower is its less aggressive adaptability, which traditional sandblasting has never really fine-tuned itself to do.

While conventional sandblasting certainly still has its place, media blasting is the perfect example of an approach that has been tweaked over time and, in the present day, is able to deliver results that the technology of forty years ago just would not allow.

Softwashing

Softwashing is a cleaning technique used to remove dirt, grime, algae, and other debris from the exterior of a home or building. It's a gentler alternative to pressure washing that uses low-pressure and special cleaning solutions to clean and sanitize surfaces. Softwashing can be a useful tool for homeowners or contractors looking to maintain a property's appearance and protect it from damage caused by algae and other contaminants. Additionally, softwashing is an excellent way to help prepare a home's exterior for painting.

Before beginning any exterior cleaning or painting project, it's essential to assess the condition of the home's exterior. If there is mold, mildew, or other growth, softwashing is an excellent way to remove it. Softwashing can also help to remove stains, discoloration, and other debris that may be detracting from the home's appearance.

When softwashing a home's exterior, it's crucial to use the correct equipment and cleaning solutions. A professional softwasher will have the necessary equipment and experience to safely and effectively clean your home's exterior. They'll also use a cleaning solution specifically formulated for softwashing, which is designed to break down and remove dirt, grime, and other contaminants.

The softwashing process typically involves spraying the cleaning solution onto the exterior of the home, allowing it to sit for a short period, and then rinsing it off with low-pressure water. Depending on the severity of the contamination, multiple applications of the cleaning solution may be necessary. A professional softwasher will be able to assess the condition of your home's exterior and determine the appropriate cleaning method and solution.

Once your home's exterior has been softwashed, it's important to let it dry completely before painting. Moisture trapped beneath the surface can lead to bubbling, cracking, and other problems with the paint job. In some cases, it may be necessary to wait several days or even weeks for the home's exterior to dry fully. A professional softwasher can advise you on the appropriate drying time for your home's specific needs.

Softwashing is an excellent way to maintain the appearance and integrity of your home's exterior. Regular softwashing can help prevent the buildup of dirt, grime, and other contaminants that can cause damage over time. Additionally, softwashing can aid in preparing your home's exterior for painting by removing any existing contaminants that may interfere with the adhesion of the paint.

If you're considering hiring someone to softwash your home's exterior, it's important to choose a reputable company with experience in softwashing. Look for a company with high-quality equipment and cleaning solutions and a proven track record of successful softwashing projects. Additionally, as with many similar types of services, it might be wise to ask for references and check online reviews before choosing a softwashing company.

Softwashing is an effective and safe way to clean and maintain the exterior of your home. It's an excellent tool for removing dirt, grime, and other contaminants that can damage your home's exterior over time. Softwashing can also help to prepare your home's exterior for painting by removing any existing contaminants that may interfere with the adhesion of the paint. If you're considering softwashing your home's exterior, be sure to choose a reputable company with experience in softwashing and a proven track record of successful projects. With the right care and maintenance, your home's exterior can remain beautiful and functional for years to come.

The Beauty of a Built-In

A 'Built-In' is a term used in construction that is right up there with the best of them in terms of those that can be confusing for whoever may be hearing it for the first time.

When someone thinks of something being 'built-in,' their mind may automatically gravitate toward something as simple as the cupholder in their car.

"I have a built-in cupholder in my car," you may hear from an excited friend.

"Oooooooo...fancy..." you may think in your head (or perhaps not).

The concept is very similar in home construction.

But whereas a built-in cupholder (to keep with this example) may be something that is fairly standard in the way that it is done across a variety of lines of cars, a 'built-in' in someone's home tends to be a bit more custom.

Though there certainly are instances in a home building where a 'built-in' feature may be one selected from a line that the builder typically provides to their clients upon request, the built-ins that I happen to more consistently run into align with something that is truly designed and constructed for the specific home that I come across them in.

While built-ins certainly may have elaborate designs behind them and take hours upon hours to create, built-ins are much more often (at least in my world) crafted by master craftspeople and cabinet folks who, although they might have a set of basic drawings that they are following as they are building the built-in, they may also not even have a plan at all and simply rely on their intrinsic vision and talent for craftsmanship that is beyond what the average person may own.

The built-in units I typically see are those that are more so on the cabinetry side, which often boasts some type of shelving system, sometimes even a window seat.

The imagination definitely is the limit, however, in terms of what the concept of the built-in is limited by.

I have seen built-in beds that drop down from a wall, built-in aquariums, built-in tables, etc.

The possibilities are endless for intertwining a variety of possible tracts for this cool feature in peoples' homes.

Not as common as a built-in bookshelf or dining room cabinet, built-ins such as the aquarium idea are usually SUPER AWESOME (the aquarium is my personal favorite!)!!

Built-ins can be worked into the design of one's home (as we have pointed out earlier), or they can be built along the way as someone is simply trying to more efficiently use a space that, for a period of time, they have had no idea what to do with.

Built-ins can be painted or finished with some type of stain and polyurethane system. If you need a fresh coat of paint, contact Lopco Contracting today!

Whatever the finish coat system happens to be, it should be quite durable (think along the lines of something that will provide an enamel-type finish), similar to what you would find associated with a solid kitchen cabinetry system.

Sometimes, built-ins blend so well with the natural state of a room that one may never even realize that the built-in was a built-in.

Other times, built-ins are meant to be the focal point of a given room (back to the aquarium example).

Whether a built-in is something you are simply looking to help out with for extra storage in the kitchen or if it is for a huge room with high ceilings whose walls (floor-to-ceiling) themselves consist of bookshelves to form a library, the two-fold purpose of usefulness and cosmetic appeal of built-ins is an age-old phenomenon which adds unique character to whatever home they happen to grace.

"I Have a Hole in My Ceiling!"

Did you ever have a problem where you thought perhaps you were the only one to have that problem and then come to find out once you mentioned it to someone, you found out that they had the same problem, and then you found someone else, and then someone else?

This could be related to a lot of things.

Maybe the most glaring of which is similarities with raising children—especially when they get to be teenagers—where you may believe that your kid is the only one who could possibly _____ , but upon happening to mention the scenario to whomever the listening party may be, you are relieved to know you are not alone in this particular boat.

While this certainly can be related to a number of different areas, in home improvement, there are endless examples.

One that we have come across more and more frequently as of late is folks with a hole in their ceilings.

On the surface, this may not seem very commonplace, but just like the teenager testing the boundaries of common sense, upon further investigation, this is a challenge that more people are working through than you may initially imagine.

Though often ignored as people pretend not to see it, they may even feel a bit ashamed (believe it or not) that they have this random hole in their ceiling, but as they gradually begin to start to mention it in conversation, they may surprisingly begin to find out that they are not alone.

So, where the heck does this hole come from?

Although there are a number of possibilities, the one we usually run into is that there is a slow leak stemming from a bathroom above the ceiling.

Often (though not always) related to the plumbing, over time, the water gradually does its damage, as it finds its lowest resting point on the backside of the ceiling and starts to eat away at the ceiling itself over a period of time—until a hole is formed.

When the hole is formed, it may or may not be noticeable at first.

There may not even be any "dripping water" per se that accompanies the hole, though it is not uncommon for 'yellowish' water staining to take place around the hole and its nearby vicinity.

A delay in addressing the hole may be nothing more than pure procrastination, or it may be related to the fear of what correcting the problem that created the hole, as well as fixing the hole itself, may ultimately end up costing.

The challenge in kicking the can down the road is that mold could obviously begin to form, and even in circumstances where the hole is tinier, airborne mold spores can begin to make their way into the living space below (clearly leading to potential health challenges which can be avoided with a bit more pep in one's step!).

Getting to the root of the problem as quickly as possible is beneficial, and as difficult as it may be to believe at the moment, a hole in one's ceiling is quite common, and the situation can often be helped to be worked through as one's homeowner's insurance may be able to aid in covering the cost of the repairs.

Whether you are the type of person to jump on a discovered home improvement issue right away or the type that would pretty much let the hole expand until when glancing at the ceiling, you are staring at the bottom of your bathtub, the sooner the hole is addressed, the better off you will be.

What is a Pocket Door?

Recently, we were working on a project where someone did what I believe they thought was a good idea at the time, but then the real-world functionality of their creative ambition kicked in, and a more practical solution was called upon to be enacted.

The center of this predicament was a pocket door that the then-owner of a condominium unit installed as an entry door at the rear entrance to their unit, coming in from a back stairwell.

While this may have seemed like a fantastic decision to the owner at the time, in reality, what occurred was simply not the most proper use of a pocket door.

We were called in to change out the pocket door for a six-panel steel entry door, which was not only more secure but, in this specific instance, much more user-friendly as well.

If you have not seen a pocket door before, it is a door that slides to open and typically becomes nestled, literally, within the wall itself.

This gives the effect of the door actually seeming to disappear when it is opened (as the pocket door rests inside the wall areas).

Pocket doors are very beneficial when there is not as much room for the swing that accompanies a hinged door.

Pocket doors open and close through the use of being attached to rollers that are hung from a track, located at the top of the door jamb and extending into the wall, and they are often kept on track by guides that are found on the floor.

The challenge with pocket doors is that they do not close as tight as traditional doors (which our fine client discovered), and there is often a larger gap between the bottom edge of a pocket door and the floor than there is with a more traditional door (which does not help in terms of limiting noise, odors, and even light from one room to another).

Pocket doors were VERY popular later in the 1800s (particularly in Victorian-style houses), and although this popularity did see a brief positive bump in the 1950s, the manner in which pocket doors were installed "back in the day" became more frowned upon by more modern building standards, as the raised tracks in the floor which often came along with them presented a bit of a trip hazard.

Pocket doors are literally made as pocket doors, and "regular" doors should not be attempted to be modified into pocket doors.

All doors can be a bit tricky to install, but installing a pocket door can be an especially delicate project, particularly if the pocket door is being attempted to be installed at some point after the home itself is built.

Although building codes and regulations these days make installing pocket doors even more challenging than they have been traditionally, and their use as features in one's home has definitely waned a bit for quite some time, as of late, there seems to be a definitive uptick in incorporating them into the stylistic approach of more contemporary homes which are striving for uniqueness in their appearance and overall flair.

Partly due to the yearning for more current versions of historically AWE-SOME features, partly due to the continuous strive to be a trendsetter, and a number of other reasons, pocket doors can add a streak of chicness to one's home; as long as you are not attempting to have your longing to be cool lead to trying to use a pocket door as an entry door into your home (whether from a stairway or otherwise!).

What is a 5-in-1?

Three decades ago, when I was breaking into the home improvement world on the painting side of the business, I was bombarded with what seemed like an endless amount of new terminology from all angles on a daily basis.

'Primer'

'Alkyd'

'Bullhorns'

You name it, it was like an entirely new language for me.

I certainly did not mind it; it was simply a lot to absorb.

One term that particularly caught my ear was the name of a tool whose importance was viewed by most painters in the same way that they would view a paintbrush.

This tool is the 5-in-1.

Now, as I was just getting used to being able to use '5-in-1' in the proper place of a sentence, I started to run into the '5-in-1's' apparent older siblings— the '6-in-1', the '10-in-1,' etc.

For myself, and I venture to guess most painters, however, a tool that looks like a 5-in-1 will always be a 5-in-1, even if it happens to be a '100-in-1'!

The term '5-in-1' references the tool's ability to be used for '5' different uses while being '1' tool.

These uses are as a gouger, a paint roller cleaner, a paint can opener, a putty knife, and a scraper.

The blade of a 5-in-1 is generally made out of stainless steel, and the handle is typically made out of wood or plastic.

I can honestly say that I could probably count on one hand the number of times that I have used a 5-in-1 to clean a paint roller or aid in puttying.

I have definitely gouged with them in the past, but out of the five most traditional common uses, the ones I have most often used a 5-in-1 for have been as a paint can opener and a scraper.

Although a true '5-in-1' may technically be intended for these five afore-mentioned uses, the list of the possible things an actual '5-in-1' can be used for is quite lengthy indeed.

Here is a short list of things that I have used a 5-in-1 for in the past:

- To help guide a piece of wood into place against another piece of wood
- To open an unlocked window from the outside
- As a shim, temporarily leveling a ladder (not recommended!)
- To hammer in a nail (with its butt end)
- To open boxes
- As a flat head screwdriver
- As a pry bar (to take old shutters that have been nailed on) off a home
- As something to aid in holding a door open and not locking behind me
- To aid in cutting a piece of string (or something along those lines)
- To help in removing wallpaper

I am sure I could go on and on.

All of these are perfect examples of why painters find this tool to be so valuable!

As you can see, a 5-in-1 can provide plenty of mileage in terms of the number of things it can help out with.

One key to its long-term effectiveness is to remember to sharpen the blade whenever it seems as though it needs it.

Another key is to not lose it! As with many tools, 5-in-1s are easily misplaced.

When breaking into the painting trade or even taking on a painting project around your home, the list of terminology related to what you are doing can absolutely be a bit overwhelming; this being said, due to its unending diversity, the 5-in-1 is one of those tools that above almost any other can be about as valuable as one can learn about and utilize!

The Toilet Paper Test

Upon first glance, when someone hears the phrase, 'The Toilet Paper Test,' it would not be uncommon for the still undeveloped far reaches of one's brain to automatically default to imagining imagery that would fall in line with that paralleling the thoughts of the great 90s thought leaders Beavis and Butthead.

As facetious as this may seem on the surface, it is probably not far off. The toilet paper test, however, is one that can be critically important to the functionality of the airflow in one's bathroom while not necessarily having anything to do with the toilet itself.

One of the more common items that we get called upon for advice about is how well one's bathroom fan is working.

A bathroom fan is a fan, often coupled with a light fixture and attached to the ceiling, whose purpose is to suck air out of the bathroom and guide it to the outside of the home.

The purpose of the bathroom fan is multi-faceted, as its aim is to guide as much moisture, humidity, and, yes, odors as possible from the bathroom to the outside of the home.

Ideally, there is a hose attached to the backside of the bathroom fan that brings the air that is being drawn out from the bathroom to the home's exterior, preferably out through the roof (as the higher the exit point, the better), though many times through an area of the home's soffit (the 'overhang' area of the home).

As surprising as it may seem, I can't tell you how many times we find the bathroom fan simply venting out into the attic itself with zero attempt visible to make an effort to vent it outside.

This is problematic on a number of levels.

In these types of cases, particularly with regard to moisture and humidity, having a bathroom fan that is vented into the attic can be the catalyst of a breeding ground for mold.

While it may take a period of time for this to occur, it is almost a sure thing that mold will begin to form somewhere in the attic in the vicinity of the backside of the fan, creating potential health challenges for unsuspecting residents in the floors below.

You may be wondering what any of this has to do with a 'toilet paper test.'

Whether a bathroom fan is correctly vented or not, sometimes people just wonder in general if their bathroom fan is truly working or not because, in all honesty, it can be hard to tell.

Enter toilet paper.

To test if your bathroom fan is even close to viably working, turn the bathroom fan on.

Next, take a piece of toilet paper and position it directly under the bathroom fan.

If the toilet paper sticks to the fan, the fan is most likely drawing in air as it should be.

If the toilet paper does not stick and instead falls to the ground, the fan is not working properly and should probably be replaced.

Super scientific, I know.

Ensuring one's bathroom fan is operating properly and vented to where it should be vented is a small exercise that every homeowner should check up on at least once or twice per year.

To me, it is fun that something known as a 'toilet paper test' can be super helpful in determining whether one's bathroom may have proper air flow or if a conversation should be had as to what has to be done to improve things.

Trapping Mildew Between Product Coatings

There is a scene in the classic original *The Karate Kid* (1984) movie where Daniel (Ralph Macchio) is being coached by Mr. Miyagi (Pat Morita) through an exercise that Daniel believes is pointless at the time.

Daniel was shown by Mr. Miyagi a technique in which he should be stroking the brush when painting a house.

As the scene moves on, Daniel is visibly frustrated as he believes that the exercise is simply a way for Mr. Miyagi to cheaply get his house painted vs. having any real value in Daniel's karate training.

These annoyances are soon squashed as Mr. Miyagi confidently walks Daniel through a demonstration of the value in the repetitive motions of the painting process and connects the dots as to how one has to do with the other.

While Daniel's concerns may have been instantaneously quelled by Mr. Miyagi's impressive show of what one had to do with the other (you have to see the movie to "get it"), my innards cringe every time I see the scene.

Though I do understand the value Mr. Miyagi was teaching, the painting genes embodied within my soul go absolutely bonkers as I watch Daniel paint directly over a mildew-covered house!

This is about as big a 'NO NO!!' of a scenario as one could put together.

Prior to any exterior paint job that we take on, we clean the outside of the building with what we call a 'soft wash' process.

This method is designed to clean the surface that it is being used on without damaging any of the substrates and without compromising whatever remaining integrity there is in the existing coating structure (i.e., paint chips are not blown all over the neighborhood).

Properly cleaning these surfaces ensures that any mildew or mold is NOT trapped in between any paint or stain coatings.

In watching this referred to scene, as methodically as Daniel works to apply the paint in the manner which Mr. Miyagi guided him to do so, my insides turn inside out every time I watch it as brush stroke after brush stroke, Daniel applies the product directly over the mildew infested surface.

Even worse, from afar at least, it appears that the product being applied is an oil product over an oil product (which would make sense given the period of time).

Because mildew particularly feeds off the properties of oil-based paints and stains, Daniel is unknowingly creating a mildew sandwich time bomb (oil coating, mildew-covered surface, a coating of oil on top)!

Once this type of scenario takes place, the mildew becomes trapped between product coatings.

Recently, I visited with a client who had a mildew-covered, polyurethane-coated front porch ceiling.

With clear coatings, this type of situation is more visible than with more solid colors.

If the polyurethane ceiling is cleaned with a mildew cleaning agent and the mildew comes off, the client is golden.

If the mildew does not come off, then at that point, the mildew is surely trapped between the coatings, and the only way to solve the issue (outside of replacing the actual ceiling boards) is to strip off the coatings and start from scratch.

Not only is mildew unsightly but with trapping mildew, mold, etc., in between coatings, even if mildew-resistant products and mildew inhibitors are used in subsequent coatings on top, it is only a matter of time before the mildew returns because mildew and mold beget mildew and mold.

Again, the only way to solve the situation at this point (without replacing the substrate itself) is to strip all the coatings and start from a clean surface.

Clearly, these are situations that can be avoided if the proper steps are taken as one is working through the project from the beginning.

It would not surprise me if, within a year, the house that Daniel begrudgingly painted was covered in mildew and mold all over again.

As disheartening as this is for me to envision, perhaps Mr. Miyagi is well aware of what most likely will occur and has some type of advanced training technique up his sleeve for Daniel to embark on a year afterward, as he is now forced to strip the coatings of the house to rid it of its mildew.

Knowing Mr. Miyagi's brilliance in the way he operated moving about things, it would not surprise me at all if this were the case.

How Wet is TOO Wet to Paint?

There are many inaccuracies that we have had to work through over the years, which combat viable and efficient production.

As in many industries (healthcare, the practice of law, you name it!), when working with a client, situations arise that should truly rely on professional expertise yet receive pushback from the client in terms of approach, to the point that the frustrated professional simply attempting to do their job to the best of their ability, may want to beat their head on the nearest wall, desk, or whatever hard surface is closest.

The Internet has certainly played a huge role in fostering these types of scenarios as at their fingertips folks can enter questions into search engines that, even though throughout history have been answered by people who have often dedicated their entire lives studying a particular subject, only to be told that they are wrong because, "I read on 'X' website that _____ should be done in the following manner."

From firsthand experience, I understand how dispiriting this is to hear and the process that needs to occur, led by patience, in order to potentially combat mistruths or old wives' tales that someone presents as factual purely by a quick lookup on their phone as they are searching for the answer to whatever the subject at hand may be.

One example in our industry that perfectly illustrates this type of occurrence is the question as to what the appropriate conditions to paint should be for someone looking to dive into an interior or exterior painting project.

While there are a number of variables involved (temperature and humidity, to name a couple), the one that we have always seemed to run up against the most is the moisture content of the surface being painted.

In other words, if it rained overnight, is it ok to paint?

If one were to look this question up online, all types of answers might pop up, but the majority will focus on the subject in general and not answer it from a scientific standpoint.

Obviously, if a surface is wet (whether inside or outside), it should not be painted.

The real answer to the question posed, however, is "maybe."

It really depends on what direction the rain was coming from, if it really hit the side of the home that was going to be painted at all, and things along these lines.

The truth of the matter is that whatever surface you are intent on painting should have a moisture content of 15% or less at the time when you are painting it.

This being said, it is absolutely feasible that you could have had torrential rain overnight, hitting one side of the home but not touching another, and the sides that the rain does not touch are perfectly fine to paint the next day.

On our end, we have instruments called 'moisture meters,' which are super sensitive gauges of moisture content that, when plugged into a surface, can instantaneously report on the moisture content of whatever the substrate (usually wood or masonry) may be.

If it is 15% moisture content or below, it is ok to paint.

If it is above 15%, it is not ok to paint, and you should wait until the moisture content meets the 15% or less threshold before proceeding with your project.

That is the science.

Just like a doctor may feel as if they may have to constantly combat diagnoses and solutions found on someone's computer vs. what the doc knows that science dictates, there are seemingly an infinite number of similar instances in the contracting world where knowledgeable contractors should simply take a deep breath and calmly lean into a scientific response countering their client's suggestion of a well-intended, yet incorrect idea if the contractor believes it warrants doing so.

Frozen Pipes

Every once in a while, we get a particularly harsh cold snap in Southern New England.

Though I'd imagine not as frequently as our neighbors in Northern New England, we still get them on occasion, and every time we do, it reminds me how much I personally dislike the cold (I'm afraid my roots are too deep at the moment to move to a place with more consistently comfortable weather!).

We had a recent extreme dip in temperatures where, though short-lived (lasting only a couple of days), winter's brute force was truly felt as I saw the temperature gauge on my truck dip to negative 6 degrees Fahrenheit, and we had at least one client who experienced negative 12—these are both BEFORE the wind chill was factored in, which in RI reached well into the negative 30s in some spots (at this same time, Mt. Washington in New Hampshire experienced a negative 108 degree Fahrenheit wind chill, the coldest in the United States since the modern wind chill scale was begun to be used nearly two decades ago).

With temperatures in these time periods pushing heating systems to their limits, it is no wonder that havoc can be easily wreaked.

There are plenty of videos online where folks go outside in these conditions, throw a cup of water in the air, and watch it freeze instantaneously.

If water is able to freeze that quickly, it certainly does not take much effort at that point to cause pipes to freeze that may be in the right conditions to allow them to do so (under-insulated cold spots in the house, etc.).

As the pipes freeze, the water in them expands, many times to the point where a seam in the pipe or the actual pipe itself bursts, and immediately water starts pouring out, or as the pipe thaws, water begins to leak.

This most recent example affected us at our shop.

As our staff was away from the shop going about their business and enjoying their weekend, our operations manager received a frantic call from the fire department attempting to get into our building because the fire alarm was going off.

Sure enough, a pipe related to our sprinkler system had been compromised, and it was effectively raining inside the shop.

Not a fun call to receive, nor a fun mess to clean up afterward.

Usually, we are the ones being called to help people out in these types of situations, and it definitely felt a bit different being on the other side of the equation.

Granted, it certainly could have been A LOT worse, but it was still not a pleasant thing to go through!

Experiencing frozen pipes and the subsequent damage that is often associated with them is far from enjoyable.

A few tips to keep these types of things from happening would be:

- Make sure your home is well insulated, specifically in areas where piping may run through

- When temps are expected to be brutally cold, be sure to turn your heat up higher than usual as your heating system is surely going to have a challenge keeping up— now is not the time to be FRUGAL!

- Have your faucets running at a slow, thin stream of water (running water should be MUCH more difficult to freeze)

While none of these is a surefire way to guarantee that your pipes will not freeze when the wind chill outside is well into the negative readings, taking potentially simple actions such as these should definitely go a long way toward helping to avoid the heartache and frustration which comes when the damage from frozen pipes is truly felt.

Mysterious Leaks

If there were ever a topic that I could write about and provide seemingly count-less examples for, 'Mysterious Leaks' would certainly be at the top of the list.

While developing a bit of a reputation over the years as an expert leak diagnoser, my list of out-of-the-ordinary leak situations definitely has grown quite long.

Clearly, there are a whole number of leaks that are quite obvious to figure out. Real-world examples of these that I have run across include:

- A satellite dish, which was held in place by brackets, drilled right through the top of a roof shingle and, when removed, left the holes behind open without filling them

- A rotted (to the pulp!) windowsill, which was fostering moisture between the walls of the home each time it rained and allowed water a free path

- A clogged gutter system that, in moderate and above rain-fall, backed up into the soffit it was hung from and subse-quently into the home from there (Reminder: when you have your gutters cleaned, flush the system as well!! Do not simply pick the debris out of it!)

These were simple ones that did not take a rocket scientist , as they say, to figure out.

A list equally as long, if not longer, are those leaks whose sources are head-scratchers on steroids to solve.

A few examples of these types of leaks include:

- A cracked sewer venting pipe situated behind a wall and in between the wall and ceiling above it

- A leaking vinyl window, where the leak stemmed from

where the side of the vinyl window met the inner sill and
then leaked to places below from there

- A leak coming from a bathroom where the initial thought
  was it was a pipe leak; two 'Plumber-of-the-Client' visits
  later, after they had "fixed" the pipes, it was learned that the
  leak was actually coming from the floor of the bathroom.

There is a system I utilize when working to nail down where a leak is coming from, and there are specific things I hone in on first to see if it is an easier
leak to figure out than others.

For instance, if the leak appears to very much be coming from the roof, I
start with what we refer to as "penetrations."

Penetrations are anything that literally 'penetrate the roof.

This could be a chimney that is not flashed properly (or that calls for a
diverter behind it but does not have one), it could be flashing around a dormer
that pops out the roof of the house, or it could be the flashing of the portion
of the sewer venting pipe that goes through the roof.

Once I go through the obvious progressions, I proceed to items that may
not be as glaring.

These could include anything that I might be able to access without tearing into the house itself—one example is a windowsill that looked to be intact
but was actually rotted to the degree that it was able to allow water in.

After this, if still not found, the next step is to recommend that ceilings
and/or walls be opened up.

Unfortunately, many times, this is the route that is necessary to take as
without approaching a leak from the backside and tracing its path, the leak's
starting point may not be able to be established (a leaking pipe is often the
perfect example of this).

Whether a leak is super simple to recognize or one that requires an entire
ceiling to come down to even begin having a shot at finding it, mysterious leaks
are often not that mysterious at all; they simply need a formalized system of
peeling back the layers to determine why they are occurring, what needs to be
done to fix them, and finally, to execute the actual repair in correcting them so
that damage that has been caused can begin to be properly repaired.

What is a Building Code?

When it comes to things that we are unfamiliar with, easing into the "knowledge" circle of things can definitely be quite intimidating.

This is true throughout almost every aspect of life, certainly within the variety of niches and spheres that comprise the very fabric of our society.

The area that I have spent the most time in over the past three decades—construction—absolutely fits this bill.

One of the areas within construction that I used to get overwhelmed just thinking about was the idea of having to address anything that has anything to do with the building code.

After all, the number of items covered by the variety of building codes within our industry appears infinite.

Where do they start? Where do they stop??

Thinking about it can easily make your head spin if you let it.

Although I do not blame anyone who wants to hide their head under the pillow, long ago, I developed a strategy to help work through code questions with ease, which is based on two simple premises:

1) Local Code is King
2) Refer to Manufacturer Recommendations

With regard to the first notion, there is no denying that there is tons of code guidance out there…International, Federal, State, Local…where, oh where, does it end?

It ends with 'Local.'

Local code, particularly that which the local building official favors, is what is going to win out in the end.

Regardless of what the international code dictates, there may be local reasoning to deviate from international guidance (in this instance), and at the local building official's discretion, this is what would take precedence.

In terms of the second point, I refer back to a situation from years ago that was driving me nuts with regard to a roofing installation question.

Though the specific question escapes me, I remember the solution as clear as day.

This particular item confused me to the point where I phoned in my question to a high-ranking state building official.

When asked the question, without hesitation, the official fired back at me, "Well, Tom, what do the manufacturer instructions say?"

"Huh?" I responded.

"Whatever the manufacturer instructions dictate, that is what we would consider code," replied my high-ranking resource.

"Is it really simple?" I asked.

"Yep! Literally that simple," they confidently responded.

I had been scratching my head for some time, researching and researching for the answer to my specific question here, and the whole time, the answer was right under my nose—go figure!

When learning the industry, those working to understand building code may at times feel as though they are facing some insurmountable monstrosity of a barrier that is put in place to make running a successful business even more challenging than it may already be.

There have been many times, particularly early on, when I sure felt this way.

But in developing the approach of 'when in doubt...' tag-teaming and following the manufacturers' instructions on whatever installation we may happen to end up doing, in conjunction with the nod of approval from our local building official of the moment, a sense of quiet confidence is allowed to set in, shoring up personal conviction that we are doing the right things, the right way.

What is the OSB Board?

In a period of time, none of us will soon forget, the late spring/early summer protesting of 2020, which in many cases turned beyond aggressive, was a catalyst for a seemingly infinite number of phenomena.

From the societally significant to things that may seem like minutiae to the majority of us, the effects were felt throughout communities all over.

Perhaps one of the tinier veins, but a piece of the puzzle nonetheless, was the effect this period had on the lumber industry, particularly when it came to the supply of plywood.

As incidents became more widespread, plywood supplies seemingly disappeared overnight.

We at LOPCO were certainly part of this as we received a frantic call from a prominent Providence hotel less than twenty-four hours after conducting a preventative walkthrough in case any type of protesting turned hostile in Providence.

While I was admittedly half-scoffing at the idea as I was evaluating what it would take to plywood up the first level of this hotel (thinking that something that I was estimating to help prevent had very little chance of occurring in Providence), sure enough, at 6 am the next morning I found myself doing another type of inspection.

This one involved me making a beeline to the hotel to assess for any damages that may have been incurred the previous night; literally a few hours after I had initially taken a peek at things, rogue protestors had done damage to the hotel.

As I was doing this, my phone began to blow up as the Director of Facilities for the hotel wanted to know how quickly we could get plywood up on the outside.

Realizing this was a legitimate situation, I put the mechanisms in place to get the plywood hung as we had been planning (I had not even finished my estimate yet) and headed straight for our local lumberyard.

I went there because I knew everybody and their mother would try to hit the box stores up first.

When I arrived at the lumberyard, I inquired as to how much OSB board they had, and after being assured they had a good amount of it, I let them know that we would purchase all of it and asked them to please deliver it to the downtown hotel.

Luckily, we were able to fasten all the OSB board up, and no further harm was done to the hotel after that.

What is an OSB board?

OSB board is a sheet of wood that looks and performs like traditional plywood but is a much more cost-efficient alternative.

Many times incorrectly referred to as 'particle board,' OSB (Oriented Strand Board) board is made from waterproof heat-cured adhesives and numerous strands of wood bonded together to form an engineered wood panel that resembles the appearance and proficiency of traditional plywood.

OSB board has many uses.

Because of its price point, it certainly is ideal for situations where board-ups are necessary; the example I used is a good illustration, but it is often used in securing vacant or fire-damaged houses being locked in over door and window areas.

Contrary to what is heard in the field, true OSB board is waterproof and is utilized in a variety of capacities.

OSB board has many applications, from wall sheathing to roof sheathing to subflooring.

The biggest disadvantage to OSB board is that if it gets exposed to significant amounts of water, its edges can greatly expand, especially if the edges have been cut (without being sealed) in the process of construction.

Both OSB Board and plywood will rot out if saturated with moisture over long periods of time.

One of the biggest construction myths involving the OSB board is that because it is more cost-efficient, it is an inferior product.

True OSB board, however, if manufactured correctly, is NOT an inferior product and actually is quite versatile, especially if its structural integrity can be maintained throughout the construction process (waterproof by correctly sealing your cuts!).

It is also a well-welcomed alternative in situations that become dire and warrant a quick response as cost-effectively as possible to guard against intrusion and unwanted vandalism, whether after a home-destroying fire or a peaceful protest that turns into a potentially compromising situation for area properties.

Low Slope Roofing

As crazy as it sounds, not all reputable roofing companies know what they are doing.

Come to think of it, perhaps that can be said about every trade.

Not all reputable _____ (fill in the trade name) companies know what they are doing.

It may even be possible to apply this to every reputable company everywhere!

In any event, with regard to roofers, my point here is probably more noticeable than other types of trades because of the way that mistakes with regard to this particular trade tend to show their face—most notably in the form of water leaking into one's home or business!

There are many different ways in which one may experience the unfortunate feeling of a roofing snafu.

From my observations, the majority of roof issues do not stem from the shingles themselves but the way that penetrations (chimneys, dormers, sewer venting pipes, etc.) are flashed into the roof.

One of the instances that I do, however, run into somewhat often with finish roofing materials is the incorrect finishing materials used for a given application.

Knowing this could translate into many focuses, what I would like to zero in on here are low-pitch roofs and the proper finish materials to utilize on them.

In roof jargon, anything below a 3 pitch should have some type of low slope roofing material on it as its finish.

"Pitch" refers to the rise and run of the roof.

A '3 pitch' would mean that the roof rises 3 inches for every 12 inches of its horizontal run.

This 'pitch' talk may sound confusing, but it is a main focal point within the roofing industry as a whole.

From ordering material to determining the overall cost of replacement, this 'pitch' concept is extraordinarily important.

Though there are different options as to what one can utilize on a low-slope roof, there is actually a type of roofing material that within the roofing industry is referred to as 'low slope.'

While rubber and various types of roof coatings are certainly terrific options, temperature plays a big role in whether or not a specific version of these can be used.

Sometimes roofers refer to periods of the year when the temperature is consistently in the 50s as 'rubber season' because that is the time period of the year when it is typically viewed as the ideal time for the glue that is used with rubber roofing systems will "take" best.

Although one has an approximate 10-degree greater lower temperature parameter with many types of 'paintable' roof coatings, the go-to when temperatures are truly a concern is the low slope (many times referred to as 'rolled roofing').

This type of roofing can be installed in the same temperatures that regular asphalt shingles are installed at, and because of this, it embodies an attractive quality in certain cooler periods of the year where temperature may otherwise be a concern.

What eats me up inside is when I see regular architectural (or even 3-tab) roof shingles used on a roof area where low-slope roofing of some type should have been utilized.

This is a disaster waiting to happen, and when I receive pictures from a concerned client who is wondering why they are having some type of challenge with a roof area such as this one described, I usually close my eyes really tight and grimace.

The crazy thing is that I have run into scenarios where some really highly thought of companies in our area have done something along these lines.

Whether due to laziness or a particular crew member's degree of incompetence and/or lack of supervision, this situation can happen to the very best roofing company if they are not carefully staying on top of things.

Regardless of the reasoning, if this type of thing does occur, the office end of the business may be fast-tracking on its way to being blindsided by a service call at some point in the not-too-distant future after the roof has been completed.

Polyurethane vs. Varnish

When it comes to wood finishes, it seems like the options are infinite in terms of what types of wood finishing systems may be the best fit for your particular project in both allowing maximum beauty and durability in balance with whatever conditions may be at play.

Two prominent finishes that, when applied properly and cured appropriately, offer long-lasting protective coatings are polyurethane and varnish.

Many times, people refer to polyurethane as 'varnish' and varnish as 'polyurethane.'

Polyurethane and varnish are actually two definitively different products, each with performance elements that differ from the other.

Polyurethane is kind of like a liquified plastic.

Polyurethane comes in either acrylic or oil-based forms.

Although resembling milk, polyurethane applies as a clear finish.

Whether acrylic or oil-based, polyurethane is very popular for many interior uses, everything from furniture to floors.

The acrylic-based polyurethane will tend to keep its clear appearance over time, whereas the oil-based polyurethanes will gradually "yellow" out on you.

The term 'varnish' is often used by people unknowingly utilizing it to describe a myriad of wood finish examples (including polyurethane).

Actual varnish, however, is an oil-based finish that, similar to oil-based polyurethanes, will cure to a faint yellow film or possibly even an amberish tint.

Due to the high-solid content of the finish and how well it holds up against moisture, varnishes are often favorite finishes for outdoor furniture, decks, and boats.

A variant of varnish—referred to as spar or marine varnish—is particularly good for guarding against ultraviolet (UV) rays.

Both polyurethane and varnishes can be tricky to apply, and if they are not used in line with the manufacturer's recommendations, they can result in finishes that are less than ideal (with the appearance of bubbling, cracking, and wrinkling becoming visible as the finish dries).

If each is applied properly, polyurethane and varnish can look absolutely stunning.

This all being said, which would I recommend for what?

I usually go by the rule of thumb that we utilize polyurethanes as part of our interior wood finishing systems and varnishes for our exterior wood finishing systems.

The idea (in my head, at least) is that polyurethanes are terrific for hardwood floors and the like, specifically because of their durability and flexibility in comparison to varnishes.

Varnishes—because of how much better they stand up to UV rays—are what we usually aim to incorporate into our exterior wood finishing systems.

Now, if you were to ask this same question to a variety of self-proclaimed wood finishing "snobs," there may certainly be nuanced debate as to what is best to use where.

This is simply the guidance from my end with the intention of keeping things simple.

One thing is for certain: the gorgeous nature of what polyurethane and varnish systems embody in their role of both enhancing and protecting a wide variety of wood species cannot be denied and is super impressive when seen 'before' and 'after' by someone who truly embraces the art of applying either one.

Egress Windows

Many folks often daydream about the types of home improvements that they would like to see on their home if they had the opportunity to do so.

At the top of the list, more often than not, is to "finish" the basement.

Thoughts of having a 'Man Cave' or shifting an older child to their own lair and the like are quite enticing and typically serve as the catalyst that ignites these visions.

Although pricey (as with seemingly everything else in life) when comparing the cost of finishing a basement to that of just a few years ago, for those with an unfinished basement, the benefits of incorporating one into the fabric of one's home are still enormously tempting.

For those brave enough and in the position to make it happen, when taking the leap toward doing so, there are a number of items to keep in mind.

Certainly, there are height requirements and other regulations and guidelines that may vary from one community to another.

Along with all of the planning that comes with this type of project, one of the biggest items of focus tends to be the egress direction that would be dictated by the local building official (remember, the more local the building code, the more it takes precedence!).

While varying in their design, bulkheads are one means of egress that are very common.

In addition to a bulkhead (or, in some instances, in lieu of—again, depending on the demands of local code), one option for egress is the 'egress window.'

The egress window is a window that is installed in one's home that literally allows egress to the exterior.

Though basements tend to be the most common area in which they are used, they can be utilized in other areas as well.

An egress window looks like a large regular window, but it opens large enough to allow the inhabitants of the space to escape in the event of a fire.

Local building officials should be consulted to double-check how large the window space actually needs to be as you are planning the project.

There is MUCH involved when embarking on the project of installing an egress window.

While it can definitely differ from project to project, here is an example of what we see usually involved when installing an egress window:

- Window needs to be ordered at the appropriate size

- Properly dug out area outside the window

- Foundation needs to be cut and the hole prepped to receive the window

- Window installed

- Finish trim installed around the exterior of the window

- Hole that was dug backfilled

- Window well installed in the hole (we always custom make these with steel and, depending on the situation, may need to incorporate a ladder into the fabrication as well)

- Crushed stone placed in the bottom of the hole that was dug

- Interior finish work done around the window with the intention of making the window appear as if it had always been there

As you can see, the process is a bit involved.

When working through this procedure, it is important that a local building official is involved to make sure that what is done meets the egress code.

Finished basements are definitely fantastic features in the homes of many. Ensuring proper egress, though, is not only prudent but an essential part of the process that should be well thought out and embedded into the overall game plan.

Horsehair Plaster

Being at an age where I find myself more and more often starting sentences with the phrase "When I was growing up...", sometimes coming across different items that we tackle daily basis truly reminds me of something that I recall from "When I was growing up" which stuck with me for some reason back then, and when I think back with what I know today, could definitely have been helpful to know!

One of these such items is a hole in the wall right behind a set of bunk beds, which I shared with one of my brothers.

This hole seemed to resonate with me as the more something or someone touched it, the larger it seemed to get.

Not only that, but behind the hole was a series of wood slats, and the hole did not seem to open up into some type of cavernous area behind it.

On top of this, I clearly remember some type of "fuzzies" being mixed in with the material the wall was made out of.

Unbeknownst to me at the time, the product that our walls were made out of was horsehair plaster.

Horsehair plaster is made out of varying combinations of water, lime, plaster, sand, and animal hair—you guessed it—most often horsehair.

Sometimes, the hair from other animals, such as oxen, donkeys, and goats, was utilized instead of horsehair.

Plants such as hemp, jute, reed, and straw have also been known to be used in place of animal hair; the challenge with the fibers from plants such as these, though, is that it is not as strong as the hair from the animals due to the protein-based qualities of the animal providing a stronger, more durable finish.

Horsehair was the "go-to" plaster for many years by many builders because it was so flexible in comparison to the other types of animal hair and plant fibers, and the finish was much more uniform.

These days, horsehair plaster is rarely utilized.

In fact, there are few practicing tradespeople around who even know how to make it, never mind working with it once it is made.

From a historical preservationist standpoint, some jobs actually require horsehair plaster repairs to be conducted with actual horsehair plaster; however, as the scopes of certain types of historical preservation projects require the project being done to utilize all building materials that are as closely in line with what was originally used as possible.

We are called on occasion to repair old horsehair plaster walls, such as the one mentioned from when I was growing up, utilizing modern-day repair methodologies.

If we were called in today to repair the hole that was behind my bunk bed as I was growing up, the first thing we would do would be to carve out any of the loose plaster around the hole.

We would keep going until the perimeter of the hole was as stable as possible.

From there, we would most likely stabilize the perimeter by screwing in plaster washers (see blog here: https://lopcocontracting.com/a-trick-to-fixing-frustratingly-stubborn-plaster-failures/) around the actual hole.

Then we can cut a piece of drywall to fit as snugly into the hole as possible, tape the perimeter and any related seams with fiberglass mesh tape, and then utilize joint compound to work the plaster repair from there (apply the joint compound to seams and perimeter, sand when dry, repeat until hole meets optimum smoothness).

After the repair is complete, things can be prepped, primed, and painted to the desired finish.

Although not old enough to have "When I was growing up..." translate into a phrase that includes the actual common utilization of horsehair plaster in daily plaster operations, I am still old enough to remember the time when horsehair plaster and its associated repair challenges were much more commonplace than they are today.

Graffiti

Believe it or not, there are quite a number of folks out there who consider graffiti to be as admired a form of art as others may view a Rembrandt or the Mona Lisa herself.

This view particularly gained steam in the 70s, specifically in New York City, and especially on miscellaneous train cars throughout the urban landscape.

From NYC, this controversial approach to art rapidly spread throughout the world and still holds a special place in the hearts of fans all over the planet.

To some, this may come as a shock, as the divisive piece surrounding this phenomenon is centered less on how beautiful many of these pieces end up being and more so on the degradation of the property where the graffiti is done.

Since its inception, there has been no shortage of folks whose efforts have been to curb the spread of graffiti, both near and far, in cities and beyond, wherever graffiti may be rearing its contentious head.

These days, if you happen to fall into the category of someone wanting to find the easiest way possible to remove an act of graffiti, you are in luck as with modern technology—to the fear of every graffiti-loving enthusiast—graffiti removal is less difficult than it ever has been.

Recently, I fielded a call from a frustrated facilities director of a local university who was calling us to review painting a structure that seemed to be a magnet for graffiti.

Due to the roughness of the wall surface the graffiti was being painted on, the school official thought that the institution really had no other choice but to paint the building that was getting pummeled by the unwanted version of this distinctive art form.

After hearing the serious concerns of this exasperated soul, I suggested a product and methodology that we have had tremendous success in removing graffiti.

It is a product called 'WipeOUT,' made by a company called 'Watch Dog.'

The way that it works is that the WipeOUT would be applied to the graffiti that one desires to remove.

The label instructions should be followed throughout this process, and ultimately, after a bit of time for the WipeOUT to kick in, the surface can be washed with a powerwasher, and the graffiti ought to come right off.

If there still seems to be some remaining, the process should be repeated again, and eventually, the graffiti should be removed.

The gentleman conversing with me was beyond thrilled that there may be an alternative solution to getting rid of the graffiti other than painting the entire building (…and subsequently repainting portions of it in the event that they got hit with more graffiti in the future!).

We have used this procedure for years with quite a bit of success.

As remarkable as this may seem to someone who has labored fruitlessly in attempts to try various methodologies for removing graffiti in the past to little avail, I assure you that I myself was a bit surprised at how well this worked when originally trying this ourselves some time ago.

Our company has even found this procedure to help remove paint from certain surfaces beyond graffiti!

Although graffiti admirers are scattered all over the globe, for those that aren't as enamored by its presence—particularly when art crosses the threshold of property damage—there may be solace in discovering that there is a solution.

Converting Interior Natural Wood to Painted Trim

_____

Although nowhere near the equivalent of a locksmith teaching a budding thief how to pick a lock, the topic of this article feels similarly dirty to me.

Doing what we do, we see some of the most beautiful natural wood trim on the interior of people's homes.

The finishes on this natural wood range from modern-day stain and polyurethane systems to ancient shellac coatings that truly are remarkable.

Once in a while, we get a request from someone who wants to paint this beautiful natural wood trim, if for no other reason than to bring the appearance of their overall interior to reflect more contemporary designs.

Each time we get asked to do this, I literally cringe.

Even with that being the case, we generally acquiesce and do a deep dive into what the potential project involves, as well as the pros and cons of painting the natural wood trim.

Once the natural wood trim is painted, THAT'S IT!!

Short of a monumental restoration process, there is no going back to the natural woodwork in anything that comes near to resembling a quick fashion.

Not only that, if the prep process is not done 100% correctly, then whoever is the owner of the natural wood trim may have a disaster on their hands.

As an example, if a step is skipped, the paint that is applied may easily get nicked and possibly begin to peel off in sheets the first time it is hit at precisely the correct angle.

The proper process (as I begin to delve into 'locksmith teaching the burglar' mode...), if one were to correctly convert natural wood trim to painted trim, looks like this:

- Lightly sand the wood trim that will be being worked on

- Clean off (wiping with a rag first, chased with a tack cloth)

- Carefully apply a coat of alcohol-based shellac

- Fill any imperfections (these will become accentuated after the first coat of primer is applied) using wood putty for any holes and acrylic caulk for any gaps in trim joints

- Apply a second coat of alcohol-based shellac

- Apply (two) coats of your desired trim finish (sanding in between coats and then wiping with a rag/tack cloth as necessary)

- Apply a third coat if it really seems like it may need it

YUCK!! I feel as though I have to go take a shower now...

In all seriousness, this is how we typically would do it.

As much as I try to talk folks out of it every time that they broach the subject with me, more often than not, people want what they want, and my word of caution seems to be appreciated but seldom sways the mission.

While my appreciation for finished natural woodwork pales in comparison to a great majority of seasoned veterans in the trades, as well as professionals with much deeper backgrounds in historical preservation, I still get irked by these types of projects.

However, as much as this is true, I do respect folks who would like to modernize the appearance of their living space, which is why we still undertake these types of tasks, even though our internal preferences may lean 180 degrees.

The Overly Annoying Woodpecker

There are few pests hitting up people's homes than New England woodpeckers.

Don't get me wrong.

Termites, carpenter ants, mice, carpenter bees, etc., are all unwelcome guests that cause enormous amounts of damage to our homes and businesses on a yearly basis, but for some reason, the tone of frustration that I have witnessed over the years with regard to active woodpeckers and the subsequent destruction that stems from their actions comparatively blasts the emotions generated by all of the other pests out of the water.

I have noticed this has become more true over the years.

While I am not sure if this is a coincidence or actually accurate from a scientific standpoint, all I can tell you is that each year, we seem to be on the phone with more and more home and business owners who are at their wit's end with these tiny, winged creatures.

It could be the constant pecking on the home, and when one goes out to scare them away, the woodpecker's departure may be short-lived as they seemingly hide in the trees and stare back at the house, waiting for their next opportunity to carry on with their incessant ruinous noisemaking.

Perhaps it is the actual damage that, unlike carpenter ants and termites, may be highly visible to anyone who might happen to pass by and glance at the house.

Or, possibly, it is the often unending mission to scare them away with some type of crazy tactic taken from the internet until one seems to work.

As tempting as it may be to call upon retired military Veteran and expert marksman 'Uncle Danny' to hide in the bushes with a BB gun, intent of picking off the feathered heathen at the first opportunity, woodpeckers are a protected species and any such discovered action would more than likely trigger the swift hand of the law to swoop down and really create a situation that will be unpleasant.

Years ago, I learned an interesting fact while visiting with a client—whom I later discovered was an ornithologist—who lived in Lincoln, RI, along the Blackstone River.

Up until this point in time, I had always thought that the woodpeckers were looking for food as they were pecking away at people's homes. On the contrary, my ornithologist client explained that they were actually looking for dates.

The wood pecking action was more along the lines of some type of mating call/ritual where the sounds that were being made on the surface being pecked on were an actual part of the attraction process for the opposite sex.

Just lovely.

While the noisemaking may be sweet sounding or a vital part of wood-pecker reproductive activity, it is far from sweet sounding or amusing to the home or business owner being affected by it.

Even worse news, no building material seems to be sacred.

We have observed woodpeckers causing harm to all different types of wood, composite material, and even stucco!

Sometimes, the damage is confined to one general area, and sometimes, it is spread throughout the entire exterior of a home.

There certainly appears to be no rhyme or reason.

As gut-wrenching as this may be to hear, the secret to ridding yourself of woodpeckers seems to be to keep trying different methodologies of attempting to ward them away until stumbling upon what may work.

If you would like to have an in-depth conversation about some techniques that we have seen used throughout the years, please feel free to reach out to our office and schedule a conversation with us.

Who knows?

We may have seen the one technique that you may not have been privy to and implemented as of yet, and it may be the technique that helps put the kibosh on one of nature's ultra-maddening dating games, which is using your home as its centerpiece.

The Hidden Rotten Wood that is Leading Your Home to be Eaten Away

Two homeowners we recently worked with have had about as good an attitude as one might imagine when addressing issues at their homes that were far from ideal.

In the first instance, we were working on the client's home and uncovered significant additional rot.

Both the client and the company knew that this was a possibility, but the client's mindset when the extent of the additional rot was revealed to be much greater than what was originally anticipated truly became clear was as ideal as one would hope to hear.

Instead of trying to encourage us to band-aid things and/or stop short of truly repairing what was rotted, the client urged us to keep going with the mindset of "It has to get fixed!"

In the second instance, we were hired to replace a rotted kickboard under a slider door, and throughout the conversation with the client, it quickly became evident to me just how savvy our newfound client was from a construction standpoint as she began walking me through what she expected us to find.

This was very pleasing to me because I am usually the one walking someone through the potential horror of rotted wood, which was very realistic in this case due to where the issue was located.

Both the client and I acknowledged that once we took that kickboard off, the sill under the door would most likely have to be replaced, which means the door would have to come out and/or be properly braced, and the vinyl siding around the door area would have to be carefully peeled back and then reinstalled after the repair was completed.

No small task for sure, but it's a perfect example of underscoring the value of addressing hidden rot.

Although in the first example, there was not any evidence of bug damage, there was plenty of evidence that this client's home was a juicy snack, ripe for the picking for the next set of carpenter ants or termites that were looking for a nice feast.

The second client was not as fortunate as the presence of termites, and their subsequent eradication was what led her to give us a ring in the first place.

As many who are in the thick of working through a termite or carpenter ant challenge are quick to find out (if they were not already aware), termites and carpenter ants gravitate toward areas in our home where wood has become moist.

This is why significant damage is often being incurred to our homes—totally unbeknownst to the homeowner.

Wood rots from the inside out.

Once you see a piece of rotted trim on your home, the chances are fairly high that the piece of trim is already rotted thoroughly on its backside, if not masking even deeper structural rot behind it.

Typically, the way this happens is that moisture gets behind the trim through some type of crack or crevice and begins to do its dirty work.

If not discovered soon enough, damage exemplified in the two examples here can surely set in before you know it.

Your best bet is to stay diligent, inspect your home twice a year (once in the spring and once in the fall) for potential rot, and reach out to a professional for further examination of anything that appears a bit concerning.

Although maintenance along the way in the form of making sure your paint/stain coatings are intact, seams are properly sealed, siding and trim are tight, etc., is the best preventative approach, if you are able to catch something that is rotted in the bud and have it corrected, you may be able to save yourself a great deal of heart and headache from if the situation were to continue to develop and you find yourself in a place which requires monumental repairs, that may or may not come along attached at the hip with a plethora of creepy crawlies, chomping away at the exterior of your home.

Acid Rain Effects on Windows

Earlier this year, we washed the exterior of a client's home and received a call of concern.

The actual washing came out nice, and the client seemed quite pleased as the home was now free from the unsightly mildew and mold that had set in and gripped her home's exterior. The challenge that arose, however, was that upon looking at their windows after things had dried out, there appeared to be a sort of clouding phenomenon occurring which the client had not previously noticed on certain windows.

When our techs went out on site, they did a quick test, and it was soon discovered that what was being observed was not necessarily anything related to the washing, but what was being seen were the lingering effects of acid rain.

Acid rain is a broad term that refers to any type of precipitation with acidic components (examples: sulfuric or nitric acid) that fall to the ground in either wet or dry forms—these include rain, snow, fog, hail, or even acidic dust! (Source: United States Environmental Protection Agency)

Air pollution is the cause of acid rain, as when gases produced from the burning of different types of fuels react with the oxygen in the air and water vapor, the acids are then osmosed into the rain that falls to the Earth.

As acid rain falls, it has widespread adverse effects, which have been known to include health problems in people, forestry damage, harmful impacts on bodies of water and their associated ecosystems, and, in our example, damage to buildings and objects.

In the instance of our window, the acid rain leaves a cloudy, grayish/white, ashy-looking type buildup on the glass in different thicknesses.

There are several solutions that may work to clean off this buildup.

If you do a search on the Internet, you will most likely come up with many methods for removing the acid rain effects from the affected areas of this glass on your windows.

Although there are a number of very valid approaches, perhaps one of the simplest and most effective methodologies is to mix one cup of regular vinegar with one quart of clean water.

After combining them and loading the solution into a spray bottle, spray the areas where the acid rain has left its mark.

Then, wipe off the sprayed areas with a clean cloth (paper towel, microfiber cloth, or the like).

It is important to use a clean portion of the cloth each time you wipe so that the dirt on the cloth does not mix with the other areas you are working to clean and leave streak marks behind.

The vinegar technique should actually produce quite a nice shine on the glass.

While not the only strategy for getting the job done, my sense is that this uncomplicated procedure will work rather well for you.

Unfortunately, the results of pollution throughout our society are not new news.

I remember being taught about acid rain when I was in elementary school in the mid-1980s, and as with many things these days, the consequences of acid rain have not gotten a whole lot better over time; in fact, the opposite may indeed be true.

No matter whether you live in an area that is greatly affected by acid rain or sees very little evidence of its existence, knowing how to recognize its presence on your home's glass and how to properly clean it may prove at some point to be a valuable tidbit of information amongst your home improvement acumen.

What Happens When You Stain Over Paint?

One of the biggest benefits of applying solid stain to the exterior of your home is that typically it does not "fail" in the manner traditional paints "fail."

When people think of exterior paint failing, what often comes to mind is visions of peeling/flaking paint that is significantly unsightly and which would ignite absolute dread when thinking about the idea of having to correct it.

After all, properly prepping and finishing any exterior surface takes an extraordinary amount of effort, even in some situations where the surface may already appear to be fairly sound.

In approaching exterior prepping and finishing, there are always cleaning efforts necessary prior to painting as well as usually some form of thorough inspection to ensure the surfaces to be coated are free from rotted wood, previous coating failure, etc.

If the previous coatings do happen to be failing, efforts to stabilize the surfaces so that they are ready to receive their next coating vary from not too much effort needed to an unbelievable amount of elbow grease required.

Making sure the surface is sound involves different types of approaches of scraping, sanding, and the like, and they are seldom viewed as fun endeavors.

Realizing this, when folks hear about the benefits of solid stains, it is easy to fall in love with the idea that maintaining one's exterior coating surface in the future is much easier with a solid stain than paint, and they might automatically desire to coat their home with a solid stain the next time their home is painted.

Whilst this may make sense on the surface (no pun intended), the feasibility of the reality of this theory may not be quite that simple.

Although the way that solid stains do eventually "fail" (gradual fading, light degradation of the coating structure, though no massive "peeling" per se) may be highly appealing for those hoping to maintain the long-term beauty of their home's exterior with minimum effort, the circumstances in which this seemingly utopic exterior coating system performs in this manner are influenced by a variety of factors.

Assuming the surface that it is being applied to is receptive to receiving exterior coatings (no presence of mill glaze or similar type of repelling factor), a solid stain is an awesome solution if used as the initial coating system or recoated over another solid stain surface.

At times, I have been asked if a solid stain could be applied over a surface that has been previously finished with exterior paint.

The traditionalist answer to this question would be a quick "no" as solid stains theoretically are meant to "penetrate" the surface they are being applied over, and if there is a paint coating already on the surface, then clearly any stain being applied will not be able to "penetrate" in the normal sense of the word.

While this is true, solid stains today are formulated much differently than solid stains of years ago.

Back in the day, solid stains were often predominantly oil-based and truly meant to penetrate the surface they were being applied.

Suggesting applying a solid stain over any type of exterior painted surface would have been virtual heresy.

These days, as a by-product of solid stains being so heavily waterborne or latex/acrylic-based, science sways things in a different direction because although the intent of solid stains is still for them to be applied as their own separate system and not applied over a "painted" surface, if the "painted" surface is sound and properly prepared, you may successfully be able to apply a solid stain over the paint.

Now, don't get me wrong.

If the painted surface that lies beneath the solid stained coating ever decides to peel, it will do so and take the solid stain coating with it.

However, if the painted surface remains intact, the solid stain will stay on the painted surface for years to come without any detrimental effect.

This all being said, applying a solid stain over paint, due to modern technology, is something that can absolutely be done, with lasting characteristics, but this will occur less because of the properties of the solid stain performing as they are historically meant to perform, but more so because of how terrifically the paint coatings underneath the solid stain being applied remain in place.

Why Having Gutters on Your Home "Should" Not Matter

Architects and contractors have been arm wrestling with each other since the beginning of time.

The reason is that architects love to hone in on aesthetics, and contractors, on the other hand, tend to focus on practicality.

In fact, sometimes, if there is not someone who serves as a conduit in the middle to serve as a mediator (I have played this role for as far back as I can remember!), things can get pretty brutal!

One great example of this is the existence of a gutter system in someone's home.

Many architects do not love gutter systems, as their thought process is they take away from the architectural beauty of the home to varying degrees.

Contractors are the total opposite (shocking!) as they, for the most part, believe that gutters are vital to a home's exterior as they work to keep water funneled away from the home.

Although I am very much of the mindset that all homes should have gutters, I do recognize that, in theory, gutters "should" be a "nice-to-have," not a "need-to-have."

The perfect example of this is a recent project that we were working on where we had taken the existing gutter system off the home in preparation for installing a new gutter system. In between the time when the existing gutter system was taken down and the new gutter system was due to be put up, a rain event occurred, and water came into the house.

I received a frantic phone call from a family member of the elderly homeowner who thought that the taking down of the gutter system was the cause of the water coming into the home.

Knowing that this could not have really been the base reason, I tried to calm the concerned family member down as best I could as we had a variety of technicians descend upon the home.

After a short investigation, it was obvious as to why the water was coming into the home.

Although the gutters definitely were helpful in catching water off the main roof and guiding it away from the home, the real reason the water was coming into the home was that at the point where the flat roof below the gutter system met the main home, the rubber that served as the roof system was not ideally flashed into the home and any water hitting this area at the right angle and the right volume would absolutely make its way into the home.

This is not unusual.

Whether it is water coming in a basement, hitting the house at an odd angle and causing the wood to rot out, or getting inside of the home as in this example where a roof was not properly terminated as it met the home, having a gutter system in place should not matter.

All of these types of situations are scenarios where, if other things were done properly, the crutch of having a gutter system really would not be needed.

Many times, when a home is not graded properly, the exterior is not sealed correctly, or some other area of construction is not carried out the way that it should have been in the first place, the lack of functionality of the existing gutter system is called into place when the truth of the matter is that if these other items were appropriately taken care of, a gutter system would not be needed.

While I still believe gutter systems are an absolute necessity for people's homes as they serve a variety of useful purposes (not oversaturating the perimeter of the home with moisture, allowing for the collection and subsequent recycling of rainwater, etc.), I also recognize that in many cases gutter systems actually aid in masking real issues on our homes that may not even be known, but that will stay hidden indefinitely as long as the luxury of having the gutter system in place to cover up these sins will allow.

When a Doghouse is not a Doghouse

When people hear the term 'doghouse,' many connotations may come to mind.

One may think of the structure that Snoopy used to be depicted as sleeping on in the old 'Peanuts' cartoons.

The picture of a more traditional type of doghouse may also be thought of, the kind that is a roughly built, literal, small, one-room "house" in the backyard with a singular opening on the front of it for both entry and exit.

Then, of course, there is also the kind of doghouse which I would venture to bet that hardly anybody in a relationship would enjoy finding themselves in and trying to work their way out of, as the cliché of finding oneself in their romantic partner's doghouse typically means that somebody is unhappy with their partner.

Although these are certainly all viable, there is another 'doghouse' that not as many may be familiar with, but if you happen to have one in your home, your mind may go directly to as a definition of the term "doghouse."

This particular variety of doghouses actually serves as an entrance to the basement of one's home and is also often referred to as a 'bulkhead entrance.'

Though very different than the traditional bulkhead entrance in that when many folks think of a 'bulkhead,' they often think of a unit made out of steel, fiberglass, or other material that is situated toward the ground and able to be opened (usually having a set of double doors or in some instances a 'hatch' opening), the doghouse bulkhead is still thought of as a bulkhead entrance.

For those who do not have a basement, there is a chance that you may have absolutely no idea what a bulkhead is to begin with.

A bulkhead simply is some type of structure that serves as an outside entrance to one's basement and is made up of two major parts:

1) Stairs that lead into the basement
2) Some type of built out protection above these stairs, providing security and guarding against elements of weather

As mentioned, a good portion of the time, the bulkhead is a unit built closer to the ground and is likely not very elaborate.

The doghouse, however, is much more built out than the units which simply serve as a set of doors leading to the stairs and heading down to the basement.

A doghouse bulkhead is one that is built up to some degree, many times, to mirror the way the rest of the house looks.

Doghouse bulkheads tend to have some type of roof, siding that matches that of the house, and a regular entry door that opens up leading into it.

Depending on the beholder, doghouse bulkheads are often viewed as more attractive than their bulkhead door cousins.

Construction of doghouse bulkheads is a bit different than simply fabricating and installing a bulkhead door ground unit, as there are potentially several construction elements involved, i.e., roofing, siding, painting, etc.

Adding a doghouse bulkhead after the house has already been built can be even more challenging, especially if the intent is to do so in a fashion that makes it look as though the doghouse bulkhead has always been there.

Some of the benefits of doghouse bulkheads are that they can be opened without having to bend over or lift up a heavier door, they can provide storage on their interior walls, and they serve as a bit more comfortable access point for getting into the basement from the exterior of the home.

While not necessarily being the first thing that one envisions when hearing the term 'doghouse,' for many people, having a doghouse in their home is a feature that they truly enjoy and are VERY happy to have.

What is a 'Break'?

Similar to many areas of life, in construction, words can have many meanings.

Perhaps a great example of this is the word "square."

A square can refer to many things.

As with areas outside of construction, a square can mean the geometrical shape in which all four sides of this box-like figure are equal in length.

A square can also be referencing a type of tool that carpenters use to execute measurements throughout the course of any given project.

The one meaning of 'square,' which, over the years, I have gotten a kick out of when I have heard contractors use it, is the meaning in which the term square refers to 100 square feet.

I have often giggled in my head when I hear the random contractor yell out, "Hey Johnny, we need 5 square of those shingles on-site first thing in the morning!"

'Square' or 'Squares' can both be plural—equally delightful!!

The term 'square' seems to sometimes be used almost as an unintentional piece of code used to test the understanding of the construction language of those around whomever may be barking out the term.

'Square' is one of those descriptors that is proudly said, almost as a badge of honor.

This interesting word which those in the society of construction trades truly understand, and anyone within earshot who may happen to hear it being spoken and comprehends what the person using the word is saying can even earn the non-construction-oriented observant some type of instant street cred within the construction brotherhood.

A 'square' can be any type of measurement of 100 square feet.

This could mean wood or vinyl siding, roofing, any type of decking, etc.

Sometimes, I hear the term being used by contractors in a manner in which I wonder if the contractor is using the term in conversation to help galvanize their trade-specific knowledge base in the eyes of whomever it is they are speaking with.

Not that simply knowing how to correctly use the word in a conversation is the be-all and end-all in terms of one's knowledge of their trade, but simply sprinkling it in a sentence here or there may indeed be a confidence builder for the tradesperson who is using it.

The ironic component of this strategy, of course, is that just as in any other occupation, using non-layman's terms can be ultimately confusing for whomever it is that you are speaking with and may actually shade one's view toward the negative on your end vs. the positive.

A parallel example may be with a doctor who spits out crazy medical terms, even if purely subconsciously. In reality, my guess is that a good portion of their patients could care less about the technical mumbo jumbo and really want to know if they are sick and what the next steps should be moving forward explained in the simplest way possible.

Construction is no different.

While it certainly is important to know the terminology of whatever industry you are in, knowing when to use certain words or phrasing and when not to use them in the most effective way possible could be just as valuable as knowing the industry-specific jargon in the first place.

How to get Paint, Tar, Gum, etc., Out of Clothes

_____

Recently, I received a somewhat frenzied call from a good friend of mine who frantically asked, "What's a great product to remove paint stains? Got some on my jacket and fighting to get it out completely."

In going back and forth a bit, it was determined that the product was a latex product, and he had noticed it soon enough that he was able to clean as much as possible of it off right away.

Fortunately for him, his first instinct was to "use water," whereas in another scenario, he could have very well picked "paint thinner" instead and totally found himself up the proverbial creek.

At this point, it is advised for someone in this situation to let the item of clothing dry out completely before doing anything else—which he did (whether intentionally or unintentionally).

The steps that my friend had taken up until this point are in line with what I would have proposed.

Here would be my exact recommended approach if finding yourself in a similar situation:

1) Figure out whether the paint product that has gotten on the clothing is latex or oil (if by chance it is a solvent-based product other than oil, either contact the supplier for direction or reach out to our office at (401)270-2664for guidance).

2) Immediately use water to clean off a latex-based product or paint thinner to clean off an oil-based product; this is where experimentation is needed to test how much water/paint thinner is necessary to get out as much as you can

3) Allow the article of clothing to dry

4) Once the article is dry, use "spray" 'Household Surface SAFE GOOF-OFF' for a dried "latex stain" or lacquer

thinner for a dried oil stain; DO NOT apply either product directly to the article of clothing; instead, put on a rag and gradually work the stain out of the article of clothing.

5) After the stain is out and after allowing the article to dry, wash with a "good" laundry detergent

By following this process, although certainly not guaranteed, you are providing yourself with the best shot possible for getting the stain out.

My friend was in luck.

He had a great guess as to what to initially attempt to take the stain out with and happened to catch me as he was entering into 'Step 3' (beginning to let the clothing dry out after the initial effort at cleaning it).

Things could have transpired much differently if he had elected to try removing the latex product with paint thinner.

This act of good fortune, combined with him utilizing the best techniques possible from that point on out, gave him a fighting chance at saving his beloved jacket, which could have very easily been on its way to a donation bin or the landfill.

What Happens When it Rains in the Middle of Exterior Painting?

Many years ago, at some point in the mid to late 90s, we were painting a home, I believe in Northern RI, and while we were working on the home, we got caught in a flash rainstorm.

It was one of those that popped up out of thin air, most likely on a day that there was minimal (30% or less) chance of rain.

Although my memory is a bit foggy on the exact details, I do recall that I was not onsite at the time, but received a frantic call from the crew that they were caught out there.

There was nowhere to run, nowhere to hide.

Everything was fine for one minute, and then the next minute, 'BOOM!!' Total devastation!!

The crew was completely drenched.

Not only were they and their equipment soaking wet, but the newly painted side of the house they had been working on caught the brunt of things as well.

The client happened to be home at the time and was distraught (as you might imagine).

He realized that the rain appeared out of nowhere, attacked our crew and his newly painted home, and was sympathetic but understandably upset, as this project that he had such a sizeable investment in just took a whack from wet weather as it was in the process of being painted.

What a DISASTER!!!

Or was it?...

These types of things happen on occasion.

As much as we do everything we can to prevent them from occurring, they still rear their not-so-pleasant heads every now and again.

I often say that meteorologists do not get paid to get the forecast correct; we, as contractors, get paid to get the forecast correct.

Meteorologists get paid to provide their best scientific analysis of what the weather is going to do, however, their paycheck is not dependent upon the correctness of this forecast.

When a contractor is working on the outside of someone's home, you best believe that they get paid to get the forecast correct.

If they do not get it correct, it can be financially ruinous to their business.

Picture the roof of someone's home being off as it is in the process of being replaced, and then the contractor getting caught in a rainstorm without things being watertight—YIKES!!!

Although perhaps not as dramatic, the same concept is true when painting the exterior of a home.

In the three decades of being in the business and the hundred of homes we have worked on in Southern New England, I have yet to see an exterior paint job that was actually "ruined" by getting caught in the rain.

Even in the example we have discussed here, the paint job was nowhere near unsalvageable.

After things had dried out, we simply had to go back and recoat the side we had been painting as the paint had set up and was merely 'water-marked,' but thankfully easily fixed with another coat of finish paint.

Still cost us a bit out of our pocket to redo, obviously, but it did not require as much aggravation as first thought to correct.

Even in the craziest of circumstances, after allowing things to dry out, we may have to prep the surface slightly in order to proceed to the next step in the process, but never more than that.

We have instruments called 'moisture meters' which we can plug into the side of a home after a storm if we ever have a question as to whether or not an area was in the safe zone (a moisture content measurement of 15% or less) to proceed with work on.

With today's technology being much more advanced than in the mid to late 90s, it is much easier to guard against damaging effects from pop-up rainstorms, as well as to guide us (as necessary) to best move forward if we do get hit with one of these unnerving surprises.

Although certainly not fun, I believe there is solace in knowing that all is not lost if Mother Nature decides to throw a soggy curveball at us while we are in the middle of painting the exterior of our homes.

If this were the opposite, I would surely have much stronger 'Chicken Little' feelings every time I felt even the slightest drop of rain.

How to Prep Peeling Exterior Paint on Modern Homes

When approaching painting the exterior of your home, it is no secret that proper surface preparation should be the single most important focus in order to best ensure maximizing the longevity of the exterior paint coating.

Obviously, there are other factors involved as well (quality of paint, etc.), but correct surface preparation, more so than any other item, is the best way to guarantee your home looks as beautiful as possible for as long as possible after your paint job has been completed.

Cleaning the surfaces being painted, utilizing caulk and putty to fill cracks and nail holes, and priming with a robust priming system are all part of this process; however, just as important (if not moreso) is working to make sure that the surface you are going to be painting is as sound as possible.

Addressing any areas of peeling paint is the largest component of this mission, and depending upon the type of peeling involved, there are a number of different approaches for executing this properly.

If the home is an older structure (built before 1978), the possibility of lead paint being somehow embedded into the fibers of the wood on the home is a valid concern, and the rules of engagement will vary quite differently than for a home built during newer time periods.

For contemporary homes, the manner of attack for making sure that any peeling paint issues are neutralized should really begin with attempting to figure out why the paint was peeling in the first place.

Is the paint peeling simply due to normal wear and tear, or is there a deeper issue involved?

In some instances, particularly with modern white cedar shingle and red cedar clapboard siding (that which was installed at some point in time since the mid-1980s), there is the possibility that an issue known as 'mill glaze' could be at play and actually could be preventing paint (or primer for that matter) from sticking to these surfaces as all.

Moisture could be a factor as well if it somehow gets behind the building material that the exterior paint is attached to.

If moisture is getting behind areas that are painted, it could be forcing the paint on the surface in front of it to peel as the sun heats up the side of your home and pulls the moisture out the front face of the painted siding or trim, taking with it any paint that may be sitting on its surfaces in the process.

Assuming that there are no major unique paint failures at play requiring special attention and that any areas of possible moisture infiltration are addressed, the process for preparing peeling paint on a surface to be painted is fairly straightforward from here.

Any of the larger areas of peeling paint should be thoroughly scraped to remove as much of the loose paint as possible.

The modern-day superpower known as 'common sense' should prevail at this point, and you should have some type of drop cloth, sheet, or plastic laid down to help protect the areas around where you are working and catch any falling paint chips.

After the peeling areas have been scraped as best as they can be, the next step would be to 'feather sand' the edges of the areas of scraped paint left behind and to work the surface so that it is smooth prior to applying primer.

When you move to the next step of 'priming the surface,' after the primer dries, you may decide that more sanding may be necessary, and if so, you are absolutely able to feather sand some more and reprime from there.

Keep working the surface until a sound surface has been achieved, and with dried primer on, it appears as though things are as smooth as they can be, and voila, you have properly prepared the exterior peeling paint and should be ready for a finish coat!!

What are Lap Marks?

Even though the exterior house stains of today perform much differently than their ancestors, they certainly embody many of their elders' characteristics.

As an example, when able to be used, stains tend not to be as susceptible to peeling as the paint is, which has always been one of the more attractive reasons for using stains.

These days, solid stains provide the appearance of paint (for better or worse) much more so than solid stains from years ago.

Some people like this, others not so much.

One aspect of working with stains, from translucent to solid stains, is the challenge of avoiding lap marks.

If you have ever worked with stain and applied the product off a ladder, then either lowered the ladder to paint to the bottom of the side you are working on or moved the ladder over (without keeping a "wet edge") and then continued to apply the product, then stepped back to admire your work and have been alarmed at what you saw, you most likely have discovered the joy of the "lap mark."

Lap marks are marks that show up as variations in color/sheen appearance (even though stains technically do not have a sheen associated with them), which look as though someone was applying product to a certain area, then stopped, then continued with the unevenness in appearance being the result.

When a lap mark is present, you are immediately in a bit of a pickle.

Correcting lap marks is going to take a bit of hard work and experimentation.

Depending upon the type of stain product that was being used, the process for fixing these unsightly monstrosities will vary.

Minimally, they will need to be sanded out to some degree, and you will have to play around to see how deep surface preparation will be required in order to allow things to be "evened out."

The ultimate goal would, of course, be to avoid having to deal with lap marks in the first place.

This can be done by simply following a couple of easy steps.

I mentioned the term keeping a "wet edge," what this refers to is keeping the edges of your product "wet" by leaving a little extra product prior to moving your ladder so that you can pick up from where you left off as you safely reposition yourself to continue applying the product.

Keeping a "wet edge" should be done in conjunction with the approach of, literally, aiming to apply product to one (or no more than three) boards at a time, from one end to another.

Put plainly, if you are able to paint one end of a board from beginning to end while maintaining a wet edge in the process, you will greatly eliminate the possibility of lap marking taking place.

This is true for both horizontal and vertical siding, decks, etc.

If this is not able to be done, there is a very good possibility that you will end up staring at the outside of your home after hours of potentially excruciating work, and instead of the gratifying satisfaction of a job well done, be confronted by a stunningly disappointing appearance of this lap mark phenomenon, which could have easily been avoided with the proper technique being utilized from the beginning.

An Exterior Caulking No-No

Many years ago, we were working on a project in Providence, RI, that as we were doing the surface preparation on the exterior of the home, we noticed there were several gaps throughout the butt areas of the home's clapboard siding.

Being an older home, this was not necessarily surprising to see.

Puffing out our chests, we thought we could fix this unsightly phenomenon by simply caulking all the gaps that we saw.

After we worked through the rest of the prepping and finishing of the exterior of the home, we stood back and admired what truly appeared to be a masterpiece.

Not only was the paint job done to perfection, but there was not a gap in sight, and we were proud to leave the job site with a finished product in place, which we knew our client was sure to enjoy for years to come.

Or so we thought…

Fast forward a year later, and our office received a call that our client's once beautiful exterior was beginning to peel in a manner in which it had never done before. The client was entirely confused as he had thought he had received the best paint job known to man.

Perplexed myself, I let our client know that I would be by as soon as I could to inspect things and see if I could figure out what was going on.

When I arrived onsite, the paint on the clapboard was peeling all over the place, and many areas that were not peeling yet appeared as though they were on the verge of peeling.

The paint on the trim was entirely intact.

The clapboard, however, particularly on the sides that were most exposed to the sun, was peeling or beginning to peel all over the place.

My heart dropped into my stomach.

This paint job was absolutely stunning when we completed it; why was this happening?

After a bit of investigating, the massive peeling on this home actually made perfect sense.

While falling under the category of learning things "the hard way," I discovered that as well-intentioned as we were in caulking the home and eliminating all its gaps, what we were really doing as an unintended by-product of our sealing things up was, literally, sealing the house up to the point its siding could not flex and breath as it could so easily do without all these gaps being sealed.

What we were effectively doing was stopping the siding from being allowed to fluctuate its shape with changes in humidity as well as preventing interior moisture's ease of passage to the exterior.

We were trapping a ton of moisture behind the clapboard, and as the sun would heat up certain areas of the home, the moisture would push its way out through the front of the clapboard and take our beautiful paint job with it.

Although cosmetically it may look terrific, you should NEVER caulk the underside of the clapboard, in between the gaps where shingle siding meets each other or any gap that could impede the natural expansion and contraction of the siding of your home or its ability to naturally allow moisture to pass from the inside to the outside.

This is an ultimate 'NO NO' when it comes to the exterior paint preparation on the outside of your home.

Some of the most valuable lessons we learn in life stem from mistakes we make and learning what NOT to do in the future.

Believe me, this is a mistake we did not enjoy fixing, but in the process of doing so, we extruded a terrific lesson in home breathability, which would prove itself extremely valuable in the future!

Do Curling, Warping, or Buckled Siding Shingles Need to be Replaced?

One of the more New England-oriented things to do when it comes to the exterior decor on one's home is to let white cedar shingle siding weather.

When using the term "weather," I am referencing literally, not (or minimally) treating the shingles.

The purpose of allowing shingles to weather is typically to allow them to achieve an appearance that has become synonymous with many "beach" communities—think Cape Cod, Block Island, Narragansett, Martha's Vineyard, Nantucket, etc.

Unlike their red cedar cousins, when left to weather, white cedar shingles will change in appearance over time.

They will shrink and "gray" out, even if treated with some type of a clear coat water protectant/repellant system.

When accompanied by white trim, a home with grayed-out white cedar shingles seems to officially be able to check the boxes and achieve this "beachy" home status.

Although white cedar shingles tend not to rot out in the traditional idea of rot (becoming soft and punky, which could happen in certain situations —above a window or door as an example—but is rare), their physical shape will be greatly changed over time.

White cedar shingles, particularly the more weather they are exposed to, will give off the vibe of a wooden contortionist.

Curling, warping, buckling, and the like are very much what one would expect as the white cedar weather.

We field dozens of yearly calls regarding this phenomenon, and folks are concerned as to whether the shingles need replacing.

My answer always is, "It depends."

If you want your shingles cosmetically to look as perfect as possible, then perhaps replacing the contorted shingles is something that may be worth looking into.

Even attempting to pre-drill holes in certain areas of the shingles (to avoid cracking) and driving stainless steel ring nails into the shingle will usually not be a viable solution in terms of satisfying the urge to "flatten" the white cedar shingles' look when they get to a certain state of natural curvy being.

From a structural standpoint, assuming the white cedar shingles were originally installed correctly, they should be absolutely fine.

Each white cedar shingle is between 18" and 24" long.

Because of the way the shingles are layered and weaved as they are installed, the only portion of the shingle that is most greatly affected by the weather is the portion of the shingle that is actually exposed to the weather (somewhere between 5" and 8" of the shingle).

Shingle siding is installed from the bottom of your home.

This means that there are many layers of protection, guarding against moisture penetration as the shingle siding makes its way up and around the house.

The shingles are staggered when they are installed, which allows for water to be shed without the worry that it will land in a gap directly below it.

I am not sure that anyone would make the argument that white cedar shingle siding bending and curving at all different angles is "pretty," but it is important to note that regardless of the way they cosmetically appear, white cedar shingles twisting six ways to Sunday over time does not necessarily warrant replacement in the interest of stabilizing the structural integrity of your home.

Is Painting Over Wallpaper a Good Idea?

Once in a while, I get asked a serious question, which is done with valid intention, but to some folks, hearing it being asked may invoke a bit of giggling until they hear an answer for it, which possibly changes their tune and gets them to nod their head in approval.

"Is Painting Over Wallpaper a Good Idea?" falls directly into this category.

If the average home improvement contractor/painter were to overhear someone asking me this question, their initial reaction might be a bit of head shaking accompanying a chuckle, as the question on its surface may seem a bit ridiculous to them.

After all, if one was going to paint a wall with wallpaper on it, wouldn't they want to take the wallpaper off first?

I mean, seriously, isn't that the whole purpose of painting a wallpapered wall properly?

If you paint over wallpaper, aren't the surfaces just going to look like painted wallpaper??

Possibly.

However, possibly not...

As crazy an idea as painting over wallpaper may appear to be on the surface, there are not only viable circumstances that may justify painting the wallpaper, but there are typically ways to paint a wallpapered wall and make it look like a regular painted wall without any long-term negative implications.

Even if it "can" be done, why the heck would someone want to paint over wallpaper in the first place?

Possibly for a number of reasons...

The person undertaking the project may be afraid that if the wallpaper is removed, the walls that the wallpaper is attached to may come off with it.

In many instances, this is a legitimate concern!

Maybe the person taking on the project is short on time and needs to get the walls painted quickly.

Or perhaps the person merely wants to paint the walls and not have to deal with the hassle of removing the wallpaper.

If the goal is to paint the wallpaper and truly have things look like what one would expect to see when looking at a normally painted wall, there are certain things that must be done in order to achieve this correctly.

The first thing one should do is to make sure that the walls are clean and that any loose paper is surgically removed (a razor knife teamed with a putty knife will work fine for this task).

After that, a prime coat of 'GARDZ' or comparable primer should be applied to the wallpaper to stabilize its surfaces and neutralize any weird reaction that the coming layers of the product might have with any adhesive used to originally hold the wallpaper in place.

Following this, I would suggest priming the walls with a latex primer, then smoothing out any imperfections and/or seams with a thin layer of joint compound or spackle, sanding the dried joint compound or spackle after it has dried, spot priming the sanded areas, and then repeating the process of smoothing out/sanding/priming until the surface appears to be prepped properly enough (smooth looking and feeling) to paint.

Then, finally, apply two coats of finish (in this scenario, my suggestion is a 'matte' sheen), and voila, at this point, you should have some pretty good-looking painted wallpaper!

Although I am certainly not advocating for painting over wallpaper as a common practice, as my preference truly is to remove the wallpaper completely prior to painting, I am simply acknowledging that contrary to popular opinion, wallpaper can absolutely be painted and is not as horrible an idea as one may initially think.

What is the Purpose of Lattice?

A number of years ago, I was having a conversation with a client, and they were excitedly telling me a story of how the previous day, they were looking for a paint product that they knew was around their home, but they just could not figure out where they left it.

Their search took them to the shed in their backyard, where upon opening the shed door, they discovered—to their heart-dropping surprise—a napping coyote!

Although beyond startled, the client had enough sense to softly close the door and tiptoe backward until they were comfortable they were far enough away and were able to quickly hurry into their home.

While not as dramatic, it would not be unusual for us to find animals taking shelter in various areas around our homes, particularly under porches, decks, etc.

One way that this can be prevented is by utilizing lattice to—in a nice-looking way—close off these areas, which are tempting for many wild animals looking for a place to hang out and set up camp.

Though lattice would not keep out mice and tinier creatures that may be able to fit through their openings, it certainly can be effective in keeping out rats, squirrels, raccoons, groundhogs, and yes—coyotes!

Lattice is a type of framework made of wood, metal, or plastic that is often used around people's homes for various purposes—not just for keeping animals out from where it is preferred they not be! It's made up of crisscrossed strips or bars, creating a pattern with open spaces in between.

Lattice is fairly easy to find for purchase at any lumberyard, neighborhood hardware store, big box hardware store, many department stores, or plenty of places online.

One common use of lattice around homes is as a decorative element. It can be attached to fences, decks, or porches to add a touch of style and charm. Lattice panels come in different designs, such as diamond, square, or oval patterns, allowing homeowners to choose one that matches their aesthetic preferences.

Another popular use of lattice is for privacy and screening. By installing lattice panels around a patio or deck, homeowners can create a sense of seclusion without completely blocking off the area. Vines or climbing plants can be trained to grow on the lattice, providing additional privacy while also enhancing the visual appeal of the space.

Lattice can also serve as a support structure for climbing plants and vines in gardens. By attaching lattice panels to walls or fences, homeowners can create vertical gardens, allowing plants to grow upwards and save space. This is particularly useful for small yards or areas with limited ground space for gardening.

Lattice is a versatile and often practical addition to homes, offering functional benefits as well as those that are cosmetically pleasing—and it can be super for enhancing privacy!

Whether it's used for keeping out coyotes, improving outdoor aesthetics, creating privacy, or supporting climbing plants, a lattice is a popular choice for homeowners looking to beautify and improve their outdoor spaces

How Does the Color Green Relate to Home Improvement?

As the luck of the Irish might have it, the color green is clearly synonymous with St. Patrick's Day.

What you may not realize, however, is that it is also VERY closely related to home improvement!

The color green is, in fact, like a secret weapon in the world of home improvement. It's not just a color; it's a whole vibe that can totally transform your living space. Let's dive into how the color green relates to home improvement and why it's such a big deal.

First off, green is all about bringing the outdoors in. Think about how calming it feels to be surrounded by nature—the green of trees, grass, and plants. When you use green in your home, whether through paint, decor, or even plants, it instantly creates a connection to the natural world. It's like having a little piece of the great outdoors right in your living room.

But green is more than just a pretty color. It's also a symbol of growth and renewal. Imagine painting your bedroom walls a soothing shade of green. It's like giving your room a fresh start, a clean slate to grow and evolve. Green has an amazing ability to make a space feel alive and full of potential.

Speaking of potential, green is all about balance and harmony. Have you ever noticed how calming it is to stare at a green meadow or sit under a shady tree? That's because green has a magical way of bringing everything into balance. Using green in your home, whether as a wall color or in your decor, creates a sense of peace and tranquility. It's like hitting the reset button on your stress levels.

But the benefits of green don't stop there. Green is also closely linked to health and wellness. Research has shown that being surrounded by greenery can have a positive impact on both our physical and mental well-being. That's why incorporating green into your home, whether through indoor plants or green accents, can make you feel happier and more relaxed. It's like giving your home a healthy dose of good vibes.

And let's not forget about sustainability. In today's world, being eco-friendly is more important than ever. Luckily, green is the color of all things eco-friendly. When you choose green building materials, energy-efficient appliances, and sustainable design practices for your home improvement projects, you're not just helping the planet—you're also creating a healthier, more sustainable home for you and your family.

So, how can you incorporate more "green" into your home? Start small with some indoor plants or green accents like throw pillows or curtains. If you're feeling bold, paint a feature wall in your favorite shade of green, or go all out and paint an entire room. And don't forget about the outdoors! Planting trees, shrubs, and flowers in your yard not only adds more green to your life but also boosts your home's curb appeal.

The color green is like a superhero in the world of home improvement. It brings the outdoors in, symbolizes growth and renewal, creates balance and harmony, promotes health and wellness, and supports sustainability. Whether you're painting your walls, decorating your space, or landscaping your yard, don't forget to add a little green—it's sure to make your home a happier, healthier, and more beautiful place to be.

How to Get Rid of Nicotine Stains

Have you ever taken a picture off someone's wall (perhaps even your own?), and there was an outline of where the picture stood, which almost made it look like the picture was still on the wall?

Although this scenario could stem from a variety of different reasonings, one very challenging situation to correct is if the staining around the picture was caused by nicotine.

Other ways that this type of thing could have happened would be prolonged burning of certain types of candles, a "puff back" from the heating system, or even soot related to a fireplace somehow making its way through the living space.

Nicotine, however, may just be the most stubborn of them all.

Regardless of how one feels about someone smoking in the house, this type of nicotine staining is quite the problem.

What often happens is comparable to the morbid myth which is heard on the occasion of boiling a frog by placing it on a stove in a cooler pot of water, turning up the heat, and bringing the water to a boil and having the frog's goose cooked before they had a chance to realize it.

As grotesque an analogy as this may be, the principal holds VERY true for those who allow smoking in their home where, over time, the nicotine staining builds up on the walls undetected until one day someone takes that picture off the wall, and it hits them as to what the condition of their walls have transpired to.

Once the nicotine staining is recognized, the question of how to fix the situation may soon follow.

If the nicotine staining is not properly addressed, it will bleed through the coats of paint that are put on top of it, and one will be chasing their tail infinitely attempting to stop the staining from bleeding through.

The funny thing about this situation is someone may live for decades without discovering this that is occurring all around them, but then once they are aware of it, getting rid of the nicotine staining could all of a sudden become an obsession.

Nicotine will seep into the walls, and its omnipresence (once identified) may seem like an immovable object unless it is properly addressed.

Once the nicotine staining has been revealed and assuming the person finding it wants to actually get rid of it, what is the correct approach?

Over the years, we have worked through quite a number of these types of circumstances, and we do have a methodology we utilize which I believe works best.

It is important when aiming at neutralizing the nicotine that ALL painted surfaces are properly hit; otherwise, it is going to be obvious that nicotine staining on the painted surfaces that were not treated abutting any surfaces that were treated.

Coating everything being painted with at least one coat (possibly two in the most severe situations) of alcohol-based shellac (our "go-to" is a product called 'BIN") is the critical component.

If things are simply gone over with what promises to be a stain-blocking oil or latex-based primer, you may be setting yourself up for some grave disappointment.

Once the proper coating(s) of alcohol-based shellac is applied, you can hit the areas with a coat of latex primer and then your desired finished coat product(s).

This will ensure that nasty nicotine stains do not push their way through fresh paint coatings and add to an already frustrating situation.

Again, the key is the alcohol-based shellac.

Once this treatment is properly executed, you will be rid of the nicotine staining forever...unless, of course, you believe allowing smoking in the house moving forward is something you are ok with, then the fresh paint job will be simply a "reset" until the nicotine staining builds up again, is discovered, and the cycle starts from scratch and repeats itself.

What is Cedar Bleed?

When painting the outside of your home, there are a number of head-scratchingly odd phenomena that can occur.

They tend to rear their heads in various forms.

Some are super unsightly.

Some are not really noticeable, but once you see them, they are hard to ignore.

These annoying nuisances run the gamut of technical mumbo jumbo names ranging from 'Surfactant Leaching' to 'Efflorescence.'

One of these types of issues, which may be visible on your home's exterior painted surfaces, is 'Cedar Bleed.'

Cedar bleed is a reddish/brownish stain that is visible (most often) on the painted (or semi-solid/solid-stained) surfaces of red cedar shingles and clapboard.

This staining is not detrimental to the paint coating itself, but it can be a bit of an eyesore once it is discovered.

Cedar bleed is another one of these items that is fairly easy to prevent before it happens, but it is a bit of a pain in the neck to get rid of once it occurs.

By priming with a cedar bleed-blocking oil primer or an acrylic primer with specifically stated cedar bleed-blocking properties at the time the home being painted is in the priming process (to exposed bare wood new red cedar shingles or red cedar shingles that are in the process of being repainted), this will prevent the cedar bleed from bleeding through the finish coat.

Even with the passing of a number of environmental laws that severely limit the contents in oil-based paints and stains in comparison with years past, my preference is still the oil-based primer for this kind of preventative measure.

Cedar bleed occurs when moisture in some way, shape, or form leaches the natural tannins in red cedar to the surface of the painted area, protecting the red cedar and allowing its remnants to sit on the front of the painted surface.

Once there, the way that we would combat it would be to prime the affected areas with a primer, such as if we were treating it as if it were bare wood, with the idea that the primer would lock in the tannin bleed.

Although finish paints blend in better than they have ever blended in the past when applied, there may be a bit of work needed in order to make sure whatever it is that you are painting is done so that the finished product is as unnoticeable as possible.

The longer the gap from the time the surface was originally painted to the time when the move is made to make the cedar bleed correction, the less of a chance there will be that the cedar bleed is able to be properly neutralized with the finish that is put on top of it blending in as optimally as one would like.

Cedar bleed is a funky happening as sometimes a surface can be painted for quite some time without the tannins in the wood being brought to the surface, and then "POW," you turn the corner one day, and it is staring you right in your face.

The lighter the color, the higher the chances that the cedar bleed will be more pronounced and easier to detect than a reddish brown, as an example, which will naturally mask the cedar bleed more thoroughly.

Even though it does not cause long-term damage to your paint job per se, cedar bleed is definitely a frustrating item to work through, particularly if it occurs on a surface that was freshly painted not that long ago.

Maintenance After the Pre-Cast Bulkhead Install

One of our favorite types of projects to tackle is when we get hired to fabricate and install a new precast bulkhead unit.

Sometimes, we are replacing an existing unit that has corroded over time.

Other times, we are hired to fabricate and install a new unit for someone's home who has never had a bulkhead before.

In each case, it can be a very complicated project as multiple moving pieces are involved.

A pre-cast bulkhead unit is an all-encompassing unit where the bulkhead "top" (the portion containing the bulkhead doors) and the bulkhead "bottom" (the portion containing the stairs leading to the basement) are steel-fabricated into one solid unit.

When installing a pre-cast unit where there has never been one in place, not only does the actual unit itself need to be fabricated and installed, but there is a series of actions that need to be followed in order to ensure proper installation.

Typically, this is what is involved:

- Some type of excavation takes place

- "Hole" needs to be cut into the foundation in order to accommodate the new unit

- The unit is fabricated and installed

- The area that was excavated around the bulkhead has to be filled back in with soil

- An entry door has to be custom fit at the base of the bulkhead leading into the basement (unless, of course, you had wanted to leave this area open without a door for some reason)

- If the entry door is installed, you may or may not wish to prep and finish the interior and exterior portions as well

- Any area around the place where the bulkhead attaches to the house that needs to be "finished off" (vinyl siding that needs to be re-fit in, etc.) is finished off to provide the appearance of as seamless an install as possible

If replacing a pre-cast unit that had already been previously installed, a very similar procedure is approached, with the exception of having to cut a hole in the foundation and possibly any work around the entry door leading into the basement from the bulkhead (the condition of the existing door would most likely dictate what, if anything, is done to the door).

Assuming everything else has been correctly completed, the most important part of the installation is the maintenance around the unit, which has to be done as the dirt that was filled back in settles over time.

As moisture (rain/snow) falls around the bulkhead, the soil that was filled back in will naturally compress, even if it is compacted as best as possible when the unit is installed.

There is an old story of a professor showing a glass jar full of rocks to his students in which he repeatedly asks if they believe the jar is full, and he adds smaller stones, pebbles, sand, and finally water while mesmerizing the students as to what he may be able to possibly fit more of into the jar.

The same type of scenario occurs around the newly installed bulkhead, compounding each time moisture hits the area around it and causing the appearance of various degrees of "caving in."

It is imperative to stay on top of this by adding extra fill when needed (perhaps saving some from the original excavation if possible).

As time goes by, eventually, the dirt will reach a point where it will no longer be compacting and will be as settled as it is going to get.

Every situation is different, as soil can vary in density, even from one yard to another on the same street.

Patience may certainly be a virtue as the soil's ultimate position around the bulkhead is achieved, but diligently staying on top of things and making sure the dirt is put back in place as it settles will be quite helpful in expediting the process no matter how long it ends up taking.

Incorrectly Overlapping Flashing or Aluminum Trim Wrapping

One of the things that we seem to have developed a reputation for over the years is being able to diagnose leak sources stemming from seldom thought-of places where moisture can penetrate one's home.

When it comes to figuring out from where uninvited water may be entering the home, there are seemingly endless possibilities.

Many moons ago, there may have been a leak source that took a bit longer to identify, but over time (with experience), the most challenging of leaks have become a bit quicker for us to pinpoint.

Leaks have been known to drive even the most level-headed of homeowners into a puddled mess of frustration, particularly when the leaks are coming from places that are not obvious.

In working to determine the origin of a leak, clearly, it is always best to start with the places that may make the most sense.

Examples of this are the overall condition of the roof or if there is an issue with what we refer to as a "penetration" (i.e., the area where the chimney meets the roof, the area where a sewer venting pipe comes out of the roof, etc.).

Sometimes, however, the leak comes from an area that is very easy to overlook.

A perfect example of this is the way the roof drip edge flashing on your home may be laid or the way that its trim is wrapped in aluminum along its peaks.

At first glance, when searching for potential ways that water is coming in from, incorrectly installed flashing or aluminum wrapping is easy to miss, especially if it is higher up off the ground.

Flashing or aluminum wrapping around the trim on peaks should always be installed with the top portion of the flashing or aluminum overlapping the piece underneath it (not with the bottom overlapping the top).

The reason for this is that if rain is hitting the flashing or the aluminum capping with the top piece overlapping the bottom piece, the rain will easily be shed off to the ground.

If the bottom piece overlaps the top piece, this could lead to some significant problems.

When the bottom piece of flashing or aluminum is laying over the top piece, it will actually serve as a highway of sorts for water to be fed directly into the home, as it effectively catches the rain as it is falling and railroads it into whatever area it may be that the flashing or aluminum capping is attempting to protect.

Depending upon how the home is constructed, some places where the water may be being fed into (often unbeknownst to the homeowner) are behind the siding of the home, into a soffit, or into the attic.

Perhaps one of the worst situations is when the flashing or aluminum capping is incorrectly installed, and water is being steered into the home, but it is also being guided in such a manner that it may not be discovered for a long time to come (if not ever!).

A specific example of this would be in the incorrectly installed aluminum trim toward the top of a home. As water enters, it is guided toward and then trapped in between the back side of the vinyl siding on the home and the sheathing of the home itself. It gradually works its way down and exists at the bottom edge of the vinyl siding, but in the process slowly rots out the sheathing the vinyl siding is attached to and creaties a breeding ground for mold that develops over the course of several years.

Scary stuff!

If you are curious if the flashing or aluminum peak trim capping on your home is installed properly, feel free to reach out to our office, and we can set up some time to have a conversation with you and review what to look for in a bit more depth.

It is annoying enough to have to chase a leak when you actually know it is occurring; however, it is a whole other level of pain, when damage from an unknown leak is found after the water that had been being let in has such a tremendous head start before even being recognized!

Why Does Wood Turn Gray?

Every once in a while, we get a call from someone who recently noticed exterior natural woodwork at their home begin to "gray out."

It does not matter whether it is a deck in their backyard or siding on the outside of their home; it could be either/or, but the question is still the same.

Typically, the question is framed out somewhere along the lines of, "I had my _____ cleaned and sealed not too long ago; why has it already turned gray?!?"

Even without seeing whatever it was that was treated, I already know the answer.

The scientific answer would be, "Radiation from the sun's ultraviolet rays breaks down the lignin in the cellulose structure on the surface of the wood causing photo chemical degradation" (source: Timbertown).

The answer in layperson's terms would be "the sun is the culprit."

This can be a very disheartening occurrence, particularly if you have put a whole lot of time and effort into restoring your natural wood deck/siding/etc.

The process of getting wood to its natural state can often be painstaking.

First, it needs to be cleaned and then prepped to varying degrees (elbow grease, elbow grease, elbow grease…) before it is ready for its finish.

Then, applying the finish can be cumbersome in and of itself, especially if the finish is being applied by brush.

Therefore, as you can imagine, the graying-out process can be super frustrating to endure.

Our approach for protecting and treating natural wood decks, siding, and the like would be to first clean the surfaces we will be applying our system to, prepping as necessary, then applying two coats of C2 Clear Guard and then one coat of Wolman Clear Water Repellent.

The C2 Guard is extraordinarily deep penetrating and is best done with two coats—wet-on-damp.

Because the C2 Guard penetrates so deeply, the Wolman can easily be applied over the C2 Guard once it is dry and be the Yin to the Guard's Yang, as the C2 Guard provides incomparable protection to the cell structure of the wood and the Wolman creates a bit of a "raincoat" to help the wood actually shed water and prevent moisture from penetrating its surfaces.

This is an AWESOME system (I personally believe the best-of-the-best!), but even with this being the case, it will NOT prevent the surfaces that are treated with it from graying out.

I always coach our clients that the way the natural wood surface looks after it is washed is the way that the natural wood will look after our system is applied to it.

The process we utilize (as described here) dries to an "invisible" finish and does NOT tone the wood whatsoever.

The only way to prevent the wood from graying out is by using a product that is more of a wood toning stain containing ultraviolet ray protection and which has an entirely different application process associated with it.

However, one has to be extremely careful of which stain they choose for their natural wood (if they should elect to travel this route), as any type of film-building application at all could result in some pretty ugly peeling down the road.

Whether it is an aged pressure-treated wood deck, clear white cedar shingles, or any type of related wood structure that is built outside and exposed to the weather in one way, shape, or form, the expectation should be there that if being left "natural," it should not be a question as to whether or not the wood will gray out, but rather how long it will take to do so.

This time element is not something that is easily defined as there are a number of factors involved.

Realizing this inevitability, though, allows you to plan for the graying out process to begin at some point in time, rather than being under the false assumption that any type of "clear" treatment will allow the wood to maintain its natural look anywhere near the length of time that you are envisioning it doing so.

To Prime, or NOT to Prime…

At times when working on the act of painting our homes, whether exterior or interior, it is not unusual to feel our inner Hamlet cause us to ask the head-scratching question "To Prime, or NOT to Prime" as to whether something should be primed or not primed prior to applying a finish coat.

As with many things, the answer is, "It is situational."

Prior to even thinking about priming, the surface in question should be properly prepared.

The surface should be prepped to the point where the surface is sound (free of any peeling paint or unwanted surface inadequacy) and clean (free from dirt, dust, etc.).

Assuming the surface is ready to go, we must now determine whether or not to prime it.

Primer is an invaluable resource in the painting systems all around us.

It is the first product that is often applied to whatever surface it is that we are painting.

The main purposes of primer are to:

- Seal the surface it is being applied to and help the finishes applied over it to appear as even and consistent as possible

- Prevent bleed-through of anything that may more easily be trying to force its way through the finish coatings on top of it if primer were not in place to block it from doing so (examples: wood tannins, graffiti, tobacco)

- Enhance bonding qualities of the surface it is being applied to, i.e., super slick metals, glass, glossy layers of previous coatings

Knowing this, it is probably easy to see why, when painting, there may be a question as to whether or not to use primer, and furthermore, if priming, what type of primer to use.

In all of the years that I have been in the painting industry, a simple rule I have always lived by when coaching someone through when they are deciding to prime something or not is simply, if there is ever any doubt, then prime it!

Technically, if a surface is sound, there is not a prevalent concern of something bleeding through the finish coat, and it is "dull" enough to accept a paint coating, then there really is not a viable need to prime the surface, particularly with today's technologies.

It would be exceptionally rare to prime a surface that didn't really require a primer and to subsequently realize some type of detrimental effect while doing so.

The greater worry would be of not priming a surface that absolutely required it.

To better illustrate…

- If you do not prime a bare plaster surface, peeling issues could come about down the road, and massive inconsistencies of a cosmetic nature will be visible in the short term

- If new red cedar—even new pre-primed red cedar—is not properly primed prior to finish coating, cedar bleed will most certainly be an unsightly phenomenon that will have to be dealt with down the line

- If an old oil-based interior trim finish is not correctly primed prior to finishing it with a waterborne coating, then it is most likely just a matter of time before the paint coating directly applied to it is triggered by some sort of minor surface abrasion and begins to peel off "in sheets"

Obviously, example after example can be listed.

Priming a surface that does not necessarily need it will most likely lead to a circumstance of "no harm, no foul."

Neglecting to prime a surface, however, that necessitates it to be primed, can lead to an annoyingly frustrating time in correcting something that could easily have been avoidable if the proper primer approach had been taken from the beginning.

While there is always the "default" act of asking your local paint dealer or calling a paint manufacturer helpline to run the question by them, really things are quite simple…if there is any doubt, prime it!

Then, simply determining which primer is the most appropriate to use is the only real item that would need to be figured out.

Why are Some Porch Ceilings Painted Blue?

Many moons ago, when I first started off in the contracting trade, one of the projects we took on was the exterior painting restoration of a cool old farmhouse in Northern RI.

I remember vividly working on this project in the sweltering late summer heat.

The home's exterior body and trim were painted in a traditional all-white finish coat, with one exception—the ceiling of the farmer's porch that made its way through a full two sides of the home.

At the time, I thought it was a cool-looking ceiling, and as I was gathering the final specifications for the project, I remember asking the homeowner what color he wanted to paint the house.

He replied that his desire was to keep the same color scheme as had been there previously.

That seemed pretty awesome, and I commented to our client as to how much I really liked the blue ceiling color of the porch and was glad he was keeping it.

"Of course," he replied, "...it keeps the bees out!"

Hmmm...keeps the bees out?

I nodded in acknowledgment while pretending I knew exactly what he was talking about and then went about researching if what he said was true.

Now, these were the days before everyone predominantly had cell phones, and heck, even getting onto the Internet was not a very easy thing to do, but I proceeded to look into this a bit further, and by golly, my Northern RI peep was correct.

What I found out was very interesting to me...

The tradition of painting porch ceilings blue was originally started in the southern United States by the Gullah people who believed that ghosts (known as "haints," pronounced 'haunts') were not able to cross water and by painting one's ceiling blue, they would be able to keep the haints away from the house (there are even colors in certain paint manufacturer palettes called 'haint blue'!).

Over time, the much more common reasoning—aligned with our Northern RI friend—of painting porch ceilings blue to keep insects away developed.

The theory was that the insects would mistake the blue ceiling for the sky and decide to set up camp elsewhere, essentially serving as easy pest control against potentially annoying nuisances.

Years ago, probably unbeknownst to most folks at the time, paint was often mixed with lye—a natural insecticide—therefore, any paint (regardless of color) with lye in it would serve to ward off the insects.

Nonetheless, the tradition of the sky-blue porch ceiling lasts to this day, and you would be very hard-pressed to find any insects building homes within the area of a blue porch ceiling.

Furthering the benefit of a blue porch ceiling, people who happen to be on the porch at the end of the day may feel the illusion the sky blue ceiling can create when they glance at the ceiling and feel the impression of extended daylight, particularly when compared with other colors which may be darker and not as prone to reflecting the light of the day as the sky blue is.

I find blue porch ceilings really fun, especially the fresher the paint!

They have always provided a serene feeling to me, and knowing that their color is viable beyond simply looking great is all the more reason to consider keeping your porch ceiling painted blue or switching to blue if you have never experienced the pleasantry of this phenomenon for yourself.

How to Save Houseplants While Away on Vacation

———————

Deep down inside my soul, I realize that I have better chances starting at center for any team in a professional basketball league than I do at being trusted with any type of garden advice whatsoever.

Recently, however, I came across some neat tips that seemed to be perfect for the interior plant enthusiast in our lives who may be taking a vacation at some point.

While some of the more truly passionate plant owners in my life certainly seem as if they would like to take their plants on vacation with them, this is obviously not realistic.

Although the plants are not able to take a seat on the plane next to you, you can be assured that they will not only survive your absence but will also be in very good condition when you get back in town.

Plants need air just as must as they need water.

Therefore, contrary to some beliefs, it is important not to simply attempt to prevent moisture evaporation by covering the plant with some type of glass enclosure.

This is an absolute 'no-no' and will most likely cause the plant to die due to lack of air.

On the same token, if you happen to have a traditional terrarium, it is equally important not to oversupply the plant because it has no design to accommodate the correct drainage.

Well then.

If a plant needs to be able to breathe and access water while away, what are the options???

One simple solution is to arrange to have someone come by once in a while to water the plants (assuming they are properly trained to do so) while you are away.

An old school trick that may be helpful would be to soak the soil of the given plant soon before your departure and then insert a heavy cardboard disk in the top of the pot that will then fit around the stem (or stems) of the plant; this will reduce the pace of moisture evaporating.

Other viable tips include:

- Adjusting the amount of light and temperature your plants will receive while you are away (with the idea that the more light the plant receives and the warmer it is, the more thirsty your plant will be over time)

- Prune the plant right before leaving (this will lead to the plant needing less water while you are away)

- A cool trick: place gallon containers or jars of water (size being dictated by how long you plan to be away) around the plant and anchor one end of a piece of twine at the bottom of the container or jar and the other end around the soil of the plant (water will gradually wick up from the container/jar and help to keep the soil moist while you are away)

Believe it or not, many folks care just as deeply about their potted plants as others care for pets or even family members!

Ensuring that their plants will be ok while they are away adds an element of peace of mind that may not be able to be described to others unless you happen to be one of these fine plant-loving folks.

Combining a number of these tips should certainly help ease concerns about leaving plants behind while away on vacation, particularly without a daily caretaker.

What is the Most Proper Way to Store Paint?

When repainting someone's home, it is not uncommon for them to want to paint it the same color it was painted previously.

Obviously, we do not expect clients to rattle off the paint formula off the top of their heads (a paint formula, might I add, that often looks like some type of ancient hieroglyphics).

What is extremely helpful, however, is if the client happens to have a can of the paint from the last time the house was painted stashed away somewhere we can draw a sample from.

The ideal scenario in this situation would be for us to be able to take a can of paint from the last time the home was painted, shake it up very thoroughly, dry a sample that would allow us to match it, and then (when we believe the color is where it needs to be from a matching standpoint) drying a sample of the freshly made paint on the house for the client to approve.

Again, this is ideal.

This process is often stopped in its tracks, though, as more often than not, the client has stored the paint can of the old product on a shelf in the garage, the paint itself has frozen and thawed out six to ten times, and the paint inside the can looks like some kind of unappetizing cottage cheese.

This is not ideal.

So then, to avoid the non-ideal circumstance, how should one best store paint so that it can be utilized without an issue if it is needed in the future for touch-ups, color matching, etc.?

The first thing I recommend is to find a place in your home that is relatively climate-controlled.

It does not have to be a coddled, spa-like room that is used to grow plants for the budding botanist; it simply needs to be in a place where the temperature does not drop below 52 degrees (my recommendation) year-round.

Most likely, this is a closet in either the basement or the main area of the home.

The next thing to do is to ensure the lid of the paint is properly secured, and then when turned upside down, no paint whatsoever will leak out.

Finally, the paint should be stored upside down.

What this does is it prevents the solids of the product from settling to the bottom of the can and sets things up so that when it is time to access the product inside the can, and the can is flipped right side up, the solids already have a head start in the mixing process and become much easier to be returned to their useful state after a rigorous mixing.

Perhaps the most critical step is to avoid falling into the trap of not following through with the proper storage process immediately after the home is painted.

This is where the law of 'diminishing intent' kicks in, and you tell yourself you are just going to "keep the paint in the garage until you have a moment to bring it upstairs."

Then you have an appointment, and you will "do it tomorrow."

Then you have to meet Aunt Betsy for dinner, and you will "do it tomorrow."

The challenge is that tomorrow seldom comes, and more often than not, we find ourselves trying to match a fresh paint color to something that looks like some type of spoiled dairy product.

The next time you have your home painted, please remember to correctly store your leftover paint.

The person who needs to access the paint the next time will be grateful for it.

The Differences Between a Wood, Steel, or Fiberglass Entry Door

We are VERY fortunate in that we are called upon to replace A LOT of entry doors every year.

The spectrum across the different types of doors we replace varies greatly.

Sometimes, we are called to replace an old wooden entry door that has served its useful purpose over the decades, and now is the time for it to be put out to pasture.

Other times, we are called in to replace a much more modern entry door, which warrants replacing either because it was a door of not very high quality to begin with and now has failed much sooner than one would have originally anticipated or perhaps a faulty installation led to its premature demise, whichever the case may be, it is now time to replace it.

Whatever the reasoning may be for replacing the entry door, one thing that is often asked is what type of material the new entry door should be made of and what the differences are between the possible options.

Certainly a viable question.

Entry doors are typically made out of either wood, steel, or fiberglass.

Although not as common as they used to be, wood entry doors are still available.

Wood entry doors can actually be more energy-efficient than many people realize, typically have a very classic look to them, and (perhaps weighing heavily on the decision), assuming the wood door is of good quality, are the most costly option of the three.

Steel doors would be the most cost-efficient option, are very highly energy-efficient, and although they can be rendered to provide the appearance (to a certain degree) of a wood door, they aren't generally viewed as the most cosmetically appealing of the three types.

Fiberglass doors are also very energy-efficient, normally fall in between the cost of a steel door and a wood door, and usually resemble a wood door much more closely than its steel cousin.

From a security standpoint, steel tends to surpass both fiberglass and wood in terms of standing up to someone trying to break in (taking tempting larger glass potential access points for someone looking to break and easily open the door from the outside out of the equation, of course...).

If anything ever were to happen to a door, the wood option is, by far, the easiest of the three to correct.

A dent in a steel door or a dent/crack in a fiberglass door is very challenging to fix in comparison.

In choosing which option ultimately makes sense for your particular situation, it all depends on what ideally you are looking for in a door...

If you are looking for a higher-end, more traditional-looking door and do not mind spending the money, a wood option would clearly be your best route.

If you are looking for a solid, secure door that is at the best price point you could probably achieve while still having a "good" entry door option, steel would be the way to go.

If you are looking for a material that looks like wood but may be a bit more energy-efficient than a wood door, fiberglass would be the clear choice.

No matter the option chosen, one thing is for sure: assuming you choose a solid quality entry door out of the three types of available choices and it is installed properly, it will be quite a remarkable contrast to the existing door you have in place which motivated you to begin looking for a new door in the first place.

What Causes Pressure-Treated Wood to Rot?

_____

One of the main reasons pressure-treated wood is used in areas of construction that may be more susceptible to moisture exposure than others is that it is much more resistant to rot than other wood used to build things, whether on the framing side or the finish side.

Even this being the case, we field calls from perplexed homeowners here and there where someone has had pressure-treated wood rot on them, and they do not have the foggiest idea why.

Their confusion is certainly well-founded.

After all, if pressure-treated wood is viewed as a rot-resistant building material, then how the heck can it rot out?

Great question!

Pressure-treated wood is a type of wood that has gone through a process where high pressure is used to inject a preservative into the cell structure of the wood.

These preservatives can vary (some even make the wood fire retardant!), but their whole intention is to disallow decay, insect damage, mold, and water damage as best as possible.

All wood is subject to rot when certain types of fungi are able to penetrate the wood and feast on it over time. As the fungi enjoy their meal, the wood gradually breaks down, softens, and rots over time.

So, the question remains: if pressure-treated wood is made the way that it is with the intention of preventing this type of thing from happening, then why does it happen?

The simple answer is that not all pressure-treated wood is created equal.

There are different grades of pressure-treated wood.

Pressure-treated wood is marketed with the lumber grades Premium, Select, Number 1, Number 2, and Number 3.

The higher the grade, the fewer challenges—including potential rot—you are likely to have down the line.

Lumber is tagged or stamped to provide a variety of info, including its grade.

Though these markings can seem like a foreign language, the information will be readily available as to what grade of pressure-treated wood one is purchasing.

If you have a project that requires lumber to have some type of ground contact or will have long-term exposure to moisture (such as the flooring on a deck), the commonsense thing to do would be to utilize as high a premium grade as possible whose rating is such which notes that it should be the type of wood utilized in such a situation.

One of the biggest challenges is that the more highly rated types of pressure-treated wood may not be available at every place one shops for wood, and that most folks are unaware that there are varying grades of pressure-treated wood to begin with.

I often find local lumberyards to be a tremendous source of knowledge and supply for these very types of situations.

If you ever have a question of whether a piece of pressure-treated wood was a high enough grade of wood and rated for ground contact, the reality of the situation is your chances of coming across a knowledgeable professional who can honestly help you out are much higher at the local lumberyard than at one of the box stores.

No matter where you purchase your pressure-treated wood, the secret is in the grade of the wood.

Although you may certainly find pressure-treated wood that seems "good," choosing the wrong type may actually lead to an unpleasant discovery somewhere down the road, and you may find yourself on the phone sounding as baffled as can be.

What Causes a Carbon Monoxide Detector to Go Off?

_____

There are few things more unsettling than a carbon monoxide detector going off in your home.

Unlike a smoke detector, where the reason why the alarm is going off is quite obvious (typically visible smoke/steam), carbon monoxide detectors are set off by an invisible/odorless/tasteless gas.

Carbon monoxide is associated with the gas that stems when using a fuel-burning appliance (think natural gas stove).

If an area is not properly ventilated, the carbon monoxide can rise to a level that is deemed dangerous, and assuming your carbon monoxide detector is properly functioning, it will trigger the alarm.

A home may normally be vented appropriately, but something (dust, etc.) may somehow, seemingly out of nowhere, block the vent, cause the carbon monoxide level to rise, and hence prompt the carbon monoxide alarm to go off.

If a carbon monoxide detector becomes expired or its battery is low, this can cause its alarm to go off sporadically.

Built-up moisture in a bathroom or similar areas can set off a carbon monoxide detector. Carbon monoxide detectors should not be set up in areas where there is a tremendous amount of steam.

Because of how energy-efficient homes are these days, sealed homes with added insulation, super weather-tight windows, and other types of things made to increase the heating and cooling factors of one's home can actually have a reverse, more detrimental effect in regard to inadvertently increasing the levels of carbon monoxide in the home, as our homes get closed up more than ever before, and hence not allowing any rising carbon monoxide to more easily escape to the outside.

One of the keys to making sure that any carbon monoxide buildup is minimized is to make sure your home is properly vented.

In the modern-day quest to achieve optimum energy efficiency, the balance between maximizing your home's energy efficiency and ensuring it is properly vented is quite the task, as with each added layer of air tightness added to your home, a natural by-product is, it becomes more difficult for it to naturally "breathe."

Carbon monoxide is a gas that has no real "safe" concentrations of it in one's home, only "tolerable" levels.

If your carbon monoxide detector does happen to go off in your home, the best advice is to open your windows immediately and leave the premises.

You should not return to the home for a longer period of time until the fire department and/or a licensed professional has had a chance to properly evaluate the situation and see if what set off the carbon monoxide detector can be determined and a plan can be put in place to mitigate the cause of the trigger.

If you experience any symptoms of carbon monoxide poisoning—headache, dizziness, nausea, rapid heartbeat, disorientation, or an overall feeling of not feeling right—in conjunction with the carbon monoxide detector going off, you should get outside immediately and be seen by a medical professional as soon as possible.

Carbon monoxide is a gas that can lead to some scary situations; however, if a way to recognize dangerous levels of it is properly in place and you are aware of what to do in the case where higher levels of it are discovered, a potentially very dangerous scenario can absolutely be a bit more comfortably managed to work through.

What is a Finial?

Working on people's homes day in and day out admittedly provides me quite the advantage when having conversations with folks about their differing projects.

Not that I am actively seeking some type of superior home improvement edge for when discussions occur centering around home items that need fixing; this just kind of naturally happens by being in the industry every day.

One clear example of this is in the terminology that is used to describe certain features of one's home.

Whereas a client may be used to walking by something for years and not quite knowing what to call it other than "that pointy thingy," doing what we do has forced me to increase my vocabulary over time, if for no other reason other than to know what to correctly order when requesting something at the supply shop, rather than referring to it as, "I need to order two pointy thingies, please."

A "pointy thingy" that often falls into this category and serves as an instance where a situation like this is logically to occur is with something called a "finial."

Finials are ornamental-type objects found at the end, top, or corner of another object.

Finials certainly can be "pointy." They can, however, be "knobish" as well.

Finials work to accent various areas around a home.

Specific locations where finials may be spotted can vary.

They can be found at the top of a post associated with a set of stairs or fence, they can be located at a decorative point on a roof, and they can be found hanging upside down at a gable end or corner of a home.

If one were to do deeper research on finials, one would discover, perhaps surprisingly, numerous stories of how they have been utilized throughout history, with applications ranging from military purposes to warding off witches.

Although the finials we often deal with are those made out of wood, many times they are made out of stone, clay, or some other type of building material.

Researching places to purchase finials from online will reveal the vast array of styles, shapes, and sizes available on the marketplace, enough to have plenty to choose from if you were looking to add a finial to the posts of a new porch you were constructing or maybe even replace finials that are already existing at your home.

When searching for a finial, it is easy to become stuck or overwhelmed with the sheer number of possibilities. Bringing the idea up to a designer can be enormously helpful with selecting the finial that is the best fit for your specific situation and personality.

While finials unquestionably are tiny features of one's home, these "pointy thingies" can add a sense of style that, when seamlessly incorporated into your home's design, can truly be reflective of your own distinctive persona.

What is a Parapet Wall?

There are some facets of modern homes that, although one might not realize it, have had drastically different uses at other points in time.

Perhaps there is no better example of this than the parapet wall.

When one sees a parapet wall on their home, there is probably zero attention paid to it at all, other than looking at it as simply another feature of the home.

A parapet wall is a small wall or rail system whose practical purpose is to prevent those behind it from falling over.

These days, parapet walls can also be worked into the design of the home as a decorative feature.

An illustration of this would be a parapet wall running around the perimeter of a flat roof above an entrance to a home in which there is no door leading out to the roof, perhaps only a smaller window.

Clearly, in this instance, the intent is not for the roof to be used as a balcony, but instead for the presence of the parapet walls to add to the decor of the home and look totally in place, even though there is no viable purpose for them.

Parapet walls throughout history have also had a primary existence as a form of protection for those behind them from some type of attack.

When thinking of this type of example, my mind cannot help but drift to a picture in my brain of a medieval town with walls surrounding it, flanked by soldiers around its top ducking behind parapet walls, defending the inner portion of the kingdom, by firing down at an aggressive enemy below who is shooting arrows towards those protecting the settlement.

Although these days we are less likely to be hiding behind a parapet wall to avoid a flesh-seeking arrow, parapet walls in non-decorative situations (those surrounding a functional porch as an example) may still serve as a place of peaceful refuge whenever one might wish to take advantage of it.

Parapet walls are constructed using a variety of different materials.

These can range from wood to metal to glass to masonry and so on…

There are also many different categories as to how parapet walls are constructed.

They can be solid or not solid (where one can see through them).

They can run flat across a roof or even run slanted up a peak of a roof.

In fact, there are so many different ways that parapet walls can be built that I can envision an architect giggling with giddiness anytime they are asked to incorporate one into the design of a building, as the sky is certainly the limit with regard to the creative ways in which parapet walls can be utilized.

Whether non-functional (adding to the ambiance of a property) or hyper-functional (helping to protect soldiers warding off seething invaders), parapet walls throughout time have served as useful elements of building design.

As with many items in construction, parapet walls (if done correctly) can be pieces of one's home that have special significance to them yet are seamlessly woven into the very fabric of home design to the point where they virtually exist unnoticed.

What Temperature Does it Have to Be to Fix Your Roof?

It is not unusual for me to be quizzed by folks as to what temperature it is ok to paint on the exterior of one's home.

Many may think this is a valid question as even the most novice of home-owners would realize that 25 degrees seems too cold to paint outside, but is 45 degrees ok?

These days, my answer to that question (given today's technology and our trial and error in the field since 1995) would ideally be daytime highs of at least 40 degrees [assuming the moisture content of whatever is being painted is 15% or less and long term (3+ days) overnight lows are projected to be 15 degrees or above, though I personally am comfortable with 35-40 degree daytime highs].

While the question of ideal minimum exterior painting temperatures may seem like a common question, particularly at certain periods of the year, one that, although not as frequent, is one we certainly get asked about is: What temperature does it have to be to fix your roof?

As you might imagine, there are a number of ways to answer this question.

If, after a bit of digging, the actual question is at what temperature does it need to be to replace the roof (a traditional shingled roof) instead of simply 'fixing' it, the answer from me could be slightly different.

We have done whole roof replacements in January with the temperatures in the teens during the day, and absolutely no issues occurring down the line.

In fact, as crazy as it may sound, these types of colder temperatures are actually quite comfortable working weather when replacing a roof as well.

There is no secret that replacing a roof is enormously arduous work.

With the temperatures being colder and the amount of physical exertion that is needed in roofing, these types of what would normally be thought of as freezing temperatures are actually quite welcome.

Obviously, there is a limit. We probably would not be replacing a roof if the temperatures were in the single digits with a negative windchill factor.

But contrary to what one may initially think, there is flexibility to replace a roof in temperatures that most would view as quite cold, as the sun hitting the roof does a surprisingly impressive job, even in colder times of the year, heating up the roof shingles enough where the product properly takes.

Though we are ok with installing roof shingles when the temperatures are a bit lower, do keep in mind that the roof shingles may take a bit longer to fully settle than at times of the year when the temperatures are a bit milder (i.e., you may have shingles that although watertight, may cosmetically have a slight ripple appearance until the temps heat up a bit and allow the shingles to fully achieve their permanent appearance).

In terms of what temperature is ok for conducting an actual roof "repair," my answer will vary.

If we were doing a repair that was in line with similar action as is done when replacing a shingled roof—examples being reflashing a chimney, installing a skylight, etc.—my answer would be in line with that of replacing the roof.

If we were doing a repair that was in line with a product that had to be "applied" to achieve some type of a patch or a sealant, my answer would be in line with that mentioned at the beginning of this article when reviewing the ideal temperatures for exterior painting.

There are exceptions to this.

Rubber roofing repairs, as an illustration, should not be conducted unless the daytime high temperature is expected to be in the 50s (except in extreme emergencies when you may not have a choice and a bit of 'dice rolling' may be necessary) as the glue needed to properly tack down a rubber roof truly needs temperatures to be a bit higher than other application-type products whose minimum temperature requirements are a bit lower.

Roofing, whether replacing an entire roof or conducting a needed repair, is no easy task, and colder temperatures at certain periods of the year definitely may complicate things.

However, it is important to realize that in many circumstances, a repair may not have to be held off until a "warmer" time in the calendar and that they can often be properly conducted in colder temperatures than one may initially realize with long-term successful outcomes.

How Long Should Plaster Cure Before Painting It?

If you have ever done or looked into doing any type of painting project around your home (whether on the inside or the outside), the chances are that you have heard the warning that surface preparation is the key to a successful paint job—both from a structural standpoint and a beauty standpoint!

There are many facets to surface preparation.

These can include filling, scraping, sanding, caulking, priming, and other actions that all help your paint job either last longer or look better.

I always venture to say, as much as the paint manufacturers may not want to hear this, that surface preparation is even more important than the finish paint you will be using for your project itself.

Although surface preparation certainly encompasses a wide variety of tasks that are super important for your paint job to come out the way you want it, there is also a task with one aspect of painting that is not something someone actually "does" at all.

In fact, this particular item is a more expanded version of waiting for caulk or primer to dry prior to painting it.

When you are having a surface plastered, it is important to wait for the plaster to cure prior to doing anything to its surface to get ready for painting.

My suggestion is two weeks.

Not to be confused with joint compound or spackle, which can usually be prepared and primed within twenty-four hours, plastering requires a longer wait time to truly make sure all the moisture that is used in the plastering process has totally gone away prior to doing anything to its surface to get it ready for paint.

Many plasterers would most likely tell you to wait three to seven days prior to painting new plaster.

This is DEFINITELY one of those subjects that if you ask ten different people, you will most likely receive ten different opinions.

My line of thinking is that a good three days is needed to allow the initial moisture involved in the plastering process to work itself out.

From there, I believe another solid four days is truly necessary for the plaster to harden up to the point that it can comfortably be sanded/adjusted as necessary to get its surface at its desired place prior to applying the product.

The curveball with all of this is that drying temperatures and conditions can vary greatly in short timespans and in the interest of making sure the plaster is as dry as possible and hardens up as much as possible before proceeding to the surface preparation process, an extra seven days is the perfect buffer to allow a safety net which one can be confident in as related to the drying and curing conditions that the newly plastered surfaces are located within.

If the proper time is not allotted for drying and curing, you could be setting up for a disastrous situation.

Improperly dried-out plaster can lead to some of the most sinister paint-peeling issues that one can imagine.

Furthermore, beginning to work with a surface that is not as hard as it should be could create a much more challenging situation than it needs to be when initially preparing the surface.

Although there may certainly be varying opinions as to exactly how long one should wait until a newly plastered surface is painted, if the plaster has not correctly cured prior to the majorly important step of preparing its surface, you may be in for a whole lot more work than should be the case in the quest to achieve as perfect and long-lasting a paint job as possible.

How to Stop Paint on Galvanized Metal From Peeling

One of the more challenging types of paint failures to combat is peeling paint on galvanized metal.

Galvanized metal is steel or iron that has a zinc-based protective coating applied to it in order to neutralize the formation of rust on its surfaces.

What often adds to the frustration of painters and homeowners alike is that unless the correct process is instilled from the very beginning, each may feel as though they are chasing their tail with regard to how to get paint to stick to a galvanized metal surface.

This is often further accentuated by different suggestions and opinions as to how to combat this odd paint failure, as nothing will seem to work and stop the peeling.

After all, the peeling nature resulting from the solutions experimented with often defy logic and conventional wisdom.

Certain primers are traditionally recommended when painting metal surfaces.

Many times, certain latex primers are recommended, and although oil products as a whole are gradually being phased out of the marketplace, there are certain oil primers that are recommended for priming various metals.

The problem is that the way that galvanized metal reacts to most primers does not lend itself to solid bonding properties.

Most primers that work on aluminum, copper, and similar non-ferrous metals (non-rusting metals) will not work on galvanized metal.

Primers that work on wrought iron, non-galvanized steel, and similar ferrous metals (metals that may lend themselves to rusting) will not work either.

So then, what the heck is one supposed to use???

Great question.

Back in the day when I first started in business (circa 1995), there was a popular galvanized metal primer we "in the know" affectionately referred to as 'GALVO.'

These days, Benjamin Moore makes a good galvanized metal primer; it is in their Super/Ultra Spec line and is called their HP04 Acrylic Metal Primer. The specific chemical formulations of these products—whether the GALVO from back in the day or the more modern Ben Moore HP04—are made in such a manner that they form a tremendous bond to galvanized metal.

We get a number of calls every year that relay that a client is having an exceedingly difficult time getting paint to stick to a metal door, light fixture, etc., and that they have tried "everything," but nothing seems to work.

Without even venturing out to see things in person, I can pretty much guess what the issue is.

With these galvanized metal surfaces, as with almost everything, the secret to getting paint to stick is in the prep (scraping/sanding/cleaning as applicable) and in the primer.

If the prep is done properly, there are a plethora of products that you can use as the finish coat.

If the prep is not done properly, the definition of insanity commonly kicks in as folks attempt to combat the peeling with similar approaches (often repeated over and over again) with (as you might imagine) similar results.

Unless the correct primer is used in conjunction with the proper prep process, preventing paint from peeling from a galvanized metal surface may continue to be a frustrating exercise in never-ending head scratching.

Whatever Happened to "Bleaching Oil"?

_____

When many folks think of New England, the stereotypical New England beach house can often be found amongst the wide variety of picturesque imagery.

These days, beach houses have often developed into edifices that could very well be said to make the average McMansion jealous.

Thinking back to a traditional New England beach house, however, the idea I have in my mind of what one looks like from the exterior is probably quite similar to what you may be envisioning.

While the shape of the home may vary, the exterior has white cedar shingle siding on it (possibly showing some age, possibly not), detailed out with white trim.

Although folks with beach houses have been known to let their white cedar shingles "weather," others choose to treat these shingles in some fashion with the interest of preserving them.

One of the more popular treatments to white cedar shingle siding over the years, for beach houses and beyond, has typically been a product known as 'Bleaching Oil.'

Bleaching oil was a specially formulated product that was designed to accelerate the natural weathering process of the exterior wood to which it was applied.

Bleaching oil contained a small amount of gray pigment and a chemical ingredient meant to essentially bleach the wood's surface.

As a product, I liken it to something between a transparent and a semi-transparent stain.

Bleaching oil had always been made by a company called Cabot (a company based out of Newburyport, MA).

Due to a number of environmental laws that have been passed over the years that dictate what can be put into paints, stains, etc., bleaching oil is no longer available on the market.

As these laws were coming into effect, attempts were made to modify the traditional bleaching oil to be compliant with the increased regulations.

Because a component of these efforts was actually adding more oils into the product, surfaces that the bleaching oil was treated with became super susceptible to mildew growth in a product that already had an elevated tendency to see mildew growth at a quicker clip than many other products on the market.

In its place, there is now a product called bleaching stain, which has come out as a water-based alternative to the traditional Bleaching Oil product.

As far as substitutes in many of these similar situations go (finding a regulatory-compliant product to sell in place of one that has been restricted), this one actually turned out pretty decent.

For one thing, the bleaching stain is MUCH more resistant to mildew growth than the traditional versions of the bleaching oil product, and certainly, the varying modified versions that had come on to the market in the time period leading up to bleaching oil being phased out.

The bleaching stain product itself absolutely appears as if it mimics its early predecessor VERY well and also holds up just as long, if not longer.

Alternatively to the leaching stain option, when clients ask for bleaching oil, we sometimes dig a bit deeper and see if we can find a product (from one of the paint manufacturers) that the client is happy with once they see a sample applied and which may provide a somewhat similar look to that of traditional bleaching oil.

Whether it is the bleaching stain or some other version, if someone is looking for a bleaching oil for their home, their options are limited, though definitely not as much as they could be if bleaching oil had been pulled off the market in its entirety without any type of similar product at all in place to replace it.

What is a Juliet Balcony?

Every so often, I hear terminology relating to a home or some type of construction that admittedly makes me stop and think, "Where have I heard that before?"

Recently, a client asked me for advice on a project involving a Juliet balcony.

When I brought the term up in conversation with a fellow tradesman to whom I was describing the project, I received a bit of an odd stare followed by them exclaiming, "What the heck is a Juliet balcony??"

It was certainly a fair question as this term is not really commonplace, even though we have our fair share of Juliet balconies kicking around in this part of the country.

A Juliet balcony often is not much of a balcony at all.

Many times, Juliet balconies are small platforms that cannot even hold a potted plant, never mind a person.

They are usually a rail system in front of a door or window that provides the protective rail and allows the door or larger window to be open and for whoever may be inside to hang out at the rail.

While they definitely can be large enough to hold a person or two, this does not necessarily have to be the case.

Sometimes, the Juliet balcony is purely decorative and cannot be accessed whatsoever.

In most cases, the rail system is made out of wrought iron; however, these days, it is quite common to see balconies made out of composite material, aluminum, or even wood.

They are called Juliet balconies, as you may have imagined, because if you remember back to that English class in high school, in the play "Romeo and Juliet," there is a balcony scene where Juliet is exclaiming, "O Romeo, Romeo, wherefore art thou Romeo," the Juliet balconies are balconies which resemble this specific balcony from where Juliet was cawing from in the play.

Juliet balconies are features in one's home that I believe to be a pretty cool detail.

In areas where outdoor space is super limited (think New York City), Juliet balconies offer folks access to outdoor space without pushing the envelope in terms of greatly extending off the building you are in and bringing into question permissible use allowances and things of that nature.

From the exterior view, a Juliet balcony adds a bit of European flavor to whatever building whose design they are incorporated into.

They can also look great from the inside, and as mentioned earlier, they are often paired with larger functional doors or windows.

Many people enjoy being able to open what often are floor-to-ceiling doors that allow plenty of light and airflow as well as a convenient and comfy view of whatever may be outside.

Although the terminology may not be used every day, Juliet balconies are neat niches within architecture that, when integrated correctly, can beautifully add to whatever home or property that they are assimilated into.

What is Parging?

New England is a part of the country where the majority of folks have some type of basement.

This contrasts with a good portion of the rest of the country, where most people's homes are built on "slabs" (most often to lessen the chances of flooding, particularly in areas with higher water tables).

The older the home, the more likely one is to have a foundation built out of a material that was assembled [brick, fieldstone, cinderblock ("block")] vs. out of poured concrete (which is the case in more modern homes).

Specifically, when it comes to fieldstone foundations (though at times with brick and block as well), the mortar (or other material that may have been used to help keep the assembled material in place) may become compromised to some degree over time.

When this happens, signs of moisture, especially during rainy periods of time, may begin to show their face in the basement.

The moisture may gradually leech its way through the walls in the form of a noticeable substance called "efflorescence" (a white, powdery substance that, if you were to touch it, would come right off on your fingertip).

Sometimes, you may be able to see the actual water itself work its way through the foundation walls in its true form and exhibit wetness in the material that the foundation is made of.

In the most severe cases of this occurring over a longer period of time, mold can develop in some form on the walls.

Usually, the moisture challenge is spotty, though it can be much more widespread at times.

Whether minor, severe, or anywhere in between, one of the best ways to combat moisture from coming through these types of walls is through a process called "parging."

Parging is a procedure where someone (often best done by a mason, though someone properly trained should be able to do so as well) takes a certain mixture of mortar and proceeds to apply it over the entire surface of the area in which one is aiming to correct these aforementioned types of is-sues—think almost like a rough skim coat, typically applied with a trowel.

The purpose of parging is not only to prevent moisture seepage into the basement but also to help solidify any cracks, visible or not visible, that may be in the process of occurring between the joints in the fieldstone, brick, or block.

This is a huge help in aiding to guard against water freezing and expanding within these joints and causing an accelerated deterioration process.

More often than not, the parging processes we have helped clients with over time have been done more so with fieldstone foundations than brick or block.

This may purely be the case of the fieldstone foundations in our region simply being older and hence even more prone to moisture challenges than a lot of the brick or block foundations that are around, though it would not be unusual for us to be called into a situation that calls for us to recommend to parge a brick or block wall as well.

Whether fieldstone, brick, or block, it is always important to monitor the walls of your basement for moisture challenges.

Knowing that a solution such as parging exists can be quite helpful for those who discover this type of issue and are not quite sure what to do to stop it.

What is Putty Used For in Construction?

When nailing up a piece of wood, composite, or other miscellaneous material, one of two things often occur.

If you are nailing with some type of pressurized nail gun, a hole is formed on the backside of the nail head.

If something is being nailed by hand, there may not be a hole but a nail head that seems as though it is resting on the surface.

In either case, the end result is not typically viewed as the most attractive from a finishing standpoint.

There is a claylike material known as "putty" that helps in "bringing home" the finished look of these surfaces.

In circumstances where a pressurized nail gun is used, many times putty can simply be forced into the hole that was created and then smoothed out so that once things are prepped and painted, no one would ever be able to tell that a nail was present there.

In the same light, when a nail is nailed in by hand and its head sits on the surface of whatever was being nailed in, if one were to take a tool called a "nail set" and use it to force the nail head a bit deeper into the wood/material being nailed, from there they would be able to use the putty to fill the hole (as in the example with the pressurized nail gun), smoothed over, prepped and finished to the point where, again, one could never tell a nail had its head previously resting on the surface.

Putty is an invaluable tool that not only helps sew things together and make finished products look smooth and pretty, but it also is part of a system that prevents water from getting into nail holes and gradually wreaking havoc over a period of time.

Whereas the best traditional putties have been oil-based, these days, there are latex-based putties that rival the best of the oil products (Aqua Glaze is one such product).

The more modern, latex-based putties have a number of advantages over their oil-based counterparts.

The latex-based putties dry faster, are easier to use, and are less brittle over time than their oil-based cousins.

The oil-based putties are still dominant in the industry due to what I would consider traditional beliefs of putty use.

Unfortunately, with the composite products that are used in many applications (the frequency of which is increasing significantly by the year), the oil-based putties are the incorrect thing to use in their entirety.

In these situations, one does not have a choice but to defer to the latex-based putties.

Since I came into the industry years ago, I have regularly heard people speak of puttying their windows when referring to the material that keeps, usually older, glass windowpanes in place.

While technically, this is correct, this specific type of putty is called glazing compound, and I tend to reference it as "glazing."

If one were to search, there are tons of uses for this wonderful material known as putty.

Although filling nail holes is what putty is thought to be mainly used for, there are quite a number of other useful applications throughout construction (glazing windows being another), for which traditional putty and variations of it prove to be highly valuable.

Painting Chimneys—
The Ultimate Roll of the Dice

If you were to take a stroll down any street in a densely populated residential area, depending, of course, upon where you are strolling, you may notice varying degrees of people who have the chimneys on their homes painted.

While I am known to say things along the lines of "We will paint pretty much anything that someone is willing to pay us to paint," there are certainly some items that I would steer people away from painting.

Chimneys are one of these such items.

Even repainting an already-painted chimney could prove to be an exercise in futility.

Recently, I received a message from a client whose chimney we had painted not too long ago and had started to peel in specific areas near the top.

When we started their chimney project, the client had recently purchased the home and did not really know the chimney's history.

Now that we had painted it, at least he had a baseline to go by.

Based on our many years in the industry, it did not take long for me to pinpoint that there was some type of hidden issue that existed and was causing the paint to peel.

The clear challenge in situations like these is that the chimney is already painted, and one's choices are rather limited in terms of what to do with it.

Basically, they could either repaint the chimney and hope for the best or strip all the paint off the chimney and leave the brick natural.

Brick, especially at the top of chimneys, can be extraordinarily finicky.

There could easily be a moisture issue due to where moisture tends to hit the inside of the chimney during certain storms, and as the sun heats the chimney and draws the moisture out of it, the moisture forces its way through the paint and gradually causes that paint to peel.

In these instances, there could also be an inter-coat adhesion issue where if the soot/dirt from the chimney was not properly cleaned off at some point along the way in the various times it had been painted in the past, then the chimney would be super prone to peeling, particularly near its top with the aforementioned additional moisture exposure.

These examples are not unusual; the 'Catch 22' with all of this is that one really would not know what entirely would happen if they repainted their chimney until they painted it and are able to monitor how long it lasts.

If there is peeling that occurs within a year or two of the chimney being painted, I can guarantee you that, more often than not, the peeling has more to do with an underlying issue than it does with whoever had most recently painted it.

When I am questioned about whether or not someone should paint a chimney that was NEVER painted in the past, my answer is ALWAYS a resounding 'NO.'

I often repeat the phrase, "We will paint pretty much anything that someone is willing to pay us to paint," when having this conversation and follow it with listing the chances someone takes when painting a chimney that was never painted before, especially the moisture content in the brick at the top of the chimney often being such an unknown factor.

If you are one of those fortunate souls who has painted or repainted their chimney in the past and never had an issue with it, count your blessings.

You were at the roulette table and ended up on the favorable side of a 50/50 dice roll.

The Difference Between a Gutter and a Downspout

In any industry, there are items that people not within that industry may mix up terminology for.

When this occurs, the person whose industry is in the middle of this verbal confusion will most often become quickly perplexed.

An example of this may be, say, if you were a firefighter and you bumped into someone that, for whatever reason, referred to a 'fire hydrant' as a 'hose.'

There is a good chance the firefighter might be left scratching their head as clearly a fire hydrant is a fire hydrant and a hose is a hose.

As funny as it may seem, throughout the few decades of my involvement in the home improvement industry, I have consistently run into this scenario with folks in conversation with me describing the two most major components of their home's gutter system.

The two major components of your home's gutter system are your gutters and your downspouts.'

For some unknown reason, quite often, people seem to refer to their 'downspouts' as 'gutters' when talking about their gutter system.

For a long time, this really was as confusing to me as having someone refer to a fire hydrant as a hose to a firefighter, as a gutter and downspout could not be more different.

Over time, as I began to notice this pattern, I have worked my very best to clarify what someone was describing as their 'gutter' while speaking with me about their gutter system, and this puzzling reference was made.

To break it down:

- Gutters:
    - » Run horizontally (parallel to the ground)
    - » Are used to catch water off the roof and funnel it to different places around the roofline

- Downspouts:
  - » Run vertically (perpendicular to the ground)
  - » Are used to catch the water from the gutters, take it down the side of the home, and direct it in some manner of fashion either into the ground or into an "elbow," etc., carrying/spreading it away from the house

I have no idea why the reverse never seems to happen—people calling a gutter a downspout.

It is always people calling a downspout a gutter.

This most often occurs when discussing painting the home and people asking if we are going to take the gutters down.

Occasionally, when this happens, the person at the crux of the conversation is asking if we are going to take the actual gutters down.

Most often, however, they are inquiring about the downspouts being taken down prior to painting and not the gutters, but they will keep referring to the downspouts as gutters unless the true context is drawn out.

If you are at all familiar with gutter systems, you can imagine how problematic this might be if the true meaning of what the person is asking is not established.

While taking down a downspout and re-hanging it is a relatively easy thing to do, taking down a gutter and then re-hanging it (making sure it is pitched appropriately and the like) is a monumental endeavor.

Truly taking someone for their word in these types of situations could lead to a nightmare of a scenario, particularly if the contractor took what the client was saying at face value and started getting into the business of taking down their entire gutter system when all that was necessary for the task at hand was taking down the downspouts.

I'm sure there are numerous cases where these types of situations occur in every industry on a daily basis.

If nothing else, this scenario underscores the popular saying "words matter" probably as well as any example one can come up with.

Why are Water Stains Brown?

Have you ever experienced the unsightly effects of a leak coming from somewhere in or around your home?

Perhaps it is a leaky roof that recently started (or has been leaking for years).

Or maybe you have a pipe that is leaking, or perhaps something funky going on with your bathtub that is causing water to leak through the ceiling areas directly below it.

Whatever the case may be, if you have experienced some type of leak along these lines, chances are that you not only had to deal with the issue of correcting the leak itself, but you also had to figure out a way to fix the damage that the leak ultimately ended up causing.

More often than not, one type of damage notoriously synonymous with leaks in our homes is that of the water stain.

Water stains may show their faces as tiny drips, or they may spread out over larger areas.

Sometimes, they are formed due to a one-time occurrence because of a random ice dam or some other similar type of anomaly.

Other times, they are seemingly "always" wet every time it rains.

Whether due to a one-time event or seemingly constantly being added to, one tell-tale sign of water staining is their brownish colors.

If it is a REALLY in-depth stain, one may even see a reddish tone working in with the brown, and for leaks that are long-term and never seem to dry, one may even see mildew or mold specks mixed in with the water staining.

All this being said, where does the brown color of the staining stem from?

Many folks recognize that the brown staining that they may see on an occasional ceiling stemmed from or is stemming from some type of leak, but few probably stop to think as to why the color is brown.

Obviously, when the leak begins, the water that is leaking is typically not brown in color.

Contrary to some beliefs, rarely does the water that is leaking come through as an actual rust stain on a ceiling (unless the water passes through an already rusted area and pulls the rust with it through the ceiling below it).

Instead, the brown stains actually come from the more prevalent building material that the water passes through on its way to show itself on the visible side of the ceiling.

More often than not, the water pulls the tannins out of the wood in the framing of the house behind the ceiling, and as it passes through the plaster, it does so in a fashion that maintains its brownish color and shows through on the ceiling as the brown water stain.

Once the leak is corrected, fortunately, the brown staining is not that difficult to get rid of.

With the help of spot-priming wherever the brown staining is located with alcohol-based shellac (using multiple coats of the primer if need be), the stains can easily be neutralized and then top-coated with the desired finish.

Where I see mistakes made is when people attempt to get rid of the stains by first priming them before finishing coating them with an oil or latex-based primer or sometimes trying to wash them away with a concentrated solution of bleach.

While these actions may help lessen the stain, unless alcohol-based shellac is used, the water stain's presence may be a long-term lingerer.

Water stains can be truly annoying to look at as one passes by them each day. Although eliminating them may prove frustrating if not tackled correctly, doing away with them can easily be accomplished if approached in the proper manner.

Popcorn Ceilings

Now and then, we get calls asking for help with a 'popcorn ceiling.'

"Help" will typically mean either how to help get rid of them entirely or how to paint them without damaging them.

Popcorn ceilings are ceilings where, for lack of a better way of describing them, there are little, tiny bumps scattered about the ceiling ('popcorn').

NOT to be confused with 'textured' ceilings, 'popcorn' ceilings have been used throughout their existence when building or renovating a home as a more inexpensive means of finishing a ceiling vs. finishing it with a plastered 'swirl' finish or using a technique providing a 'smooth' finish.

Popcorn ceilings that are older (for example, done in the 1950s, 1960s, etc.) tend to have their 'popcorn' firmly in place and, while being easy to maintain, can be a bit more difficult to get rid of (if so desired) than newer popcorn ceilings.

More modern popcorn ceilings are much more challenging to paint (as when doing so, a good portion of the 'popcorn' can be pulled off on your paint roller and are best done by having their finish 'sprayed' on by a professional), but are a bit easier to convert by having the popcorn removed if that is what you would like to do.

The best way to get rid of an older popcorn ceiling is to either hang a new ceiling over it (the most common approach we take is hanging over it with a 3/8" blueboard and plastering over the blueboard to the finish one aspires to).

Sometimes, folks elect to try to skim over the popcorn with a process allowing them to smooth it out; I am not a fan of this, however, as in my mind, no matter how stable the older popcorn ceiling appears, in the back of my mind I am always worried of the new skimmed over coating somehow coming off at some point due to some type of bonding issue with the ceiling it was put over.

Of course, the other way you can convert the ceiling is by taking down the existing ceiling and hanging a new ceiling up altogether. The demo using this method, however, can be quite messy.

Speaking of messy...

If working to get rid of a newer popcorn ceiling, a chaotic situation can certainly ensue.

Similar to the older popcorn ceiling conversion, the path of either hanging a new ceiling over the existing ceiling entirely or removing the existing ceiling and putting up a new ceiling altogether is applicable here as well, and there is also another technique that can be used.

If prepared properly—everything removed from the room and/or covered extensively—the newer popcorn ceilings can actually have their popcorn removed by being carefully wet down and then scraped off (as the popcorn will come off and get everywhere and be extraordinarily dusty if it is not wet down first).

After this process is done, the ceiling may need a procedure in place to be skimmed over in order to smooth out the ceiling.

The procedure would most likely look something like:

1) Prime the ceiling
2) Patch the ceiling wherever needed
3) Sand the patches appropriately
4) Spot prime the patches
5) Then keep repeating until the surface reaches the "smoothness" that you are looking for

Popcorn ceilings are certainly something we run into fairly often, and there are various ways to help people achieve their preferred finish.

Depending on the age of the ceiling and the desired result, the methodology for getting people there absolutely ranges from the "not too bad" of a project to SUPER intense!!

Why is it so Hard to Find a "Good" Contractor These Days?

Even before the recent pandemic began to take over all our lives, finding a contractor did not seem to be the easiest task to do.

Some may say that it would have been easier to find a unicorn than a good contractor.

With the advent of decades of students being steered away from the trades, most contractors had been increasingly put in a bind over the years, as not as many newer generation students had been entering the trades.

Add the pandemic into the equation, and things went from a dire situation to one of its own pandemic-like proportions.

Not only were contractors facing their own challenges related to COVID—being able to manage the effects of the virus within their existing staff and client base, working through virus-related supply change craziness, etc.—but many also suddenly faced actual staffing shortages with the ability to find new hires instantaneously going from overwhelmingly difficult to almost impossible.

Couple all of this with actual demand for contractors being at an all-time high—on the residential side because folks were home more than they have ever been home in recent history and were literally inventing home improvement projects (as they stared at their walls every day) and on the commercial side because many facilities worked to take advantage of a time period with people not around as often and being able to concentrate and get things done in a more comfortable fashion than they typically would be able to—and the property improvement industry instantly had a huge issue on its hands.

Demand for contractors was at an all-time high, and supply for contractors was at an all-time low—A PROBLEM INDEED!!

Almost two years into COVID taking a foothold in the United States, this phenomenon does not appear to be drastically improving.

Now, when we say the word "Contractor," this is a broad term that can be applied across the various trades (electricians, plumbers, painters, etc.) and also encompasses the quality of the individual contractors across the board—good, bad, and in between.

The term good contractor is certainly open to interpretation.

A phrase I often get a kick out of hearing is when someone asks a particular friend of mine for a contractor referral.

He always responds: "Good, fast, and cheap. Pick two. I'll be able to send you a contractor that embodies two out of the three. Just not all three."

In almost thirty years of being in the trades, I have never heard a more perfect way to describe what I have come to know the contracting world to be.

Good, fast, and cheap—you can get two out of the three, just not all three—PERFECT!!

No matter what your definition of good is, however, these days, finding almost any contractor—even those that simply only pass the mirror test (if you place a mirror under their nose and it fogs up, hence letting you know they are alive and real) can be an exercise of epic frustration.

What is the Best Floor Covering for a Bathroom Floor?

When deciding to renovate/update your bathroom to any degree, one item that folks often contemplate over what the best approach would be is: what in the world do we do with the bathroom floor?

Clearly, there are almost infinite answers as to what someone might want to put down.

The recommendations I try to convince our clients of when faced with this dilemma are either ceramic tile or sheet laminate.

Yes, there certainly are several other options that others really believe in and preach about—everything from self-adhesive vinyl tiles to actual hardwood flooring, etc.—each of which I personally have varying degrees of reservations about.

Ceramic tile and sheet laminate, however, are both avenues that I believe are the cream of the crop when it comes to bathroom floor coverings.

The biggest reason is that both offer optimum protection against any type of water causing deterioration to the floor in the long run.

Sheet vinyl is, by far, the most cost-effective of the two.

Sheet vinyl, when laid by a tradesperson who is adept at doing so, is a seamless way to not only waterproof the floor but also do so in a manner that is actually pretty attractive in comparison to earlier versions of this material from years ago.

Literally, the only thing that even somewhat mimics a seam is the area around the edge of the laminate where it meets different portions of the bathroom (for example, the walls, toilet, vanity, and the like).

Ceramic tile, although a more intense and costly operation to install, can provide a stunning look to the bathroom floor while (again, assuming everything was done appropriately) waterproofing the floor in a manner that should last a long time.

If, for some reason, a tile ever cracks/gets compromised, assuming you have extra tiles and grout (from when the project was originally done) on hand, things can easily be corrected.

These days, styles are quite diverse regarding one's possibilities of selections for either of these two ways of doing things.

If someone were to say that they would rather not have one of these two options as part of their bathroom project, we are always receptive to what someone may propose and, after pleading the case for either ceramic tile or sheet laminate, may acquiesce to the non-preferred method of bathroom floor covering installation and although installing one of these alternatives to the best of our ability, we will do so, being very mindful to sternly underscore the negatives of choosing to proceed with this particular chosen perspective in the process.

One of the most notorious examples of this is putting hardwood flooring in the bathroom.

Similarly to how strong my opposition is to people wallpapering the walls in their bathrooms, installing hardwood floors in your bathroom is something I look at as a VERY big 'no-no'!

Though hardwood flooring can look absolutely amazing—even in a bathroom—its beauty may be relatively short-lived as the hardwood flooring may not only be highly prone to rot and deterioration from constantly being exposed to moisture, but this phenomenon can also lead to undesirable mold growth in a fashion that could easily have been prevented.

As with the other options that I would not necessarily recommend, even with advanced warnings, many times, people still insist on having their way and end up having the flooring of their choice versus one that would make more long-term practical sense.

As the old saying goes, "You can lead a horse to water..."

Being Mindful to Keep Snow from Critical Areas

Every winter is different.

Some years, we New Englanders flirt with record snowfall totals as the winter progresses.

Other years, the most snow-hearty of us are disappointed in the lack of this white stuff.

No matter where we fall on the snow lover scale, falling snow can easily drive us batty before, during, and after any major snowstorm that may hit.

Regardless of what your emotional connection to snow may be, it is certain that any time we have any type of impactful snowstorm, almost all of us are diligent in making sure things are properly cleared away afterward.

When cleaning things up after a snowstorm, there are obvious places we all have to tend to.

Clearing our walkways, driveways, and general areas of most frequent foot traffic is an unarguable necessity.

Beyond these areas that any New Englander may naturally gravitate toward attacking are the not-so-obvious places that, if they are not properly monitored after a good size snowstorm, can have remarkably detrimental effects.

The most common area not taken care of, believe it or not, is the foundation area around the perimeter of the house.

This is most likely because as people work their way around the perimeter of their homes, they move through areas of their property that may not be as easily accessible, especially when there are several inches of snow on the ground.

The problem is that as the snow starts to melt in these areas, the melted water may begin to work its way inside toward the basement if it is able to find a way to do so.

The areas around foundation windows, particularly in older homes, can also be susceptible to this type of occurrence, specifically if we ever happen to get a storm where fallen snow is measured in feet instead of inches.

While maneuvering around the foundation, it is also important to gently clear away snow from heating system-related pipes to help eliminate potential carbon monoxide buildup.

THE CARE AND MAINTENANCE OF A NEW ENGLAND HOME

Another key area is any area where your downspouts drain into the yard. If these areas are "blocked," they can lead to possible damage as water/ice may back up inside of the downspouts and, in the most severe cases—when things are REALLY cold for an extended period of time—can lead to water freezing inside of the downspouts, expanding and severely damaging them.

In the same breath as mentioning the frozen downspouts, we would be remiss if we did not discuss ice damming.

Ice damming and the damage resulting from it is something that none of us could possibly ever enjoy experiencing.

In 2014, we had a winter where ice damming was as bad as I have ever seen it in these parts and created significant damage in thousands of homes across New England (2015 was bad as well, though not quite to the level of 2014!).

As ice dams in your gutters are formed and work through their lifespan, the damage is caused not only to the gutter systems but often to the interior and exterior of the homes as water makes its way in as part of the damming process.

To help prevent this, many folks subsequently installed various (most often cabled) low-voltage heat systems in their gutters, which would help keep them free of snow during each snowfall (the key is they would have to be turned on prior to the snow starting to fall).

Although not easily able to be freed of snow if the presence of one of these systems is not in place, depending on how one's roof is situated, it may be a good idea to have someone (or to do it yourself if you are capable) free the roof of as much snow as possible either by shoveling or through use of a roof rake. Unless you are extremely able-bodied and experienced on roofs, however, I strongly suggest you venture down the roof rake avenue if doing it yourself and hire a professional to clear off the roof if you truly believe that this should be done.

I am one of those who is wired as such that I enjoy snow for about five minutes as I watch it fall during a storm—five minutes is definitely my max, though!!

No matter how much you enjoy or despise it, keeping spaces such as these in mind when cleaning up after a storm—and not just focusing on the most commonly thought of locations (walkways, driveways, etc.)—could possibly save a tremendous amount of headache in the long run!

Converting a "Normal" Closet to a "Laundry" Closet

Every once in a while, I see certain trends emerge through conversations I have with potential clients.

One of the more popular recent ideas that have been the basis of quite a number of discussions has been the desire to convert a "normal" closet to a "laundry" closet, which would house a washer and dryer unit as well as perhaps some shelving, etc.

There could be a number of reasons for folks exploring the idea as to whether this makes sense to do or not and what it ultimately takes to execute the conversion, which is a bit more involved than many folks realize.

Most of the time, people look into a project like this to make things "easier" for them.

It could be for an immediate concern or preparation for the future.

This type of undertaking may be for someone who is working to make things a bit more convenient as they age, or simply because they are just plain sick and tired of having to go "all the way" into the basement every time they want to do the laundry.

Whatever the reasoning, the act of pulling off the conversion typically requires several trades.

An electrician will be needed to run a dedicated circuit to enable the new closet to have the proper juice it needs to function appropriately, and then the actual receptacles for the appliances need to be installed (as well as if the person would like any additional outlets added).

A plumber would obviously be necessary to perform the behind-the-scenes (rough) plumbing that is needed in order to make things happen and properly conduct the plumbing finish connections.

A carpenter would most likely be needed to modify the existing closet to accept the new use as a laundry area.

A roofer may be needed if any venting is being incorporated in order to properly integrate a vent hood on the roof to allow any venting to make its way outside (assuming this was needed).

Someone skilled in drywall and plaster/joint compound might be required to help make the space look as if it had always been set up the way it is being prepared.

A painter could be needed to make sure all finishes are properly done through completion.

In some cases, a flooring specialist may have to be called in to work the flooring on the inside and outside of the closet and ensure that the flooring areas are all finished the way they should be.

Finally, after all this, the space is ready to accept the washer and dryer appliances.

Every situation is definitely different.

Rarely, sometimes things really are as simple as running a few connections and the new space being good to go.

This truly is the exception rather that the rule, however, at least in my experience.

When converting a closet to a laundry area, the majority of the time, the project is very involved, with many of these layers intertwined within it.

Although an operation like this can become a bit intricate, when complete, it can absolutely make a huge difference in someone's life, no matter if it is for luxury or necessity!

What Affects the Price of Wood?

In the summer of 2020, I needed (3) 20' long, 5/4" x 6" pieces of pressure-treated decking for a deck repair we were doing in Providence, RI.

Let me emphasize the number '3.' I literally needed three pieces of wood. These pieces of wood, however, were nowhere to be found.

One of the things I pride myself on is the relationships I have been able to cultivate over almost thirty years of being involved in the construction industry.

This being said, no matter what relationship I worked to lean on, these pieces of wood seemed nowhere to be found.

When I finally found them, I felt as if I had struck gold.

Thinking back on it now, not only should I have felt this way because of their scarcity, but I should also have felt this was because of the price I had to pay for them at the time!

Although I may have wanted to faint, I had to pony up because of how much in need I was.

This similar situation played out repeatedly throughout the recent pandemic for seemingly anybody embarking on a home improvement project.

With supplies being so scarce, the industry price increases were, naturally, a result of what was occurring.

Though there have been some price reductions since things were at the non-COVID vaccine era height, I would be shocked if the pricing of wood ever came close to its pre-pandemic levels.

The hard-to-get nature of wood in this specific environment ultimately was the biggest reason for lumber prices to be jacked up so high.

At the time, we not only had the pandemic, which slowed production as the various mills producing the lumber went in and out of virus-related stopping and startings but there was also a HUGE demand for the lumber that had never been seen before.

People at home were taking on more home improvement projects than ever.

The riots that were occurring throughout the country at the time sucked up a huge amount of plywood as folks worked to board up and protect their homes and businesses.

As an example, I remember being hired by a hotel in Providence at the time to board up their entire first floor.

I went to the lumberyard and bought ALL of the 1/2" plywood they had.

I was one contractor for one hotel, and I ate up all this popular lumberyard's plywood in one fell swoop—and this was something that was occurring all over!

Then, at this particular time, there were also a ton of historic wildfires in the Pacific Northwest, which burned hundreds and hundreds of square miles of lumber.

This is a part of the country where we forest much of the lumber we use for home improvements.

If you add all of this together, it equals a perfect storm that decimated the lumber industry and forced the lumber prices we all experienced to astronomical levels.

Clearly, all of these events occurring at the exact same time were a coincidence of Biblical proportions.

Nonetheless, these instances provide insight into the influence of outside forces on the cost of lumber.

In our current situation, instances that will have a resonating impact for what I believe to be quite some time to come.

A Trick to Fixing Frustratingly Stubborn Plaster Failures…

_____

Strolling down the aisles in many hardware and big box home improvement stores can prove to be quite an interesting exercise.

While the majority of items very well may be commonly recognized, there are some items that the unfamiliar may understandably stare at and wonder, "What the heck is THAT thing used for??"

Normally, when someone says this (whether out loud or in their mind) upon stumbling upon one of these objects, the item that is causing them to scratch their head is often an object that is not only extraordinarily useful but something that ultimately may in fact be a stroke of genius as to its being invented whenever that may have happened to be.

One of these items definitely could be a certain 'disc-looking' object with holes all over it.

This may, in fact, actually be the perfect example!

When glancing at it for the first time, the average person may truly wonder: what in the blue blazes could this possibly be used for?

However, this particular item, although not widely known outside of plaster repair circles, is crucial for many folks who do repairs to plaster on a regular basis.

Whether old horsehair plaster or more modern plaster/drywall scenarios, these discs do an amazing job at saving certain plaster failure situations that otherwise might turn into huge undertakings.

If you have ever tried to do a horsehair plaster repair, one of the first things you may come to know is that the old horsehair plaster, once compromised, is highly unstable.

What may appear to be a small hole on the outset can turn into a large hole REALLY quickly if you go poking at it.

By properly screwing in a number of these discs directly into the unstable areas around the hole, you will have a compacting action and tighten up the plaster, which will allow you to correctly fix the hole or the crack, etc.

With newer plaster, especially with ceilings, sometimes the plasterboard (or drywall in some cases) may have a seam loosen up and form a crack all along it.

When you push on either side of the crack, you may notice that the ceiling or wall has a lot of "give" to it, so much so that trying to fix it by simply carving out the crack, taping, and replastering/compounding the crack may not do the trick in the long run, as the crack may end up returning.

If you notice this circumstance occurring as you go to push on the ceiling or wall, and you are able to utilize these discs along either side of the crack and then perform your more traditional repair, you will, again, better stabilize this area and most likely give yourself as best shot as possible in making sure the crack does not return.

As part of the repair processes, once screwed in, the discs can then either be merely patched over or taped and patched over in order to hide their being there.

There are tons of similar little knick-knacks out there that are tremendously useful when the situation calls for them.

Knowing of their existence and being able to incorporate them can feel fulfilling, in particular when you realize you know tiny little tricks to help work through predicaments that normal folks would typically not have a clue about.

Exterior Paint Application: Spray vs. Brush and Roll

As with many items in home improvement, if you ask ten different folks their opinions on the "best" methodology for applying exterior finishes to wood siding (shingles, clapboard, vertical siding, etc.), you may very well indeed get ten different answers.

Being in business since 1995 and starting as someone whose primary focus was exterior painting, as you might imagine, I have experimented with many different finish application methods over the years.

After a long time of trying these differing application strategies, I can say with a high degree of confidence that the most longevity to be gained out of one's exterior wood siding "paint" job will be if the finishes are applied with a brush and roll strategy.

For the sake of our conversation here, when I mention the term "paint," I am also wrapping in solid, semi-solid, and semi-transparent stains.

Certainly there are exceptions to this, but since we guarantee everything that we do for five years after we do it, you can bet your bottom dollar we are going to do everything we can possibly think of to maximize the longevity of any coating that we apply.

This being said, why is this?

When spraying your finish application on wood siding, even when "back-brushing/rolling" (the act of using a brush or roller to work the finish in after it is applied by spraying), the millimeter (mil) thickness of your coating will be markedly different throughout the wood siding surface being sprayed, due to the way paint ends up being absorbed varyingly by wood siding.

The closer to the center of the spray gun, the thicker the paint typically lands on the surface, and the further away from where the product is being sprayed from, typically the thinner the finish.

This is especially true the higher up on a building that one goes, particularly when spraying off a ladder.

No matter how well-intentioned the applicator is, there is just no possible way to ensure an entirely even finish when approaching things in this manner due to how wood siding varies in the way it takes the product that is being applied to it.

Contrast this with applying your product with a brush or roller, and you literally have more than 99% control over the entire structure that you are coating.

This is HUGE as it enables one to make sure that whoever's home is being finished is receiving as close as possible to an even and consistent finish coat throughout and systematically helps to ensure that the finish coat's life is enabled to be maximized for as long as possible.

As mentioned, there are anomalies to this theory.

While I am the first to admit that coating the exterior of the home is much different than coating a car per se, there are instances when I am a believer in utilizing a sprayer to apply a finish coat (one example is when similar to a car, one is painting aluminum or vinyl siding).

If you finish coating shutters, lattices, or something similar, spraying is absolutely the way to go.

These types of items are quite easy to ensure even and consistent finish coatings when being sprayed due to their tighter size when compared to the entire outside of a home or building.

Another ideal situation to utilize a spraying application is when applying certain types of non-film building water protectants, repellants, and sealers where mil thickness consistency is not a concerning focal point.

I am quite sure that there are many out there who would debate me profusely on this to one degree or another, which I am perfectly ok with.

After paying close attention for decades, however, it is quite evident to me what the best approach for guaranteeing the optimum life of one's exterior paint job on wood siding is.

It may be easy to work up an argument against me, but it is not as easy to work up an argument against the evidence.

How Many Coats of Paint Should be Applied to the Exterior of Your Home?

As I work meeting with folks throughout the year planning exterior painting projects, one of the more intense parts of our discussions can often be the conversation about how many coats of paint should be applied to their home's exterior.

I often have to re-wire in people's minds what seems to have become a rather conventional approach toward this question.

When we begin talking about how many coats should be applied, it is not unusual for someone to 'demand' that they get two coats of finish on the exterior of their home…that is, until I ask them, "Why?"

When posed with this question, they usually have either no answer at all or respond with something along the lines of "Because that is what you are supposed to do, no?"

Whether it is from people working to educate themselves on the Internet or relying on their brother-in-law 'the painter' or basing their feelings on a young sales rep from a national company who told them that is what they are "supposed to do," I tend to gently push back and enter into a further conversation as to why just slapping two coats of paint on your home every time it gets painted can do WAY MORE harm than good.

The reason for this is that the answer to the question of how many coats of paint should be put on the home is more of a situational endeavor as each side of your home weathers differently than others.

Assuming all of the surface preparation is done correctly and that the finish being used is a GOOD quality finish (although exaggerating, if you are using a lesser quality finish, five coats might not be enough!!!), my thoughts on this subject in terms of providing guidance, are influenced by several factors including if there is a color change involved and how the finish coat is going to be applied.

If there is a color change involved, with few exceptions, you definitely would need (minimally) two coats of finish.

Our finishes are generally applied by brush and roller (vs. spraying), and I make this clear to the client when having these types of conversations; applying the finishes by brush and roller allows better control of the evenness of mil thickness (millimeter thickness, the measure by which paint film thicknesses are evaluated) distribution.

Again, not to be underemphasized, each side of your home weathers differently.

If you were keeping the same color and approaching it with a blanket "two coats on everything" wave of paint, it is quite possible that you may be prematurely building up the mil thickness of the paint coating on your home well beyond what is necessary, to the point that premature failure could come into play because of the weight of the paint coating on the home's exterior.

This all being said, normally, the north side of your home would have the least amount of wear. Assuming proper prep and going with the same color as last time, this side would usually only need one 'maintenance' coat.

Compare this to the south side of your home, which typically wears the heaviest, and this side may or may not need two coats (again, assuming proper prep and the same color being used), depending on a variety of environmental factors.

The east side and the west side wear in varying degrees (in comparison to the sides facing the other directions), and the number of coats I would recommend really depends on what else may be going on (number of trees/ amount of shade, proximity to neighbors, etc.).

I am a firm believer that if your exterior absolutely needs two coats, be it in its entirety or solely certain sections, then it should surely receive them.

However, if you only need one coat to properly protect your home while avoiding unnecessary mil thickness buildup, then that is exactly what I am going to recommend.

My goal when I have these conversations with people is to lead them down the path toward what I truly believe is in the best interest of their home, even if it conflicts with widely held opinions that attempt to dictate the opposite.

Cloudy and Foggy Glass Windowpanes

One of the best benefits of modern windows is how energy-efficient they are.

Among the many reasons they are so energy-efficient is because of the way the glass is set up in them.

The glass panes of these windows are typically made with some version of two panes of glass with gas in between, usually argon or krypton. Though, just to err on the side of caution, I am not sure if Superman would have krypton in his windowpanes or not....

These glass panes come in the form of what is called Insulated Glass Units (IGUs), which double the R-value (a measure of how well an insulated material resists the flow of heat; the higher the R-value, the better the insulating ability) of a glass window.

In this specific case, energy efficiency refers to keeping temperature-controlled air on the inside of your home (vs. having it leak out and heat up the neighborhood!).

If you happen to see a cloudy or foggy window, the culprit is a seal that has been compromised in the pane of glass you are looking at.

The seal can become damaged for a number of reasons.

Exposure to water, particularly after a flood or in a situation where the seal is subjected to frequently getting hit with water, can lead to the seal weakening.

Being subjected to heat over time can also lead to the seal failing, especially with direct sunlight, where the sun's ultraviolet (UV) rays tend to accelerate things.

As windows age, the seal may also naturally wear out.

Moisture from air escaping from the glass panels can lead to condensation and ultimately the cloudy or foggy look that is observed in these types of situations.

If you happen to notice a cloudy or foggy glass pane, contrary to some opinions out there, the entire window unit itself does not need to be replaced.

The approach we most often take toward correcting this type of issue is replacing the individual pane which is exhibiting the problem.

When done by a skilled technician, this can be accomplished in a manner in which the replaced pane looks like it was original to the window itself (or at least to the point where unless one is laser focused on discovering it, will not be noticed).

The best way to not have a cloudy or foggy window issue is by doing what can be done to stay ahead of it happening.

Inspecting your windowpanes at least once per year for cloudy or fogginess can be quite beneficial in this regard.

Making sure your home is well ventilated is very important in general and can certainly help lessen the chance of premature wear on your windows.

Alleviating potential moisture challenges can be invaluable. This may mean utilizing a dehumidifier on the interior of your home in areas that seem to be overly humid and ensuring that your window areas are not exposed to unnecessary water on the exterior (a leaking gutter constantly spilling/dripping water on to a window, etc.).

Another option may be purchasing window film kits to add another layer of protection to your windows, although this can be done by the average homeowner, one has to be super particular while doing so, or else they can easily have a mess on their hands!

Cloudy or foggy glass panes can surely be annoying, especially if they are located in a spot of your home that tends to draw your eye.

Aiming to prevent them from occurring in the first place can be extremely helpful in terms of avoiding this unsightliness, but if cloudy or fogginess in your windowpanes does happen, this is a situation that is fairly easy to address.

Why Your Home Has Mice

Most everyone I know has some type of "fear" that totally skeeves them out.

For some people it is spiders, for some it may be cockroaches, or it could be any other of a wide variety of creepy crawlies.

For me, it is mice.

If I see one of these tiny beings, I will totally freak out and run for my life!

Throughout various properties I am responsible for, I use differing methods of control in order to disallow mice from working their way in and setting up shop.

Although these methodologies have proven to be quite effective, the big question always is, how do the mice get in there in the first place??

Valid question.

The simplest answer is—any way they can!

In general, mice do not need that big of a hole whatsoever—typically not bigger than a dime—in order to make their way inside a home or business and start exploring.

With the alternative being getting overrun with these tiny creatures, in many properties, some type of mouse control is vital.

In addition to control measures, here are some tips in terms of limiting access points:

- Old bulkheads (basement doors) – make sure these are very well sealed; these tend to lose their tightness over time and can develop into great entry points for mice

- The weather stripping at the bottom of entry and garage doors – if these are not solidly tight, mice will very easily work their way in

- Holes in the foundation or a gap where your foundation meets the main exterior siding – these entry points are especially tricky to neutralize because mice can (as an example) enter from one area (i.e., just above one's sill plate) and begin to work their way in behind your siding until they gradually find a path into the house

- Gaps associated with windows – mice will often work their way around a property until they find a weak link around a window; many times, this ends up being an unknown space large enough to fit the mouse yet tiny enough to be undetected

- A gap around a pipe that enters the home – this could be a water pipe, a gas pipe, or the likedefinitely an attractive possible entry point!

To prevent the unsettling feeling of seeing a mouse scurry across the room as you are comfortably watching television on any given evening, proper prevention tactics (as with most things) are critical.

I believe the best way to go is to bundle a mouse control plan with an approach of making sure that any potential entry point is as limited as possible.

It is good to have a mouse control system in place, if able to be done, it is even better to stop the mice from getting in altogether.

The key is to eliminate any semblance of a gap that mice might be able to squeeze their little bodies through.

This includes making sure any rotted wood that can easily be gnawed through for access is properly replaced.

Unfortunately, prospective areas of ingress can be seemingly everywhere, the more possibilities you are able to eliminate though, the less of a chance you will have that random startling encounter with this tiny animal, which has been known to make even the bravest of heart jump up on tables in order to avoid them!

Redoing a Ceiling: Better to Go Over Existing or to Start From Scratch?

There are a number of reasons why someone may want to replace a ceiling.

Perhaps their existing ceiling has some type of texture to it that is overly annoying to them.

Maybe they have a large section of the ceiling that is damaged (think someone falling through a ceiling while putzing around in the attic!).

Or they may have an old calcimine ceiling that gives them a fit every time they go to try to fix some peeling paint on it and the paint seems to keep peeling and peeling and peeling and peeling...no matter how thoroughly they prep the ceiling before painting it.

Whatever the reasoning, once the decision has been made that the ceiling needs to be redone, there are two different ways of doing so.

One method is to go over the existing ceiling with a new ceiling.

In the Northeast, where blueboard and plaster—particularly in residential settings—is king, the general approach would be to hang new 3/8" blueboard over the existing ceiling and then plaster over the blueboard to whichever finish one desires (smooth, swirl, textured, etc.) over it.

If there is crown molding that surrounds the room, a ceiling fan, certain types of light fixtures, or the like, they may have to be very carefully removed prior to the ceiling being hung and then properly re-installed (or have an updated version installed) after the ceiling has been completed.

The other method is starting from scratch.

This method entails, literally, taking down the existing ceiling in its entirety and hanging a new ceiling—again, assuming the Northeast typical residential construction approach—in this instance with ½" blueboard and then plastering over the blueboard to whichever finish one desires (smooth, swirl, textured, etc.) over it.

In both methodologies, one can certainly substitute sheetrock (vs. the blueboard) and its accompanying process of taping the seams and joint compounding the seams and screw holes and the entire process that is involved with this particular procedure.

Most often, however, in this part of the country, blueboard and plaster is what is utilized for this project the majority of the time.

If there is an existing "bow," even a slight one, with the existing ceiling, if going over the ceiling with a new ceiling, the bow will most likely NOT disappear as the new ceiling will simply follow the contour of the old ceiling once the new ceiling is hung over it (whereas taking down the ceiling in its entirety clearly provides an opportunity to possibly correct what may be causing the problem).

With this all being said, which angle is "better"?

As with many things, there are pros and cons to each.

The biggest con with hanging a new ceiling over the existing ceiling is one will lose about a ½" of ceiling height (which for some folks is a big deal, for others not so much).

The biggest con with demoing an existing ceiling when replacing it, is the demo process can be a bit more cumbersome and messier (as well as costly if you are hiring someone to do this for you) than simply going over the existing ceiling (even when taking into account any crown molding or fixtures that might have to come down and go back up over the existing ceiling).

The biggest pro of hanging a new ceiling over the existing ceiling is it is a bit easier than having to trudge through the messiness of taking down a ceiling in its entirety.

The biggest pro in completely removing a ceiling is that no ceiling height is lost.

With me, the optimum choice is truly situational.

While some folks may be more strongly opinionated than others on this topic, I believe there are some times when going over the existing ceiling makes more sense, and there are other times when taking down the ceiling in its entirety and starting all over again might be the better way to go.

If you have a ceiling that is bothering you and you are hemming and hawing over which path to travel down, feel free to reach out to our office and set up some time to chat on the phone; we would love the opportunity to dive into a deeper conversation regarding your specific situation with you!

The Challenges of Exterior Structural Repairs

Some of the more difficult issues to work through while addressing areas in need of repair on the exterior of your home are those that come along when tackling repairs of a structural nature.

Exterior structural repairs present a unique set of challenges that require careful consideration and expertise to overcome. From accessibility issues to regulatory compliance and safety concerns, addressing the structural integrity of your home's exterior often demands meticulous planning and execution.

Accessibility plays a pivotal role in the difficulty of exterior structural repairs. Unlike interior repairs, which can often be accessed relatively easily, working on the exterior of a home many times requires specialized equipment and techniques. Taller or multi-storied homes present particular challenges, frequently necessitating the use of scaffolding, cranes, or lifts to reach the affected areas safely. The logistics of mobilizing and setting up this equipment adds complexity to the repair process, as does the coordination required to ensure that whoever is working on the repairs can properly access all necessary locations.

Weather conditions further compound the challenges of exterior structural repairs. Repair work conducted outdoors is subject to the whims of nature, including rain, wind, extreme temperatures and sunlight. Inclement weather can disrupt work schedules, compromise worker safety, and hinder the effectiveness of repairs. Moreover, certain materials and techniques may be sensitive to environmental conditions, requiring careful planning to ensure that work can optimally proceed.

Structural integrity is another critical consideration when undertaking exterior repairs. Issues such as cracks, corrosion, or deterioration on the exterior of a home may indicate underlying structural problems that need to be addressed comprehensively. Identifying the root cause of these issues and developing appropriate repair strategies demand expertise in structural construction. Failing to address underlying structural concerns adequately can lead to recurring problems and compromise the long-term stability of the home.

Regulatory compliance adds another layer of complexity to exterior structural repairs. Homes are subject to various codes, regulations, and permitting requirements governing construction, alterations, and maintenance. Depending on the location and nature of the repair work, permits may be required from local authorities, historic preservation boards, or other regulatory bodies. Ensuring compliance with these regulations necessitates thorough research, documentation, and communication with those directly involved, which can contribute to project delays and costs.

Safety concerns loom large in the realm of exterior structural repairs. Working at heights or in precarious conditions pose inherent risks to the well-being of those working on the repairs. Falls, struck-by accidents, and other hazards are primary considerations that must be addressed through proper safety protocols, training, and equipment.

Materials and techniques used in exterior structural repairs also present challenges. Matching existing materials, preserving architectural details, and ensuring compatibility with the home's construction require specialized knowledge and skills. Moreover, the selection of materials and techniques may be influenced by factors such as climate, usage, and aesthetic considerations. Balancing these factors while adhering to budgetary constraints can be a delicate task that requires careful planning and decision making.

Exterior structural repairs are challenging due to a combination of factors, including accessibility issues, weather conditions, structural integrity concerns, regulatory compliance, safety considerations, materials and techniques, and cost considerations. Successfully addressing these challenges requires expertise, careful planning, and effective coordination among all involved in the repair process. By understanding and navigating these challenges, it's possible to undertake exterior structural repairs that restore the integrity and functionality of homes while ensuring the safety and well-being of those working to fix things as well as those living in the home.

Structural repairs, although often difficult to execute, are as important to take care of as they are arduous.

Without correctly addressing them as quickly as possible once they are recognized, it can lead to significantly greater damage down the road that will be even MORE burdensome to undertake!

Why that Old Steam Radiator Heats Up so HOT!!!

_____

Have you ever been in a building—an old home, apartment building, school, or other building of the sort—where the ancient, cast-iron radiator in whatever room you happen to be in at the time heats up to the point where the heat is seemingly unbearable and, literally, forces you to open a window?

Ever wonder why the system was designed this way?

Getting past the notion that there are more modern-day systems that allow temperatures to be controlled by zone (heck, even room by room if one wanted to pay to have their heating system laid out like that), why were these archaic systems designed like this in the first place?

Believe it or not, it was quite intentional and related to a similar situation as the most recent pandemic we have all painstakingly been making our way through.

Theories of how to control the spread of the previous pandemic in 1918 and 1919 led to the design of these systems, which a great number of us can still hear loudly clanging and blasting out tremendous amounts of heat to this day.

With recent events bringing much of the concepts of circulating air in buildings, etc., to the forefront, the idea as to why these radiator systems were developed is difficult to ignore.

In theorizing that air from outside, when brought into buildings, would help combat airborne pathogens, the Board of Health in New York City at the time ordered that all windows should remain open, even throughout the winter.

With this being the case, engineers quickly devised heating systems that would blast out heat to extreme measures, including being able to heat a building while its windows were open on the coldest day of the year.

As crazy as it may sound, all these years later, on a cold winter day when the heat is on in one of these buildings and folks inside are forced to open the windows because it becomes so balmy, they are duplicating an action that engineers from just over a hundred years ago were hoping to occur.

During the times of the previous pandemic, fresh air came to be looked at as even more of a necessity than up until that point—even throughout winter—and concerted efforts through heating system design continued to be made to influence people (without them even realizing it) to open their windows while their heat was on.

There are obviously pros and cons with anything, but the design of these older systems, blasting out the intense heat that they do, certainly made me tip my cap to these engineers of old when stumbling across an article reviewing this all, as well as the reasoning behind it.

The elementary schools I grew up learning in definitely had these systems in place, and I vividly remember the windows being open on freezing winter days.

While this particular example of engineering may have caused many folks over the years to wonder why heating systems like this were developed and still in existence in this fashion, in the days of COVID with school districts, etc., nationwide trying to figure out how to better ventilate their buildings, particularly in winter, this old school method of forcing in fresh airflow while at the same time keeping the building warm may in actuality be nothing short of pure genius.

What is the Difference Between Red Cedar Shingles and White Cedar Shingles?

On the outside of our homes, there is clearly a wide variety of what exists in terms of siding options.

Over the years, many have opted for vinyl, cement board, masonry, or some other alternative style of sided home.

Traditionally, in New England, when a home is sided out of wood, there are two main players.

While occasionally, there certainly may be an outlying T-111 or selection of pine-oriented siding; these are exceptions rather than rules.

Typically, when a home is sided in wood, it is sided with some form of either red or white cedar.

With red cedar, one tends to have either shingle, clapboard, or vertical siding.

White cedar (in New England, at least) is predominantly present in the form of shingle siding.

There are several differences between red cedar and white cedar shingles.

Cost-wise, white cedar has always been a much less expensive option than red cedar.

This has been true throughout time, until the recent pandemic.

In New England, our white cedar shingles primarily come from Canada, and our red cedar shingles are from the Western United States.

Due to extended Canadian challenges relating to the pandemic, the cost of white cedar shingles has skyrocketed from their resulting scarce availability.

While white cedar shingles are regularly as common as everyday printing paper, there were long stretches during COVID times when a single white cedar shingle could not be found in a lumberyard or box store from Maine through (at least) Ohio—I know this because a contractor buddy of mine relayed his exasperating quest, where he contacted over 400 hopeful sources of white cedar shingles throughout this region, with a grand total of zero to show for it.

Taking this time period out of the equation, there are numerous other points of differentiation.

While both are stealthily resistant to rot and being chomped on by bugs and subsequent insect damage, any similarities pretty much stop there.

Red cedar shingles tend to keep their form over time, whereas white cedar shingles shrink, curl, and can even warp.

Even though white cedar may contour with weather exposure, this does not compromise their integrity from a structural standpoint, but surely can make them cosmetically unpleasant to look at.

Red cedar shingles tend to hold paint and stain coatings MUCH better than white cedar shingles.

In fact, due to the way that they are milled (particularly over certain portions of history), white cedar shingles may be susceptible to a phenomenon known as mill glaze, which essentially makes it impossible for any type of coating to penetrate its surface unless some type of aggressive surface preparation (preferably some type of media blasting) is performed.

Due to their distinctive composition, red cedar shingles are more environmentally friendly and energy efficient than white cedar shingles.

As with many building products, when comparing one with the other, there are definitive pros and cons to each.

Although traditionally a tad pricier, my preference is always red cedar shingles. The reasoning for this is I enjoy how they hold their form as time passes as well as how receptive they are to paint and stain finishes.

Someone, on the other hand, who is looking for a more cost-effective approach and/or may just like a shingle that they would want to have installed and naturally weather as time progresses (many of our clients refer to this as the 'Cape Cod' look), white cedar would be the choice that wins out.

Regardless of which route one takes regarding either red cedar or white cedar shingles, they can have comfort in knowing that each option provides ample protection against rotted siding and damage by annoying pests as their home gracefully ages.

Arguably the Most Delicious (and Perhaps Most Dangerous!) Turkey One Could Possibly Have!

Recently, I was in attendance at an all-day meeting, and during a break in between sessions, a couple of colleagues and I started bantering about a number of holiday mishaps we have witnessed over the years.

Whether somewhat comical or extraordinarily serious, there seemed to be endless numbers of examples.

One tangent we drifted into had to do with what, when done safely, might possibly be the tastiest way to cook a turkey I have ever had the pleasure of indulging in.

When not done safely, however, this particular cooking procedure of this holiday staple could quickly turn into a complete disaster.

I am, of course, referring to deepfrying a turkey.

There are no video shortages on the Internet of deep frying a turkey gone bad.

From deep frying a frozen turkey in a garage to doing the same thing on a second-floor deck located two feet from the house, there are some approaches to tackling this method that seemingly defy logic.

I can honestly say that perhaps the most delicious turkey I have ever eaten has been a deep-fried turkey prepared by an employee and friend who passed away a while back (RIP Keith).

This was years ago, and I can still taste that delectable first bite as it absolutely melted in my mouth.

Although potentially dangerous, if proper steps are taken, deep frying a turkey can be surprisingly easy to do.

Just as on the Internet, there are numerous ways that exhibit an attempt at making this holiday meal one to remember, which ends up turning into one that one might not like to remember; there are most likely just as many, if not more, showcases of how to correctly make this experience a good one!

We receive calls on occasion where we are asked to come in and help put back together an area that the person calling in may be a tad embarrassed about.

With the old adage of hindsight being 20/20, after someone sets fire to an area in their home while deep frying a turkey and has to call a contractor to help sew things back together, I assure you that the call is often made with the person's tail surely being between their legs.

When they look back on what they did, they typically openly acknowledge that it probably was not the smartest thing they have ever done.

Similar to anything else, many times when accidents occur with this angle of cooking a holiday turkey, they often do so when someone is not following instructions that are right in front of them or while they are trying to take a shortcut.

A deep-fried turkey is not only a tasty alternative to other more traditional ways of cooking it but also a much quicker way...unless, of course, your attempt goes wrong due to some foolish decision that could have easily been avoidable.

In a case like this, not only might you lose out on the main piece of your holiday meal, but the loss may end up being much greater!

If you do choose to deep fry a turkey, please do so safely to ensure that you are truly able to enjoy the fruits of this unique way of cooking!

Gobble Gobble!

How to Stop that Annoying Chirp from the Smoke Detector

If you have not had the pleasure of being woken up from a cozy sleep by a seemingly annoying chirp, you have no clue of the enjoyable experience you are missing!

The chances are that we have all had to deal with some variation of this annoying sound at some point in our lives.

Sometimes, when we hear it, we immediately know what it is.

Other times (perhaps simply not thinking of it right away), it may take a bit for us to figure out where this specific noise is coming from.

I am not sure how, but I have known friends of mine who have just let this beeping persist for so long that it almost seems to become part of the fabric of their home, and they live with it, being totally oblivious to the irritating chirp that happens every few seconds.

Again, I have no idea how this constant peep does not drive them absolutely bonkers, but for some reason, it does not!

For me, even if I am at a complete stranger's home, at the first sign of this infamous "chirp," as politely as possible, I ask if the person whose presence I am in at the time minds if I help them eliminate this dastardly distraction.

Call it my obsessive compulsiveness. This sound is one pet peeve, though, that bothers the heck out of me—which is probably what it is intended to do (rightly so!).

In any event, the reason why the smoke detector beeps like this, is to provide a warning that the battery needs to be changed.

Even a smoke detector that is hardwired has a battery backup and at some point will need to be switched to a new one.

Once the battery is changed, the smoke detector may continue to beep until its internal codes are cleared.

The way the battery is changed is usually two different ways...

First off, most smoke detectors these days take 9-volt batteries, though some do use AA batteries.

For a wide variety of reasons, it is probably a good idea to have some type of household battery storage place that you can draw from any time you need a battery of any type.

If the smoke detector is a battery-only smoke detector, you would simply have to detach the bottom portion of the smoke detector, change out the battery with the appropriate size, and reconnect the smoke detector to its base.

For hard-wired smoke detectors, there is one extra step.

With hardwired detectors, in the process of disconnecting the base, you will also have to unclip the portion of the smoke detector that is wired to its base and then reconnect it once the battery is swapped out.

The entire process should take less than ten minutes.

Clearly, if you have a smoke detector that is located much higher up, the process will be a bit more involved.

On certain occasions, you may have to reach out to someone (family friend, handyman, contractor, etc.) to help out to access the smoke detector because of the height or its location.

The chirping from a smoke detector may indeed be one of the more maddening sounds one might endure—definitely my opinion!—but as mentioned earlier, it is most likely meant to be that way in that it ultimately may motivate someone to change the battery out as quickly as they can to help better ensure a safe environment for all those in the household.

What is the Difference Between Drywall and Blueboard?

When it comes to building materials, there are some items I have always noticed clients seem to refer to when possibly actually referring to another.

One classic example of this is gutters and downspouts.

I have had many occasions in the past when clients were discussing their downspouts and, while doing so, kept calling them their gutters.

Another example is when someone asks us to "plaster" a hole in one of their walls when technically they would like the hole fixed with some type of material, and while saying "plaster," they may actually mean spackle or joint compound.

In this same category of contractor lingo confusion is 'drywall' and 'blueboard.'

These two materials are quite different from one another, though, as in the above examples, many folks often interchange them.

Drywall is a type of wallboard covered in paper and then, after being hung, is meant to have its joints "taped" and then properly covered with joint compound.

Blueboard, on the other hand, is a type of wallboard that is more absorbent than drywall and specifically designed to bond with a veneer plaster.

In New England, drywall is most often used in commercial settings.

Drywall has a rougher appearance to it and is typically not able to achieve as smooth a finish as its plastered cousin.

Drywall also takes a number of days to truly have an install complete, as there are a number of steps of sanding and re-application of joint compound prior to the finished joint compound application being considered "finished."

Drywall typically provides better insulating qualities than blueboard, whereas blueboard is a better barrier for sound than drywall.

Drywall is definitely the more cost-efficient option of the two and less labor-intensive overall.

The plastered finish that goes on blueboard is viewed as much more of a "high-end" finish than drywall.

After hanging blueboard, it can conceivably be prepped (seams taped and initial coat of plaster) and completely plastered the same day it is put up.

Unlike drywall, one does not have to wait a day between steps; however, once plastered, prepping and finishing painting should not occur until at least one to two weeks after the plastering has been done.

This waiting period allows the plaster to properly cure after it has been applied.

Blueboard and plaster is especially popular in residential settings in New England.

In some areas of the country, folks have not even heard of blueboard and plaster (which many in New England may find this difficult to believe).

Where aesthetics may be critical, blueboard is certainly the superior choice.

Though at a much heftier price tag, the finishes that can be achieved with a correctly done plaster wall over the blueboard strongly overshadow anything that can be done with drywall.

Although very different, it is not unusual for a contractor to hear a client referring to drywall as blueboard or blueboard as drywall.

It is important when having a conversation about a project with a client that contractors ask clarifying questions to make sure that they understand specifically what their clients are referring to.

Similar to as frustrating as it may be for a contractor to hear a client call a downspout a "gutter," having teaching moments like these can be surprising opportunities for contractors to tactfully show their industry expertise by guiding folks through actual correct terminology.

What Causes Gutters to Leak?

Leaking gutters can be caused by a variety of phenomena.

For the purposes of our conversation here, we will be referring to aluminum gutter systems (vs. copper, wood, etc.).

When discussing a leaking gutter, I am alluding to the actual gutter (the horizontal piece of the gutter system) and not the downspouts (the vertical components of the gutter system)—although many folks do like to refer to downspouts as "gutters" (a pet peeve of mine!).

Downspouts can certainly leak, too, though.

When downspouts leak, it is often simply because the parts of the downspout that are connected to each other are connected upside down (with the piece that is supposed to be dipping into the bottom hung with the bottom going over the top).

If the downspout is hung this way, water is naturally going to come pouring out of it with each rain.

There are a number of reasons why gutters may leak.

Gutters can leak if the sealant that is located in its corners or seams dries out over a period of time and begins to fail.

If this occurs, the leak can be neutralized with a simple resealing of the area utilizing the proper sealant.

Another way a gutter system can leak is if the gutter system is made out of a thinner gauge aluminum and becomes pitted over time as it oxidizes and eventually develops pinhole-type leaks.

In theory, these leaks can be fixed with a few different products and processes available on the market (Geocel and Gaco are a couple of good ones), but when a gutter reaches this stage, it is most likely time for it to be replaced.

Perhaps the most notorious reason a gutter system "leaks" is not really a "leak" at all.

Instead, this particular "leak" is caused by the gutter system becoming clogged and water essentially "spilling" over the front or rear of the gutter.

If this occurs and water flows over the backside of the gutter, it is conceivable that it could make its way into the house and show its face as water staining on a ceiling or dripping through a window.

If this occurs and water flows over the front of the gutter, depending on how the gutter system is positioned will dictate whether the water will be coming over the edge as a thin stream or cascading like a waterfall.

Either situation can be easily prevented by making sure your gutter systems are cleaned and flushed every so often.

This does not mean putting a ladder up and picking the leaves and debris out of your gutters once or twice per year.

This means actually testing things by running a hose every so often and making sure that water is properly flowing through the gutter system.

Better yet, the incorporation of a gutter debris protection system can be most beneficial (I prefer the Gutterbrush system).

When clogs occur, they seem to frequently happen at the point where the gutter empties into a downspout below it; it is SUPER important that these points are clean and free of debris.

Gutters can be an invaluable asset for catching and helping to guide water away from your home.

If they are not inspected a couple of times per year, however, challenges that stem from a "leaking" gutter can have a serious negative impact on your property.

Why Re-hanging Things is Often More Involved Than it May Seem...

Have you ever taken down a nail used to hang a picture, shutter, or like item, and the nail that you initially used to hang it up with did not seem to quite do the trick when you went to re-hang the item?

This can be a frustrating experience.

It may be likened to if you ever have seen wood clapboard siding on the exterior of the home have a nail pop out, and when the nail is attempted to be banged back in, success is only temporary as the nail pops back out a short time later.

Why does this type of situation occur, and how can it be avoided?

This phenomenon happens because the nail that is used to rehang whatever it is that is getting rehung is essentially sliding back into a hole that has already been formed, and it is no longer tightly held in the wall area around it.

The nail, ever so slightly, had to be loosened out of its original hole (even if it did not feel as though one was loosening it significantly when it was being taken out of the hole).

When this is done, the initial nail instantly becomes obsolete, and there is no logical way for this nail to be reutilized in its same hole moving forward.

This same type of situation occurs outside of the home in the siding example where although nature did the loosening, the same nail cannot be reused and possibly be expected to correctly fasten down the siding.

In all these types of instances, the only way to successfully rehang the picture or correctly tighten the siding, etc., would be to use a nail that is either longer or wider than the nail that was used in the first place.

By working in a nail that is either longer or wider, you are forcing your little hanging system to either go a bit deeper or expand around the shaft area to truly hold whatever it is that you are trying to hang/fasten.

Be careful of situations in newer homes where the plaster is much tighter than the plaster of older homes (where horsehair plaster was frequently used).

In these newer homes, if you try to reuse an existing nail, the plaster can often give the false initial impression that it has "grabbed" your nail and that whatever was hung can be safely rehung.

All is fine and dandy until BOOM!!—the family portrait that you have treasured as the centerpiece of your home for years comes crashing down!

Truly, the safest way to avoid this type of disheartening scenario is to remember this rule of thumb—when rehanging an item where a nail has been taken out or if you ever are trying to put a nail back in place (whether it is on the exterior or interior of the home) that has come out of its original hole for one reason or another, always use a nail that is either longer or wider than the original one (assuming you are putting it back in the same hole it came out of).

Approaching things in this manner will provide comfort that the nail will correctly hold its place and steer you clear from a situation where something potentially very valuable to you or your family gets unintentionally smashed to smithereens!!

Two Traditional Societal Norms that Have Transitioned into Modern-Day Superpowers

---

One of the more interesting by-products of my 3+ decades of being involved in business is the ability to have a chance to reflect on consumer behavior over this time period.

These days, this observational privilege is compounded by the number of different businesses I am fortunate to own and the very different clients that we service in each one.

I am not sure whether this is magnified by everything that we all have been through in the recent pandemic or if it has been something that has been gradually brewing for quite some time, but there are two definitive, glaringly waning societal characteristics that I have noticed as of late which cannot be ignored.

While I have certainly observed these on my own, my feelings continue to be co-signed by numerous business contacts I have conversations with across a number of different industries.

These characteristics are those of patience and loyalty.

The 'patience factor' is something that I have heard mentioned for a long time but have seen hit our industry extraordinarily hard over the past couple of years, as we all experience supply chain challenges that no one really knows when they are going to improve, the across industry lack of qualified employees to help in almost every facet of business, and in at least our specific industry as of late, weather that has not been anywhere close to conducive for getting work completed anywhere near a fluid manner.

Admittedly, I do feel I am showing my age a bit when I remember a time when patience, in general, appeared to be much more prevalent—almost superpower-like!

I believe the same can be said for loyalty.

Whether it is a career situation or simply a brand-loyal consumer behavior, loyalty just does not seem to hold the value it once did.

Regardless of switching jobs or switching kids' sports teams, the loyalty quality that once was so dominant in our lives seems to be valued less and less by the day.

Perhaps they are tied together?

While I do not mean to philosophize, I do see an overlap that is impossible to ignore.

I see and hear of scenarios on a daily basis where a company "messes up" some aspect of their daily business, and instead of patiently working through to correct things, the "huffy puffy" gene of many folks quickly rises to the surface and proceeds to almost encourage the individual to torture said company and quickly look for an alternate means of receiving the same service employment.

A teenage worker accidentally gives the wrong flavor of ice cream at the neighborhood ice cream store you have been attending for years after you have already waited in line for half an hour—time to look for a new ice cream shop!

You don't like the fact that your athlete is "benched" for non-performance, and instead of encouraging them to work hard to get better and retake their spot, you look for another place for your athlete to participate.

Even though we are all aware of the monumental delays in shipping these days, the monthly vitamins you have ordered from your favorite vitamin company for years all of a sudden start arriving later than ideal, and instead of patiently adjusting your ordering habits, you decide to change your "go to" vitamins altogether.

Where does it end?

I personally have no idea.

I do know that these are real items that businesses have to work through and come up with real strategies to combat.

As with many things in life, patience and loyalty are not what they used to be, and those businesses that are able to embrace this concept and adapt to this alarming trend in our behavior are sure to be ahead of the curve.

How exactly to go about doing so may be an almost Rubik's cube-like mystery to figure out.

What is a Water Table in a House?

Any time there is some type of flood showcased in the news, while digging deeper into the event, you might notice the mention of the term 'water table' in the story.

Perhaps you have heard this phrase in conversation with a friend, realtor, contractor, or the like referencing something having to do with a water table at someone's home.

So, exactly what is a water table in a house?

The water table is a boundary located underground in between the area where groundwater saturates the spacing between sediments and cracks and rocks and the soil surface above it.

At this boundary, water pressure and atmospheric pressure are equal.

Below the water table lays a saturated zone where water fills all spaces between sediments and within the rock itself.

The height of this water table can be very different in areas and even within the same area...does that make sense?

In other words, it is not inconceivable that the water table levels within someone's same property can vary; it all depends on the geology of the property.

The water table can also vary in levels at different points in the year.

As an example, in New England, during late winter and spring, when snow melts and precipitation may be high, the water table will rise.

During summer, on the other hand, the water table goes down as days are a bit drier, and plants take up water from the soil surface prior to it sinking down toward the water table.

When the water from melting snow or falling precipitation hits the soil, there is a bit of a lag from the time that water starts sinking into the soil (as the water has to trickle down and fill the spaces between the sediments), and the water table rises.

The saturated zone below the water table is called an aquifer—basically a big storehouse of water.

This water is what is referred to as groundwater.

While melting snow and rain events are terrific avenues for replenishing groundwater, because of the time it takes for water to sink down through the soil and reach the aquifers, too much moisture, too quickly can oversaturate the soil and lead to the flooding that is often experienced with certain storm events.

If an area has a higher water table, it will be easier to flood as the area below the ground will become overly saturated with water at a quicker pace.

Homes with basements built in areas with higher water tables should strongly consider having some type of basement waterproofing solution in place (including but not limited to a proper sump pump system) in preparation for a time when they may be more prone to flooding.

There are companies that specialize in waterproofing basements, and the more reputable ones should definitely be leaned on for guidance on how to best protect your basement.

The knowledge of water table location is also useful in construction as one is building a home, particularly when it comes to homes that will draw their water from a well or deciding on a location to build that may be less susceptible to flooding.

While not something the average person may need to think about every day, the knowledge of what a water table is and how it may affect things such as flooding might be useful to be aware of, particularly if you live in an area that has seen its share of flooding in the past.

The Secret Power of Underutilized Shoes

Chances are the majority of us have some old shoes kicking around that are not doing much but gathering a bit of dust or holding a place within our minds that is saying that we will wear them "someday" and that having them in our current collection still makes sense to do.

If by some chance there is a way to somehow part with these shoes, there may be someone out there who can truly put the shoes to "good," if not more regular, use.

One awesome vehicle for providing these currently underutilized foot-pieces a terrific home is a local competitive cheerleading gym in Providence, RI—Cheer UP Athletics—which has teamed up with an extraordinary or-ganization—funds2orgs—to put these gently worn, used, and new shoes to fantastic use!

The fundraiser, with good reason, has even drawn the attention of local media outlets which are helping to get the word out.

One, the athletes that call Cheer UP their home benefit from the drive as they receive funding from funds2orgs based on the total weight of the shoes they are able to gather in their outreach efforts.

The funding is then used to help offset the cost of different gym-spon-sored, team-building events, which, in turn, bring everyone closer together (something that is perhaps needed now more so than ever!).

funds2orgs then takes all the shoes that are raised and donates them to be repurposed around the world by distributing them to micro-entrepreneurs in fledging countries, who, in turn, take the shoes to their local village markets where they set up shop with this welcomed boost from abroad, and take solid steps forward in helping raise themselves out of poverty.

Finally, the obvious benefit is in the ultimate end users, who gain a diverse alternative in footwear to what they would normally have the opportunity for in their places of living.

Perhaps you have never known such a thing as a fundraiser designed spe-cifically for collecting shoes, which may be just kicking around (no pun in-tended), even existed.

THE CARE AND MAINTENANCE OF A NEW ENGLAND HOME

This is the perfect time to take advantage of this type of situation and clean out that shoe closet or pile of shoes accumulating under the bed and get them in the hands of a truly valuable cause.

Whether it is one bag of three pairs of shoes or several large contractor bags full of shoes, all of the donations are very much appreciated.

To donate the shoes, you can call or text message Cheer UP Athletics at 401-215-7022.

The Smithfield Times in Smithfield, RI, is also a drop-off location, and a drop-off can be arranged there by calling 401-232-9600.

Or if you were to reach out to us at LOPCO Contracting at 401-270-2664, we can help to arrange for the shoes to reach the folks at Cheer UP Athletics.

Thank you for any help you could provide as well as anything you might be able to do to help spread the word about this absolutely wonderful fundraiser!

Can I Paint Without Sanding?

Finish painting is the easy part.

Many folks say that painting is extraordinarily therapeutic, peaceful, and almost zen-like.

Chances are those saying this are not referring to the prep portion of their projects.

It is not unusual to contemplate whether sanding should be involved with the prep process for your particular project.

With few exceptions, sanding is almost ALWAYS necessary.

The reason is by sanding, you not only eliminate roughness and set the stage for the magnificent paint or stain system you are about to apply, but by doing so, you also allow the surface to be in a position to "hold" your coating in place for a long time to come.

On the exterior, sanding is often necessary to eliminate the edges of peeling paint and to make sure that unsightly imperfections are as limited as they can be given an individual circumstance.

On the interior, sanding is necessary to smooth out plaster, joint compound, or spackling that has been applied, allow for "bite" in between coatings of paint or polyurethane, or scuffing up older finishes to cut down glossiness.

If lead paint is present (in homes built prior to 1978), it is generally advised that sanding should only be done by a certified professional who has the proper equipment to appropriately work with this type of situation.

Another instance where sanding should not be done is with certain types of wood decking and the deck finishes that are associated with them.

This is because by sanding certain types of wood that already have tightly dense wood grains to begin with (Ipe as an example), sanding these surfaces would cause the wood grain to tighten up even further and, as crazy as it may seem, disallow any stain applied to its surface (seemingly no matter how thin the stain maybe) to correctly penetrate.

As far as what we are all traditionally taught in terms of preparing surfaces, this may appear to be quite the 'Catch 22'!

There are other nuanced situations where sanding would not make sense to do; these are the exceptions rather than the rule, however.

To truly prepare any surface that you will be painting or staining, sanding should be planned to be included in some capacity nearly 100% of the time.

When sanding, it is important to not only use the proper equipment but also to wear the proper personal protection (the correct facemask, eye protection, etc.) that is necessary to help guard you from harm.

When sanding, there are different "grits" associated with the variety of sandpaper you may use.

The higher the grit, the smoother the sandpaper (typically used for final sanding or tasks that do not need as rough a paper).

The lower the grit, the rougher the paper (typically for tasks that require a "heavier hand," i.e., exterior surface prep).

It is easy (with good reason!!) to envision the idea of sanding as being an excruciating task that is neither fun nor relaxing.

While some types of sanding are certainly more of a workout than others, the fact that the act of sanding is an overall vital part of the surface preparation process when it comes to painting may be the unfortunate realization for any lazy bone who may be approaching a painting project and desires it to come out as best as possible.

Exterior Decking Floors— To Coat or Not to Coat

When the majority of folks have a natural wood deck as a feature on their home, at some point in time, they will most likely come to a crossroads.

The question will pass through their mind as to whether they should treat their deck floor surfaces with some type of coating.

Now, obviously, if the deck already has some type of coating on its flooring, this is not a question that will arise, as whatever maintenance pattern the deck is in would clearly be present.

But if the deck flooring has never been treated before, it is understandably common for one to ponder if they should treat it in one capacity or another.

After all, shouldn't the deck be treated in order to ensure it lasts as long as possible?

The short answer is—not really.

Most wood decks are made out of either pressure-treated wood, mahogany, or Ipe.

Each, in its own right, would be perfectly fine for years if left untreated with any type of coating.

Yes, they will weather.

If left unfinished with any type of application, over time, they will develop a grayish tone and possibly incur varying degrees of mold or mildew growth.

However, if maintained properly, i.e., cleaned when these types of phenomena set in, they will rarely experience any type of "rot" per se and will maintain their structural integrity indefinitely.

If this is the case, then why do people often treat their deck flooring with some type of stain or porch and floor enamel?

Great question.

The most logical answer I can come up with is that they believe that by doing so, they are employing good practice from a maintenance perspective; they enjoy the way the application looks on their deck surfaces or a combination of the two.

While there definitely is not anything wrong with applying some type of coating to your deck surfaces, it should be done with the correct expectation that in applying any type of coating system to your deck—particularly horizontal surfaces such as flooring—you are committing yourself to some type of long-term maintenance of the deck.

It should be further noted that the more solid the coating system (a porch and floor enamel as an example), the more potentially involved the maintenance will ultimately be.

Meanwhile, wood toning stains are fairly easy to keep fresh looking (needing a simple cleaning and recoating every now and again).

The more solid the application, the more of a chance that the coating will peel at some point (especially if the surface is not properly prepared/etched prior to being applied).

If a situation is in place where the product utilized is prone to peeling, it will be much more of a chore to keep looking good year after year than a system that is more likely to simply need some "light" refinishing.

I would never tell someone NOT to apply some type of coating system to their deck.

Many coating systems look absolutely stunning when done and cared for properly.

I would simply caution whoever is applying the application to fully understand what they are signing up for.

Crown Molding

One of the decorative features of homes that I have seen homeowners get most excited about over the years is crown molding.

I don't know if it is the way the word 'crown molding' slides off one's tongue or the vision that folks think of when having a conversation about it in their homes, but when discussing crown molding, it is not unusual to hear how much homeowners genuinely seem to enjoy conversation surrounding this particular element of their homes.

Crown molding is a type of molding that hugs the perimeter of the room, and it is located at the point where the wall meets the ceiling.

Not to be confused with its cousin 'picture molding' [a similar molding, but one that leaves a small space (traditionally for hanging pictures) in between the ceiling and the top of its molding], crown molding touches both the ceiling and the wall area below it.

Most crown molding these days is made out of wood.

'Back in the day,' when crown molding designs were much more elaborate in comparison to today's standards, crown molding was very often found to be made out of plaster.

Sometimes larger, more intense crown molding is created by layering different types of molding to fabricate a fashionably unique appearance.

Crown molding is often integrated into the design of newer homes.

Some love it so much they work to incorporate crown molding into as many rooms as possible!

Others prefer to have it located solely in one room (the living room as an example).

Crown molding can be what I consider 'standard' crown molding, where the molding itself is one straight shot of trim.

Crown molding can also be a bit more detailed, as is the case with 'dentil' crown molding.

Crown molding is installed either with its corners meeting up, ideally with 'pretty' miters, cut and installed by an experienced carpenter, or with blocking installed into the corners (which can add a little spice to the crown molding layout design and that makes the crown molding installation a tad easier to do).

Crown molding does not necessarily have to be installed when first building a home, and we are hired all the time to install it on homes that have never had it before.

When most people think about crown molding, they think of it being installed on the inside of one's home.

The reality, though, is that crown molding is just as often (if not more often) to be found on the exterior of one's home.

Whether being installed at the time a home or addition is being built or later on, after the home has been lived in for years, and whether on the inside of the home or the outside of the home, crown molding installation can be extremely tricky.

To bring it to a truly finished look, whether the finish is going to be some type of paint or enamel or a natural stain/polyurethane combination, it can be quite the process to make sure everything in and around the crown molding is filled, caulked, prepped, and finished to the point that enables the crown molding to look as "perfect" as possible.

Crown molding can truly add a spectacular ornamental component to the areas in which it is installed.

Though there certainly is skill involved in properly installing it, its mere presence in an interior room or as a beautifying feature on one's exterior is frequently a source of delight for many a homeowner.

Unintentional Damage by the Well-Intentioned

Recently, I had a situation with a client that was truly heartbreaking to work through.

The client had lost her husband within the past year and was currently fighting health challenges of her own.

Since her husband had passed, a mysterious leak had developed within her home.

The leak did not happen all the time but seemed to line up with rainstorms of a certain nature.

Not too long ago, we had a significant storm that was brewing.

As you can imagine, the client was extremely nervous due to the direction from which the storm appeared to be coming.

Right before the storm hit, the family's longtime handyman unexpectedly showed up on the doorstep with a tarp that he wanted to put on the roof, over a skylight in the area that he was convinced the leak was coming from.

No water appeared to come through in the storm.

The degree of relief the client felt at that point was beyond measurable, and she was extraordinarily grateful to this kind soul for stopping by out of the goodness of his heart and tacking the tarp down prior to the storm.

Several days later, I came over for a meeting that had previously been scheduled for some time to review the leak predicament.

After looking over things and hearing what had happened, my heart fell ill.

Shouldn't my heart have felt "full" instead of "ill"?

Well, you see, in this situation, not quite so.

Upon investigating things, it was clear to me that the leak had absolutely nothing to do with the skylight.

Instead, the leak was stemming from where one of the three sewer venting pipes in the vicinity was penetrating through the roof.

We have a flashing correction system that we install for these types of leaks, and all three of the sewer venting pipes could have used it.

Although there seem to be few who know how to detect this, once someone knows what to look for, these are relatively simple leaks to diagnose.

Now I was faced with the task of relaying this to the client as well as the unsettling fact that while the handyman was extraordinarily well-intentioned with what he did at the last second before the storm, there is now a good amount of additional damage to correct as a result of all the areas where the tarp was nailed into the roof.

Not a good scene.

After running through all of this with the client, she seemed receptive to what I had said but also said that she thought she might look to seek another opinion.

I thanked her for allowing me to come out, sent her a blog I had written a while back about this specific type of leak, and encouraged her to get as much feedback from people as it made her comfortable...but I also asked her to please not give whoever comes out the "answers to the test."

I have no idea if this particular client will end up hiring us to fix these issues.

While we would welcome the work, if she does not end up hiring us, my only hope is that she hires someone who is very well-versed with these types of leaks.

This is definitely a challenging circumstance for all involved; however, the lesson learned from the unintentional damage incurred by an extremely well-intentioned individual should not be lost on any of us.

Opening Pandora's Box

Anyone who owns a home with even a little bit of age to it (and quite many times, even much newer homes!) is susceptible to the idea of opening 'Pandora's Box' any time they go to repair a piece of rotted exterior wood on their home.

When taking off the rotted components, there is a chance that the wood behind the wooden trim (the structural framing) has rotted on some level.

Unfortunately, there is no way to tell the degree (if any) that rotted structural work exists behind rotted trim work until the rotted trim work is removed.

This makes planning for these types of circumstances extraordinarily difficult.

I have seen situations in the past where something looks like a simple corner board replacement turns into a massive repair situation.

I have also seen many occasions where something on the surface looks shot beyond belief and the structural items behind it ended up being in very good shape, with no additional structural corrections necessary.

Although there is no surefire way to know when one is more likely to stumble upon structural repairs needing to be done than others, there does often seem to be a common thread—areas allowing moisture to get in behind the trim work for extended periods of time!

When moisture is allowed to get behind the exterior finished areas of the home, it can gradually deteriorate the structural components to which they are attached.

This is because of a variety of reasons.

The moisture itself—without being able to properly dry out—can lead to decay, mold growth, etc.

The moisture being there is also a sort of magnet for carpenter ants, termites, and the like, which are constantly searching for damp, wood areas where they can make a home and utilize for sustenance.

When structural rot is discovered behind any rotted trim work, the first thing we always look for is signs of insect damage.

If it is found, we urge the homeowner to get things treated as soon as possible, and we are at a standstill in terms of correcting the rotted structural members until any wood-damaging insects are eradicated.

Once it is assured that any existing tiny guests that are causing this type of ruckus are no longer a threat, it is ok to begin to properly replace the structural areas that have rotted.

It is important that these types of repairs and corrections are only conducted by someone who knows how to properly stabilize them.

While this may seem like common sense, you may be surprised to learn how many repairs we come across in the field that we have to re-correct what someone else had previously done to structurally "fix" something.

Opening Pandora's Box and discovering a plethora of items that one was not counting on addressing is bothersome enough.

However, having to correct a structural repair that was not done properly in the first place is astronomically unsettling!

Caulking Your Foundation

If you have a home in New England, there is a good chance that you have some type of "foundation" associated with your home.

Foundations are found at the base of your home and serve as a solid structure on which your home can be built.

There are many analogies across life that reference the importance of building a strong foundation; what we are discussing here is the actual, real-life application of these popular metaphors.

Foundations can be built out of brick, cinderblock, stone, or any other masonry material.

As important as properly constructing a foundation is when it is originally built, equally as important is making sure that it is well maintained as it ages over time.

Some folks like to paint their foundation, while others do not, and instead, they may elect to apply some type of a clear waterproofer to it or elect to leave it "natural."

Although I am not the biggest fan of painting a foundation, I do realize that many people LOVE painted foundations (or even if they are ambivalent about their foundations being painted, they may inherit them when they purchase a home having one).

As long as the paint is well-maintained and exterior and interior moisture is regulated appropriately, there is nothing technically "wrong" about having a painted foundation.

Whether painted or not, one item that is imperative to stay on top of is making sure that exterior moisture is not allowed entry into the home from cracks forming in the foundation itself or at the point where the foundation meets the ground.

If a crack forms in the foundation itself and it is not painted, having the mortar appropriately corrected (sometimes with the help of an experienced mason) by properly repointing it is necessary.

If the foundation is painted and cracks in the foundation form, utilizing some type of caulk meant for caulking the joints in your foundation would absolutely be fine.

In this scenario, it is important to determine whether or not the caulk is able to be painted prior to its application.

Another area of the foundation that is super critical to avoid cracking from existing much longer than after the point in time it is discovered is the point where the foundation itself meets solid ground that is built upon with asphalt, concrete, cement, or a similar material.

If cracks are found in these areas, there are specialty caulks that should be used to correct these nuisance gaps.

"Regular" caulk should never be used.

My "go-to" product in these situations is a product called Dymonic.

Dymonic is solvent-based, which essentially means that you should have paint thinner on hand (vs. water) to help clean any excess Dymonic if needed.

Dymonic comes in tubes as traditional caulk does, but the way it is formulated makes it the perfect caulk to be used in these situations.

A Dymonic dealer can be found with the help of a simple online search or inquiring about it at your local lumberyard.

Exterior moisture penetration is something that can lead to very expensive foundation repairs down the line.

Carefully inspecting your foundation every once in a while (at least once per year) can be extraordinarily helpful in staying ahead of things and helping to ensure that your foundation remains solidly intact for years to come.

Reglazing Windows

Of all the things that can possibly be undertaken as they relate to painting, whether it be interior or exterior, there are two tasks that I have always despised more than others.

One is removing wallpaper.

Removing wallpaper is a grueling chore, and every time I have had to do it, it has always felt as if I had been assigned this tortuous punishment for some type of unruly crime that was committed.

Right next to this, I would place reglazing windows.

Reglazing windows is far from an easy thing to do.

It is a special skill set, however, that very much feels in line with many other trade-related skills in that fewer and fewer are able to properly execute them these days in comparison to years past.

The term "dying art" certainly applies here.

The actual action of reglazing windows is fairly straightforward, and although there may be different variations of doing it correctly (the whole "there is more than one way to skin a cat" idea), for all intents and purposes, the actual procedure should look somewhere along these lines:

- Remove all loose glazing

- Clean areas being worked on

- Prime all mullions (the areas of the windows that the glazing is attached to) and any remaining glazing that is still tightly bonded

- Reglaze areas in need using proper glazing techniques; traditionally, many have used oil-based glazing for this; more recent strides in technology have allowed water-based glazing to be more comfortably used while maintaining comparable quality

- After glazing hardens/"skins-over" to a reasonable level, prime all mullions with an appropriate primer

- Finish coat with two coats of the preferred quality finish

- Clean all glass panes associated with the areas being worked on (using a combination of razor blades, Windex, perhaps a tiny squeegee, and paper towels)

Seems simple enough, no?

For me, as beautiful as the end results usually are (typically, especially when compared to what things looked like prior to the project being done), the process itself is extraordinarily mundane.

Most "not-exciting" is the actual act of the glazing itself (this is where my obsessive compulsiveness kicks in!), as I have always striven for perfectly smooth, balanced runs of glazing with the perfect thickness.

Years ago, I hired a college student who had been attending the Rhode Island School of Design as a sculpting major at the time.

Needless to say, his feelings about glazing were completely 180 degrees from my feelings about it.

He absolutely loved it!

Obviously similar to working with clay, once trained, he was absolutely wonderful at it and really did seem to enjoy every moment.

It is interesting to me how one person can dislike doing something so much and another person can find the same exact task highly enjoyable.

I'm sure this can be compared to many things in life, but one thing is for certain: glazing is NOT something that many folks these days are able to do and do well.

Fortunately, reglazing windows is an activity that a number of our staff have become quite adept at over the years, and they have saved me from having to force myself through these types of projects when we are hired to do them.

Although clearly not as prevalent as in years past, there are still a TON of older windows that need reglazing every so often, and if the intent is to keep them around, reglazing them is something that at some point will have to be done—whether the person doing the reglazing likes doing it or not!

Surfactant Leaching

As New England summers gradually move forward and the calendar advances, there is a phenomenon that occurs with painting outside, which is often a head-scratcher when it is seen and can lead to various forms of panic.

Annually, we tend to receive at least a couple of calls from clients who reach out to us with concerns that something "weird" is happening with their paint.

This "weird" occurrence (when it happens) is frequently noticed in mid to darker-toned colors—though it can surely happen in lighter colors!

Its appearance is such that it looks like the paint is reacting in a type of odd way in the formation of brownish and/or glossy (even amongst flat finishes) spots that are tacky and/or oily to the touch.

When someone first sees this, thoughts of having to completely repaint something that has just been painted can race through the observer's brain.

Fortunately, this type of situation is an extremely easy fix.

Years ago, however, I was the one who experienced an anxious alarm when I received a frantic call from a client relaying their concerns.

My guess is the year had to be 1995 or 1996.

We had just completed the project, and the homeowner said that they were frazzled because what looked extraordinarily beautiful one day was covered by this weird brown streaking the next, and they were not sure what caused it or what to do.

At the time, neither did I.

I reached out to my manufacturer's paint rep and set up a meeting at the site.

As soon as our rep looked into the issue, he calmly let me know what was occurring.

When latex (water-based) paints and stains, at certain periods of the year (often as summer wears on and heads into and through fall), are in their curing process after they are applied and are mixed with the natural moisture that can occur overnight or with rain in conjunction with other weather influences, this circumstance known as 'surfactant leaching' can take place.

Surfactants are water-soluble ingredients in paint and can be brought to the surface of paint coatings ('leached') as curing conditions are slowed down if moisture (something as simple as overnight dew) lays on the paint surface.

Although if the conditions are there, surfactant leaching can take place interiorly as well (most often in bathrooms or interior environments with a higher humidity level), I have mostly run into it on the exterior.

The way my rep explained it at the time, the surfactants are very similar to the surfactants one would find in soap (hence their oily feel).

The fix for a situation like this is to do either one of two things.

If one were to gently wipe the surfactant leaching with a warm, wet rag, it would absolutely come off.

My preference, however, has been to encourage homeowners to let nature take its course as, over time, the surfactant leaching will certainly go away as the paint cures and begins to form its permanent barrier to the weather.

Although definitely unsightly, all is not lost if one is to experience surfactant leaching, and (as with many things) patience can be an absolute virtue in waiting for it to work its way out and your paint coating to naturally mold itself to the pinnacle of its beauty—which was envisioned when the paint color was first decided upon.

Interior Peeling Paint

While it is certainly not unusual to see peeling paint on the exterior of someone's home, it is a bit less common to see peeling on the interior of the home.

It would even be safe to say that seeing peeling paint on the exterior of a home is eventually an expected sight at some point during an exterior paint job's life cycle, not so much on the interior.

Now, there are those rare phenomena that can make sense for peeling interior paint to be present.

Examples would be when old, calcimine-influenced ceiling coatings do not allow the paint to adhere properly or when there is a leak somewhere within a home's structure that subsequently causes paint coatings to peel.

But what about in newer homes, where paint is seen to be peeling on the interior for seemingly no reason whatsoever? Why does this happen??

Peeling interior paint can occur for a variety of reasons.

One such reason, and perhaps the most obvious, is if the correct bonding primer was not used when the walls were originally painted.

Another reason could be that the surface that was being painted may have had an elevated moisture or humidity level at the time it was painted.

This is a tricky one because even if a moisture meter (a tool used to measure the moisture content of a surface its prongs are "plugged" into) is utilized prior to preparing a surface for painting, its measuring needles may not be able to penetrate deep enough to where moisture may be lurking within the surface that is being painted.

As this moisture gradually works its way out, it can cause the paint coating to come off with it.

This type of situation can occur in basements or areas that are prone to being particularly damp.

It can also happen when surfaces are painted during times of the year when there is naturally more humidity in the air (i.e., summer).

Still, another reason for interior paint peeling is if there happens to be some type of foreign residue—often invisible to the naked eye—sitting on or within the surface when the painting takes place.

As one can see, there are quite a number of reasons why peeling interior paint can happen.

Although these are the most common, on rare occasions, interior paint can peel as a result of a "bad" patch of paint.

These types of incidents are EXTREMELY isolated, but it certainly is feasible that a micro percentage of the time, this could be the culprit.

If you do find yourself in a situation where you are dealing with interior peeling paint, all is not lost.

Once it is evident that there is an interior peeling problem, the issue should be able to be rectified by traditional surface preparation approaches (removing the peeling paint areas, filling/sanding as necessary, and properly priming).

If you work to rectify the issue and, at some point, this nuisance returns, the recommendation would be to find the most reputable, knowledgeable paint expert possible to review the situation with (even if you may have to pay to do so!).

Interior peeling paint can be quite an annoyance once it is discovered.

What will be even more annoying, though, is if it is left to simmer and is not properly addressed to rid its menacing existence.

Mill Glaze

Peeling paint can be one of the more unsightly things a homeowner has to contend with.

Not only is it unsightly at first glance, but once discovered, the peeling paint has the tendency to draw the homeowner's eyes to it like a magnet every time they pass by the portion of the home that the peeling paint may be located on.

Compounding this challenge is if the correct solution to neutralize the peeling paint is not identified at the time the homeowner decides to fix the peeling paint.

The mother of all peeling paint challenges stems from a phenomenon known as mill glaze.

Peeling paint resulting from mill glaze, although a problem with a good-sized presence amongst housing stock in certain areas of the country (New England is one such example), is a problem that VERY few know how to truly recognize and properly correct.

Mill glaze is a scenario that occurred in wood siding stock coming out of the mills in the mid-1980s through the early 2000s—primarily the most affected being bare red cedar clapboard, vertical siding, and white cedar shingles—where a thin layer of "invisible" wax became embedded in the fibers of these wood materials as they were being milled into the shape (clapboard/vertical siding/shingle) they would be going to the market with.

Mill glaze is undetectable to the naked eye.

However, once a paint/stain system is placed on top of it, it is typically only a matter of time before challenges can occur.

It is not unusual for the mill glaze issue to go undiscovered for years and years.

The mill glaze may not show its face until something—a water pocket, air bubble, etc.—somehow begins to trigger the peeling process. Once this occurs, usually, all heck breaks loose.

As time goes by and the more paint coatings are put on the home, the greater the likelihood that the peeling challenges associated with mill glaze will show their faces.

Once these mill glaze-influenced peeling issues arise, the tail chase typically begins to figure out what exactly is going on.

In my experience, folks often try to blame whoever painted the home last prior to this odd peeling challenge showing its face.

"They didn't prep/prime it correctly!" is what I often hear.

If a rep from a paint company comes out, as surprisingly as it may seem, the vast majority of the time, they do not know how to recognize the issue either, and their default reasoning tends to be either a "moisture" issue or the "prep" logic that the homeowners often steadfastly convey.

The reality of the situation, of course, is that neither moisture nor any other type of traditional prep-related catalyst is the true cause of mill-glaze-oriented peeling issues—which can develop into something quite severe.

Essentially, when a mill glaze peeling issue arises, it does so in a fashion that may only show its face on certain sides of the home, although it obviously exists on the entire exterior wherever the like siding was used.

Basically, the coatings put on top of mill-glazed clapboards, vertical siding, and shingles "float" on top of the siding and are never allowed to truly penetrate into the wood.

The paint/stain coatings, where they are peeling, peel back to bare wood, oftentimes in a sheet-like appearance, where if one were to pick at a piece of the peeling coating, they can often keep pulling and pulling, and the coating would keep peeling and peeling.

Unfortunately, there is no easy fix for this.

The most drastic fix is to re-side the home entirely with new siding (whether that be with non-mill-glazed wood siding, cement board siding, or vinyl siding, etc.).

The only other option is a VERY intense prep treatment that very few paint companies know how to truly execute (it is one that we actually specialize in).

If nothing is done, though, one thing is for certain: the peeling challenge will continue to get worse over time, and the finger-pointing will often become more passionate and confusing until someone who truly knows what to look for and is able to properly diagnose it comes along and is able to offer the proper guidance.

Roof Leak Frustrations

Recently, we had a client who reached out to me who was extraordinarily frustrated over a situation they were having with a leak.

At one point over the past several months, we had done a repair around a pipe that was penetrating through their roof.

This repair was beyond necessary as the sealant around this particular pipe had worn away and was clearly taking on water.

We repaired the issue stemming from around the pipe and assumed all was ok until we received a frantic call that the leak had either returned or had never quite stopped leaking.

It was obvious to me at this point that there was more than one point of entry.

After revisiting the roof, we discovered quite a number of possibilities of where the leak might be coming in from and offered a 'next step' plan, as well as the ultimate recommendation of solving the problem once and for all and installing a new roof entirely (for sure a hefty price tag, but worth the investment if it was able to happen).

Chasing leaks is not an easy task.

We always start with the most obvious entry point in accordance with where the exit point of the leak is being observed from and then proceed accordingly from there.

At some point, the process can definitely seem like shooting basketballs blindly.

When it comes to diagnosing leaks, there are only (2) surefire ways of conclusively neutralizing the situation:

1) Re-roofing entirely—essentially ripping the band-aid off—
   assuming that your roof is installed properly, this should absolutely fix any leak that is stemming from a roof area

2) Opening up ceilings, walls, etc., from down below and pinpointing the exact point of penetration from the inside out

Short of these two items, tracking down leaks is a methodical exercise that may take quite some time to positively nail down.

This is due to a variety of factors.

One such factor is that many times, multiple leaks can occur from different parts of your roof, but because of the way that gravity functions in line with the way your home is constructed, they all exit from the same place.

This is why, in instances where one knows there is a place where a leak is coming from and this area is fixed, the leak still shows its face.

As one might imagine, this is the point in time when head games might be played...

"Was this specific leak point fixed correctly?"

"If the leak was fixed correctly, how many other places are things leaking from?"

"Do I need a new roof?"

These are all very valid questions.

As one searches for solutions, ultimately, there are very few choices in terms of paths to venture down.

You can either keep experimenting down the path of logic, hoping that pay dirt is hit and the leak is discovered and able to be fixed.

Or you can go the "drastic" route and either re-roof entirely or pinpoint things by taking areas apart from the inside and tracking the leaking area(s) down.

When it comes to nuisance leaks, no matter which path is ultimately taken, something certainly has to be done.

Not only can leaks be annoying to one's psyche, but if they are not found and neutralized, they can lead to much bigger challenges down the road (rot, mold, etc.)!

Where is Asbestos Found?

Asbestos is a natural mineral made up of delicate and flexible fibers that are impervious to heat, electricity, and corrosion.

These qualities are what have made asbestos a "go-to" building material prior to society eventually figuring out how harmful it actually was.

If your home was built prior to 1987, you may be surprised as to where asbestos may have been used in your home.

It actually seems like an endless list of areas where it could have been found!

Even for seasoned pros, the list may be a little shocking.

As an example, there is a good chance that those in the trades are very well aware that it has historically been utilized as insulation around various pipes, siding shingles, roof shingles, and vinyl floor tiles.

However, many veteran home improvement specialists may be stunned to know that asbestos has also been known to be found in gutters, fencing, carpet underlayment, and kitchen backsplashes, just to name a few places!

Asbestos becomes hazardous when it releases dust or fibers into the air.

When it is intact, asbestos is generally not considered hazardous.

When it is in a form where it is able to be breathed in, this is where it can be extremely dangerous!

Once in the body, particularly once the asbestos dust/fibers have lodged themselves into someone's lungs or body tissues, it is not able to be removed.

There are a number of health challenges that can result from taking asbestos particles into the body.

Asbestosis, lung cancer, mesothelioma, and other cancers can all stem from this type of scenario.

If you find yourself in a position where asbestos needs to be removed from your home for any reason, it is extremely important to have someone who is well-versed in asbestos removal come out to help you.

The consequences of not doing so can, literally, be life-threatening by this potential slow, silent killer.

Unfortunately, one cannot tell if a material contains asbestos by simply looking at it (unless it is clearly labeled).

When in doubt, have an expert come out to work through a process for sampling the material to see if it contains asbestos.

The awkward, ironic challenge with this, of course, is that if the surface you are inquiring about does indeed contain asbestos, disturbing the surface to run even a tiny sample by a lab for analysis could potentially put someone around it at more risk than if the surface was left alone.

If the asbestos material is in good shape, you probably should not mess with it at all (unless it really needs to be removed as part of a larger home renovation project—i.e., converting the exterior siding to wood shingle siding, etc.).

If the asbestos material is in disrepair, it should probably either be repaired by an experienced authority or a professional methodology should be put in place to remove it entirely.

The decision as to what to do with possible asbestos at your home could certainly lead down a few different paths.

The most important thing to remember is to be sure to approach likely asbestos-containing material with respectful caution if the plan is to disturb the area in any way, shape.

How Do You Replace a Bulkhead (AKA Cellar) Door?

Depending upon where you live in the country, if you were to ask someone if they had a 'bulkhead' on their home, they may provide somewhat of an odd stare back at you.

Bulkheads are a term used to describe an entrance to the cellar from the exterior.

Another way folks refer to these is cellar doors.

In many parts of our country, cellars purely do not exist as homes are built on cement slabs (for a variety of reasons).

Homes in New England are where you are certainly apt to find a basement.

Building code can vary from place to place, as local building code (believe it or not) will supersede even International Building Code, but in many situations, it is required to have an exit to the outside from the basement.

Sometimes this is required, but at the time the home was built, it may not have been, and folks decided to add the exit later on.

If someone is adapting their basement for any type of finished purpose at all, at least two forms of egress are a must.

This may be in the form of a bulkhead, a window, or an alternate type of entrance, but it would be absolutely critical to exist.

After a bulkhead has been in place for a number of years, naturally, it may run the course of its useful life.

When this occurs, what typically happens is the weather/elements cause the bulkhead to rot out over time.

Even when properly maintained, it is not unusual for the bulkhead to gradually deteriorate.

Signs of this type of deterioration are recognized by the evidence of moisture and/or creepy crawlies (mice, snakes, etc.) being found within the bulkhead opening.

As the time to replace the bulkhead arrives, it is important to ensure that the bulkhead is changed out correctly, and as with many things, there are a number of ways this can be done.

What is available on the market today is perhaps much different than what was available when the bulkhead was first installed years ago.

As an example, there are fiberglass models today, whereas the technology was not in existence to make them years ago in this fashion.

Sometimes, people get creative and transform what previously was a bulkhead into something much more elaborate (for example, a fully built structure attached to the house with a roof over it, etc.).

For those wishing to stick with a more traditional bulkhead model, there are a couple of different options.

One option is to use an "off-the-shelf" model, which can be purchased from one of the box stores or through your local lumberyard and is available in a number of standard sizes.

The challenge with this option is that although one of the standard sizes may fit properly, it may not fit "like a glove."

The other option is to have one of these traditional steel units custom-fabricated (this is the way we do it).

The biggest advantage of replacing your bulkhead door with a custom-fabricated steel unit is that the new bulkhead can literally be made to fit EXACTLY how you need it to.

This can be done whether the unit is one that is installed by sitting on a cement apron or one that is a pre-cast unit (which is a version that extends wholly underground).

No matter what type of bulkhead is installed, it is extraordinarily important that it is flashed into the house properly, that the area around the bulkhead looks as natural as possible as things are completed, and that the installation itself looks as seamless as possible (preferably as if it had always been there).

Although not something needed to be wary of in a good portion of the country, the importance of a properly maintained bulkhead and correctly replacing one when it is time to do so should be a home maintenance item that is not overlooked if your home happens to be one that has a bulkhead associated with it.

Is it OK to Powerwash a Roof?

A question that has been asked of us quite often over the years is whether or not it is okay to powerwash your roof.

The answer is: sort of.

In terms of actually POWERwashing the roof, as in using a ton of pressure, I believe this should NEVER be done.

Roofs, in general, have a tendency to grow a variety of all types of interesting items on them—algae, mold, fungus, mildew, to name a few, particularly when facing certain directions or being exposed to certain environmental conditions.

So, if washing with a bit of pressure is NOT how I would recommend approaching things, how then would I suggest someone clean their roof?

After all, wouldn't the ability to clean your roof prolong the lifetime of the roof?

Of course it would!

Instead of washing with pressure, I recommend washing with a 'soft wash' process utilizing organically-based chemicals that are meant to get rid of the aforementioned unsightliness without damaging the roof itself.

There are different versions of these types of organically-based products, all with varying degrees of success, but success nonetheless.

Treating your roof with this type of soft wash process may require multiple applications.

Once the treatments are concluded, they should prevent the type of growth that they were being used to eliminate for years to come.

These processes are able to be used on all types of roofs: 3-tab shingles, architectural shingles, low slope roofing, wooden shingles, etc.

We help work with clients who find themselves in very confusing predicaments all the time.

These are folks whose roof seems to be structurally sound but looks like it has been put through the wringer because of all the disgusting-looking microscopic organisms congregating on its surface.

The soft wash process works absolute wonders.

Where an average roof may easily cost $10,000-$15,000 to replace, a soft wash procedure can typically be done for much less than $2000.

This type of process not only makes the roof look amazing once the method is complete and set in, but it preserves the roof from a shortened life cycle by getting rid of these tiny beings that literally eat away at their surfaces.

If you ever hire someone to conduct this type of treatment for you, it is imperative that it is done correctly.

If anyone goes to wash a roof and is not experienced in doing so, a whole lot of damage can result.

I would never recommend someone to wash their roof—soft wash process or not—if they have never tried their hand at washing a roof before and/or been trained to properly do it.

If the correct technique is used, a roof can absolutely be safely washed without causing any damage, and it will be accompanied by eye-pleasing results that will have a protective, stabilizing effect on its surfaces for years to come.

What Makes a Home Considered "Historic"?

Somehow, over the years, we have developed a reputation of being a type of "expert" in working on historic homes.

I have no idea how this happened.

In the same way, I suppose that if you search the term, a video of me pops up describing a bunch of lead paint-oriented items.

These types of reputational development scenarios are quite perplexing to me.

Since 1995, we have always had a knack for restoring these potentially intimidating structures, which many steer clear of.

Restoring older homes, or anything related to them, is definitely NOT for the faint of heart.

As one example, speaking of Hearts," recently, while scrolling through an awesome Facebook group that showcases items from Rhode Island's past, I came across an old photo of 88 Benefit Street in Providence, RI, from 1952.

Unbeknownst to me, Edgar Allen Poe's love, Helen, lived here when he was seeing her (a fact that was shared amongst the group).

Ironically, we had just refinished the exterior of this home.

A finished picture from our records of a similar angle, I think, is extremely interesting when viewing it next to the older one.

In both pictures, you can see the RI State House as well as the Cathedral of St. John (Episcopal Diocese of Providence) in the background.

I believe this to be very neat stuff and an unsolicited, gentle reminder for me as to some of the awesome feelings associated with being fortunate enough to work day in and day out on historic homes such as this one.

This all being said, many folks often wonder what makes a home considered "historic" in the first place?

The answer is quite simple…

There are generally thought to be two qualifying factors.

One is that the home has to be at least fifty years old.

Folks from other parts of the world where their history, literally, goes back centuries, obviously may laugh at this, but in this country, this is the starting point.

Secondly, it must meet one of four qualifying factors:

- Be associated with an important historical event

- Be associated with the life of a noteworthy individual

- Be thought of as the embodiment of a particular architectural historical style

- Has provided or is likely to provide significant historical information

One of the reasons I have always enjoyed working on older homes is the pure idea of any of these factors in conjunction with something that is quite aged. It has consistently created this fantastic inner feeling inside of me, challenging to explain but eerily magnetic nonetheless.

For me, one factor does not necessarily supersede the others.

Other folks, though, may have a passion for historical figures or historical types of architecture, etc.

I am hugely honored whenever someone puts their faith in us to work on homes of a historical nature in whatever the capacity may be.

Not only because there is often such a dramatic difference from 'before' we started working on the project in comparison to what it looks like when things are completed, but also because of the actual underlying historical significance of the home we are humbly working on to fix.

How to Get Pet Urine Smell Out of Hardwood Floors…

You may or may not fall into the category of folks who are faced with a certain head-scratching dilemma, which can be the bane of existence for some.

Even if you are not personally experiencing this, there is a strong chance you know someone who has had to deal with it.

The scenario I am referencing is having beautiful hardwood floors in your home that have been affected in one way, shape, or form by pet urine.

Although you may not even notice it (somehow you may have gotten used to the odor over time), I guarantee (whether they share it with you or not) that if you have guests that come through the house and pet urine has hit your hardwoods and not been treated, they more than likely detect it.

It may be something that has been there for a long time, and you simply have not found a way to get rid of it yet.

You may have only recently discovered it by taking up an old carpet and in doing so, released the reek of ancient urine that had been trapped for decades beneath the layers.

Regardless of how cognizant you are of the odor and for how long it has been there, your options are somewhat limited as to how to truly address it.

If it is a pre-finished floor from a factory, you face an even stronger uphill battle as the urine, which may have been on top at one point, creeps in through the seams and allows the urine to gradually saturate in between things.

Site-finished flooring at least leaves you with a fighting chance.

There are homemade concoctions that folks can find on the internet, which contain some measures of vinegar, baking soda, and hydrogen peroxide that many appear to swear by as solutions to combat pet urine.

There, of course, also are a number of commercialized products that promote themselves as urine slayers.

The age-old adage of testing in small areas before applying to a wider area definitely applies here.

If the odor is really bad and none of the home-based or commercial solutions seem to be working, there is the refinishing process, which should be pretty effective in getting the odor out.

A particular methodology may work in terms of neutralizing the odors, but if there are dark urine stains involved, those will not come out.

There, unfortunately, is NOT a silver bullet for completely eliminating the annoying essence of pet urine odor; there are certainly a number of possibilities, though, that will go a long way in winning the fight and making it so that guests are less apt to stereotype your home in associating it with what can really be an awful stench.

How Long do Toilet Wax Rings Last?

Before answering 'How long does a toilet wax ring last?' it may be helpful to know what the heck a wax ring has to do with your toilet in the first place.

A wax ring for your toilet is precisely what it sounds like: a ring made out of a very tacky wax which aids in forming a watertight seal at the point where the bottom of the toilet and the top of the sewer pipe meet.

A plumber by the name of Paul Thies is credited with inventing the wax seal in the mid-1950s.

There have been a number of modifications to this handy methodological device over the years, but all with the same intent—to minimize the potential for leakage at this crucial juncture where the bottom of the toilet meets the top of the sewer pipe.

So, what happens if the wax ring does leak?

This, of course, should be answered in the context of the fact that water needs only the slightest bit of a compromise at this critical meeting point to begin seeping out and leaking toward whatever may be located below it.

A leak in a wax ring may be noticed soon after it occurs, or it may literally take years to be discovered.

These types of leaks are most often learned about, as was the recent experience realized by a client of ours this past week, when a ceiling below the toilet begins to show some signs of water staining.

In theory, the wax ring should last the lifetime of the toilet or certainly twenty to thirty years.

We come across situations all the time, however, where wax rings are in need of replacing well short of this scenario.

Besides leaking, signs that the wax ring may need replacing could be an odd odor stemming from the area where the toilet meets the floor or if the toilet itself feels wobbly.

If a toilet is not properly secured, it may get loose to the point where the wax seal gets damaged and subsequently begins leaking (obviously, it IS possible to catch the wobbliness prior to the wax seal being broken).

If a wax ring needs to be replaced because it is found to no longer be functional, my recommendation is to have it done by a professional.

Could an average homeowner replace the wax ring? Of course!

Because of the expertise involved, though, I personally would not recommend it.

I have seen a number of times in the past when folks thought that it was easy enough to do and attempted to do it themselves with disastrous results.

Either a plumber has to be called in to properly correct things, or a leak occurred where the damage needing to be corrected is super-involved, or some combination of both!

I have seen non-knowledgeable, well-intended homeowners caulk around the base of the toilet (where it meets the floor), attempting to solve what truly is actually a wax ring repair-oriented leak.

To a plumber, I imagine this type of homeowner attempt would be "cute" but entirely ineffective.

While extremely appealing because the entire material cost of the wax ring fix might be $10 or less, the priceless knowledge of a seasoned professional is worth its weight in gold!!

What is a Drip Cap?

———

Door, window, and water table (aka skirtboard) areas are parts of your home that are potentially prone to water infiltration if their installs are not conducted correctly.

Compounding their already natural vulnerability of allowing water into your home (due to the fact that these areas are all obviously "open" areas of your home without the door, window, or water table taking up the corresponding space!), is the horizontal tops of the trim in each of these types of areas which, if not properly protected, are an inviting entry point to any form of moisture that would like to make its way inside.

So, how does one guard against moisture coming in from the tops of these areas?

The answer would be with the proper installation of a type of flashing known as a drip cap.

Drip caps can come in various sizes, depending upon the thickness of the piece of trim that it is being put in place to protect.

One can make drip caps themselves if they are handy with a metal-bending brake.

Above doors and windows, the drip cap is placed above the top of the topmost piece of trim of the door or window (the piece that horizontally travels across the door or window).

If you were to look at the side profile of a piece of drip cap, it would look like the side profile of a chair, except without its back legs.

Imagining this, the horizontal portion of the drip cap sits on the top of the piece of trim one is working to flash.

The top of the drip cap is tucked into the back side of the siding directly above the piece of trim that is being flashed.

The bottom of the drip cap comes slightly down in front of this piece of trim—this allows for the "drip" of any moisture that hits the top of the piece of trim as it is prevented from working its way behind the trim and made to shed off the front of it.

These days, drip caps are most commonly made out of aluminum, but they can also be made out of copper or plastic.

Another possible material that drip caps can be made out of, and how it was done "back in the day," is lead.

When lead used to be the more common material to make drip caps out of, it tended to be positioned a little differently than today, as many times, the lead did not extend over the edge of the trim it was being installed over.

I have never been a big fan of stopping at the edge, as I feel more comfortable knowing that any moisture hitting the top of a piece of trim we are installing has a clear path to be allowed to "drip" off of it.

Believe it or not, in the field, we come across many cases of non-existent drip caps, which is quite annoying.

When we find a scenario like this, our attention is often drawn to these areas due to wood that has rotted away in some capacity, and when backtracking to figure out the cause, we discover that the drip cap is not properly where it should be.

A drip cap is EXTREMELY important!

If it is not accurately placed above the door, window, or water table areas, rotted wood is something that is bound to happen and is never a question of "if" but "when" the moisture, being allowed to penetrate the backside of the trim, will rear its ugly head, in the by-product of these rotting wood situations that could have easily have been prevented.

What is the Best Waterproofing for Wood?

If there is natural wood in one form or another around the exterior of your home, at some point in time, you may have wondered, "What is the best way to go about making sure it is protected from moisture damage?"

Perhaps you are one of those folks who is ultra-diligent and uber-protective of your home's exterior and is always looking for ways to help protect it and make it better.

Or maybe you are one of those folks who really does not think about the exterior of your home, except every ten years or so when you just happen to randomly think one day, "I should probably be doing something to keep up with the exterior of my home!"

Whatever best describes your approach to the exterior, the truth is something probably needs to be done at some point to protect it.

The exterior of many of our homes is painted or protected with some type of wood toning/pigmented stain.

In many cases, though, folks have a good amount of natural wood exposed.

This natural wood could be in the form of siding or trim, or maybe your deck is left in its natural wood state.

In the cases where these types of products are left to weather, they are typically ok without any type of product applied to them.

In fact, some people NEVER apply any product to these natural wood surfaces, and the surfaces actually perform fine over the course of time.

Seldom do these areas (whether they be cedar shingle siding or some type of pressure treated/hardwood decking) truly rot out even without any treatment to them.

If this is the case, why should someone think about applying a water protectant to these types of natural wood surfaces if they would not rot even if a treatment were not done?

Although these areas may not ever technically completely rot on you, there are a ton of other types of damage and unsightliness that can be avoided if the wood is properly protected.

If the wood is guarded as best as possible against moisture, it will help ward off cracking, splitting, and warping and even help to lessen mildew and mold issues.

With this being said, there are a TON of waterproofing solutions on the market. I believe they all work in varying degrees.

Over time, we have developed a system that is as solid as one will find for helping to protect wood from the damaging effects of long-term on and off moisture exposure.

The first thing we do is clean the wood.

After cleaning it, we apply a product called C2 Guard for Wood.

This is a clear solution that goes on with a milky appearance and dries to an invisible coating that should be applied with two coats, wet-on-damp (basically, you chase the first coat with a second coat right after it appears that the first coat has absorbed into the wood).

This C2 Guard product penetrates deeper into the wood than any other product I have come across on the market; it forms a flexible polymer barrier and amazingly becomes part of the wood's cellular structure.

After this has dried, we apply one coat of Wolman Raincoat Acrylic Clear (which, again, goes on with a milky appearance and dries to an invisible coating). Although not penetrating as deep as the C2 Guard, it is the perfect complement to the C2 Guard application as its qualities allow for a repellant to be formed on the surface of the wood, causing a barrier that forces water to bead up as it hits the surface.

Both of these products are excellent in stunting mildew and mold growth as well as the overall protection of the wood surfaces they are applied to.

The way the wood appears after it has dried after being washed is the way the wood will appear after both products are applied.

In fact, if someone does not literally watch us apply the product, they may not even believe that we have applied the treatment!

This system can be utilized to protect both vertical and horizontal wood surfaces.

Horizontal surfaces may require treatment a little more often as this protection may wear out sooner on areas that are exposed to sitting water, foot traffic, etc.

Whether it is the system I reviewed that we have utilized with tremendous success or an alternative system, it is SUPER important to make sure that any type of natural wood siding or deck surface is secured against water damage!

What is a Lavette?

"Lavette."

Sounds fancy, doesn't it?

If you have had home improvements done to your home in the past or even just planned on a future home improvement, there is a good chance you have heard the term used in the past.

But what really is a lavette, and why is it called this??

A lavette is essentially a half-bathroom or powder room. Lavette is a derived word that basically means 'small lavatory.'

If one were to do a bit of research on the Internet about the term, one would find the expression was popular in the 1930s and was often used to describe these smaller bathroom areas, often found under a stairway or in place of a large clothes closet.

Interestingly, articles I found have said the term itself did not endure over time. I certainly would like to beg to differ on this one. I have actually found the term lavette to be quite commonplace.

For years, I have heard various clients use this term to describe these handy restroom areas.

Some families are constantly using their lavettes, while other families have lavettes that hardly get any use.

Regardless of how much or how little a lavette is used, it definitely is a handy room to have in one's home, particularly if someone has a larger family or enjoys entertaining.

Lately, we have worked with a number of clients to modernize their lavettes.

It is amazing how much of a difference it can make when upgrading these areas, similar to any room that one might delve into, bringing up a more contemporary feel.

Upgrading could mean simply changing out the vanity or upgrading the paint. Anything to provide a little bit of a different feel.

For the more adventurous homeowner, there is also the idea of adding a lavette into a space where one previously did not exist. Clearly, this is a MUCH more involved undertaking.

Where tiny upgrades to a lavette would typically require minimal carpentry, electric, and/or plumbing work, adding a whole new lavette requires a good number of trades to make the plan become a reality.

Lavette is a fun word to use in conversation with your friends when discussing features of a home.

When I used to hear the word, I almost used to think whoever was using it was trying to prove that they knew what the word meant, and on the same token, when I heard the word, I always used to pretend I knew what it meant and kept going with the conversation.

If you were previously similar to me in this capacity, now you no longer need to pretend!

What is Hardware Cloth?

One item we were asked to help out with at a recent job was to replace the screening that had been in place behind a client's attic gable vent windows.

Typically, the screening that is used behind these windows when they come from "the factory" is not necessarily the most impenetrable type of screening.

It is usually a pretty thin screening and most often not really fastened in the most ideal fashion.

We get quite a number of calls asking for our help to come up with a solution for replacing the screening in a manner in which it is a bit more solidly in place and also a bit more robust with regard to what it would offer, for protection from potential intrusive visitors (bats, squirrels, birds, etc.).

My go-to solution in these cases has always been hardware cloth.

Hardware cloth is a smaller, strong and durable, mesh-type product sold in rolls at both local hardware stores and at the big box stores.

Think chicken wire on steroids.

I prefer hardware cloth to chicken wire because hardware cloth is sturdier than chicken wire, and its holes are much tinier.

It would be very challenging for any rodent to get to the other side of the hardware cloth, assuming it is properly fastened.

There are several uses for this material.

I usually use it when attempting to keep rodents from getting into a certain area.

In addition to the earlier example, I also have used it in the past to keep varmints from digging into the bottom of a shed.

I have seen folks use it to keep animals out of their gardens, I've seen it used on deer fencing, and I have seen it used to help patch holes in walls.

Because it is such a strong material, I have seen people get creative with it and use it for such things as making fruit/vegetable baskets, making bird feeders, and even creating wall-hung storage racks (the strength of the areas around hardware cloth's holes are ideal for hanging things).

It certainly is a very diverse building material.

When working with hardware cloth, be sure to have a good pair of wire snips, gloves, and some stronger plier-type tools (to help in handling/bending it).

If using it to keep rodents out from somewhere, to help in keeping the tiniest of creatures out (if that may be a concern), double back the hardware cloth with some version of a smaller type of screening; the outermost layer should be the hardware cloth itself, as this would be the stronger of the two layers.

I believe hardware cloth is an awesome product!

I stumbled across it years ago at a local hardware store, and every time an opportunity pops up to use it, do so without hesitation.

What is the Single Thing You Can Do to Help Sell Your Home— FAST!?

_____

I preface this all by solidly stating that I am NOT a realtor. Nor do I claim to be anywhere near an expert in the real estate field.

That being said, I have experience dealing with thousands of folks who were in the process of selling their home.

Whether you are selling your home because you are interested in buying a much bigger property, you are selling it to "downsize" , or any possible reason in between, out of all the things I have observed people in these situations undertake, in order to aid in the process of selling their existing home, painting, by FAR, appears to be the most impactful.

It may sound crazy, but from what I have noticed, doing a major bathroom or kitchen remodel is typically not going to have as much of an effect on how fast your home is sold as painting your home.

Painting your home may not add a ton of actual value to the home, but it will certainly go a long way to help it sell as quickly as it possibly can.

Don't get me wrong.

If your home is extraordinarily dated on the exterior with paint that has not been addressed in quite some time, which in turn has led to rotted wood, then yes, painting very much could add to the overall amount you are able to sell your home for.

After all, if you were a homeowner looking to buy a home, what would you be willing to pay a bit more for in a market where the number of homes for sale in your area is not really that high (such is the case in the Rhode Island real estate market at the time I am writing this), a home that has a solid paint job with a neutral color or a home that is going to need a ton of work prior to moving in?

I have had multiple conversations with bewildered individuals over the years whose homes had been on the market for quite some time, with grossly dated paint jobs (whether it was the interior or the exterior), and were trying to sell their homes but could not figure out why nobody to date had given them respectable offers on them.

There are absolutely a ton of reasons why homes may have been taking so long to sell.

However, ask any seasoned realtor, in general, what would be an ideal situation to sell in.

A home that looks like it was recently painted with a non-polarizing color or a home whose paint looks like it was barely holding on, faded, and/or with a color that would make even the most eccentrically-wired brain shudder in its place?

I think the answer is obvious.

We noticed this phenomenon a long time ago, and we even went as far as to make our five-year warranty transferable to whoever may be buying one of our client's homes, with the intention of adding peace of mind to whomever the home was being sold to.

Life changes and selling your home can be a nerve-racking, stressful thing. Why make it more difficult than it already may have to be?

Paint your home. Have it be as presentable as possible to the market.

Although not a major renovation, painting is the one thing that can be done to help things move along more quickly for you and perhaps even add some value to the overall sale of the home along the way.

What is Roof Decking Code?

The famous line from Forrest Gump, "My mom always said life is like a box of chocolates. You never know what you're gonna get," can be applied to roofing, particularly in older homes.

In my opinion, to properly replace a roof, it should always be stripped to its roof decking when delving into things.

Though most local building codes these days do allow for two total layers of roof, I personally do not prefer layovers whenever possible.

That being said, similar to Forrest's box of chocolates, when you strip off all the existing roof shingles from someone's roof, you often obviously have no idea what the roof decking underneath it all will look like until you get it off.

Although you may be able to gather somewhat of a sense from looking at the underside of the existing roof decking by venturing into the attic and seeing how things appear directly underneath the decking, you will not have a true sense until the old roof is off.

Once it is off, either one of three things will happen:

- The roof decking will be perfectly conducive to fastening the new roof system on top of it.

- The roof decking will have areas that need shoring up, but overall, it will be in good shape.

- The roof decking will be a total mess, and it will need to be overhauled in some capacity to properly put the new roof on.

The roofing code states that a new roof system must be applied on top of a solidly sheathed roof deck (a roof deck with a minimum of 3/8" sheathing, installed with no more than ¼" spacing between sheathing panels).

When an existing roof is taken off, and it is found that the roof decking beneath it is compromised to some degree (either some type of rot has set in over a wide span or the spacing between the existing sheathing is too wide, etc.), new roof decking needs to be laid.

As long as when you are fastening the new sheathing over the existing sheathing, you are doing so in a manner in which it is appropriately fastened to the roof rafters or trusses and can properly carry the new roof system through the most common severe weather conditions of your particular region, it is perfectly fine to do so.

It is SUPER important to make sure your roof decking is solidly sheathed.

The whole goal of a solidly sheathed roof is to make sure that your new roof system can properly "grab" onto the area it is being fastened to.

If ever thinking about getting a new roof done, if whoever is doing the roofing work has any doubt that your existing roof decking is conducive to receiving the new roof system once the existing roof is stripped, a conversation should be had as to what the possible cost would be to install a new sheathing system over the existing roof decking if need be.

Again, this is something that is often found needing to be done for older roofs (in homes 50+ years old) and is less likely to be found needing to be done on more modern homes.

What Causes Wood to Rot?

One of the items that pops up in conversation most frequently about painting the exterior of their home is rotted wood.

Obviously, rotted wood is not something that you want to paint over. It is something that should be addressed.

Perhaps the situation is one where the rotted portions can be carved out, and then some type of epoxy system can be put in place and then shaped, prepped, and painted.

The situation may also call for an actual replacement of the piece of wood that is rotted.

As these possible solutions are being worked through, part of our conversation may center around what causes wood to rot in the first place.

This is an excellent question.

Wood rot itself is a form of decay.

What sets off the decay is prolonged moisture exposure combined with fungi (microscopic organisms).

In order for the fungi to get comfortable and start rotting things away, the wood must be continuously damp.

Fungi will not grow on dry wood; it just won't happen.

There are countless types of fungi that exist all around us, and there is no way to really get away from them.

My experience has witnessed that wood often rots from the inside out.

In other words, you could have a piece of wood trim that appears perfectly solid one day, and then a few months later, the wood seems to have rotted to the core.

The reality of the situation is that this did NOT happen overnight; instead, the wood had gradually been rotting from the backside toward the front, until one day, it finally broke through the front side of the wood.

So, how does this type of thing happen where the wood gets wet without someone even knowing?

Actually, fairly easily ... Water does not need that much space to begin gradually creeping in and starting to hang around for a while.

As one example, when water is able to get through the inside crevices of wood trim, it is usually able to nest in an area that will not allow it to easily dry out, hence the reason these dark areas can become an attractive place for fungi to come on board and start doing their thing.

Preventing this from occurring amounts to checking around the exterior of your home once or twice per year (I recommend once in the spring and once in the fall) to see if you can spot any signs of rot or any places where rot may be able to begin to stem from if not addressed.

Simple preventative measures fighting the possibility of rot taking place can go a LONG way, such as:

- Making sure that the joints in your trim are properly caulked
- Making sure there are no visible holes in your trim where water can rest
- Making sure your gutter and downspout systems are properly functioning
- Making sure to limit the amount of time wood trim sits in the snow in the winter or piles of leaves in the fall
- Making sure that flashing is properly in place where necessary
- Making sure that the grading of your yard is such that it steers water away from the home
- Making sure vegetation around the home does not rest directly on the home

In short, the more you are able to ensure the exterior of your home stays as dry as possible, and any prospective areas of allowing water to creep inside are eliminated, the longer you will be able to enjoy not having to replace wood that has rotted away and potentially set you up for even larger repairs if it is not caught and corrected as soon as possible.

Why Does Siding Get Chalky?

_____

Have you ever leaned up on a house, and when you came off of it, either you or someone else noticed the back of your shirt was covered with a mysterious, white substance?

That substance is chalk.

I remember this happened all the time to us growing up, as we were playing games and leaning up against houses.

Fast forward to adulthood, and doing what I do, I see this happen frequently as I am constantly rubbing my hands on people's homes to check for this phenomenon.

So then, why does this happen? Great question!

Chalking happens on vinyl siding, aluminum siding, and siding that has been painted.

Oxidation occurring during some type of damp weather is the culprit.

Oxidation refers to a reaction that happens when something somehow becomes chemically combined with oxygen.

When these reactions take place with the correct amount of moisture, it leaves behind this chalky residue on these various styles of surfaces.

Over time, this residue can build up.

The more the residue builds up, the more difficult it is to remove.

Chalking can be extraordinarily frustrating when working to remove it.

In fact, it may take multiple efforts to remove the chalk.

Hand washing with a scrub brush or dual-sided sponge could definitely do the trick.

Powerwashing can also work if done safely and correctly.

When washing, my suggestion would be to use some type of detergent to assist you.

Because mildew is often intermingled with chalkiness when we are washing someone's home, we typically use a diluted chlorine solution.

If getting rid of the chalk is the main objective, I would suggest a degreasing dish detergent (though I have heard of some folks using laundry detergent).

Although I am admittedly very biased, the best way that I have found to neutralize the chalk from returning is by painting the surface it is forming on...

(Yes, if it is forming on vinyl, believe it or not, vinyl can be painted).

This certainly is not a guarantee that the chalk will not return.

This does, however, totally refresh the surface and, with today's technology being what it is, it is tougher for chalk to form on the surfaces of the highest quality exterior finishes than it ever has been before.

It all comes down to how much the chalkiness bothers you in combination with how much effort you want to put into making sure that the chalkiness is as limited as possible in the future.

If the chalkiness is just something that "exists" and is merely a once-in-a-while type of nuisance to you, you may not even want to do anything with it.

But if the chalkiness is something that is constantly somehow getting on people's clothes and bodies and has become more than annoying, you may want to look at, minimally, attempting to wash it off and, on a grander scale, perhaps even look into getting things painted to limit the chalky presence as much as possible going forward.

How Do You Get Rid of Carpenter Bees?

Some pests are pestier than others!

The more challenging it is to get rid of a pest that is causing damage to your home in one way, shape, or form, the "pestier" it is than others. There are all types of creepy crawlies that many folks refer to as pests that create damage around the home—carpenter ants, mice, termites, you name it.

Perhaps near the top of the pestiest of them all, for me, would be carpenter bees. As far as bees are concerned, carpenter bees are not really that harmful.

The males may appear to be a bit feisty (they do like to dive bomb beings that they feel are coming into their territory), but they do not even have stingers (and they would not bite per se!).

The females have stingers but will only resort to trying to sting if they are being bothered.

The carpenter bees create damage by burrowing into various areas around the home (I usually see them in trim areas high above or various areas around porch ceilings, etc.).

Carpenter bees are unlike other bees in that they do not live in colonies.

To a degree, they are loners, and when you see their damage, it is typically the females chewing circular holes to make places to lay eggs and protect their larvae as they develop.

These holes can be quite extensive and are often noticed when a homeowner happens to stumble upon varying degrees of carpenter bee excrement, which is often found in the area of a home directly below a place where carpenter bees have been burrowing.

The crazy thing about these pests is that although they can cause quite a bit of damage to your home, they are extraordinary pollinators! Knowing this, I come across situations where people are often torn as to how to address them. Assuming you would like to be rid of them, they are not very easy to stop, as even with pest control treatments, they often come back to the same spot, or a spot nearby, soon after a treatment has been done. There are a variety of recommendations throughout the Internet on how to stop them.

My recommendation is that if you do move forward with some type of pest control for carpenter bees, do not close their holes up right away. Instead, keep an eye on the area that was treated and its nearby places to make sure that the carpenter bees are indeed gone. Once you are convinced that the carpenter bees are no longer around your home, wait until later in the fall to work toward correcting any damage that they may have done. My further recommendation is to replace the damaged wood with pressure-treated (or some other chemically treated) wood or composite material where possible and to keep all painted surfaces properly maintained. Carpenter bees sure can create a dilemma between their usefulness in pollination and the damage they can cause to someone's home. Believe it or not, there are systems out there that try to attract carpenter bees away from areas in the home that they may be in the process of damaging.

Whatever the case may be, out of all the pests I typically come across, carpenter bees present the most challenge in terms of quickly stopping them from damaging someone's home over the long term.

Is Step Flashing Necessary?

Recently, I stepped out on a roof at a client's home, and it was a roof that led up to a wall for another part of the home.

As I got closer to the wall that the roof led up to, something did not feel right under my feet.

I mean, it was not totally squishy, but something just did not seem correct.

By this, I mean I felt a weakness in the roof underneath my feet.

What started out as a project I was called into to review a problematic area of painting and some minor repairs led to my recommendation to the client to have a serious conversation with me about their roof, which did not appear to be that old.

After investigating the situation further, I determined that the roof was not step flashed properly, was allowing water to leech in under the roof shingles, and has caused at least a portion of the roof sheathing (the portion of the roof system that the shingles themselves are attached to) to weaken.

The client had also recently noticed that with certain types of rain storms, the roof appeared to leak into the home in the vicinity of this area.

Step flashing is used to stop water from getting into walls as it flows down the roof.

Step flashing has been required for asphalt shingled roofs at places where roofs meet walls as far back as the 1986 Council of American Building Officials Code Book for One And Two Family Dwellings.

Step flashing makes sure that any water that makes its way under a shingle will still end up on the top of the flashing that is on top of the shingle on the next course directly below it.

The water is then allowed to safely drain away without migrating into unwanted places.

Step flashing is basically a series of bent metal pieces that span connections between asphalt roof shingles and adjacent walls.

In the particular case I could tell that the leaking problem had been an issue in the past, as someone had attempted to neutralize the leak by caulking a piece of clear silicone at the joint where the roof shingles met the wall.

I have seen this many times in the past. I have seen people use silicone, caulkable black tar, and almost any other type of caulkable material that promotes itself as eliminating leaking.

The problem with trying to approach things in this manner is that no matter how tight the seal appears, it will most likely be compromised in a short period of time after it is done, as the roof and the wall are constantly expanding and contracting with fluctuations in temperature and humidity. And it is only a matter of when, NOT if, somewhere along this caulked seal develops a gap large enough to start allowing water to work its way into the wall.

A correctly step-flashed joint is the only way to go.

If you notice a leak under a place located beneath an area where a portion of your roof meets a wall, my first suggestion would be to question the condition of the step flashing (or perhaps lack of step flashing entirely), more often than not, I guarantee this most likely will be the culprit!

How to Caulk Large Gaps

Have you ever been in a position where you had an extraordinarily large gap to fill, and you were really not sure how to do it?

This may have been the case with wood, concrete, on the interior, or on the exterior, but the challenge was still the same!

A gap large enough to seemingly be able to fit three tubes of caulk, but incorporating that particular solution just did not seem correct.

I used to wonder about the exact same thing while in this position.

So what is one to do when confronted with this daunting quandary?

Enter backer rod.

A backer rod is a foam-type, cylindrical "string" that comes in various diameters. It could be ½", ¾", 1", etc.

A backer rod is used by taking the most appropriate thickness of the backer rod and, with the help of a putty knife or a 5-in-1, stuffing it into the crack that you are attempting to fill, leaving a very small portion of the gap unfilled.

Once the backer rod is set in place, you can then caulk the gap as you normally would.

Once the caulk is dry, you can paint or finish over it as you may have already planned to do.

Keep in mind this is meant in situations where caulk would normally be used, and it is not meant to be a solution for gaps that are ultra-wide and would require finishing with a material other than some type of caulk.

I have seen backer rods used for a number of scenarios ranging from gaps in trim, cement, window and door applications, and so on and on.

If, for some reason, a backer rod is not an option, you may indeed have to go the multiple layers of caulk route.

Though certainly not what I would prefer, one could also fill the gap with layers of caulk, letting the caulk dry or set each time before covering it again with another layer of caulk.

This would be a painstakingly slow approach but, in theory, could get you to where you need to be.

When using a backer rod, it is important to be sure to use a backer rod whose width is a tad wider than the crack you are using it to fill.

A backer rod can easily be cut with a utility knife or a razor to trim it to the length that is needed.

It is important not to fall into the trap of thinking that the backer rod is ok solely to stuff and leave in a gap without filling around it.

By using the caulk, you will not only be able to form a proper seal around the backer rod, but you will also set yourself up for being able to leave a smooth finish over the gap itself.

Seeing what at first appears as a monstrous gap can be a little bit of a head-scratcher as to how to correctly fill it; having a backer rod at your disposal, however, will make this initial discouraging nature of the task quickly go away as fast as the gap that you are filling in the process.

What is a Calcimine Ceiling?

We often get calls from folks who are really confused about a particular ceiling issue that they are experiencing.

It is centered around a peeling challenge that they keep having with a ceiling of theirs.

Once all possible traditional potential causes of the peeling are neutralized, the person reaching out to us when they cannot nail down why their ceiling continues to peel. They may have done everything that they can think of that "the book" says to do to fix it.

They clean, they scrape, they sand, they prime, they use great quality finishes, and yet, the ceiling still peels!!

After they work to correct it, the ceiling may remain intact for a week, a month, or a year, but eventually, the same problem resurfaces, and the ceiling peels again.

This obviously can be super annoying.

The fact of the matter is that the reason their ceiling continues to peel actually stems back to many, many years ago.

Back in the day, there was a product that a lot of people used to treat their ceilings with.

The product was called calcimine.

Calcimine was basically a chalk-type finish that folks used as a cost-efficient, fast method for finishing plaster, particularly on ceilings.

It was widely available and highly popular.

Calcimine ceilings lasted and lasted, even with the introduction of oil and latex-based coatings. Everything was hunky dory until it wasn't...

Problems with calcimine ceilings start to arise once the finish coat on top of them is compromised for one reason or another.

Many times, this initial peeling issue is caused by a water leak or something along those lines, and the ceiling starts to peel.

This is when things go south.

Once a ceiling that has a more modern finish on top of the calcimine starts to peel, it is a wrap, and the chase is on.

Once one part of the peeling ceiling is fixed, another part of it often starts to peel.

It soon becomes like that old Bugs Bunny cartoon where Bugs plugs a crack in a dam with his finger, and then another crack forms, and then another, and then another... With each crack that forms, Bugs uses another part of his body to stop the leaking.

Needless to say, soon Bugs runs out of body parts.

Though there are suggestions out there on how to correct this specific peeling issue (which may work to varying degrees but are typically far from permanent fixes), the only surefire ways to truly fix the issue for good are to either go over the existing ceiling with blueboard and finish it appropriately with plaster or to take down the ceiling entirely and hang a brand new one.

Literally, those are the options.

As drastic as they may be, either one of those two routes would be the only way that we could guarantee the ceiling fix.

Outside of that, anyone would DEFINITELY be fighting the tide (or, like Bugs, the increasingly cracking dam...) attempting for a real deal, long-term fix to their difficulties with their peeling ceiling!

Why do Deck Stains Peel?

Deck stains are perhaps THE most challenging product to adhere long-term to any surface on the exterior of anyone's home.

Well, there are a few factors involved, which also tend to be intertwined.

Let's start off with the obvious: most deck stains cannot be applied to all six sides of a piece of decking once it is in place.

If this type of treatment is not done when the deck is initially installed, it would be pretty much impossible to do afterward.

If the deck is not sealed on its underside and butt ends, moisture (both when it rains or snows and natural moisture from the ground below the deck) can easily be absorbed into the unsealed portions of the wood and loosen up any coatings that may be on the sealed portions of the deck as the deck dries out.

If this process occurs enough, it will do so to the point where the coatings will start to peel.

The majority of decks do not have wood that is super receptive to receiving ANY type of coating.

In fact, the harder the wood (mahogany, Ipe, etc.), the more challenging it will be to get any type of product to properly absorb into it; even pressure-treated wood, as soft as it is in comparison to the harder types of decking, is not easy to get stains to properly penetrate.

Unless the deck surface is roughed up enormously (glass blasting is the only true process I am aware of that 100% allows for this), there is a shot that the pores of the decking are not open enough to comfortably receive whatever stain product is being applied to them.

Simply sanding a deck is not necessarily the complete answer because although it is a necessary part of the surface preparation process, if not done correctly, can actually tighten up the grain of the wood TOO much.

Because of this, unless someone is willing to undertake the expense of glass blasting their deck, I typically advise folks to use as thin a stain as they are okay with using along the thought process that the thinner the stain, the easier it is going to be to penetrate the wood.

This may be counterintuitive to other information that is out there, but in 25+ years of wrestling with these types of projects, this is what we have found to work best.

When staining a deck, one should be prepared to put a maintenance coat on it yearly if need be.

Depending on individual situations, deck coatings could absolutely last more than three years but should not be banked on to do so.

Having a deck with any type of coating system associated with it is not for the faint of heart.

Decks can be beautiful centerpieces of one's home. If they are not properly maintained, however, they can develop into an eyesore that is the bane of existence for many a homeowner.

Does Vinyl Siding Decrease Home Value?

_____

Often a potential client is wrestling between vinyl siding or painting their home and which route makes the most sense.

This seems to particularly be the case with our paint systems that, although guaranteed for five years and VERY different from all else in the industry, tend to be MUCH more of an investment than a more traditional paint job.

In other words, the client has a tough decision to make.

Although vinyl siding is still a bit more of an initial investment than even our systems, folks looking to weigh the pros and cons of our paint systems vs. vinyl siding are certainly tempted by the notion that they would, in theory, never have to do anything to their home's exterior again after it is vinyl-sided.

My warning to them is to be very careful about delving into the vinyl route, as vinyl siding can devalue the home in a number of ways.

Any fire department will tell you that a fire in the home becomes deadlier for any home with vinyl siding on it; there are a number of studies that confirm this.

Simply being aware of this is usually enough to deter many from making the plunge into vinyl.

If that were not enough, though, there are also other factors that add to the devaluation of homes with vinyl siding on them.

If your home is anything close to historic or uniquely decorative in nature and it is vinyl-sided, any value associated with these often sought-after characteristics goes right out the window.

Perhaps one of the more commonly relatable deterrents of vinyl siding one's home is the fact that when it eventually is time to put the home in question on the market for sale, and it is vinyl-sided, one significantly limits their potential pool of buyers with the vinyl siding.

The reasoning behind this is if your home is vinyl-sided, you better hope that whoever is thinking about buying it is ultra into the way the vinyl siding looks.

If the home is not vinyl-sided, the prospective buyer could always vinyl it themselves if they wanted to. They could change the color more easily and, in general, make the exterior of the place more in line with how they ideally would like it vs. being held hostage in terms of the options of what they may or may not be able to do with it if it is vinyled.

At the end of the day, if someone deep down wants to vinyl their home, ultimately, they will most likely do so and not think twice about it. The day when one of these scenarios (or others like it) that were laid out comes to fruition and then the decision to go the vinyl route will obviously be WAY past too late…

How Many Years do Wood Fences Last?

During periods of time when we spend longer stretches at home (the best example of which may be most recently when folks have not had a choice but to spend longer stretches at home!), we obviously have a higher tendency to notice "things."

Particularly if the weather is nice, we may be working in the yard and subsequently just happen to catch specific "things" that we may not have noticed if we were caught up in the typical hustle and bustle of what, until as of late, would have been considered our normal, busy lives.

By being forced to press the pause button on our usual routines, situations that may have gone unnoticed before are suddenly brought to the forefront.

Once discovered, it is often tough to shake them from our heads.

I have often said to clients that if you stare at something long enough, you can make the case in your mind that "something" should be done to it.

Whether it is rotten wood or the paint job on your house, when more time is spent at home, there is a greater chance for something to be added to the "to-do" list that was not thought of before.

Sometimes, it is not staying at home more often, and sometimes, the weather forces our hand, grabs our attention, and forces us to pay attention to things that may not have been seen before (such as the wind causing accelerated damage to something that was hanging on by a thread, to begin with).

Sometimes, it is a combination of both of these circumstances.

This past week, I had this exact type of scenario happen to a client of ours. She had been at her house more than usual as her job had asked her to work from her home. While working from home, there was a day that was quite windy and caused a branch to fall in her yard. The branch hit her wood fence and knocked two sections of it down.

The fence had been aging for some time, and as our client went about her business day in and day out, she never really noticed how old it was getting until the branch fell, called her attention to the fence, and she then, while looking at it, realized how old it had gotten.

She reached out to us to help her out, and a question was raised, similar to what many clients have asked us in the past, "How many years do wood fences last?"

The answer, as with many home improvement items, depends on how well it is maintained.

Wood fences tend to be structures that, once erected, are often seldom thought of again until the years pass by, and for some reason, as in the case of our client, they are rotted to the point where it does not take much for them to fall down.

So then, what is the best way to make sure your wood fence lasts as long as possible?

My favorite way of preserving wood fences to maximize their lifetime is a pretty simple process:

1) Clean the fence
2) Apply two coats of C2 Guard (wet-on-damp)
3) Apply one coat of acrylic Wolman water-repellant

This is with the idea that the intent is for the fence to stay natural looking in its appearance.

I would highly discourage folks from applying a solid stain or a paint system to the fence (only because this will end up being much more involved from a long-term maintenance perspective as the fence ages).

Another decent possibility would be to stain the fence with some type of light-bodied (i.e., a product having very few "solids") wood-toning stain.

Although this process is a bit more involved from a long-term maintenance perspective than applying the clear coat system I had recommended, it is a lot less involved than having to maintain a solid stain or a paint system in the long run.

If your wood fence is properly cared for, it should last indefinitely, really until the portions of the wood posts located underground that the main sections of the fence are attached to gradually wear out.

If the bottoms of the fence posts do rot out, one can often just replace the post and put the fence back together.

If your wood fence is not properly preserved, however, and is just left to age and rot over time, it may only take a short number of years for the wood fence to get to the point where it needs to be replaced.

As with anything else, the life of your wood fence will be dictated by how much is put into its care and protection as it matures.

Where Do Bathroom Vents Go?

One of the more interesting questions I like to ask when walking through any type of bathroom project with a client is, "Do you know where your bathroom fan is vented to?" Perhaps not surprisingly, most folks don't have a clue—nor should they!

After all, most people who move along through life as homeowners generally assume that when the home was built and along the way, things were constructed properly, and everything should be functioning fine.

Unfortunately, this assumption could not be further from the truth.

For purposes of this specific discussion, let's center things around the way a bathroom fan is vented.

Now, if you were to ask where "should" bathroom fans be vented to, the answer is to the outside of the house.

My preference is through the roof whenever possible (and, yes, if installing a roof vent, it should obviously be properly flashed).

In some cases, through the roof may not be logically feasible; in that type of circumstance, whatever way can be found to get the fan vented to the outside in a place that is least likely to lead to mildew or mold growth (around the exterior vent that is installed) should be done (hence, the ideal situation where it is vented through the roof and the moisture can more easily be directed away from the home).

Even though it is imperative to get bathroom moisture to the home's exterior, you might be shocked to find out that in a large percentage of people's homes, the bathroom fan is vented directly into the attic.

This is a "No-no!!" for a variety of reasons, not the least of which is that this type of methodology can lead directly to unwanted mold growth on the inside of the attic.

Even beyond situations where the bathroom fan installer is purely ignorant, lazy, or careless and does not relay the importance of venting the fan outside, there are accidental situations that may lead to a fan unknowingly being vented into the attic.

An example of this would be someone going into the attic who mistakenly, without knowing it, bumps into, shifts, and causes the duct system leading from a bathroom fan to the exterior vent to be dislodged.

If this occurs and is not checked to make sure that everything is secure, the next time the bathroom fan is used, it will be vented to some degree into the attic.

This could happen because of any reason, from a tech (HVAC, electrician, etc.) going into the attic to perform some type of service to a homeowner going into the attic to move something there for storage.

Asking a client where their bathroom fan is vented to is DEFINITELY a question that almost always causes the individual to then immediately ask themselves in self-reflection, "Where DOES my bathroom fan vent out to?" In fact, as you read this, you may even be asking yourself that question.

Hand Sanitizer Paint?

Have you ever read on a bottle of hand sanitizer how it says it kills 99.9% of germs (or some variation of this statement)?

My thought is if you had not heard that prior to very recently, perhaps now you may have with everything going on with the whole wave of media attention on coronavirus as of late.

Imagine if there existed a paint that behaved similarly to hand sanitizer. Believe it or not, there is.

I make it a point to never solely have blinders on when it comes to manufacturers and deciding which paint to recommend to a client for whatever situation they may need their paint for.

In other words, I am not married to any specific paint manufacturer.

Conversely, I tend to recommend what I believe to be the best product to help in each specific situation, given what a particular client is working to achieve.

That being said, not too long ago, Sherwin Williams came out with a product called 'Paint Shield.' Paint Shield is an amazing product as it exhibits two unprecedented features (as referenced from the Sherwin Williams website):

- First EPA-registered microbicidal paint that kills greater than 99.9% of Staph (Staphylococcus aureus), MRSA (Methicillin-resistant Staphylococcus aureus), E. coli (Escherichia coli), VRE (Vancomycin-resistant Enterococcus faecalis), and Enterobacter aerogenes within two hours of exposure on a painted surface.

- Continues to kill these disease-causing bacteria for up to four years when the integrity of the surface is maintained.

Basically, the hand sanitizer of paint products. This product has come out fairly recently and is certainly pretty impressive.

Although originally meant for hospitals, healthcare facilities in general, nursing homes, public gyms, etc., if more folks were to find out about it, my sense is that its usage could have a lot more of a potential market.

While its technology is obviously groundbreaking, it appears to have quite a ways to go to be fully positioned in the light as a household name.

As with anything, the more Sherwin Williams is able to promote the proven benefits that are associated with this product, the more folks will find out about it, and the more Paint Shield may become a viable resource for people who, possibly more so than others, might be a bit more concerned about the types of scenarios the product was developed for.

Essential Home Improvement

Given everything occurring in our world these days, the term 'Essential Home Improvement' sure may seem oxymoronic.

After all, what the heck type of homeimprovement could be considered 'essential'??

Contrary to this particular opinion, there are seemingly tons of home improvement projects that we are able to help people with on a regular basis, which are actually pretty essential.

I will provide a few examples...

Recently, we helped a client through a situation where their previous contractor dug out an old bulkhead in her yard, leaving a HUGE hole in its place, as well as a fairly flimsy interior door at the entrance of her home underneath this area. EVERY TIME it rained, her basement flooded.

We stepped in, custom-made and installed a bulkhead along with a custom steel door at the entranceway, and now she no longer has her heart drop in her stomach each time rain is in the forecast.

Lately, we have had a number of projects we have been working on with clients that are SUPER important and cannot come to completion soon enough. This is because of a position that has developed within their family makeup, where a family member from a medical standpoint, needs the home to be modified in order to accommodate a specific health condition—often with urgency attached to it.

Examples of these types of projects typically tend to be adding a handicap ramp or modifying a bathroom or bedroom to provide critical living space changes that are suddenly necessary and often appear to come out of nowhere.

Yet another illustration of an essential home improvement need would be someone who has something occur from a disaster standpoint that must be addressed IMMEDIATELY!

We are currently helping a number of families through these predicaments that range from a compromised roof letting through a bunch of water in a storm and significantly damaging the ceiling below it to a situation where mold has been discovered in someone's home, and we are working with a mitigation company, ensuring the mold is removed, and things are properly put back together again afterward.

I could go on and on…

Although at first glance, with VERY good, obvious reasoning, the home improvement industry, in general, is certainly not as important as some of the other industries that are at the forefront of things, particularly these days, when it comes to relating it to illnesses, life-threatening scenarios, and anything first responder related.

If you were to ask any doctor, nurse, or first responder, however, if they thought a good home improvement contractor would be helpful to know as their basement was flooding due to the unfinished work of a contractor who had abandoned them, as their elderly parent was going through an unexpected life change that required a "sooner rather than later" living space correction, or as their ceilings were caving in due to a roof that had begun massively leaking from a storm, I believe they would say—ABSOLUTELY!!!

What is the Difference Between a Carpenter Ant and a Termite?

While working on people's homes and businesses, it is not unusual for us to encounter insect damage, either actively occurring or from some time in the past.

Most often, this damage is done typically by carpenter ants or termites.

It is not unusual for people to unintentionally use the terms 'carpenter ant' and 'termite' interchangeably when describing or referring to the type of damage they have incurred.

While I totally appreciate this, especially in the heat of the moment when a massive amount of insect damage has been uncovered on someone's property, it is obviously incorrect as there really are two different types of insects that are definitely distinct from each other.

There are at least a few similarities in that both carpenter ants and Termites swarm while mating (swarming is the only time that both carpenter ants and termites have wings), are attracted to moisture about your property, and cause damage to wood as we have mentioned.

There are absolute differences between the two, however.

Carpenter ants DO NOT eat wood. Instead, they make their homes in the wood by burrowing, creating tunnels, and the like; one may often recognize carpenter ants' damage by the wood shavings they leave behind.

Termites, on the other hand, actually eat the wood (they need the cellulose contained in the wood to survive), and they certainly would not leave any shavings behind.

Carpenter ants will wander about looking for food (their diet consists of sugars and proteins); you may very well see them gallivanting around your property as they hunt for food.

Termites may never be spotted (unless you happen to encounter a swarm); you are more likely to see signs of termite damage than actual termites.

Finally, their body types are both very different.

- Carpenter ants have a narrow waist and segmented elbow antennae and, when winged, have large forewings and small hind wings.

- Termites have a broad waist, straight, bead-like antennae, and, when winged, have two sets of wings that are uniform in size.

Whether you come across carpenter ants or termites when working in or on the outside of the home, it is NEVER a fun situation.

Knowing a little bit about their similarities and differences, though, could be quite helpful in navigating through the process of how to correct things.

What is Efflorescence?

Way back when I first started my career in the home improvement industry, I heard the term 'efflorescence,' and it immediately intrigued me.

I don't know if it is because I enjoy the way the word rolled off my tongue (say it—'efflorescence'—pretty fun, no?)

I don't know if it is because when I learned what it was, I started pointing it out in meetings with clients when I happened to notice it and then felt pretty fancy knowing something of this particular nature.

If you have ever noticed a white, powdery substance on any masonry (brick, cinderblock, cement, etc.) on the inside or outside of your home or business, it could be on bare masonry, or it could be on masonry that has been painted in the past, chances are that it is efflorescence.

So, what EXACTLY is efflorescence??

Efflorescence is something that occurs when soluble salts and other water-dispersible materials come to the surface of concrete and mortars.

Efflorescence is prompted by low temperatures and moist conditions (think condensation, rain, dew, and water).

Efflorescence is something that builds up over a period of time.

I have seen it in the form of a light coating, and I have seen it super chunky.

Efflorescence by itself is not a harmful situation, but it can be an indicator that there is some issue with moisture developing behind or within the areas it is stemming from.

How does one get rid of efflorescence?

Well, assuming that you are convinced that there is no ongoing moisture challenge behind where the efflorescence is congregating, there are a number of methods that could be used.

However, if there is the possibility of a moisture problem causing the efflorescence, my recommendation is to remedy the moisture challenge prior to removing the efflorescence, or you may be spinning your tires as the efflorescence may soon return.

Once you have determined the approach from a dealing with the moisture challenge standpoint, the efflorescence can be addressed by a variety of different means.

You can try washing it off with a mild detergent and a stiff scrub brush. You can also attempt carefully powerwashing it off.

However, if it is deeply embedded within the masonry, your only real option may be to glass blast (or some other type of media blast) it off, at which point you should probably have a professional come out to evaluate it.

If it is a painted surface or even if it is not, you may prefer to prep and paint the surface after the efflorescence has been removed.

Efflorescence.

For me, certainly a fun word to say, although the process of addressing the phenomena itself obviously may not be as enjoyable!

Ever Wondered About the Plastering Process?

If you live in New England, I don't really have to tell you that our part of the country is very unique compared to other areas of the United States.

This applies across many fronts—cultural, architectural, religious, environmental, culinary... You name it!

One facet that is different than other places around the country is our construction processes.

Many of our construction processes are quite similar to what you may find elsewhere.

Some aspects of it, though, certainly appear to be utilized more in our area and are not as customary in other regions.

One specific example of this is the plastering process.

Although other areas of the country absolutely use the plastering process, it is not nearly as dominant as it is in New England.

Most areas of the country use drywall, taping, and compound as a means to construct and maintain their wall systems.

In fact, in our area, this is the system that is most often used in commercial settings. In residential settings, however, the plastering process definitely reigns.

Why is this?

Most probably because if the plastering process is done correctly (properly mixed and applied), the finished product is a much more durable finish than regular drywall would allow you to have.

As an end product, plaster is more resistant to being damaged by being hit or knocked into than drywall.

So, if plaster leaves a higher-quality finish, why isn't this taken advantage of more often throughout the country?

This is a great question, and there is certainly some good discussion to be had about the roots of each system (plastering vs. drywall) and their histories.

From a cost standpoint, what we would bill out to blueboard and plaster a room would be very similar to drywalling, taping, and compounding one.

I am just philosophically opposed to not using blueboard and plaster.

A number of years ago, we were called in to assist with a rare, new residential home on Cuttyhunk Island in Massachusetts.

The contractor working on building the home was from California, and his client insisted on drywalling, taping, and compounding through every room in the beautiful structure.

I literally told him that I truly believed that blueboard and plaster was the correct route to go in their situation, and I stuck to my guns.

The project was one that we did not end up working on because of this insistence, and although it would have been an awesome home to incorporate into the portfolio, I simply had no interest in doing something that I did not believe was the right solution given the circumstances.

Don't get me wrong. We use tons of joint compounds in the process of fixing repairs that we believe warrant it.

For larger expanses, however, I really do believe utilizing blueboard and plaster is the way to go.

Certainly, if one is looking for a harder finish on their walls, NOTHING beats a true, well-done plaster finish, regardless of what area of the country one may live in!

FIX YOUR LEAKY PIPES!

Recently, we had a client reach out to us who experienced a huge flood in her home.

I felt very bad about her being in this particular predicament.

Apparently, her upstairs tenant had been experiencing a slow leak under the sink in her kitchen but neglected to inform our client of this.

The tenant had a small container underneath the sink, which she allowed to gradually fill up. She would then empty it and put it back under the sink until it filled up again.

The tenant probably was only minorly inconvenienced by the slow drip and didn't think too much about it.

Had she informed our client, our client could have addressed the issue.

Instead, what happened was the problem with the pipe gradually compounded to a larger challenge, even to the point of affecting the piping beneath from where that specific pipe ran out.

The next thing you know, our client had a waterfall in her kitchen and the rear entrance located directly beneath the tenant's kitchen.

Subsequently, there was a tremendous amount of damage to the ceiling and wall areas where the water had come down and situated.

Our client messaged us to see if we could help, and we were over the next day tearing open the ceiling and wall areas to allow the plumber to be able to go in and fix things.

Even if a situation like this is covered and put through your homeowner's insurance, who wants to endure horribleness like this if they do not have to???

The answer to this dilemma? Fix your leaky pipes!!

Even more importantly, however, would be to coach those around you to let you know if they ever have an issue with things needing to be fixed.

In this situation, it was a leaky pipe, but it obviously could always be something else—a light that does not activate when a light switch is turned on, a piece of rotted wood, etc.

Whether it is a tenant, a family member, or anybody else who may be in the position to let you know of a smaller issue, it is critical that they do so, as smaller issues can easily develop into bigger issues over time.

Pipe situations are notorious for this. Pipe leaks do not fix themselves.

Sometimes, we get spoiled as there is evidence of something bad happening in the form of water staining, discoloration in your paint coatings, or something along those lines.

In our client's instance, she really would have had to rely on her tenant to warn her that she had noticed a pipe leaking.

Because this did not happen, a disastrous mess ensued.

That being said, it is impossible to fix something that you are not aware is broken, and it is hypercritical to check with the other folks on your property once in a while to make sure that all is okay.

Short of the tenant thinking that she should have reached out to our client and let her know that she had a problem with her sink leaking, there was nothing our client could have done to prevent this.

Unfortunately for our client, not only is she forced to fix the pipes that were the original culprit, but she now has a very expensive mess on her hands that is certainly going to take some time to correct and put back together.

Why are GFI Devices Used?

There is a wide variety of things that should be paid attention to when renovating a kitchen or bathroom, which are very different than every other room in the home.

One of the most notable of these items is obviously the plumbing aspect always associated with kitchens and baths.

Whether you are just changing out a sink or gutting the kitchen or bathroom entirely, plumbing is a component that is often connected to someone's main desire to embark on one of these types of projects in the first place.

An important facet to pay attention to that is directly related to these kinds of projects, even though it is an entirely different trade than plumbing, is the appropriate electrical applications being laid out that safely wire up your newly improved kitchen or bathroom.

One of the more important components of the electrical portion make-up of your kitchen or bathroom is the proper utilization of GFI (or GFCI—Ground Fault Circuit Interrupter) outlets.

So, why are GFI outlets used?

GFIs protect us from being electrically shocked by faults in the electrical devices we use in our homes.

GFIs work by comparing the input current on the "hot" side to the output current on the neutral side.

It is an electrical code for a GFI outlet to take the place of a standard outlet at any location that may be exposed to moisture.

GFI outlets can be recognized by the addition of two buttons that control the GFI functionality—labeled "Test" and "Reset."

The "Test" button literally tests if the GFI is working. By clicking the "Test" button and plugging something into the outlet, if the device you plug in does not work, the GFI is functioning correctly.

To make the outlet active again, either after a test or after the GFI "pops" in a real application scenario, click the "Reset" button, and you will be good to go.

The GFI will not allow itself to be reset if it is not safe to do so.

Although I see debate all the time as to people trying to rationalize which outlets in a kitchen or bathroom require a GFI and which "technically" do not, I refuse to participate in them.

Maybe it is my deep-down fear of electricity.

Whatever the reasoning, I always say that if the electrical outlet has the slightest chance of being exposed to moisture, be sure a GFI is there—especially because of any relatively small, incremental cost in using a GFI compared to a traditional outlet.

I would much rather err on the side of caution.

GFI outlets are there to protect us and should be approached as such. In my opinion, if anyone is trying to talk you out of using one in a place where it should really be used, they should be ignored, and the proper, safe action of installing the GFI should absolutely be done.

When Should You Replace Your Front Door?

Whether it is your front door or any other exterior-facing entry door of your home, there is typically a "useful" life component attached to any type of question as to how long one of these should last before needing to be replaced.

There are a variety of factors that play into when it makes the most sense to look at replacing an entry door.

One area of focus could be whether it seems like you are losing energy through the door.

Whether it is heat in the winter or cool air in the summer, most folks would prefer the energy to stay within their household and not release it into the neighborhood if at all possible.

Do you notice any major warpedness or disfiguration with the door?

Although it is not necessarily unusual for doors to change their original form over a period of time, there certainly is such a thing as "too much" of a shape change.

Rotted beyond repair door rot is also one of the easiest ways to recognize that your door needs to be replaced.

I am not referring to the trim around the door, as usually the trim can fairly easily be changed out if ever necessary.

Instead, I am referring to either the door itself or, what most commonly happens, the exterior-facing portion of the door jamb (which is the side of the door frame that the door runs into perpendicularly).

The rotted door jamb conversation often gets me into what I consider a losing battle discussion with highly capable mastercarpenters, who plead with me that the rot in the jamb can be surgically removed and a new piece of wood installed in place of the rot.

Technically, they are correct. My mentality, however, is that when the jamb starts to go, the door is "toast."

With the door products that are available on the market today—fortunately or unfortunately (depending on how you look at it)—it is more cost-efficient to pay for a new door and change it out than it would be to buy some time by repairing the old jamb which, in my mind, is only temporarily delaying the inevitable.

The exception to this would be a really "solid" older door where you simply would not be able to replace it with what is on the market today. The age old saying, "They don't make them like they used to," is highly applicable in door replacement.

As an example, a solid wood door made fifty years ago will be light years ahead in terms of durability in comparison to anything that most consider reasonably priced on today's market.

The reasons for this are a combination of the raw door-making materials not being as readily available in the modern world, along with the fact that it is nearly impossible for manufacturers to produce these doors in a manner that would allow them to sufficiently sell them to consumers, at a volume which would make it worth it for them to do so.

Although it is difficult to pinpoint the exact moment of when it is best to change an exterior entry door, there are absolutely various signs that one can rely on which help determine when it might be time to do so, subsequent to any LARGER issues developing that extend outside of the door in question itself.

Natural Wood Cabinetry Refinishing and Restoration

As cabinetry ages, whether it is in the kitchen, bathroom, or another room, it typically begins to show signs of wear and tear.

This is especially true if the cabinetry gets a good amount of use.

Assuming this occurs and the owner of the cabinetry grows a bit concerned about this happening, a tough decision is often involved at this time.

Should the cabinets be replaced? Should the cabinets be repainted? Should the cabinets be refaced?

Or, along the lines of what I personally have found to be the most gratifying solution, should the cabinets be refinished? Certainly, any of these options could be a great choice.

Replacing the cabinets provides the "sky's the limit" type of option, as you could really take this anywhere you wanted with regard to what the cabinets are replaced with.

Repainting the cabinets, if done correctly, could change the entire look of the room they are located in and provide its own "WOW!!"-factor.

Refacing the cabinets is a nice option, though probably my least favorite (although they absolutely may come out awesome, I am just not particularly a fan...).

This brings us to refinishing.

From a cost perspective, assuming we are, minimally, having a conversation about "good" cabinetry, it is most in line with the painting systems we would utilize when painting cabinetry, possibly a little bit more.

Restoring natural wood cabinetry typically would cost a lot less than replacing them, but it is usually a bit more than refacing them.

Why do I like the refinishing option so much? That is actually a really tough question to answer. Maybe it is solely the purist in me.

I love it when our craftspeople can take something that is seemingly worn out and, with a bit of time, energy, and effort, literally resurrect things to brand-spanking new fashion.

Even cabinetry that only has bits and pieces of its set that are a bit tired looking can, with the correct individual performing the restoration work, be brought back to look right in line with the existing finish of the rest of its set.

Restoring cabinetry is A LOT of work.

From the stripping, sanding, and overall prep to the staining and polyurethane finishes, cabinetry restoration is not for the faint of heart.

Cabinetry restoration is also, unfortunately, a dying art form where there are a limited number of people who truly are 100% in tune with what is involved with actual cabinetry restoration and are able to professionally execute it from start to finish.

With all the above being said, if you are someone who would very much prefer to have your cabinetry restored versus one of the other options available if the right person is performing the restoration work, the results can be remarkably stunning and leave the owner of the cabinetry with a feeling of satisfaction and pride, that would tend to simply not be there with replacing, repainting, or refacing the cabinetry.

The Dirty Little Secret About Solid Deck Stain...

Earlier this past week, I was watching a video of a contractor talking about how excited they were about applying a solid deck stain to a deck in the backyard of one of their clients' homes.

They could not wait until they applied it to the deck surfaces (which had previously been bare), to sew together the paint job that they were in the process of completing on the rest of the home.

After the coating was applied, the contractor beamed with satisfaction as they truly felt that they had just accomplished something absolutely awesome for their customer. I cringed.

To the contractor's credit, they are not alone; I believe most contractors fall into this same trap.

There is a dirty little secret about solid deck stains these days that the majority of contractors are oblivious to, and most homeowners scratch their heads about after the fact.

The Dirty Little Secret?

Solid deck stains, especially in New England, typically do not last for more than one year.

In fact, any conversation about applying a solid deck stain to someone's deck should also be conducted in conjunction with a conversation about how reasonably long the application will last (realistically, 6-12 months before the solid stain starts to peel in some capacity) prior to needing a maintenance treatment.

It does not matter whether the homeowner or the most talented painting contractor on the planet does the application. It does not matter whether it is an oil-oriented solid deck stain or a latex-oriented solid deck stain. It does not matter if it is being applied to pressure-treated wood, mahogany, or fir.

So, if this is indeed the case, then why are solid deck stains positioned in the marketplace as long-lasting, and why do many contractors continue to recommend them on surfaces that do not already have a solid deck stain in place?

Great question!!

If the surface already has a solid deck stain in place, unless you plan on stripping the existing coatings off of the deck, you have no choice. It, unfortunately, makes the most sense that another solid deck stain system should be applied (with the expectation, again, that it will not last for more than one year until issues start to surface).

If you were to approach a deck application by traditional means (wash, scrape, sand as necessary, and two coats of finish), you are directly in line to experience some type of failure with your coating system within a year after it is done.

If you harshly rough up the deck surfaces as part of the process—i.e., by means of some type of abrasive/media blasting—you would have somewhat of a fighting chance at extending the life of the system sometime beyond the gloomy one-year outlook.

Blasting is a bit of an intense process, but it does absolute wonders toward TRULY roughing up the surfaces and making them HIGHLY receptive to whatever type of coating system might be being applied to it.

This is hardly ever done, however.

Blasting should never be performed unless executed by an experienced professional, and it can be quite an investment.

One of the biggest reasons solid deck stains do not last is the wood grain they are applied to is way too tight to properly receive the product.

Combined with how highly susceptible to moisture the deck surfaces are to begin with, and you have the recipe for an absolute disaster waiting to happen.

When prepping the deck, professionals and homeowners alike tend to unintentionally make the wood grain even tighter by sanding through a process of traditional means (by hand, with a palm sander, belt sander, random orbital sander, etc.).

There could certainly be an unending diatribe coming from me as to why solid deck stains should not be utilized on deck surfaces in New England that have not had a solid stain previously applied to them.

My preference in these situations falls back on wood toning stains and possibly an occasional semi-transparent.

If you would like to have a more in-depth conversation about what I might recommend for your particular situation, please reach out to our office, and they will be happy to set up some time for us to discuss things.

Deck coatings and getting them to last might just be the most challenging component of the exterior portions of our homes that sometimes receive some type of protective coating system.

Setting proper expectations and long-term maintenance plans in place is key for their beauty and longevity, even if it may take a contrarian approach to achieve them.

What are the Benefits of Epoxy Flooring?

Many of us have concrete flooring around our home or business in one shape or form.

A few examples of this are concrete flooring that can be found in our basement, garage, or shop areas.

In a good number of instances, people elect to leave the concrete bare. This could be for a variety of reasons. Maybe they are concerned about the long-term maintenance of it if they were to put some type of floor covering over the concrete.

Maybe they are concerned about the permanence of the floorcovering once it is installed over the concrete.

Maybe they just like the look of the bare concrete.

Whatever the case may be, there is certainly nothing wrong with leaving the concrete bare.

For some people, though, the desire exists to make the concrete as durable as possible without laying a solid floor covering (carpet, floating floor, etc.) over it.

For these types of situations, an epoxy flooring system may be the perfect solution.

An epoxy system, when installed properly, protects the underlying concrete from grease, miscellaneous staining, moisture, and even cracking.

There is typically a limited choice of colors to choose from.

If the epoxy system is not installed properly, one could certainly have a bit of a disaster on their hands to fix it.

When an epoxy flooring system fails, it fails by the system peeling off in sheets from the concrete, and what is required to correct the failure is nothing short of a nightmare.

To correctly install an epoxy system, the concrete should be etched prior to any application.

This can be done with some type of abrasive blasting or acid etching, which is EXTREMELY important in order to allow the epoxy system to properly "bite" and absorb into the concrete.

I have found that the best epoxy flooring systems are sold in two-part kits (what we refer to as an 'A' and a 'B'), where the two parts are mixed together and then applied the way the manufacturer lays it out on their labels.

These epoxy paint kits generally do not stretch very far and are usually a bit pricey.

The coating system is ordinarily comprised of two coats.

After roughing up the concrete surface via blasting or acid etching, the first coat is applied and should sink really nicely into the floor surface.

The second coat is applied and should finish it off beautifully. Some systems even come with fancy speckles that you can add in conjunction with the second coat to add a bit of flavor to things.

There is a pretty good variety of epoxy floor systems on the market, but no matter which system is chosen, the most critical step is properly preparing the concrete before the system is applied.

If done properly, an epoxy floor system will not only make your concrete floor look super sharp, but it will robustly protect it for years to come.

If not done properly, however, one can certainly chase their tail as they work to correct the mess on their hands, which often could have easily been prevented by properly preparing the concrete surface prior to applying the epoxy system!

Deck Project Ideas

If this is the year you are planning on working a deck project into your home improvement agenda, NOW is the time to get your ducks in a row, particularly if you live in New England.

Why is this the case? New England weather is as finicky as it exists in the country.

You may believe you are comfortably planning on starting your deck project in March, but before you know it, it is mid-October, and your deck project STILL has not been completed.

Even if it is a relatively simple project (such as re-staining a deck), with the weather needing to be correct, the project could easily drag on for months.

Here are a number of deck project category examples:

- Building or rebuilding a new deck from scratch
- Converting an existing deck from wood to composite
- Expanding an existing deck
- Repairing a deck
- Staining or re-staining a deck

Any of these take a good amount of planning.

For example, if your project is simply re-staining your existing deck, the process would look something along these lines:

- Wash/clean the existing deck surfaces
- Properly prepare the surfaces you will be re-staining (to make them suitable to accept your stain system)
- Apply the desired stain system

Even a project as seemingly straightforward as this could linger for weeks if the correct weather is not realized [solely in applying the stain, we recommend (assuming the proper temperature) the weather being free from precipitation the day before you do the project, the day of the project, and the day after the project to allow the stain to properly set].

For more involved projects, if you have not gotten the ball rolling by now, my assumption would be that you are not particularly in a rush to get the project done and that you are ok with getting it done at some point this coming year, not necessarily ready to go come springtime (with the idea that spring in New England could mean March, it could mean June, or anywhere in between).

When building a deck from scratch as an example, in its most basic form, the process could look something like this:

- Dig out areas for footings
- Position and pour footings
- Frame out the deck appropriately
- Install deck flooring
- Install deck finish work (the rails, spindles, trim, etc.)

Even when helping one of our clients, this process could take quite some time with A LOT of starting and stopping due to what the weather allows us to do or not do.

Regardless of whether the project you are undertaking is something you're tackling on your own or hiring a professional to do, my sense is that now would be the time to work to get things together.

If hiring a professional, from our experience, deck projects are amongst the most challenging to schedule, as shown by some of the variables we have reviewed here.

It is not unusual to have a deck project remain in our scheduling queue for months on end, waiting for the most ideal time for us to attack it.

If deck project ideas, the planning process behind them, or any other related questions may be something we can help you out with, please reach out to us.

Decks can often be one of the more enjoyable facets on the exterior of your home.

Getting them prepared so that they are at the point where they are able to be most vibrantly utilized during the nicer months can sometimes be an unexpected, painstaking exercise that, if jumped on early enough, can easily be overcome.

A Holiday Disaster!

_____

This is a joyous time of year for many of us.

In fact, it is not far-fetched to say that for many people, the holiday season late in the calendar is their favorite time of year (though mine is the fourth of July; perhaps I am an anomaly??).

Through the diverse array of holidays that folks may celebrate this time of year, things may happen that those celebrating may not have counted on occurring, therefore putting an unplanned twist to holiday celebrations.

In this instance, I am not necessarily referring to medical or life-threatening related occurrences, although those could certainly be relevant to this type of conversation as well.

I am referring to crazy things that may happen around the home.

It could be that cousin of yours whose brilliant idea it was to deep fry a turkey in the garage and subsequently set the garage on fire.

It could be your niece/nephew/grandchild, etc., that used an entire roll of toilet paper while using the upstairs bathroom and subsequently flooded the kitchen downstairs below it.

It could even be that tech-savvy relative who got overly ambitious with that new drone they just got for a gift and accidentally flew it through that brand-new window you just installed.

Whatever the case may be, these types of incidents can lead to costly property disasters.

Many moons from now, you may be able to look back and laugh at the family cat who decided to chew through the Christmas tree wires and unintentionally lit the tree on fire.

You may be chuckling as you read through these examples, or you may not be, depending on how much any of these unfortunate scenarios are applicable to experiences that you have lived through!

If you do happen to live through any of these happenings that may someday make a great story but, in the meantime, are an annoying inconvenience, feel free to keep this column handy, reach out to our office. We will be happy to guide you through putting things back together as efficiently as possible.

Selling Your Home? To Repair or Not To Repair?

Whether your home or family home is getting ready to be placed on the market, there is always the question that comes up as to what should be done and what should not be done.

Recently, I looked at a home for a client who was put in a position of needing to sell a home for a family member pretty quickly.

They wanted to hire us to repair a window that was a bit of an eyesore and had rotted out long ago.

Visiting with the client and putting my eye quickly on the home, I noticed that there were actually quite a number of things that a potential buyer might raise as a concerning issue before electing to move forward with a sale.

The challenge is that when a potential buyer is looking at a home to purchase, one never knows what is most important to that individual.

What might be entirely important to one person may not be the least bit important to another person.

In the example I provided, our client was guessing (through no fault of their own) that whoever was buying the home may take issue with the window that was in grave disrepair.

The prospective buyer buying the home, however, may be doing so with the intention of replacing ALL of the windows on the home and perhaps could care less as to whether this particular window in question was repaired or not because, in the end, it was going to be replaced anyway.

On an even larger scale of this example would be folks who engage in major kitchen or bathroom remodels prior to selling.

I usually advise STRONGLY against doing so, as kitchens and bathrooms tend to be rooms that folks often tailor toward their own taste while moving in or after moving into a new home.

A while back, we painted kitchen cabinetry for a client who was in the process of selling a home.

The client's realtor was ultra-skeptical as the investment in having us do so was $10,000-$15,000.

The cabinets were quite dated, and professionally painting them changed the entire look and feel of the kitchen to something ultra-modern.

The realtor patted our client on the back afterward and said they took back what they said and thought the cabinet painting job we did actually helped in selling the home as quickly as it did for the price it sold for.

This is the exception rather than the rule.

The principle of this situation is what I would like to focus on.

Instead of playing a guessing game, my suggestion is to work with a reputable realtor to help develop a list of what to focus on.

This can often be done in conjunction with a pre-listing home inspection by a reputable, professional home inspector.

The more guesswork you are able to take out of it, the better.

Although it is possible you may be able to nail down on your own things that may indeed need to be addressed in the best interest of selling your home the quickest for the most money, I would feel much more comfortable with a client working with a professional (or team of professionals) to truly determine what should be focused on and what should not.

Holiday Interior Painting Ideas

Perhaps you have been hosting some faction of the holidays at your home for quite some time.

Perhaps this is the very first time you have been called upon to host (which you gleefully accepted...even though now you may be wondering what the heck you have gotten yourself into!).

Whatever the case may be, you may be looking for different ways of making your home more cozy and inviting for whichever guests may be popping over for a visit.

Whether just a friend or dinner for thirty, it is always nice to create as welcoming an environment as possible for whoever may be coming by.

There are a number of things that could be done to help with this.

Obviously, de-cluttering and decorating are at the top of the list.

If you wanted to do something a little "more," though, some interior painting may go a long way!

No matter if you do it or if a professional does it, if properly approached, clean, crisp interior painting in just the right places can make a HUGE difference.

Here are some areas that may make sense to focus on:

- Mudroom
- Foyer
- Stairway
- Living Room
- Dining Room
- Common Bathrooms
- Ceilings and trim, in general

There is no real pecking order to this, just areas where your guests may be most likely to frequent.

New paint can be extraordinarily soothing.

Not just for the times during the holidays when you may be entertaining, but also for the time after the holidays when you are able to truly enjoy that one area that has been bugging you for years of wanting to get painted!

Picking the most appropriate color can certainly be an obstacle for some people and could even prevent them from pulling the trigger on a paint job right before the holidays.

If possibly talking to and maybe hiring us for any interior painting project you may be contemplating doing makes sense, all of our paint jobs come with a professional color consultation with no additional cost to our clients.

The holidays are a terrific time to catch up with family and friends about what has transpired in everyone's life since the last time you have seen each other.

What can make it even more terrific, though, is doing so in an environment (perhaps freshly painted!) that adds to the special feeling of the occasion.

Do You Enjoy Shoveling Snow?

I am not sure I have ever asked a more rhetorical question to open up any home improvement snippet I have written.

My Dad always said that he enjoyed shoveling snow because of the workout it provides.

I am not sure if he euphemistically looks at it that way in order to motivate himself to conquer the task at hand or if he really does enjoy the test it provides his body, especially with the heavier types of snow.

If he does indeed like doing it, I would venture to guess he would be in the minority of folks who begrudgingly stare this daunting task in the eye each time it is presented in front of them.

I, for one, certainly do NOT enjoy shoveling snow (not even close!).

Although I will agree that there is a distinct sense of accomplishment once you have worked hard for a while carving out paths around your home (even if sometimes this sense is short-lived once the snowplow comes trucking down your street!).

Regardless of the emotions you feel every time a path needs to be shoveled, the fact remains that the path still needs to be shoveled.

After coming to this realization, there are two things that can happen: you could shovel yourself. You could have someone else do it.

If you do tackle the task yourself, it is important to:

- Keep your feet spread the same distance as your hips

- Use your legs as much as possible by bending your knees and keeping your back straight

- Try your best not to twist your upper body when shoveling

- Be sure to shovel small bits at a time, and do not overdue the amount on your shovel

- Stay hydrated—as you may already know, this is quite the workout!

If you do elect to have someone else do it, make sure that you are very clear on what is and is not being done and the methodology involved while doing it.

For example, LOPCO Contracting does not plow driveways.

We will, however, shovel someone out through the use of shoveling and/or a snowblower (if you would ever like to talk to us about getting on our service list for this, please reach out to our office).

If you are anything like me, you will acknowledge that shoveling snow is neither easy nor fun (sorry, Dad!!).

Unfortunately, living in New England, each time a "shovelable" snowfall hits, our options are fairly limited in terms of how to combat it!

What is the Best Month to Perform an Exterior Paint Job in RI?

If you were to ask any exterior painting Contractor what the best month to paint the exterior of your home or business in RI was, you would most likely get one of two answers...

You may get the ambiguous answer, where the contractor kind of dances around the question and, instead of providing a specific month, lists the various conditions as to when exterior painting work is optimally performed.

Or you may also get the answer, which, although not perfect, is a bit more fair of a response, which basically would state that around these parts, you would not know for sure until the specific year was all the way through (because technically it could have been March or it could have been August...), where you would have the luxury of looking back and seeing what actually transpired.

In this day and age of information being at your fingertips, we see homeowners constantly, not just in painting but with regard to home improvement items in general, believe they have discovered the secret answers to whatever home improvement question they may have in mind, simply by inputting some data into their smart device or computer and resting their solid belief of the answer on whatever the technology happens to spit out, in conjunction with how it satisfies the individual's comfort level in the response.

It is actually one of the most common questions I have been asked in my time in the home improvement industry.

Although obviously, the safe answer would be that one would not know until the calendar year has passed, I pretty much have a more direct answer.

November.

Huh? But, but, but...

I apologize if I offended you by suggesting this, but from my experience, I have found this to be 100% correct.

How could this be?? After all, just as recently as the November I am writing this in, we have heard the weather forecasters whisper that four-letter 'S' word (snow) and have experienced a couple of fluke cold fronts!!

True, but on average, I very much believe (if backed into a corner) that the answer is November.

Here's why…

- The average daytime high in November is 52.4 degrees Fahrenheit, and the average nighttime low is 35.1 degrees Fahrenheit, which is perfect with regard to providing applied coatings the smoothest cure time (not too long, not too short)

- Rain averages throughout the year have little variance, 3-4.5 inches depending on the month; every year is different, but with there not being that huge of a difference, I would remove this variable from the equation (contrast this to temperature fluctuations, as an example, July's average high temp in RI is 82.6 degrees—a difference of about 30 degrees!)

"But Tom, you all painted my home in July six years ago, and everything has lasted great!"

We typically paint exteriors in dry weather conditions and allow the coating we are utilizing to cure as correctly as possible, as long as we are doing so on a surface with a moisture content of 15% or less.

Certainly, there are an enormous number of times during the calendar year that you would be absolutely fine doing exterior coatings; if I personally had to pick a month, though, it would be November.

We offer a five-year warranty that I consider the strongest in our industry, and we obviously would never coat anything that would put us in a position to have to entertain a warranty service call, as the next time we come out to paint or do something at someone's home, it would preferably be something new, not reworking something for free that could have been avoided doing so.

As much as I believe this to be true, it seems we work through annual November challenges with clients whose projects pop up in a queue and are hesitant about not moving the project to the spring.

I absolutely do not knock on their concerns. With the amount of messaging out there—whether it be the Internet, a "friend" in the industry, or even their local paint store—there is a plethora of contrarian information out there that may sway them to disagree with what I say.

While I appreciate the sentiment, at the end of the day, these individual influencers are not the ones who tend to stick their livelihood on the line by actually providing a long-term guarantee for the type of work we do in the time period we believe is good to do it in.

If you ask ten different people, you may/may not get ten different responses to this question. I would be curious to see, however, how many would respond with the answer we would provide, as well as the track record to be willing to back it up for five years afterward.

Why You are Getting Water in Your Basement…

One of the more unsettling things any home or business owner can come across is water in their basement.

This is particularly nerve-racking when you may come across it for the first time.

If you have ever had this happen to you, you know exactly what I am referring to.

You innocently head downstairs to change out the laundry, check the furnace, etc., when you see a tiny puddle of water.

Upon further inspection, you notice it is coming from the wall

You then think to yourself, "Uh-oh, this isn't good."

You may have lived in your home for decades and never had water in the basement before, and all of a sudden, you come across this situation.

You may have just bought a house, and from the moment you bought it, it seems like every time it sprinkles, you get water in the basement.

Whatever the case may be, whenever water coming into the basement is noticed, the faster you can neutralize the root of the problem, the better off you will be.

By addressing things as soon as possible, you certainly lessen the chances of mold growth, and you will just be able to sleep easier at night.

One thing is for sure: if you ever go to put the property on the market to sell, there are few things that chase away potential buyers faster than once they know the basement is susceptible to taking on water.

So then, where the heck is this water coming from??

There are quite a number of potential answers to this question. Here are a few…

- A leaky bulkhead

- Water leaching in from a window or door opening

- An extremely porously passive foundation that easily allows water to seep through

- A higher water table that gets raised during a specific rain event and causes water to come up through the floor

- A leaky roof (Yes! Water can leak in from the roof and make its way all the way to the basement!!)

- A leaking pipe

These are just a snapshot of some of the possibilities that we come across most often. There are always more rare reasons, too.

Since 1995, we have been scratching our heads with home and business owners, working to figure out why water is getting into basements and the solutions of how to stop this from happening.

Although not always easy to discover and rectify, the sense of relief that accompanies the accomplishment of doing so really cannot be put into words—though if you have been fortunate enough to make it to the other side of one of these circumstances, you know EXACTLY what I am talking about!

If you or someone you know is having a challenge with water in their basement that they would like an outside opinion on, please feel free to reach out to our office, and we will be happy to have a conversation with you about it.

When is Rotted Wood NOT Really Rotted?

As the old saying goes, "If I had a nickel for…"

In this case, the second part of this sentence would be, "…every time someone told me that they had rotted wood that needed fixing, I would be a rich man!"

So then…

If I had a nickel for every time someone told me that they had rotted wood that needed fixing, I would be a rich man!

One would think that if someone had rotted wood that needed to be corrected, it would be just that, rotted wood.

Technically, this is true.

However, our office constantly fields calls asking for help fixing some type of rotted wood situation where the wood, it turns out, is not really rotted.

I do not blame the person reaching out to us in this situation, though.

Many times, people are explaining things to the best of their ability, and they simply do not know how to describe what they need fixed, other than something being "rotted."

There are other times when even we, as contractors, are fooled.

Sometimes, wood appears to be rotted, but when we go to check it, it is actually not rotted.

Properly identifying rotted wood can be a tricky thing.

There are also many times when something appears to be perfectly fine, but when we hit the area with some type of tool, our tool goes right through the wood, and it is rotted to its core.

Because wood often rots from the inside out, this situation happens more often than you might think.

I believe it is VERY important to inspect the exterior of your home or business for areas that may appear to be rotted at least twice per year… (once in the spring and once in the fall).

It is very important that an effort is made to diagnose these types of situations, as rotted wood trim or finished siding can lead to rotted structural wood behind it.

Rotted wood can also attract carpenter ants, termites, etc., because of how much it holds moisture.

Rotted wood can also encourage mold and mildew growth because of this type of dampness.

Although upon inspection, what appears to be rotted wood may not end up being rotted at all, I would strongly suggest that you err on the side of caution and examine your home or business' exterior every so often as thoroughly as possible.

If you would like some help or guidance in this area, please feel free to reach out to our office, and we will be more than happy to assist you!

Why Does the Paint on My House Bubble?

_____

Recently, I had two different conversations that essentially asked pretty much the same thing.

"Tom, why does the paint on my house bubble?"

The answer to each was a question from me.

"When you see it bubbling, what else is happening at that time?"

Although there are numerous reasons as to why paint might bubble, I am going to address the two specific reasons why the paint was bubbling in these particular circumstances that I was asked about.

In the first example, the individual mentioned that she was in the process of painting her home, and everything seemed fine for a week, but then, about a week after it was done, she noticed that the house seemed to be bubbling. After speaking with her further, there were no obvious signs of moisture involvement, and it only seemed to bubble in areas that the sun shined on, and only when the sun was actually shining on it.

In this case, I believe that something two-fold was occurring.

I believe that the paint coating that was applied was not fully bonded to the coat beneath it (this could be for several different reasons).

Typically, it takes at least thirty days for paint to fully cure. Although these days, paint may dry to the touch fairly quickly, it still does not maintain its full hardness for some time afterward.

If a paint coating is not fully bonded to the coating/surface below it and the coating has not yet achieved its full hardness, a little heat from the sun will typically pull any air in between the coating and the surface directly below it to a point (or several points...) and cause it to bubble.

In the second example, after asking the person some questions about the circumstances of their issue, it seemed that somehow moisture was working its way in behind the paint coatings.

The coatings had already been on the house for quite some time, so a coating needing to cure did not appear to be part of the problem.

This particular home was quite old (about 175 years old or so), and sometimes, in older homes, moisture can creep behind places in peculiar ways.

When the moisture crept behind the wooden clapboard that the paint coatings were attached to, as the surface heated up, the moisture would tend to be pulled and gathered in certain areas to points, which would create bubbles.

In fact, if you were to pop one of the bubbles, water would come out of it.

To "trick" the moisture, we ended up breaking the seal at the butts of the clapboards and using a wedge (basically a tiny shim) directly behind the areas where the bubbles were forming.

The idea with this is that as the climate moves to pull the moisture to the various points, instead of trying to find its way out through the paint coating in the front of the clapboard, it would have a much easier escape on the backside of the clapboard.

Though these are just two examples, paint coatings could form bubbles on the surfaces they are attached to for a wide variety of reasons.

If you are experiencing bubbling on your exterior paint coatings and haven't the foggiest idea as to exactly why it is happening, please feel free to reach out to our office and set up a conversation with us, and let's see if we can work together to figure it out!

If You Have a Chimney in Your Home, THIS is NOT Optional!

_____

We all hear the horror stories.

Someone enjoying the warmth and aura of their fireplace on a cool fall or cold winter night when all of a sudden, they hear a loud popping and cracking noise, perhaps accompanied by dense smoke.

With their heart pounding, they immediately call the fire department, which comes out and informs the unfortunate homeowner that they were experiencing a fire in their chimney.

This is actually the MOST fortunate scenario in this particular type of situation. The REAL unfortunate event would occur if the fire began to spread beyond the chimney, which is NOT uncommon.

How does something like this happen?

Your chimney is a significant ventilation system that allows smoke, toxins, and dangerous fumes to be released safely from our homes.

When a chimney is clean, these hazardous fumes, smoke, and various toxins can easily escape our homes.

When a chimney is not clean, things such as creosote (a flammable tar) are generally built up on the inside of the chimney flute and can lead down the path to the scenario described earlier where, at BEST, the fire department is at your home putting out a chimney fire.

So, how is this type of situation prevented?

Quite simply? By having your chimney swept once per year.

A chimney sweep's job is to remove built-up creosote, soot, and other blockages from the inside of your chimney.

By doing this, you are not only preventing an obvious fire hazard but also increasing the efficiency of the chimney itself.

If you have not had your chimney swept in more than a year, I would suggest having it done in the fall (before the time of the year when it typically gets its most use).

From a maintenance perspective, the ideal time to get on the schedule would be to have your chimney swept every spring when there is usually less of a wait.

This is NOT something that should be played around with, however.

If your chimney has not been swept in a while, it REALLY is imperative to do it before winter arrives.

Otherwise, you may be relaxing in the warmth of your home on a cooler day when you start to hear popping and cracking coming from your chimney and the sure-to-follow chaos that could have been prevented by merely having your chimney cleaned.

If you or someone you know would like to have a discussion about cleaning your chimney, please feel free to reach out to us, and we would be happy to have the conversation with you.

When is the Best Time of Year to Clean Out Your Gutters?

As fall creeps in across New England, I believe many would agree it is truly a blessing to be able to take in the beauty of the colorful foliage that takes shape in the process. The gorgeous patterns of brilliant autumn colors can absolutely be a breathtaking sight to anyone who is able to take them in. With this annual passage of seasons comes another yearly event that is typically not as pleasant.

As these magnificent leaves begin to fall, they end up in every place imaginable (if you have ever had the pleasure of manually raking leaves for any length of time, I am sure you would agree!).

Among the places where folks really would prefer the leaves, NOT land, is in the gutter systems of our homes and businesses.

Although this can be a fairly preventable thing to occur by utilizing an appropriate gutter debris protection system (I personally recommend the GutterBrush system), if this type of system is not in place, one should have a plan for cleaning out all of this annoying buildup!

The big question obviously would be, "When is the best time of year to clean out your gutters?" Believe it or not, the answer may not be clear-cut.

If a gutter debris protection system is not in place, I recommend cleaning out your gutter systems twice per year, once in the fall and once in the spring.

I also recommend not simply picking out the leaves that may have fallen inside the gutter systems. I believe that the gutter systems should be flushed each time the gutters are cleaned out as well.

The gutter system can be flushed by running water through the gutter system through the use of a garden hose.

It is EXTREMELY important to make sure that the water flows freely through the downspouts and any clogs that may exist are freed up and removed entirely—even if it means completely disassembling the downspouts in order to do so.

Timing can be challenging as sometimes the leaves are not completely down until sometime in December when overnight temperatures can make it a bit more difficult to flush the systems if any moisture in the gutters freezes the leaves together.

Ideally, temperatures should be at least in the forties when cleaning and flushing your gutter system is done.

In the spring, temperatures are less of a concern as things are trending warmer at that time.

It is important to clean and flush the gutter systems in the spring in order to free up any debris that may have been collected over the winter.

Staying on top of the functionality of your gutter systems is critical, as blockages in the system can often cause water to back up into your home or business and possibly create a substantial amount of damage—sometimes even leading to an insurance claim!

The Magical Leak

If you live in New England, the chances are that you have experienced a Nor'easter, even if you have not realized it at the time.

A Nor'easter is a very unique wind and precipitation weather phenomenon.

Most often in New England, our "stormy" weather approaches from the south/western area.

With Nor'easters, the storm approaches from the north/eastern area.

Even in New England, when the term 'Nor'easter' is heard, it is most often associated with snow events.

As rare as Nor'easters are, a Nor'easter being a rain event is even more of a distinct occurrence.

When Nor'easters arrive, if rain aligns with them in some capacity, they can test the structures that are built for our homes and businesses in ways they are not normally tested.

Because of this, "magical" leaks, water stains, etc., often appear out of nowhere.

Throughout my time in the home improvement industry, I have had numerous conversations with people who call into our offices and (paraphrasing) say, "I have this weird leak; it does not happen every time it rains, only during certain rain storms when the wind may be blowing the rain in a certain way."

Usually, this mysterious leak will only show its face during a Nor'easter, and it could possibly be VERY challenging to figure out where it is coming from.

Even if the general area where the leak is stemming from is able to be nailed down and a normal water test is done (where the area is saturated by a garden hose in an attempt to pinpoint the leak), the leak may not be able to be found because of the absence of the wind conditions that often happen with a Nor'easter.

These types of leaks are often the most difficult to correct. If the point of entry is not identified, the leak obviously cannot be fixed.

The "natural" test that needs to be done may only happen any time a Nor'easter rolls through.

You can imagine the accomplishment one must feel when one of these types of leaks is actually neutralized!

Do You Need Surgery?

Well, now, it seems like it is quite a personal question to ask, doesn't it?!?!

In this case, though, I am referring to if you may need surgery on your home.

I was on the phone recently with someone who had surgery to repair a long-hindering challenge with their back.

It not only affected their overall mobility, as the issue affected their sciatic nerve as well as their back, but it also had a HUGE influence over the quality of their everyday life.

I asked them how they were feeling sometime after they got out of surgery, and their response was, "I have no pain in my back or legs. First time in thirteen years, at least. I have walked the corridors. You wouldn't recognize my walk. I am walking how I walked years ago. I am so looking to become who I was again."

I think you would agree; that must be an overwhelmingly powerful feeling.

When they said this to me, I started thinking (which is usually a dangerous thing...) that this seems pretty similar to what I have noticed many of our clients feel about their homes over the years.

Obviously, someone's health is drastically different in the grand scheme of things than the place where someone may live, but believe it or not, a similar overwhelmingly powerful feeling can occur when something that has been nagging at you for years is finally repaired or replaced at your home.

Maybe it is that stress crack stemming from the top of that door that has been eating away at your insides every time you look at it.

Maybe your gut turns inside out every time you pull into the driveway and stare at that peeling paint all across the side of your home.

Maybe you feel like you get electric shocks to your heart every time you hear it start to rain because your roof is leaking from somewhere, and you just cannot seem to figure out why.

Whatever the case, and there are tons of examples, when the day comes that any of these types of things do get corrected, you will most likely feel a tremendous load lifted off your shoulders.

Similar to the example of the surgery relieving years of built-up demoralization with their physical health, correcting things needing to be repaired around the home, no matter how large or small, can have a comparable effect on oneself once the repairs are completed, and you are allowed to breathe SO much easier!

How to Save the Destruction of Your Home for $2.87...

Ok, so maybe the headline is a bit drastic, but believe it or not, it is not too far off!!

Over time, we have come across a variety of damage on people's homes—some monumental—that could have been prevented for $2.87 or less.

I just got off the phone with a local paint store and asked them how much it costs to buy a good tube of caulk; after tax, the total was $2.87.

Knowing that prices vary, whatever the actual cost may be, this puny investment could potentially save thousands upon thousands of repair costs in the future.

The old saying goes, "An ounce of prevention is worth a pound of cure." This is absolutely 110% correct when it comes to preventing major certain types of catastrophes from occurring in our homes.

This one tube of caulk, if used properly, can guard your home against two of its most vicious predators—water damage and insect damage.

The two are actually VERY closely related.

The most destructive insects that attack your home (carpenter ants and termites) tend to destroy areas of it in their quest for moisture.

The easiest places for insects to find moisture are areas that have rotted out, are in the process of rotting out, or are retaining moisture and getting ready to begin to rot out.

Moisture often creeps in from areas on the exterior trim of your home that are not properly sealed.

The most notorious culprits are gaps around doors and windows and the corner boards on your home—though rot is not solely synonymous with these areas of trim alone.

By caulking gaps in these areas, moisture is prevented from getting behind them and beginning to rot things out and attract wood-eating insects.

One of the many unfortunate characteristics of rot is that it tends to rot from the inside out.

In other words, by the time rot is discovered, it is often waaay too late to correct things without some type of significant investment of time, energy, and money!

A while back, in East Greenwich, RI, we ended up taking down and reconstructing a three-story bump-out on a home that was less than twenty years old due to water damage that occurred simply because the contractor who installed the exterior window trim never caulked the trim as he was putting it in place around the windows.

Just recently, we have been working on a home in East Providence, RI, that has multiple areas of rot and associated ACTIVE carpenter ant and termite damage, all resulting in some major structural defects needing to be corrected around the home!

I could go on and on...

The crux of each example is the same, though—easily avoidable, astronomical damage that could have been prevented by investing $2.87 in a tube of caulk.

What is Home Improvement Serendipity?

One definition of serendipity is when you unexpectedly, but fortunately, discover something by accident.

Over time, I have heard numerous examples of this in all walks of life.

Perhaps the most amazing instances of serendipity occur in the medical field.

We have all heard various stories about this type of situation.

A while back, one of our employees was shopping in a retail store when his son somehow got hit in the head with a bike.

Our employee took his son to the emergency room, very upset at what had happened.

When they arrived, and his son went through testing, something did not seem right to the doctors examining him.

They did a bit deeper testing and ended up finding a cyst on his brain.

This may be an extreme case in point, but it is a powerful showcase of serendipity.

If his son never got hit in the head with the bike, they may never have found the potentially deadly growth on our employee's son's head.

Today, he is perfectly fine, in high school, and doing exceptionally well.

When it comes to home improvement, we run into serendipity all the time.

We actually had two recent instances of this!

In one case, we were scheduled to replace a piece of crown molding high up near a roofline.

In order to get a better view of the crown molding, our guys went up on the roof above it.

When they did so, they ended up finding several punctures in the rubber roof above the crown molding.

If the crown molding never rotted, the punctures may have gone undetected for a long time to come.

In another situation, we were at another site replacing what appeared to be a piece of rotted soffit, and we found severe structural damage to beams behind it.

Again, if we never pulled back the soffit, the structural damage could very well have gone unnoticed until, literally, the house fell down.

Could something around your home be setting itself up for serendipity? I would say, quite possibly!!

The next time you see a piece of trim rotting out, or maybe a water stain pop out of nowhere, try to look at it as a positive sign, for you never know what will be found when closely probing into this area that happened to catch your attention in the first place!

Are Doorbells Falling by Way of Shutter??

_____

Over time, things that were SUPER purposeful during one time period may fade away into obsoleteness, to the point where they may be really cool to look at but don't serve much purpose beyond that.

One example of this in our homes would be the shutters many of us have hanging on our exteriors.

Where once upon a time, these shutters were tremendously useful in guarding windows from approaching storms, today, I would venture to say that north of 95% of the shutters we see are not functional at all.

The shutters are still nice attributes on homes, as many think (as do I) that they look really pretty when utilized in an appropriate capacity.

If we look around us, not only could we probably find things in a variety of areas of life that fall under this same umbrella, but we may also find things that are in the process of (for lack of a better term) working through a similar fate.

What comes to mind for me in this regard would be the doorbell.

As I have had the fortunate opportunity to visit hundreds of homes over the years, I have met people and discussed various projects with them, and I have also rang hundreds of doorbells.

Even before the advent of smartphones and similar advances in modern technology, I have noticed that only a portion of doorbells on homes today are actually operational in the first place.

If you are reading this and your doorbell does not work, I assure you that you are not alone.

We have helped numerous folks over the years get their broken doorbells back up and running.

Instead of fixing them, because of the intricacy of a wired doorbell, many years ago, people began to shift to doorbells that worked off a radio frequency.

I was one of these people until, of course, the neighborhood kids discovered that several of us on the same street had the same type of radio frequency doorbell and that when one doorbell was rung, all of us would come out at once to answer the door.

Apparently, they thought this was funny (can't say that I blame them!) and used to ring one of these such doorbells and then hide, sometimes repeatedly, so they could get everyone coming to run and answer the door at once.

The most modern versions of doorbells include features that alert us on our smartphones when someone rings the bell, and they can then see who it is on video, along with a bunch of other bells (no pun intended) and whistles that can make them super fancy.

I enjoy having a working, hard-wired doorbell in my home. It could be just me, though. I would be the type of person who would love fully functional shutters in their home as well!

The reality of life today, however, seems to be that people use the doorbell as a thing of the past.

(Incidentally, I used to get annoyed when people would honk the horn trying to get someone to come outside; this is pretty much a thing of the past as well!)

With smartphones gaining steam in almost every aspect of our lives, a quick call or a text message often takes the place of the use of the doorbell. I expect this trend to continue…

Nowadays, when the doorbell is rung, people seem to get quickly on their toes as it just MUST be somebody trying to survey them or sell them something, correct??

Obviously, I could be incorrect, but my take on the situation is that as useful as doorbells once were, today they are heading toward the land of purely decorative features that no longer are relied upon to do what we once relied on them heavily to do—seemingly very much in line with the 'shutter'!

Does Your Gutter System Have Seams?

———————

To a degree, I would expect any property owner that has gutter systems in their home or business to believe the question as to whether or not their gutter system has seams to be a bit rhetorical.

After all, assuming someone is at least a little bit cognizant of gutter systems, they sure could quickly think/reply, "Of course, my gutter system has seams, silly!"

In theory, they would be correct.

The definition of a seam (according to the Google Dictionary) in the case of gutter systems would be "a line where two pieces of wood, wallpaper, or another material (components of a gutter system) touch each other."

Technically, any place where a gutter system has any type of cut and is joined together would constitute a seam.

Examples of this with regard to a gutter system could be their endcaps and inside and outside corners (or "miters" if a particular run of a gutter system might have them). I usually consider these places a "given."

When I ask the question of whether a gutter system has seams or not, I am most often referring to longer stretches of gutter that have had multiple straight runs of gutter spliced together to make the entire run vs. having a long, seamless run.

As with many facets of construction, the fewer seams you are able to have when constructing something, the better.

In the case of gutters, every single seam that exists presents an opportunity for a leak at some point in the future.

Seams that exist on endcaps and miters are unavoidable.

Optimally, seams that are part of longer gutter runs that have been spliced together should be eliminated, if possible, the next time the gutter system has passed through the course of its useful life and is ready to be changed out to a new one.

In the meantime, I believe it is important to periodically check all of the seams of your gutter system to make sure they are not leaking.

One of the biggest sources of rotted wood and peeling paint we find on people's homes are areas behind seams on gutters that have sprung a leak over a period of time.

Although a relatively easy thing to keep intact, if you do not even realize that your gutter system has seams, it is obviously going to be a bit challenging to stay on top of.

Are You Unintentionally Making it Difficult for Your Home to Breathe?

_____

Believe it or not, all of our homes need to be able to breathe.

In other words, they have to be able to allow moisture to escape from the inside of the home to the outside of the home.

Sometimes, people are really well-intentioned, but their actions for doing what they believe to be positive things may have unintended, damaging consequences.

The negative effects of some of these types of "improvements" that I am referring to, can be something as simple as paint peeling prematurely on the exterior of the home to something as overwhelming as creating an environment that is ripe for rapid mold growth on the interior of the home.

Sometimes when painting the exterior, one might be tempted to caulk in between any gaps amidst their shingle siding or in a gap where the butts of their clapboard siding may meet the course of clapboard below it.

While cosmetically, this certainly could look "nicer," the adverse effect of doing this type of thing would be the siding of the house would then effectively be sealed tight.

If this occurs, when moisture attempts to pass to the outside of the home through the exterior walls, it will have no natural egress point and gradually force its way through the paint coating on the front face of the shingle or clapboard. I know this because many moons ago, this happened to me.

One time, while believing I was doing something in the best interest of the client, I had our crew caulk all the gaps on the underside of the clapboard siding of this one particular home.

The home looked GORGEOUS. Not a gap to be found ANYWHERE!! Which was great until the siding paint started peeling everywhere, and I had no choice but to correct the problem by tearing out all the caulking we had worked so hard to put in and painstakingly prepping and repainting the siding.

Sometimes, we learn the hard way.

I have seen the even more drastic version of tightening up one's home earlier this year.

Our client had done what they thought was a good thing.

They vinyl-sided the exterior, changed out all the windows, and put a new roof on (without any type of venting, but a new roof on nonetheless).

The house looked BEAUTIFUL. The end result, however, was dramatic mold growth throughout the home's entire interior.

The home was sealed up so tight, and in this particular case, only utilized for certain periods of the year, that mold grew enormously quick and heartily in so many places.

It was gut-wrenching to see.

The way that I ended up advising to correct things was installing roof venting, ripping out all the ceiling on the main portion of the interior, getting rid of all the mold (including moldy insulation), installing exterior soffit venting, installing insulation baffles in between the roof rafters after the ceiling had been taken down, re-insulating, putting a new ceiling up, and using mold resistant paint systems wherever we could possibly use them.

In other words, quite an extensive and expensive procedure.

I understand that reading these couple of examples might stimulate certain types of intimidation when thinking of your next home improvement project.

While I would appreciate this sentiment, there is no reason to be hesitant about doing any type of home improvement project that you may already have lined up.

I do recommend being super-cognizant, however, of the methodology of things being done and to follow up and make sure that they are done with the intent of allowing your home to continue to breathe the same, if not better than it is breathing already.

Does Your Property Have Proper Drainage?

Perhaps one of the biggest nightmares of any property owner is taking on any type of unwanted water to the inside of their property.

There are a seemingly infinite number of ways in which this can occur,

The roof may need replacing

There may be some type of flashing challenge

A pipe could have burst, etc…

One potentially damaging way that is preventable is to make sure that your property is set up to drain properly.

If exterior moisture is not directed away from any building, there is a good possibility that, over time, water can infiltrate areas you would rather not.

In New England, this most often means the basement, though this obviously is not necessarily always the case.

If exterior moisture is not draining properly, it could absolutely back up into your property from higher-up areas as well (from the roof to any point downward!).

So, what are some examples of things that can lead to water not being shed correctly from the property? I thought you would never ask…?

A gutter system not operating as it should is due to:

- Improper pitch

- Downspout connections that are not properly set up

- The system itself draining into an underground drain system that has somehow been compromised

- The landscaping is not set up to properly shed water away from the property

- The landscaping HAD been properly set up, but some type of issue occurred that changed the landscape and, subsequently, its ability to shed water (a fallen tree, a retaining wall getting hit by a car, etc.)

If water is not appropriately guided away from your property, the chances drastically increase that some type of ensuing damage can occur.

Immediate and gradual harm are both definite possibilities!!

Some drainage corrections can be quick, easy, and inexpensive (such as a loose downspout that needs to be tightened up).

Other drainage corrections can take a while to do, are fairly complex, and require a good-sized investment (such as correcting the overall landscape of a property).

Of course, there are also tons of examples that are in between!

Whatever the case may be, water that drains properly away from your property greatly reduces easily avoidable future moisture damage headaches.

The Wonderful World of Exterior Door Finishes

One of the more interesting things I learned to appreciate when venturing into the home improvement industry was how much pride people took in the appearance of their exterior doors—particularly their front ones!

I learned REALLY quickly just how important a feature these were to the majority of the homeowners I began to work with.

The exterior door finishes (again, most specifically, the front doors) seemed to be a reflection of the homeowner's personality.

Sometimes, it may only be a matter of color.

Recently, we worked with a client who was simply in love with the color red when it came to accenting things around her home.

Not just any color red, however, but the color red that those big plastic cups we all often see at parties.

This particular client masterfully incorporated this specific red in key places around her home, including her front door.

I will absolutely admit that she utilized this color perfectly and that using this red as her front door color could not have made more sense.

Another recent client had a stunning wood door that had an exceptionally old finish, which had certainly seen better days.

We had our top wood refinisher work on it, and he was able to restore it beautifully to a super impressive finish!

The client could not have been more genuinely happy for what transpired as their front door regained its prominence as the centerpiece of a gorgeously restored rural home.

Still, another example of a modern finish on exterior front doors was a hybrid new door/older door combination of a home we had recently been working on.

The door finishes seemed to be the cherry on top of the sundae, as the client elected to go with a super high gloss black finish that eventually led to stunning finishes rivaling the appearance of mirrors.

These finishes solidified the vibe of the home's exterior, bringing home a project that was a bit of a renaissance in combining new with old and further allowing older portions of the home to be sewn together seamlessly with newer portions of it.

Whether you live in the middle of the city, deep in the woods, or right on the ocean, picking the correct front door finish can allow your personality to show through in a nuanced manner, where anyone who passes by your home might not have a choice but to notice!

Painting Brick Foundations

"Why would anyone ever want to paint a brick foundation??"

I have been asked this question many times in the past.

The answer to me is no different than why someone would want to paint natural cedar siding, redwood trim, or vinyl siding, for that matter—because they enjoy the way it looks!!

Painting brick is a bit different than painting wood.

Repainting a previously painted brick foundation is different than painting a new brick foundation.

The methodology is a bit different.

In terms of a brick foundation that has been painted before, my suggested approach would be:

- Be super cognizant if the coatings on the brick may contain lead paint or not; if they do, all applicable lead prep precautions should be utilized

- Wash the areas that you are aiming to paint with the appropriate solution

- Be sure that all mortar joints in and around each brick are sound and NOT loose or crumbling

- Scrape any peeling paint (in many circumstances, a wire brush would work best to do this)

- Prime any bare, cracking, or overly glossy area with the proper latex primer

- Finish coat with 1-2 coats of a good quality waterborne paint

As with many types of home improvement-oriented items, prepping and painting a new or non-previously painted brick foundation could be accomplished through a variety of different methods, depending on whom you are asking; here is what I would do:

- Make sure the surfaces being focused on are clean

- Treat all areas that are to be painted with a coat of masonry conditioner (this helps better adhere the paint finishes to the brick)

- Be sure that all mortar joints are tight and there are no loose or failing areas (properly address them if there are)

- Carefully and thoroughly finish coat all areas with two coats of a good quality waterborne paint

Whether it is a previously painted foundation or one that has never seen a coating before, there are many folks who LOVE the look of a painted foundation.

Contrary to many myths one might hear, it is perfectly ok to paint your brick foundation—as long as it is done correctly.

Gutter Trough Copper Repairs

Upon hearing the words 'Gutter Trough Copper Repairs,' you might think what you are about to read next may be boring/not interesting, and you might even stop reading further... unless, of course, you are one of the unique individuals who has a gutter trough system on their home, that has been searching near and far for someone to fix it, with absolutely no success whatsoever... then, you may be focused on reading what was next perhaps more than you ever have focused when you were reading before...

Gutter trough systems are rare finds these days, and they are hardly ever built on newer structures.

They were, however, pretty prevalent at one point in time and served the same purpose as modern aluminum gutter and downspout systems serve today.

One of the bigger differences between the more historic nature trough systems and today's modern systems is that the old trough systems are part of the structure themselves, whereas today's systems are separate entities attached to the structures.

Being part of the structure makes repairs on them very challenging as, in my mind, there is only one way to do them correctly.

Sometimes, people elect to eliminate the trough systems altogether and convert to more modern systems. There is nothing necessarily wrong with this (unless, of course, you ask a preservationist...), but if this is done, it definitely eliminates some of the original character of the building you are doing it to.

Sometimes, people try to "patch" these trough systems with "lexonite," roof cement, or some other type of patching material.

Still, other times, people try to take shortcuts in repairs that they believe "should do the trick"—lining the trough system with rubber, aluminum panning, or even lead-coated copper panning.

I have a family member in the Navy who travels all over the country inspecting different factories where components for submarines are manufactured.

In a conversation about how cool it must be to see what he sees, he agreed, and although he could not really go into detail (for obvious reasons), he said that there are some components that cannot really be improved beyond the way they were first developed decades and decades ago and are still made that same way to this day.

Lining these trough systems, I believe, falls under this category.

I am a firm believer that the correct way to line these wooden trough systems is with copper panning, specifically made for that specific trough system.

There are a few around that do this correctly. We are fortunate that this is a niche we have become quite well known for over the years, as our coppersmith hails from a family of coppersmiths that has done the trough systems for generations.

Although certainly not something that is seen every day, it is beyond fulfilling to be able to help someone who did not think they were going to be able to ever find anyone who was not only capable of restoring their wooden trough system to what it once was but to do so in a manner that would allow it to be fully functional for years to come.

What is Behind that Drop Ceiling?

I am fairly certain that the majority of people reading this have seen a drop ceiling in the past.

There is also the possibility that you have even seen them before and not recognized what you were looking at was a drop ceiling.

Drop ceilings (or 'acoustical ceilings' or 'suspended ceilings' as they are often also referred to) are usually utilized to provide a ceiling below the "main" ceiling while at the same time providing relatively easy access to the piping, wires, etc. (what we in the trades often reference as 'mechanicals') behind it.

Sometimes, drop ceilings are hung simply to lower the overall ceiling height for energy efficiency purposes (with the idea that there would now be less space to heat or keep cool).

On some occasions, drop ceilings are hung simply to hide a not-so-cosmetically appealing main ceiling. Drop ceilings are found in people's homes and in commercial buildings as well.

Perhaps you may even have one in your own home!

In the week leading up to me writing this piece, we worked on drop ceilings in someone's home and a commercial one.

In the home version, we were hired to remove the existing drop ceiling frame below the "mechanicals" and install a new "regular" ceiling in its place.

In the commercial version we removed an existing drop ceiling for the Omni Hotel in Providence, RI, allowed for the installation of a new air conditioning unit, and then replaced it with a new drop ceiling below it.

There is nothing that necessarily says that someone "has to" have a drop ceiling (or a "regular" ceiling, for that matter) in their home or business.

Drop ceilings are often convenient, particularly when there is a lot of piping or wiring attached to the main ceiling that is not that pleasant to look at.

A drop ceiling can potentially be much more pleasing to the eye than having to stare at a bunch of piping or wiring while at the same time allowing you to access the piping and/or wiring if you ever needed to in an emergency or just to rework these areas.

Whatever the reason for having a drop ceiling, having one installed by a professional might be the best way to go—although you can absolutely do it yourself!!

How to Know Which Colors to Pick for Your Home

One year, many moons ago, we had a booth at a couple of local home shows, and I was trying to come up with an idea for a theme for the booth.

I stumbled across a book at a paint store titled 'What Does Your Birthday Color Say About You?'

Brilliant!! I decided to build the booth around that theme.

I had bought two copies of that little book, and I probably could have bought many more as the book turned out to spark many conversations about color.

Color is one of the most critical components in home improvement.

Whether it is interior or exterior painting, roofing, or even accent features for your home, the colors around your home are a way for you to express who you are.

There are so many ways in which color can be used to make your home feel modern, comfortable, and truly like YOUR home.

Sometimes, people are very confident in picking colors on their own.

Other times, they feel good about doing it, but they appreciate someone's outside opinion as to whether they are heading in the correct direction.

Still, other times, people are, often admittedly, completely clueless about what color to pick for whatever it is they are looking to do.

No matter where they stand on this scale when we work with them, we always make a color consultant available to aid in color selection at no additional cost to them.

If someone wanted to hire a consultant on their own, they can obviously certainly do so.

If choosing to hire outside help with regard to color consulting, my suggestion is to ask your local paint or hardware store for a reputable referral.

The color consultant may also happen to be an interior designer but does not necessarily have to be.

If choosing to hire a color consultant, good ones typically start at $75/ hour or higher.

Whether hiring someone to help in color selection for your project or working through the variety of colors available on your own, choosing a color for whatever it is you are doing may actually be the most challenging part of your ENTIRE project.!

Have you Ever Smooshed a Plant?

If you work around the exterior of your home fairly regularly, your chances of unintentionally causing some type of collateral damage are probably pretty decent.

As a company that typically works on a good number of homes on a week-ly basis, in the "good" weather months of the year, we are no exception to this.

As careful as we aim to be and coach our people in the field, the obvious risk of inadvertently smooshing a plant, damaging a bush, or clipping a tree is constantly there.

Once in a while, this type of situation occurs.

Admittedly, I have most likely the least green thumb on the planet.

On occasion, when one of our staff damages some type of vegetation at a client's, we have an action plan in place for what to do.

The first thing we do is sincerely apologize to the client as we truly do not mean to ever harm anything in their yard and feel extraordinarily awful every time it happens.

Whether it was an extremely meaningful plant or one that is a dime-a-dozen perennial that is just kind of "there," we do not enjoy this experience at all nor having the conversation that has to be had with the client afterward.

The next thing we do, assuming the client is OK with us helping to rectify things, is get on the phone with one of the landscapers we work with.

From there, the landscaper will typically come out, evaluate what hap-pened, and then perhaps even reach out to one of the nurseries they work with for suggestions.

The vast majority of the time, all is not lost, and the plant is able to be salvaged.

In the cases where the plant does have to be replaced, our landscaper will still use their expertise to salvage the planting while adding another one of the same types in its space.

It seems that most often, the type of plant that we run into (no pun intend-ed…) is a perennial that normally returns on a yearly basis.

If this is the type of plant that sustained the damage, our landscaper will either stabilize it as best they can for the rest of the growing season or cut it back as one would usually prune it at the end of the fall or the beginning of the spring.

Whether you or a professional working around your home happens to accidentally damage any plant life that is growing around it, as frustrating and deflating as the incident can be, more often than not, there is something that can be done to treat the plant and make sure that it will be able to mend itself.

How Valuable is that Old Ladder?

A HUGE number of homeowners have ladders lying around their homes in one place or another.

Some are constantly used.

Some may be used once per year.

Some may just be sitting around collecting dust, with the intention of being used, but never end up being utilized for anything.

Whatever the case may be, there may come a point in time in a ladder's life when the decision is made to find a new owner for the ladder.

If this time comes, there could be some questions as to what amount of money makes sense to sell the ladder for.

Being fortunate enough to be in the home improvement industry, we are in a position where we are constantly buying ladders and have formulated a pretty good sense as to what a ladder is worth.

Over time, as I have seen ladders for sale, I have noticed that they are placed for sale all over the price scale.

Now, I am sure that this may certainly be true with whatever used item is being sold anywhere.

I thought it might be useful though, if perhaps I shared what we generally thought of as fair prices for ladders we generally deem best to go after.

I preface this by saying we do not use wooden ladders at all.

We also do not use aluminum stepladders whatsoever.

Here would be what I believe to be the most fair pricing with the corresponding most common kind of ladders that we generally go after (it should be noted that these are regardless of ladder type—Type I, IA, II, etc.):

- 6' Step (fiberglass): $25
- 8' Step (fiberglass): $50
- 24' ladder (aluminum or fiberglass): $100
- "Little Giant" (aluminum, all sizes): $100
- 32' ladder (aluminum or fiberglass): $150
- 40' ladder (aluminum or fiberglass): $200

Obviously, there are a lot more potential ladder options out there, and these are just the most common ones.

Do you have an old ladder sitting around the house, collecting dust, that you have no idea who might be willing to buy it from you?

Well, if you do get stuck, we would most likely be willing to take it off your hands.

Heck, now you even know what we would be willing to pay you for it!!

What in the WORLD is the Purpose of Shutters?

Many of us have shutters on the exterior of our homes.

I'm sure many of us—correctly, I might add—also assume that once upon a time, shutters were pretty commonplace and used to protect windows during various types of bad weather.

With the advent of modern technology, what once was a very useful fixture on the exterior of our home has become obsolete to a degree.

In the place of protection from shutters, the dramatic improvement of the sturdiness of windows, the introduction of storm window systems, and other advances have gradually made shutters a non-factor when it comes to protection from storms.

This is so much so that actual functional shutter systems that remain from a time when they WERE extraordinarily useful are still maintained in many capacities because of their aesthetics.

Believe it or not, this is pretty much the only purpose for any type of shutter these days.

Even if they are fully functional, I'm not sure if I have ever seen anyone over the twenty-five years I have been in business use them as protection from an approaching storm.

These days, shutters are typically made out of vinyl or plastic, though there are quite a number of wood shutters bought and installed on a yearly basis.

These shutters are purely decorative, as they often add an accent color to the home.

When they are in someone's home, they are always (with VERY few exceptions) hung on the front of the home.

Many times, they are also hung on whatever side is visible from the street.

Not as common, but still done, are when someone hangs the shutters all the way around their home.

For someone who would like to get ultra-creative (and does not mind making a bit of an investment), wood shutters with custom wood "cut-outs" can be done that reflect the personality of the client.

We had a client spend in excess of $8000 not too long ago to have new wood shutters made with a custom "cut-out" of an anchor. He was a person who loved being on the water and captaining his own boat. The shutters were placed all around his home.

Although once upon a time, they were an extraordinarily useful component to a home's storm defense system, today, they are, in well above 99% of occasions, used as decorative pieces to liven up the exterior look of your home.

The Evils of Using Tape on Home Improvement Projects!

When embarking on any number of a variety of home improvement projects, the pull (no pun intended!) to use tape in different capacities can be pretty great.

Many contractors (including ourselves) even use it as a safety net to help protect different types of surfaces.

There are so many different applications for tape, as well as types of tape, on the marketplace, and it can be a little confusing when to use it, when not to use it, and when using it, what type of tape to use.

- Tape can be used to aid in the protection of adjacent surfaces when painting or staining.
- Tape can be used to help stabilize different types of floor protection (resin paper, Ram Board, etc.) when protecting floors that you are working around.
- Tape can be used to protect exterior surfaces in a whole diverse fashion as well.

It definitely seems like there are tons and tons of uses for tape in home improvement.

What type of tape is best recommended for whatever project you are working on will certainly vary—especially these days when there are so many choices to choose from on the market.

What one has to be ultra-proactive about when using tape, perhaps more so than anything else, would be the surfaces the tape is being applied to and what lays beneath these specific surfaces.

Recently, we experienced this important factor in a couple of different projects we were working on.

It was essentially floating on the plaster!

Until something like the tape is attached to it and pulling on it is done, it may never be tested, and one might never know that the coating that the tape is attached to is not bonded correctly.

Once the tape pulls that paint off, things can certainly be fixed (and we did that); it is just a total pain in the neck to do so.

Another recent time when we had a significant challenge with tape was while protecting floors while working on a major repair project.

We used tape to tape down Ram Board to hardwood floors throughout the home.

When the tape and Ram Board were taken up, the tape pulled up the polyurethane that it was attached to all the way to the bare hardwood floor underneath it.

Just as in the paint example, the surface that the tape was taped to had an adhesion issue associated with it. In this case, the polyurethane was not correctly used when the floors were initially coated.

The floors (most likely pre-finished when they were originally put in, possibly not, though) should never so easily have their polyurethane ripped up simply by having tape on them.

Just as in the paint example, this can be fixed, and we have been in the process of doing so. It is absolutely not a fun thing to have to do, though.

In both of these cases, it is not the tape's fault.

Nor do I believe it is necessarily our staff's fault, as the intent to protect was in the right place.

The actual action occurred because the surfaces the tape was attached to were not correctly done when they were originally painted and polyurethaned, respectively.

Where we did err is by actually trusting the surfaces the tape was attached to in the first place.

Although the tape that you may be using is a great quality tape, and it may be being used in the correct application, if the surfaces that the tape is being attached to are not entirely sound and bonded all the way through to their original substrate (plastered wall, bare wood floor, etc.), you may have a similar challenge on your hands that we had the unfortunate experience of recently going through.

Using tape to help protect areas while doing home improvement work is altruistic and obviously well-intended; however, it is extremely important to be conscious of what type of surface the tape is being attached to and the potential problems that may exist while doing so.

Tips for Cleaning Your Walls

Most people are generally aware that they are supposed to clean their floors, windows, and furniture fairly regularly, but they don't always show the same kind of attention to their walls.

You may have hired some of the best house painters in Rhode Island to give your home's walls a fresh coat of paint. Obviously, it would make sense then that you would want them to look their best.

It is not uncommon for homes to have walls covered in fingerprints, marks from a child's crayon, or any other blemishes that seem to appear randomly.

Part of the reason why so many homeowners don't clean their walls as regularly as they should is because they may not know how to go about it. While you can always hire professionals (such as us at LOPCO Contracting) to take care of your walls when they get really bad, perhaps considering these tips may be helpful if you desire to keep them even reasonably clean...

Clean Fingerprints as They Appear

One of the best ways to keep your walls clean is to tackle any fingerprints or other marks as soon as you notice them. Painted walls can generally be cleaned with a soft brush attachment from a vacuum cleaner and wiped clean with a soft cloth or a cloth-covered dust mop. You can spray the dirty wall with a dusting agent or mild detergent for best results, but avoid using TOO much soap and water on most painted walls.

Know Your Finishes

You should know what kind of paint finish is on your walls when it comes time to thoroughly clean them. An eggshell or satin finish—such as what you might find on a living room or bedroom wall—is typically fairly fragile; this being the case, you may not want to scrub at it too harshly with a lot of water or degreasing agent. Wiping away spots with a mildly damp sponge should be enough.

THE CARE AND MAINTENANCE OF A NEW ENGLAND HOME

If a wall has a glossier finish, you can usually get away with using a more harsh degreaser to clean the bigger messes. You may even need it, too, as most glossy paints are used in the kitchen and/or trim and will probably be subject to bigger messes or exposure to dirt and grime. Keep in mind that glossy paint can still scratch, so stick to using soft sponges when you wipe up your messes.

Finally, latex paint can be cleaned with a gentle all-purpose cleaner. Simply wipe down the wall with a mixture of the cleaner and some water with a soft sponge. More troublesome spots, such as areas with plenty of fingerprints, can be cleaned with a paste made from baking soda and water and a non-abrasive cleaning pad.

Why "Natural Finish" Deck Staining is SUCH a Finicky Undertaking

---

When I first got involved in the industry, we had some historically SUPER sweet natural finish deck staining products that were the backbone of many of our deck staining suppliers.

As time progressed, however, I personally have witnessed revolutionary shifts with regard to these types of products, as environmental laws have tightened up and become more restrictive than any of the natural finish deck stain producers could have possibly anticipated.

As this has occurred, normally ultra-reliable "go-to" natural finish deck staining products have seemingly overnight become the source of application issues in the field as well as potential service challenges on the backside of things.

As our industry has done its best to adapt and keep pace with these dramatic shifts, we have done a tremendous amount of trial and error on our end to be able to recommend and put into effect what we believe are the very best natural finish deck staining methodologies for our clients.

Although not perfect and still ever-evolving, I do believe we have (knock on wood) the best systems in place for ensuring that our clients have what is best available in terms of natural finish deck staining technology for each of their absolutely individual deck requirements.

There are many variables when it comes to properly getting a natural finish deck staining job done correctly.

Although it is not able to be controlled, the weather is at the forefront of everything.

We prefer it being bone dry the day before you stain, the day you stain, and the day after you stain.

We try our best to communicate this to our clients.

In New England, with particularly challenging stretches of on-and-off wet weather, we understand that it can be difficult for clients to remain patient as they wait for the ideal time to stain.

Nonetheless, proper weather conditions are VERY important.

Another VERY important thing to pay attention to is the way that the stain is applied.

My recommendation is that the stain should be applied one board at a time, end-to-end, while always maintaining a wet edge.

For best results, we either brush, rag, or brush/rag in tandem with our natural stain applications.

If ragging, be sure to store all used rags in a bucket of water (if you want to know why I say this, feel free to reach out to us and set up some time to chat with me, and I will be happy to fill you in...).

We typically utilize one-coat natural finish deck stains.

Before any product is applied to the deck, the deck should be thoroughly cleaned and prepped to bare wood as best as possible.

If the deck was previously coated, there are a variety of techniques that can be utilized to ensure that the finish you are applying will be as beautiful as ultimately possible.

It is important to note that all horizontal natural stain finished deck surfaces (floors, stairs, and the top of handrails) should receive a maintenance coat, minimally, once every one to three years, depending upon how they weather and a few other factors.

As you can see, natural finish deck staining is not the easiest to plan or execute.

If done correctly, though, your deck can easily be the envy of all who may see it and can be protected to maintain its SWEET-looking state for a long time to come!

What is Lurking Behind YOUR Walls?

One of the areas of one's home that the goings-on within is pretty much completely unknown to every homeowner is that space in between the exterior walls of their home and the interior walls of their home.

This "invisible" area would pretty much never need to be accessed unless, of course, it needs to be accessed.

So when, might you ask, would this area need to be accessed? Great question!!

Once in a while, as unpleasant as it is to think about, an animal may unfortunately pass away and start decomposing within the wall.

You will certainly notice this as a very pungent smell emanates from the wall, and you will probably be scratching your head as you try to figure out where this is coming from.

Another example is sometimes a pipe can develop a leak and start to drip behind the wall.

Depending upon the route the water takes, it may or may not be easy to tell where specifically the leak is coming from, other than "someplace in the wall."

Still, another example is that it might be recognized that something is wrong with the wall itself.

We ran into this recently when a client was about to have some work done on the home, and she noticed her entire wall was swaying back and forth when she pushed on it.

Very unsettling, as well as uncommon, but it does happen!!

In each of these cases, the only way to get to the root of the issue is to open up the wall where it makes the most sense to do so and start investigating.

These types of situations (and I'm sure you can most likely think of more!) are beyond annoying, as not only does the wall have to be opened up, but then the problem has to be eradicated, and then the wall has to be put back together and finished.

As much of a hassle as these circumstances are, they are a necessary evil, so to speak, in terms of taking care of the issues mentioned.

As in the examples above, there could be quite a number of things going on within our walls that we simply would have no idea about until the time came when something grabbed our attention and pushed us to venture into these parts unknown!

Historical Artifact Adventures!

On a recent Friday night, I was on my way home from the shop and trying to figure out what to do.

It was an odd situation as there was some type of mix-up with my 5 pm appointment, all of my most immediate paperwork was seemingly caught up on, and our staff had wrapped things up for the week.

On the home front, everyone apparently had things going on, from school dances to work obligations, etc.

I all of a sudden found myself alone with nothing pressing to do. VERY weird!!

As I was thinking about this, I happened to glance at my phone and noticed a missed call from someone in the community who we typically help out with a wide variety of things.

I called her back, and the next thing you know, I was in the middle of a park in Providence, RI, where we had volunteered much time in the past.

I was there looking at what, to me, appeared to be some type of ancient object.

The massive cast of a being turned out to be an extremely rare, unique type of safe that was utilized decades ago in an old factory that used to stand on the site of the park.

Hence the phone call to me.

When I arrived, we worked on a plan to restore the exterior of the safe as best as possible and to figure out plans to protect it from possible graffiti vandals (an unfortunate necessity with these types of situations).

This is not the first time we have been called in to help restore a neat piece of history.

As another example, we also restored a historic caboose in West Warwick, RI, in the past.

Couple this with the long, storied experience of working on some of the most historic buildings one can find, and I would certainly say that things like this are something I thoroughly enjoy being a part of.

Being called in on a free Friday evening to help with a sweet restoration project like this one is definitely much more appealing to me than most other things I can think of.

Common Historic Restoration Mistakes

We would all love to be able to restore a historic building to its former glory—or at least hire the right historic restoration contractors to do the job—but it's never easy. You're essentially fighting against time itself whenever you're restoring a historic property, and many of the materials and techniques used to build any given historic structure simply might no longer exist. Even the best Rhode Island historic restoration contractors will have their work cut out for them.

Since the historic restoration of any Rhode Island property is always very difficult, mistakes are quite common. Some of these are fairly simple and easy to fix, but others can practically derail a promising restoration project. If you're somehow involved in restoring an old property, here are a few common mistakes that you should avoid.

Choosing the Wrong Paint

Working to be one of the premier painting contractors in Rhode Island, we understand how important it is to choose the correct paint for a project. Unfortunately, many in our industry like to choose "cheaper" paint that works well with a new structure but does not work at all for historic restoration. If it is up to you to choose what kind of paint is going into a historic restoration, we encourage a few extra dollars to buy high-quality paint that will last longer than much "cheaper" products.

Poor Waterproofing

Waterproofing an old building sounds like a great idea, but it can do more harm than good. Many historic buildings were built before modern waterproofing techniques were being widely used, but they were built in such a way that minimizes water damage. They are built from many different materials that intersect at lines of unequal expansion and contraction. Modern waterproofing can eventually force moisture into these lines, and the results can potentially be disastrous.

Using the Wrong Mortar

Failing mortar joints are common in older buildings, so it makes a lot of sense that any restoration project would require contractors to possibly repair brick walls and fireplaces. One problem with this is that much modern mortar is based on Portland cement, while older mortar is lime-based. Portland cement is very hard and doesn't transmit water very easily, which is why it is so popular in modern construction. The challenge is that it does not work well with older bricks. In fact, it can cause these softer bricks to start to deteriorate and cause even more damage to the structure. Portland cement also tends to look different from lime-based cement when it dries, and it often stands out when used in restoration projects.

Historic restoration is far more challenging than people realize, and it is easy to make mistakes.

The right team of house painters and carpenters, however, can do a great job and make even the oldest buildings look like new.

Finding a company that specializes in historic restoration is extremely important if you want the job done right.

Termites, Carpenter Ants, and Other Wood-Boring Insects... Oh My!

When the landscape around your home is saturated with moisture, you will most likely not see these pesky insects as they would have plenty of moisture sources to choose from.

When the sun and its accompanying warmer temperatures eventually return the moisture around people's homes will gradually dry up.

When this happens, these types of insects begin the search for moisture in order to survive.

This quest for moisture often leads them to begin exploring places in and outside of your home itself.

Carpenter ants you will usually see poking around on the outside of your home.

Termites, you will not.

They can absolutely cause an enormous amount of damage before you know what is happening.

Oftentimes, we only happen to stumble upon structural members of our client's homes that are being eaten to pieces after we remove what appears to be just a simple piece of rotted trim wood that needs to be replaced.

There are two major things that can be done to combat these situations:

1) The first is to make sure your home is getting regular treatments of carpenter ant, termite repellent, and the like by either yourself or a professional.

2) The second is to make sure any rotted areas around your home are properly repaired/replaced and that nothing funky is going on behind them.

It is also not a bad idea to caulk trim joints and eliminate potential areas where insects can crawl in behind the trim when journeying for moisture sources.

I can guess with much confidence that we will pretty much all be extraordinarily happy when the sun finally comes back.

It may not be a bad idea, though, to be cognizant of what else may come back as the pleasant weather makes its triumphant return...

When is the Best Time to "Blank"?

It is no wonder people are outside fixing, planting, and replacing things.

I often get asked, "When is the best time of year to _____?" Where "?" it could mean paint. . it could mean replace your roof... it could mean a wide variety of other home improvement-oriented items that are prevalently dependent on the weather being conducive to doing them.

New England being New England, the answer I usually give is that it very much depends on the year.

We have some years that if I looked back on the calendar year on December 31st, the best time to paint the exterior of one's home might have been in February (with the temps happening to be consistently in the 40s, without dropping too frigid at night, and a dry, non-precipitative stretch of weather).

Now, if I generally went around these parts recommending February as the best month to paint the exterior of someone's home, I would most likely get odd stares.

However, the reality of the situation, although rare, could very well have this be the case.

It is often said that if you do not like the weather in New England, wait five minutes.

I TRULY believe this!!

Although the weather currently outside is stunningly magnificent, unfortunately, we are not able to bottle it up and spread it over other periods of the year.

We can play the weather cards as they're dealt to us, though, and keep an open mind in terms of when we aim to get work outside our homes and businesses done—and be EXTREMELY patient with the process.

Gorgeous days like the one we are experiencing now are not easy to come by, particularly in this area over the better part of the last year.

When we do stumble upon nice stretches of weather, it is great to be able to maximize the opportunity to get stuff done outside—whether it be a freakishly nice stretch in February or a terrific day in May that all of us in New England might have been waiting quite some time for!!

Getting Your Home Ready for Spring

If you are at a loss as to how to get started with your spring cleaning, here are a few tips that should hopefully make the process a bit easier…

Start With Your Exterior

The best place to begin your spring cleaning is outside of your home. It's the part of your home that's exposed to the elements, and it has almost certainly taken a beating from some type of harsh winter weather. Take a walk around the outside of your home and see if there is any damage that needs to be repaired. This may include damaged gutters, peeling paint, dented or rotted siding, and anything else that might catch your eye. You should be able to clean off some of the grime that has accumulated with a power washer, but more extensive damage may mean seeking out professional painting and carpentry services.

Check Your HVAC System

You might not need to turn on your AC right now, but you should still get it ready for the hot summer months. Check your air filters and change them if necessary. Clear your main outdoor AC unit of debris and get an HVAC service person into your home to make sure that everything is in good working order.

Start Cleaning Inside

Once your home's exterior and your HVAC system have been addressed, it's time for some interior spring cleaning. Wash all of your windows on the inside and outside, dust off ceiling fans, and clean out your fireplace (if applicable). This is also a great time to take a look at your walls to see where they need to be cleaned and/or re-painted. Cleaning your walls usually involves a soft sponge and very little soap and water, but walls with a glossy paint job or latex paint can be wiped down with a mild degreaser if they're really bad. If you want to repaint your walls, the spring is a great time to do so.

Many would agree that spring is absolutely an EXCITING time of year; a little bit of spring cleaning injected into it (although perhaps not the most fun thing you may do) can often make it an even more enjoyable season!!

Does Your Home Have Hidden Mold?

Probably one of the things that any home or property owner cringes at the thought of as it relates to existing within their living or operating space.

Mold can create a plethora of health challenges.

I, myself, am very fortunate when it comes to health overall, but I am apparently allergic to some rare type of mold that shows itself with exterior climate changes and triggers an annoying cough that sounds absolutely horrible...

It also seems to surface when I am in certain types of buildings for extended periods of time (think at an all-day seminar in a hotel).

Over the past twenty-five years since I have known of the cough's existence, I still have not found a solution for it (and believe me, I have tried seemingly EVERYTHING!).

But if all I get is a nuisance cough out of it, I consider myself lucky.

Some have much more severe reactions to mold.

Now, imagine if a harmful mold were lurking in your home and you were sleeping with it around you every night.

This scenario is not good for healthy people, and never mind if your body is prone to have highly adverse reactions to exposure to certain types of mold, to begin with.

We certainly run into mold in homes and businesses often enough.

Usually, the mold we come across stems its growth from either moisture or humidity.

Mold can begin from a leak that has/had allowed exterior water to come into a home or building for a length of time and congregated in an area that did not allow it to dry properly.

I have seen other instances (one recently) where mold grows with a sudden drastic change in the environment of a building (think an old, uninsulated home that all of a sudden gets vinyl siding installed on its exterior and a new roof put on without any type of proper venting or internal humidity control installed at the same time).

There are quite a number of things that can stimulate mold growth.

If you spot mold and are curious as to whether the mold is potentially harmful, there are companies that can come out and run tests to tell you if the mold should be a cause for concern.

I have found that most folks spotting any type of mold, however, seem to want to mitigate it as soon as possible though and typically could care less about the extent of its 'technical" harm.

The thought of mold anywhere around the home is stomach-turning for the typical home or property owner.

Fortunately, there are a number of ways to combat this uncomfortable phenomenon should it be found, no matter how small or large the issue may be!

How to Stop a Bleeding Knothole

You may have dealt with this before...

A knothole in a piece of wood that you are trying to paint that, no matter what you do to stop it from bleeding through your finish coat, just seems to magically keep reappearing.

Why is this???

In a nutshell, the knothole bleeding through is a result of the sap from the wood continuing to bleed out through the knothole.

As the sap continues to push, the natural resins of the wood begin to stain the topcoat.

What occurs from here is what could be a tiny bit of insanity, as people often try every trick on the planet to contain the bleeding knothole.

Pine is a wood that is notorious for this unsightly phenomenon.

Most of the time, what we have found does the best job of neutralizing the knothole from bleeding, which is a nice dollop of shellac.

Zinsser makes a REALLY fine product for this, and it is their 'BIN' product. This alcohol-based shellac sure does seem to work wonders!

For more stubborn knotholes, I would suggest two coats of BIN

If the knothole is really, really stubborn, my suggestion would be two coats of BIN, followed by one coat of a great oil primer (available from most major paint suppliers).

Few things are more discouraging than having bleeding knotholes pop up on freshly painted surfaces a short time after they are finished coated.

When I first came across this type of failure years ago, I experimented with a number of different products to solve the dilemma.

Through this experimentation, I have found the above-mentioned procedure to be the absolute best way of nullifying the bleed-through.

Perhaps the Best Spring Gardening Tip Ever

Although surely not everyone celebrates, for those that do, Easter is a very special time! Not only for spiritual reasons, but Easter often seems to symbolically run parallel with the beginning of spring.

Although not always the warmest of days, this year, with Easter being a bit later than it often is, folks who garden are most likely well on their way toward situating things in place.

Being a home improvement contractor, I guess gardening is something that somehow can technically fall under the category that our industry envelopes me into.

Honestly, I am probably the last person on the planet who should be offering any type of gardening advice.

My thumb is about as green as a piece of mahogany.

So then, what makes me think I can write a column about the best gardening tip ever?

It's quite simple, actually!!

My best gardening tip ever is to PROTECT your gardens, particularly those with vegetation growing within them that may be particularly yummy for different types of animals passing through your yard.

Whether it be deer, groundhogs, rabbits, etc., properly guarding your hard-earned brewing harvest is of utmost importance.

In fact, if you do not take proper precautions to defend your up-and-coming greenery/vegetation, why even aim to attempt growing things in the first place?

To the veteran growers, this may seem like common sense, but you would be surprised at how many clients we have who are heartbroken by a compromised or destroyed garden that could have easily been safeguarded.

Depending on how your yard/garden is configured, there are a number of ideas that can be found all over the Internet for helping out.

Once in a while, we have a client that hires us to help them construct some type of screening enclosure to help ward off potential vegetative pilferers…

Sometimes, they are simple, sometimes, they can be very complex…

Whether hiring a company like ours to construct some type of protective housing that the architects of Fort Knox would be jealous of or simply utilizing one of the wide variety of home remedy-type suggestions found readily online...

The message is the same... Protect your hard work!!

After all, the feeling of internal fulfillment after gathering a bountiful harvest is MUCH better to have than the feeling of loss after one of our furry friends made off with your tomatoes right before they were fully ripe!!

The Importance of Storm Windows!

With the advancement in window manufacturing technology today, one would think that the traditional storm window market may be falling by the wayside.

This is very much not necessarily true.

Although when folks update the windows on their homes and businesses, they do seem to steer towards windows that do not require storm windows, there are a whole lot of people who still have a need for storm windows.

This is especially true on buildings with older wooden windows, where the property owner enjoys the cosmetics of the older wood windows but needs a little added protection in order to more properly insulate their home, as well as help better preserve the life of their wooden windows.

Storm windows add an element of energy efficiency to people's homes.

Storm windows also protect the exterior-facing portions of the wood windows that they are placed over. By simply having storm windows in place, I believe you triple the life of the paint cycle related to the windows.

In other words, if you paint your home once every ten years, the windows that the storm windows are placed over should not really have to be touched from a repainting standpoint for at least thirty years!

Storm window technology has certainly advanced over time.

The more traditional style of storm windows is still available from storm window manufacturers, but most storm window manufacturers have also developed lines of storm windows that are more robust, more energy efficient, and more easily operable than the conventional models.

Replacing and/or installing storm windows is a part of our business that we truly enjoy doing!

When we replace storm windows with newer ones, we typically greatly improve how well a home retains heat in the winter and keeps cooler in the summer.

We also take comfort in knowing that the storm windows we install will greatly protect the windows we are installing the storm windows over for many years to come!

If you are curious about storm windows and their functionality, or perhaps it may be time to update yours or someone you know, feel free to set up a conversation with us.

Is Composite Trim Truly Maintenance-Free?

_____

When someone replaces rotted wood trim on their home with some type of composite trim, initially, there may be a feeling of satisfaction knowing that what they just installed will never rot on them again.

They may even have a slight feeling of invincibility at first as they may like to believe that what they have done has even created a maintenance-free situation for them.

I believe this to be at least partially true.

Yes, the composite trim that was just installed will not rot on you.

Maintenance free?

Well, that is another story...

It depends what you mean by maintenance free.

Technically, after installing it, you could leave it alone and not have to touch it ever again.

However, depending on the situation, there may actually be a bit more than meets the eye from a maintenance standpoint.

If the rest of the trim on the home is painted, then the majority of folks would elect to paint the composite trim to match.

Some folks may want to paint the composite trim due to the way it may look after the nail holes are filled assuming it is shot in with a nail gun or fastened in such a manner where some type of nail (or screw) is showing.

Or, even if it is fastened with a no-show nail/screw system after it is caulked in place, some may not like the way the caulk appears after it dries.

Composite trim will actually hold paint better than wood trim will.

Composite trim does not hold moisture behind paint coatings as wood trim does, and when painted with the correct system, its coatings will tend to have a tighter bond than a similar system may have to wood trim.

Even if you do not elect to paint it, composite trim may shrink on you over time and may have to be re-caulked.

To properly prep and paint composite trim, I suggest the following:

- Fill nail holes
- Caulk in trim
- Use the appropriate bonding primer
- Apply two coats of a latex/waterborne, high-quality, appropriate grade (exterior/interior) paint product.

After painting it, it really should not peel; it should simply be repainted to freshen its look each time the house is painted going forward.

Composite trim is a WONDERFUL product!

We often use composite trim when we replace rotted wood for clients.

We do typically prep and paint our composite trim after we install it.

Although not absolutely necessary, painted composite trim can be very beneficial to do cosmetically, and after it is painted, it is virtually impossible to tell whether it is a piece of painted composite one is looking at or traditional wood trim.

Proper Exterior Painting Surface Preparation Expectations

Perhaps one of the diciest questions for exterior residential painting contractors to navigate (when asked by a potential exterior painting client) is:

What do you do for surface preparation prior to painting?

This can be such a daunting question to answer for the contractor because there are so many different possibilities in terms of the exact approach, and most well-meaning ontractors want to make sure they are on the same page as the client when it comes to surface preparation expectations.

I believe pretty much everyone can come to an agreement that the way you prepare the surface prior to finishing the coating is going to dictate both.

How long the exterior painting job will last? How good will it look cosmetically?

Over the years, I believe that I have narrowed the approach down to three different categories:

1) The 'Fluff and Buff' approach.

This is where the surface is scraped as best as it possibly can be wherever there are peeling areas. This approach tends to be the most cost-effective but yields the least longevity for the paint job and the least cosmetically appealing of the approaches.

2) The 'Super Solid' approach.

This is where all the peeling areas are scraped, and all blemishes/highs-and-lows are sanded as best as possible with the proper equipment. Although you may not entirely achieve the look of a brand-new painted surface, this option should provide you with the next best thing. Approaching things this way will allow your exterior paint job to last eons longer than the 'Fluff and Buff' while letting your home look as good as your home can possibly look without completely stripping off its coatings in their entirety.

3) The 'All-In' approach.

This is where ALL the paint is entirely stripped off of whatever surface that is being painted. This approach is always QUITE the investment, and although it will last the longest in the end and definitely look the nicest (as you are essentially starting with new surfaces at this point), it is hardly ever the route chosen because of the tremendous expense always associated with it.

There are, of course, much more technical terms for the methodologies I listed as well as several varying degrees of each.

Paint purists will probably roll their eyes at how simple I present something as important as surface prep here, but this is truly the most simple way I feel that I can break down such a vital part of the painting process.

Spring is Springing! Now, What Do I Do?

Well, the first thing we should do is take a look around the exterior of our properties to see if anything is at the point that needs to be fixed and try to get ideas of how much it would cost to fix this.

Although this is a service we provide when called upon (it would be a $150 consult fee to come out and generate a list of visible repairs and the costs associated with them), this is absolutely something someone could do on their own.

Here are some key points of focus:

1) Exterior Washing of Home – does your home have dirt, mold, or mildew on it? This is a great time of year to get it washed!!

2) Window Washing – many people clean their windows twice a year (once in the spring and once in the fall). If embarking on this yourself, remember to use a squeegee vs. just a paper towel/newspaper/etc. by themselves.

3) Spring Yard Cleanup – remove leaves/debris that may have gathered over the winter, trim bushes/trees, and de-thatch the lawn. Spring is a great time to set your yard's foundation for the rest of the year.

4) Gutter System Check – make sure all downspouts are properly connected and clean/flush the gutter system to make sure there are no leaks, and the system is functioning as it should be.

5) Inspection of Paint and Stain Coatings – inspect anything that may be painted or stained outside. This includes the house itself, deck areas, sheds, detached garages/other buildings. By doing this, if any issues of peeling are noticed, they can be nipped in the bud so that they do not

lead to bigger issues (rotted wood, a paint job needing to be entirely re-done sooner than ideal, etc.).

This is definitely a broad list, but it should be able to serve as a starting point for some key ideas to pay attention to.

How to Get Your Contractor to Treat You Like GOLD!

I have been fortunate to run a contracting business for a LOOOOONG time.

Through observation over the years in dealings with our clientele and listening and watching others' situations, I have had the opportunity to pay attention to what really motivates contractors to take extra special care of their clients.

I am not simply referring to doing the best job they possibly can in line with what was originally agreed to be done.

I am referring to what are the general motivating things that make a contractor go above and beyond what they were originally scheduled to do, and happily so, at no additional charge to the client.

What I have found is quite interesting.

I was out of town but was in contact with our staff, who kept me updated as to how things were going.

We actually had two snow events while I was away (one on Saturday and one on Monday).

As I was getting ready to leave, I had a meeting with a client whose house we were in the process of finishing up.

We still had a day or two left, but because she knew I was leaving out of town, she pretty much paid the final bill in full with the exception of a few hundred dollars (she gave me $6000, and there was around $500 she was still holding toward the end).

Obviously, she did not have to do this.

Do you think her gesture went a long way? Does a one-legged duck swim in a circle? At that point, we did not know it was going to snow like it ended up doing.

For each of the two snowstorms, I instructed our staff to shovel the client out like they had never shoveled for anybody before and not charge her a dime.

Not only that, but there were a number of extra things our staff made sure they went out of the way for that were not in the original agreement, but we were more than happy to do them.

Certainly, you would have to have a good relationship with your contractor to be able to do a kind thing like this comfortably, and I appreciate that.

Most situations are along the lines where clients stick to exactly what was listed in terms of expectations in the contracts, and contractors, in turn, typically will do the same thing.

If you have a good relationship with your contractor, however, and would like to do an experiment and see how far your kindness may go, here are some tips for small actions that may end up with you being pleasantly surprised by what your contractor does in return:

- On hot days, leave a cooler full of cold drinks for the crew.

- A pot of hot coffee or access to good drinking water is always appreciated.

- Donuts, cookies, and other treats are typically looked at as exceptionally delightful!

- Buy them lunch, and you will have friends for life.

Smiling and coming across as having a nice attitude provides welcoming feelings; contractors LOVE working for nice people.

If a payment is asked for, try to work with your contractor as best you can to provide them payment. This is the ultimate and will often make your contractor forever grateful.

These are just a few quick hints.

The Golden Rule: Treat others as you would like to be treated should always be in play.

This should definitely work both ways, and I would like to think your contractor is treating you as they would like to be treated as well. Home improvement projects can be stressful situations for all involved.

A little grease in the gears in the form of varying types of kindness, though, can be worth its weight in gold in terms of assuring, above and beyond, the best outcome of any home improvement undertaking.

Navigating a Home Improvement Nightmare!

This past week, I walked into a situation that I had, sadly, seen many times before.

I had a client reach out to me who had hired someone to help them out with a home improvement project who ran into some challenges, and they kind of left the homeowner with a started but never-finished project.

The contractor was a family/friend type of referral and, from what our client knew, had done good work in the past prior to working on their home.

I had another client recently reach out to me that had some roof damage, which subsequently led to more damage to the living spaces underneath it. (As it effectively rained inside their home for quite some time on each occasion of precipitation that fell after that).

The Contractor that originally started to work on the project put a tarp on the leaky area (well after it probably should have been put on...), argued with the insurance company for the better part of a year, and now the client has a bit of a mold problem to contend with as things never really got settled.

This situation, again, was a family/friend type of referral.

After some digging, it became quite evident that this specific contractor did not seem used to working with insurance companies in these types of situations, and the client and their home ended up being put through the wringer as a by-product of things.

Fortunately, I believe LOPCO will be able to help both of these clients through each of their situations.

Unfortunately, these types of experiences often seem to be more of the rule than the exception when it comes to contractors.

We have seen very similar situations occur again and again.

I understand that not every project is going to run smoothly.

Heck, every now and again, we run into situations on projects where things just happen that we have no explanation for.

We then have to work really hard to get to the end of a project with our client while remaining on as amicable terms as possible!

I believe the difference is the experience of the contractor hired for a particular type of project as well as the systems that are in place on a company level that will help navigate through rough spots in project schedules.

This past fall, we had more rain in Southern New England than we have ever had.

Combine that with an August that was hotter and humid than normal (making outside working conditions pretty unbearable), and we had a recipe for a very uncomfortable several-month stretch, working through any project with an exterior component.

We had projects scheduled for August that did not get completed (or even started, in some cases) until much, much later.

The whole time we were facing this situation, we tried to be as accessible to our clients as possible to reassure them that they were in very good hands and that we would get them tightened up as soon as we possibly could.

I had several face-to-face meetings myself with clients, working to reassure them of things.

We even had a number of projects that had to be moved to the spring because we just simply ran out of acceptable weather to complete things.

As hectic as it was, we worked to stay the course.

Accordingly, I certainly feel bad when I hear of homeowners working through situations where they may have been taken advantage of to some capacity or the contractor that they were working with was way over their head with what the contractor thought they were getting into.

There are obviously many reasons why nightmarish home iImprovement circumstances occur.

I personally feel really good when we are able to lend a hand and help someone who has had a pit in their stomach for quite some time and is going through horribly unsettling situations that they feel they have nowhere to turn.

National Home Warranty Day?

If folks want to acknowledge one day a year as 'National Home Warranty Day,' I am TOTALLY all about it!!!—most specifically because I believe that we have the STRONGEST warranty in our industry.

We are the only company I know of that has been in business as long as we have and offers a five-year transferable warranty (in the event the property being warrantied changes ownership during the warranty period) on what we do for your home.

At first glance, 'National Home Warranty Day' seems to encompass and be meant for appliances (washing machines, stoves, refrigerators, etc.) and home electronics (TVs, video game systems, various components run by apps on your smartphone, etc.),

I would make the case that it is also meant to celebrate warranties like ours as well.

Painting and repair work on the home may not be thought of as something that is guaranteed and protected by a warranty, particularly for an extended period of time, but in our situation, this is CERTAINLY the case.

With this all being said, I urge you to celebrate. It is as important a holiday as there ever has been one (...even if I myself have no idea how to celebrate it!!!).

The BIGGEST Painting Mistake I Ever Made?

_____

As a business owner, I understand that when coaching an employee through things, sometimes thoughts may cross their mind as if I am one who doesn't make mistakes.

Every now and then, I have one of them mention this to me as I am walking through something, and I usually cannot help myself but chuckle.

Whether they believe it or not, I tell them (and I REALLY mean it!) that I make more mistakes on a daily basis than probably all of our employees combined!!

If I were to be asked what my biggest mistake in my actual painting days was, there would be several VERY good candidates!

My biggest mistake as a painter, however, I would have to say occurred way back in the year 1995... I was just starting out in business, and we were working on a new construction home.

The home was sided in cedar clapboard. There were a ton of nail holes that had to be filled throughout the home. For some reason, I thought it would be a good idea to fill all the nail holes with caulk. The home was painted with a medium-tone olive color on the body.

When the painting process was complete, and I stepped back to admire our work, the house was covered in dark-colored dots as EVERY nail hole that was filled was MUCH darker than the color all around it!!

What was determined to be the best way to fix it was to literally;

1) Dig out the caulk from every single nail hole!
2) Spot prime the nail holes.
3) Fill all the nail holes with the proper putty.
4) Spot prime the putty that was put in.
5) Completely prime all of the siding.
6) Apply two coats of finish.

As one might imagine, this was a VERY expensive problem to properly correct.

To this day, I really don't think the homeowner ever caught the mistake, as the crew jumped right on fixing things, and the home looked beautiful in the end.

My guess is that the client just thought we had an EXTREMELY extensive prep process?

The Next Big Thing in Home Improvement

Whether it is home improvement, fashion, automobiles, etc., trends come and go and usually come back around again.

One good example of this in home improvement is residential wallpapered walls.

Wallpapering one's walls used to be enormously popular as there was quite a long period of time when you would be hard-pressed to walk into someone's home without seeing some type of wallcovering somewhere, if not throughout the home.

In the last few decades, wallpapering in the home has seemingly lost its luster as more and more homeowners were opting to remove the wallpaper and paint the walls (with a few exceptions, like perhaps a bathroom).

In recent years, wallpaper (at least as it has seemed to me...) is making a bit of a comeback as more and more people are incorporating wallcovering back into their homes (the challenge now is that, because it was in such less demand, there are very few folks who know how to properly hang it in residential settings).

I am fortunate that we are one of the outfits that have kept this unique skill up...

But that is an example of a trend. Something that was popular at one point died down and then came back around again.

Between trade shows, relationships with vendors, and real field observations, I see many new and exciting things that are always popping up in our industry.

What seems to me to be the next big thing in home improvement appears to be anything that can function from an app on a smartphone.

This phenomenon has been gaining steam for several years now.

Whether it is opening your garage doors as you are pulling up to your home, controlling your home's heating/cooling system from far away, or monitoring your home through a surveillance equipment app while vacationing on a Caribbean island, the only limit appears to be the imagination!

Just as UBER and the like have dramatically changed the transportation industry, home improvement apps are chomping at the bit to affect their industry as well.

There are companies in EVERY industry aiming to be the next 'UBER.'

While I have not found a singular app that can claim this clear-cut title in our industry, I can say with great confidence that app development, and its penetration into home improvement across the board, is absolutely the 'Next Big Thing' and will continue to be so for the foreseeable future.

How Can I Best Find a Wall Stud?

If you have ever gone to hang a TV or a heavy mirror and just tried to simply nail/screw your mounting hardware randomly onto the wall, you may have been rudely awakened by the object crashing down on you!

The safest way to secure items such as these as well as pictures, plaques, memorabilia, etc., is to do so by nailing/screwing in your mounting hardware directly into the studs that are behind your walls.

A stud is the vertical support portion of your wall's framing inside the wall that the wallboard and plaster on the inside of your home are attached to (as well as what your exterior wall system is attached to).

There are electronic devices called "stud finders" that, when passed over a wall, can help you find a stud.

Many prefer this method of locating studs. Although certainly not a bad technique, it is not always my particular method of preference.

When possible, I personally like to use a strong magnet and pass it over the wall.

The magnet will be attracted to the nail or screw that the wallboard is hung by, and because the nails/screws will typically be on either side of the front of the stud, the stud should easily be able to be found by marking two nail/screw points within a couple of inches apart from each other horizontally (though most likely at different points vertically) and nailing/screwing in the middle of them.

The above-mentioned method will work like a charm in newer homes.

In older homes that did not use today's building methodology, you may have to be a little more creative.

In older homes, I would say to use the above-described "magnet"-finding methodology on the baseboards of the room as the trim carpenters often made sure they were nailing directly into the studs.

Another way would be, knowing that your electrical outlets are either fastened to the left or right of a stud, measuring 16" from the left and right sides of the electrical outlet (from both sides of it), and drilling tiny test holes with a small drill bit that is fairly long. You should hit a stud at one of these measured points.

If you are still having a challenge and are able to get in the space above the walls (attic, crawl space, etc.), you may be able to locate the studs from there.

Finding studs in order to properly hang something on your walls can be an enormously frustrating task!

However, as frustrating as it is, it is MUCH less frustrating than having a TV or large mirror come crashing down on you after you thought you might have it hung the correct way but were not properly locked into a stud after all!!

What Does it Mean to Re-Point a Chimney??

Chimney maintenance is something that is often unintentionally neglected.

After all, they are made out of brick, right? Shouldn't they be maintenance-free???

This, unfortunately, could not be further from the truth.

If we were just referring to the bricks, yes, they themselves certainly could last decades without really needing anything at all done to them.

The challenge with brick chimneys, though, is not necessarily with the bricks themselves but the mortar that holds them all together.

Weather-exposed mortar typically will last about twenty-five years before it starts to break down.

Obviously, the more weather that is able to consistently reach the mortar on any particular side of the chimney, the more accelerated the wearing process for that more weather-exposed mortar.

To combat this, the process of "tuckpointing" or "re-pointing," as it is often referred to, must be undertaken.

The way re-pointing is done is basically the old mortar is "ground" or "routed" into a depth that is uniform and then re-mortared through a mortaring process (typically by a skilled mason) that enables the mortar in between the bricks to become stabilized.

Re-pointing really is a procedure that is crucial to ensuring the longest life of the chimney possible. Re-pointing aids in preventing water from entering the chimney structure while stabilizing any weaknesses within the chimney.

Yes, it is a bit of an investment to re-point your chimney.

Re-pointing your chimney, however, is FAR more cost-effective than completely tearing down and re-building your chimney, which is EXACTLY what can happen if the mortar joints are allowed to decay to the point of no return!

What Home Renovations Provide the Most Value When Selling?

Often, I am brought in to work with a client who is thinking about putting their home on the market in perhaps the not-too-distant future.

The client typically aims at picking my brain in terms of what they can do to maximize the value of their home as cost-efficiently as possible in order to sell their home for as much as they can get, as quickly as they can sell it for when they decide to pull the trigger.

Many times, clients believe that upgrading their kitchen or bathroom is going to add an immediate large sum of value to what they are hoping to sell their home for.

Unfortunately for them, plunging a lot of resources into remodeling a kitchen or bathroom does not guarantee that you will get a huge positive gain in doing so.

Furthermore, many times, the people who end up buying the home may very well elect to demo the kitchen and/or bathroom areas in their entirety in order to more appropriately align them with their own tastes.

Based on my experience, I believe there are a number of things that can help make the sale happen quicker and, at the same time, increase the profit on the transaction.

Here is a quick list:

- Eliminate all signs of water staining (#1 red flag...)

- Eliminate any mold that might be visible around the home

- Wash the exterior of your home

- Eliminate any peeling paint on both the exterior and interior of your home

- Eliminate any "loud" paint-colored areas (neon green walls, etc.) with more neutral colors

- Do some simple landscaping (eliminate weeds, cut the lawn, trim the hedges, etc.)

- Neutralize any leaky gutters

- Perform minor interior maintenance (repair broken cabinetry, fix that dangling toilet paper holder, etc.)

- Clean the inside and outside of your window glass

- Get rid of clutter

A good number of these items may not cost you anything to do, while for some of them, you may need assistance from a professional.

Whatever the case may be, it is definitely important to put some thought into what you may be contemplating doing to your home in order to help with the sales process.

The one question I suggest asking yourself when trying to figure out whether or not to do something would be, "Does doing this either increase the margin that will be made on the home, or does it help speed up the sales process?"

I really do think it is as simple as that!

Why Winter is the Best Time to Sell Your Home

Obviously, I am FAR from a realtor.

Because of the way my business operates, though, a strong pulse on the real estate market is a by-product of which provides me tremendous insight as to how the real estate market (at least in Rhode Island...) tends to flow.

One of the people whose words I gravitate toward the most in history is Earl Nightingale, who once said, "Watch what everyone else does—do the opposite. The majority is always wrong."

Typically, I love to apply this to my business as often as I can, but in this case, I believe it applies to residential real estate as well.

I hear time and again that when people decide when exactly they aim to put their home on the market, they aim for the spring or somewhere close to it.

The problem with that?

Everyone is aiming for the spring.

Granted, in more robust sellers' markets, this may not seem like a big deal.

I believe if one truly would like to maximize the dollar amount and quickness of the sale of their home, winter would actually be the best time to work to do so.

I say this after having conversations over time with a number of realtors about this subject.

In winter, there is less competition from others trying to sell, and the buyers that are out there are VERY serious.

Beyond this, in prepping to sell the home or when a buyer buys it, lining up contractors to help in either case is a lot easier in the winter than it is in other parts of the year as, frankly, contractors, in general, are just not as busy in the winter (and, hence, can get to you quicker and you will have a better chance of your project running more smoothly than at other times of the year).

I'm sure this is definitely a debatable topic.

If you or someone you know is contemplating putting their home on the market, however, I encourage the decision to not be based on the fear of winter or relying on the seemingly ideal time of spring to put it on but to be bold and do what no one else is doing and take advantage of a perhaps golden opportunity that so many others are letting pass by them.

A Simple, Sure to be Often Overlooked Home Maintenance Initiative

_____

I sat down earlier today to work at my desk, and my desk chair literally fell apart underneath me.

It certainly could have been because I ate one too many tasty treats during the holiday season. It could have also been because the craftsman (me!) who originally assembled it was not on his 'A' game the day he put it together. Or, the option that I really believe to most likely be the case, after a period of time of use without "checking the connections," the wear on the chair sneakily crept up on me until I almost ended up on the floor this afternoon.

During the winter, when the majority of us spend more time indoors than at any other point in the year, it may not be a bad idea to take some time (probably only an hour or less) to take a spin around the home or office and just tighten up things that need to be tightened up.

This could be something similar to what I experienced earlier today, where a simple maintenance check (making sure the screws were tight) every so often would have undoubtedly kept my chair together.

It could also mean things such as checking that everything around your home or office needing batteries is properly powered and that there are re-placement batteries (that may be needed in a pinch) in a drawer or on a shelf somewhere to take the place of any dead batteries that may be found or may be on their way toward dying.

Last weekend, I was at a friend's house, and the batteries in their remote control died just as a command came up on the TV to press the 'X' button or the TV would shut down because of 'X' reason—normally a simple task, unless, of course, your batteries die as you are attempting to do the TV's bidding...

It would probably be best to make a list of simple things that one can tackle before just randomly running around guessing as to what might need some TLC.

The list could serve as a road map for all those pain-in-the-rear things that would be nice to catch before they influenced something annoying to happen that could have been prevented with a simple maintenance tweak beforehand.

From personal experience, it is much better to have an extra battery for the smoke detector on hand and a step ladder for reaching it BEFORE the annoying 'beep' starts to occur that so many of us have experienced in the past!!

Rust

Rust, perhaps one of the more unsightly things that one might see, can really take away from the cosmetic appearance of any given finish, but it can also, if left untreated, cause extraordinarily expensive repairs.

Rust forms when an iron or an alloy that contains iron (such as steel) is exposed to both oxygen and moisture over a period of time.

Another name for rust is 'iron oxide.'

If you were to search it out, you could most likely find rust everywhere—rusted nail heads on the front of someone's home, rusted steel windows, bridges, etc.

Corrosion due to rust is no joking matter.

Dealing with rust can be particularly frustrating because the rust can gradually sneak up on you over a period of time.

Left untreated, replacing an item that is rusted to the point that it needs to be replaced is normally quite an expensive endeavor.

We deal with it quite frequently as it seems like we are constantly replacing steel bulkheads, wrought iron rail systems, and the like, which have rotted out on our clients and now have to be changed.

The best way to prevent rust is to appropriately coat rust susceptible surfaces with the correct paint system right from the time they are installed.

This will ensure that these areas are rust-free for years and years without having to be tended to.

If rust has set in, all is not lost, especially if you catch it in time before it does any extensive damage.

To deal with rust that has already set in, we recommend sanding/grinding all the rust off the surface it has formed on.

From there, a good quality "rust oxide" (a term we coined years ago) primer should be applied, and then the surfaces should be properly coated with a finish that was made for these types of metal surfaces.

If not treated in this manner and, as an example, just simply coated with regular primer and finish paint, the rust will surely pop its head back up again.

Rust certainly is not pleasant to look at, nor is it pleasant for the structural integrity of the surface it is forming on.

If it can be prevented or if it can be neutralized early enough, though, rust can absolutely be kept in check!!

Should Old Siding be Removed Prior to Vinyl Siding?

As the realization of just how high home improvement costs have escalated over the past several years sets in, it is not unusual for a homeowner looking to do a vinyl siding project to approach us with the idea of leaving the previous siding on instead of stripping it completely, in an effort to save costs.

Removing old siding, however, before installing vinyl siding is an essential step for several reasons. While it may be tempting to skip this step to save time and money, doing so can lead to a host of problems and compromise the overall quality and longevity of the vinyl siding installation.

First and foremost, removing old siding allows for a thorough inspection and assessment of the underlying structure. The presence of old siding can mask potential issues such as rot, moisture damage, insect infestations, or other structural problems. By removing the old siding, any underlying damage can be identified and addressed before the installation of the new vinyl siding. This ensures a solid and stable foundation for the new siding and prevents future problems from arising.

Secondly, removing old siding provides an opportunity to improve insulation and energy efficiency. Older siding materials, such as wood or aluminum, may not have the same level of insulation properties as modern vinyl siding. By removing the old siding, it becomes possible to add insulation layers or upgrade the existing insulation, which can result in improved energy efficiency and reduced heating and cooling costs over time. This step is especially important in older homes that may not meet current insulation standards.

Furthermore, removing old siding allows for proper preparation of the exterior surface. Vinyl siding installation requires a smooth and even surface to ensure a tight fit and proper attachment. Old siding may have irregularities, such as warping, bulging, or damage, which can affect the installation process. By removing the old siding, the underlying surface can be inspected and repaired as necessary, ensuring a seamless and professional installation of the vinyl siding.

In addition, removing old siding enables the identification and resolution of any moisture-related issues. If moisture has seeped behind the old siding, it can cause mold, mildew, or rot to develop over time. These issues can compromise the structural integrity of the walls and lead to costly repairs down the line. By removing the old siding, any moisture problems can be detected early on, and appropriate measures can be taken to address them, such as repairing or replacing damaged sheathing or applying a vapor barrier.

Moreover, removing old siding allows for aesthetic improvements and customization options. Vinyl siding comes in a wide range of colors, styles, and finishes, offering homeowners the opportunity to refresh the look of their home and increase its curb appeal. Removing the old siding provides a blank canvas for the installation of the new vinyl siding, allowing for greater design flexibility and customization.

As you can see, removing old siding before installing vinyl siding is crucial for multiple reasons. It ensures a thorough inspection of the underlying structure, allows for the improvement of insulation and energy efficiency, provides proper surface preparation, identifies and resolves moisture-related issues, and enables aesthetic improvements.

Although it may require additional time and cost, removing old siding prior to vinyl siding installation is a wise investment that enhances the overall quality, durability, and appearance of the home.

Top 10 Reasons Why Smoke Detectors Commonly Go Off...

There is no secret of the importance of having smoke detectors throughout your home or business.

Whether battery-operated units or units that are hard-wired to the local fire department should they be set off, their purpose is the same: to alert us as quickly as possible if there is a potential fire in the area where the smoke detector has been set up.

The intent of smoke detectors is obviously to help save as many lives as possible in the event of a fire. Here is a quick 'Top 10' list of the most common reasons a smoke detector's alarm is triggered:

1) Burning food on the stove
2) Smoke from the fireplace
3) High humidity
4) Insects
5) Burnt toast
6) Low batteries
7) Chemical odors
8) Dust
9) Steam
10) An actual fire!

Knowing the above can help you perhaps stay ahead of the game and limit your smoke detector from going off for reasons other than true emergencies.

Obviously, if there is an actual fire, I am sure we all want the smoke detector blaring as annoyingly as possible.

However, short of an actual fire, I believe most people would rather limit the number of times the sound of the smoke detector alarm occurs.

Simple things such as making sure that the toaster is not located directly under a smoke detector or that your smoke detector batteries are changed out frequently (to avoid the maddening chirp that can occur as the batteries gradually run their useful life) can be helpful in limiting your smoke detector's alarm from sounding.

Other things may not be as controllable (such as a random insect somehow getting into the smoke detector and setting the alarm off).

Whether easily preventable or not, I am hoping this list may be helpful in providing some type of guidance as to the variety of things that may be responsible for activating the blaring alarm of a smoke detector in your home or business.

Sprucing Things up for the Holidays

Here are a number of home improvement ideas that may provide an even more hospitable feel to what may already be a welcoming setting:

- Wash the exterior of your home, particularly if you have mildew and mold around your home or moldy walkways that can often become slippery when wet.

- Paint/refinish your front door or front entrance area – This is the area that seems to get more focused on during the holidays than at any other point in the year, as sometimes folks, literally, only use certain entrances during the holidays.

- Repaint your kitchen, dining room, common bathroom, or other areas that guests may spend much time on while they are over.

- Change out carpeting in common areas or rooms where people may be hanging out.

- Wash your windows – This may seem silly, but dirty windows, depending on how your home is set up, can easily get the attention of a guest if the right light hits them.

- Make sure the hardware on doors your guests may be using is working properly and that the doors open and shut correctly – There are few things worse than being at someone's home and the common bathroom door has a lock that does not work, or its door does not close all the way…

- Have your heating system serviced – This falls under "Murphy's Law"…one of the more inopportune times for your heating system to malfunction is with guests over; having it serviced may easily help prevent a disaster.

Some of these items might be things you were planning on doing already. Knowing that you have guests coming over can often expedite getting things done that you had previously been contemplating doing for a while. I'm sure there are many other items that can be added to this list. These are just a number of them that popped into my mind.

Oil vs. Latex

Perhaps the longest-running technical debate that I have come across is the discussion of which is "better" oil or latex when it comes to exterior and interior home paint and stain products.

This is probably a subject that I could literally write a book on, as I believe it really has many different answers.

One of the things to keep in mind while speaking on the subject is that the paint manufacturers over the past few decades have had to navigate through increasingly stringent laws regarding what they are able to put and not put into oil-based primers, paints, and stains.

Most notably, the management of their VOC (Volatile Organic Compounds) content.

While doing all of this, I have noticed, more so now than ever before, that exterior oil-based finish coatings seem to encourage the growth of mildew, and I do believe there is a direct correlation with a lot of the tweaking that has been done to their chemical makeups.

With all that being said, in a nutshell, if someone were to ask me at the time of my writing this, which situations would I recommend for "oil" and which situations would I recommend for "latex," here is what my very short, abbreviated list would break down as...

Latex:
- Priming new bare wood
- Priming with the intention of neutralizing tannin bleed
- Any natural wood stain that will be top-coated with a polyurethane
- Polyurethane in certain situations
- Certain types of deck/natural exterior stain coatings (with the expectation that mildew growth may be apt to happen sooner than you might like, even with mildew inhibitors added in, and the expectation that the surfaces will have to be washed to get rid of the mildew every so often)

Oil:

(I am also including acrylic and waterborne formulated-based products in this category without getting into a deep, technical discussion about the differences between them all):

- Exterior and interior general finish coating
- Polyurethane in certain situations
- Specialty primers aimed at neutralizing specific types of exterior and interior peeling situations
- As a primer over the aforementioned specialty primers (to serve as a "bridge" primer to the finish coat)
- In place of more traditional oil-based enamels as an interior trim finish
- As a clear, water protectant

Regarding polyurethanes, there are certain situations I would recommend using oil-based polyurethanes and other situations where I would recommend using latex/acrylic-based polyurethanes. Oil polyurethanes will "yellow out" on you over a period of time, but latex/acrylic-based ones should not.

This is meant to be my brief, humble opinion on this subject.

However, it is definitely one of my most asked questions, and I thought it would be nice to provide the overview.

What is a GutterBrush?

For years, I sought out and tested different gutter debris protection system methodologies with the aim of helping our clients avoid the hassle of ensuring that their gutter systems were free, clear, and allowing water flow as best as possible throughout the year.

However, it seemed that whatever system I found, there was always a blemish in its armor.

Whether it was they easily became detached over a period of time, they allowed birds and insects to fly in through the sides of the gutter and nest in the gutter systems, or them being too "permanent" and required a bit of hoop-jumping by the manufacturer if it ever had to be removed for any type of maintenance to the gutter system, etc. there always appeared to be some type of challenge with it.

Enter GutterBrush.

While far from being a GutterBrush spokesperson, I am a GIANT advocate of the system.

GutterBrush is a cylindrical-looking brush—I often tell clients to picture the brush you used to clean the beakers out with in chemistry class being on steroids—that I find to be absolutely phenomenal!

It acts as a type of filter that allows water to flow into the gutter yet keeps leaves, pine needles, the "spinny" things that fall from oak trees, and the like from clogging the gutter.

It is super easy to install and allows very easy access if it ever needs to be removed for any type of gutter system maintenance.

The brush takes up the entire inside of the gutter, making it difficult for creatures to nest and even more challenging for ice dams to form (not its intent, but an apparent by-product of the system, along with its "black" color which helps to "warm" the gutter areas in the winter).

More information about the system can be found at www.GutterBrush. com, and I also found an informational video on YouTube!

I am certainly glad I stumbled upon GutterBrush at a trade show a number of years back.

GutterBrush has helped tons of our clients thus far, and if I have anything to do with it, it will hopefully help tons more in the time to come.

If a Piece of Wood Furniture Has a Natural Wood Finish, Can I Just Paint Right Over It?

Well...Can I?

As crazy as it may sound to some, there are times when someone may want to paint a piece of old furniture to give it an entirely new look.

This may sound odd to people who might consider themselves purists when it comes to their "wood-looking" furniture.

After all, the furniture in question was originally finished this way for a reason, no?

If it were meant to have a painted finish, then it would have had a painted finish.

If it was finished with some type of stain and polyurethane or varnish-type system, then it should ALWAYS keep that type of finish associated with it, isn't that correct?

I am one of these individuals who would be very hard to convince to paint a piece of natural-finished furniture.

However, if, for some reason, someone convinced me to help them paint their natural wood furniture, there is definitely a way that I would recommend doing it...

The most obvious starting point for me would be to make sure the piece of furniture is clean, and I recommend cleaning it with mineral spirits first.

Next, I would recommend making sure the existing coating structure is stable and that any nicks or peeled areas are sanded/buffed out.

From here, the correct binding primer should be used.

I personally recommend an alcohol-based shellac ('BIN' by Zinsser would be my "go-to" product in this situation).

I would then lightly sand the piece and apply two coats of good quality enamel, similar to what one would use if ever painting cabinetry.

There are a number of really good ones on the market.

My preference (at this point in time) is one put out by Benjamin Moore called 'ADVANCE.'

You would now be able to enjoy your painted piece of furniture.

Although not what I would typically necessarily desire, there are, without question, people who, on occasion, love to give natural wood furniture pieces a "painted" makeover.

What is the BEST Way to Remove Old Wallpaper?

_____

When it comes to working on clients' homes, there are two things that I absolutely personally despise doing more than any other...

One is re-glazing old windows. The other is removing old wallpaper.

I am very fortunate that I have been able to surround myself over the years with some very hardworking, talented people who are able to relieve me of what, for me, are the most painstaking of painstaking tasks.

Of the two, taking down wallpaper is obviously the one that is the more interior-oriented.

'Arduous' is one word that many use to describe this "fun" activity, and I think it hits it right on the head.

Elbow grease is essential when taking down wallpaper.

Over the years, we have found there to be a few other tools that may be able to assist in the process (once the wallpaper is perforated, so that these tools will be truly effective)...

1) Wallpaper steamers can be very helpful. Clearly, not everyone has a wallpaper steamer kicking around their home. If you are able to borrow or rent one, although a little cumbersome to set up and clean up, many find them extremely useful.

2) Concentrated or ready mix wallpaper removal solutions from the local hardware, paint, or box store we have found to work to varying degrees depending on the type of wallpaper situation that is being stripped (vinyl or paper-backed, paste or adhesive, how many layers, etc.).

3) A home "remedy" that you may find on the Internet (fabric softener or vinegar mixed into differing concoctions with boiling hot water as one example) could possibly be an alternate type of way of approaching things.

Taking down wallpaper is not an easy task whatsoever.

Many times, it is a process of trial and error to see what the best methodology is for a specific wallpaper removal situation.

Out of the numerous possibilities, believe it or not, our best wallpaper guy for years has sworn by just using… Boiling hot water!

No matter how you cut it, the process is the same:

- Perforate wallpaper.

- Apply "solution" (steam, wallpaper removal solution, home remedy, hot water, etc.)

- Use a putty knife or scraper to take off the wallpaper.

- Use a sponge to help remove as much of the adhesive residue as possible, and repeat until everything is all off.

At the end of the day, there is no magic button.

Good old-fashioned hard work is the most essential part of the entire process, and there is no escaping that!

How do you Clean Painted Walls?

_____

If you have painted walls in your home, there is a good chance that you have wanted to clean them, for one reason or another, at some point in time.

We have some clients who love to literally wash their walls every once in a while because it is something entwined in their DNA, and they feel like the walls should be washed now and then.

We have other clients that never wash their walls but may get an occasional mark on them from cooking grease, someone bumping something into them, or (my personal favorite) kids using the walls as an easel for their latest "art" project, etc.

No matter what the reasoning may be, there are certain ways that one should go about approaching this task.

If you are fortunate, the wall will have at least some sheen to it, which will allow for whatever it is that you are cleaning off the wall to come off more easily.

No matter how shiny or un-shiny the wall is, a test should always be done in an inconspicuous area to make sure the process used to clean the wall does not strip the wall of its finish.

For general wall cleaning, I recommend Dawn mixed with warm-to-hot water.

Dawn is a degreaser (there is a reason that biologists utilize it in cleaning up wildlife after an oil spill...) and will work wonders in terms of helping to get off oily handmarks and the like from the walls.

In removing miscellaneous spots, the first thing to determine is what it is that you are trying to clean up (a crayon mark? a tar mark? and so on...).

I then typically recommend starting from the least harsh solution possible and then proceeding from there until what you are looking to accomplish has been satisfied.

First, try some hand sanitizer on a paper towel/napkin or a rag.

The alcohol in the hand sanitizer tends to break down the characteristics of many things that may have marred the wall and allows them to be easily wiped away.

If the hand sanitizer does not work, I would try putting Windex on a rag and then wiping the area. From there, I would gradually try Goo-Gone, Oops!, and Goof-Off, in that order.

I listed them from what I have found to be least harsh to harshest, and they all should work, but all may affect the wall finish to varying degrees.

If you are not able to find the finish or get the finish appropriately matched, repainting the wall may be your only option at that point.

Whether you habitually clean your walls every so often or are just looking to clean off that unsightly smear that is driving you bonkers, it is important to have a gameplan of the right methodology for doing so, or you may end up unintentionally damaging the finish of the wall while attempting to clean it.

When is a Cricket not a "Cricket"?

If someone asks you if you have a cricket on your roof, your first inclination may very well be that you really have no idea what a cricket might be doing on your roof, but you do not believe so...

However, you may actually have one and not even realize it!!

Many times, people have chimneys that fall within the angle of their roofline, either along the roofline itself or smack dab in the middle of their roof.

When the chimney is placed in these areas, it is a prime target for water to bash the back of the chimney as it glides down the roof and somehow finds its way into the house.

Even seemingly properly flashed chimneys can fall victim to this flow of water as water does not need to have that big of an area to squeeze through and gradually work its way into your home.

A cricket, or a water diverter as some often refer to it, is a little hump that is built into the roof directly in the back of the chimney and shingled over as the rest of the roof system would be.

Once the cricket is in place, any water that heads towards the back of the chimney will easily be "diverted" around the chimney and allowed to continue its path off the roof.

If a cricket is not there, a chimney that is indeed 100% water-tight on its backside can gradually lose its effectiveness as it is beaten up with water crashing up against it over a period of time.

A cricket will help preserve the chimney's flashing and allow it not to have its normal life expedited by the constant streams of water that are natural by-products of precipitation events.

Although a cricket, in my opinion, should be built when the roof is constructed in the area where the chimney would be going, this is far from the case.

We deal with quite a number of calls from frustrated homeowners every year who have water staining near the chimney, are confident in the chimney's flashing, and are absolutely bewildered as to why the water is coming into their home.

After a brief conversation with some pictures, the light bulb often goes off, and the concept of the cricket and its benefits is immediately recognized. Though the sound of a chirping cricket on a late summer evening may be peaceful or annoying depending on who you ask, the absence of a cricket behind your chimney can lead to something that almost everyone can agree is TRULY annoying—water penetrating into the interior of your home!!

Mice, Squirrels, Raccoons—Oh My!!

_____

These "guests" take the form of many different tiny beings—none of them typically a pleasant experience to come across!

The list runs the gamut as to what they could be: mice, squirrels, raccoons (We had a client just this past week call into the office with one of these!!), and many, many more begin to make their way to warmer environments, and YES, this does include the inside of our homes.

Once they are in your home, you pretty much have three choices:

1) Welcome them with open arms as the newest member(s) of your family.

2) Try to get rid of them through some means of your own.

3) Call a professional pest control company to help you alleviate the issue.

What really may be the most helpful (and this is perhaps the most critical time to do it!) would be preventative maintenance.

There are a number of items that can be done in this regard:

- Place bait stations around the exterior and interior of your home (a professional can help with this as well) in areas where you may have seen activity in the past or in an area that you believe, for some reason, you may be susceptible.

- Do a thorough inspection of existing holes and make sure they are plugged by either yourself or a professional contractor using some viable means (keeping in mind that mice have been known to squeeze their bodies through holes that are no bigger than a dime).

- Find any area that is not an existing hole but that can easily be made into one with little effort. This includes rotted wood areas (both near the ground and higher up), weak areas in roofs, loose flashing, etc. The raccoon call we got this past week stemmed from a hole the raccoon was able to bust through the client's roof. A legitimate contractor or home inspector can certainly help you identify these areas (and the contractor should be able to help you correct anything that needs to be corrected before the little visitors are able to make their way in).

- Be sure that any trees that may be close to the house and serve as bridges for squirrels and the like are properly trimmed back. This is perhaps the easiest way for squirrels, raccoons, etc., to get access to higher areas of the house and start poking around.

- Perhaps the simplest way is to make sure that potential food sources around the home (open garbage containers, bird seed, fruit from trees dropping on the ground as a few examples…) are addressed so that they are not luring visitors that you do not want on your property.

Fall is a gorgeous season in this part of the country, and it is definitely one of the big reasons why I hear from people that they love New England so much.

Fall is also a time when non-humans seek comfortable shelter for the upcoming winter.

Maybe you enjoy them around or in your home, or maybe you don't.

However, if the prospect of waking up and seeing a fury blur run in front of the doorway of the room you are about to enter (or dozens of other potentially creepy scenarios) does NOT interest you, it may be a good time to try to get out ahead of things before you unintentionally have a home that is serving as a pit stop or more permanent living space for any one of these zealous creatures.

The Correct Treatment of Wrought Iron Rails

Wrought Iron Rails can be a BEAUTIFUL aspect of a home.

As with most areas of your home, if you are fortunate enough to have these often underappreciated works of art as decorative pieces, proper maintenance can ensure they add a touch of beauty and functionality for many, many years.

Wrought iron rails themselves are often put in places where some type of rail system is necessary (whether of wood, metal, composite material, etc.) to aid in moving about; whether it be up a walkway or up a set of stairs, they are certainly a helpful tool in helping people navigate around areas where they often walk.

An added bonus is what many consider their beauty and classic appearance.

Wrought iron rails that are located on the exterior of your home should be inspected at least once per year for any signs of rust.

The portions of the iron rails that would most likely be the place that rust would stem from would be the portion of the rail system that connects with the ground (typically a rail tied into cement or concrete) or the very top of the rail system (where your hand would touch as you held on to the rail).

To treat the rust,

- One should sand/grind off as much of the rust as possible and then prime the rusted areas with a good, rust oxide primer (a primer usually deemed "For Use on Heavily Rusted Metal").

And then,

- A good finish should follow with a product that was meant to be used on this type of metal.

Once your iron rail system has a good finish,

- Then, it is just a matter of making sure it is free of mold and that you are able to minimize (as best you can) situations where the wrought iron is "soaking" in moisture.

- This could mean keeping wet leaves and snow off the system or anything along those lines.

What the HECK is a "Stink Pipe"?

You may or may not have heard of the term "Stink Pipe" before.

If you have heard of it, there is a good chance it was in passive conversation with someone in your circle of family or friends who works in the construction trades.

A "stink pipe," as crude a term as you might think it may be, is a term used quite often in the construction trades to describe the pipe that vents out your home's sewer gasses through your roof.

The more "technical" terms for these pipes are either 'plumbing vent' or 'vent stack.'

However, I think those of us in the trades like to use the term 'stink pipe' because deep down inside each of us, a little giggle occurs every time we say it.

Stink pipes are important because they remove gas and odors from your home as well as allow fresh air into your plumbing system.

As important a feature as they are to the overall efficiency of your home's sewer process, they can also lead to an entry point for water to come into the home if they are not properly flashed or if they develop a leak over time.

I have been called out to many leaks at a client's home where they cannot figure out where a specific leak may be coming from, and after a quick examination, I determine that the leak is stemming from where the stink pipe is protruding through the roof.

In these instances, a correction has to be made by someone with experience dealing with this challenge (as with most things, if not addressed properly, the problem could get worse).

Quite often, it is a simple matter of re-working the flashing around the pipe, and then the mystery is solved as the leak, over time, is found to be neutralized.

So, if you did not know before, you know now! Sink pipes are a critical part of your home's plumbing system, and they should be maintained properly to ensure that this critical component does not develop a leak at its base as it ages.

If nothing else, you now have a new piece of trivia to bring up at your next family dinner!

Where in the WORLD are these Water Stains coming from?

Possibly one of the most disconcerting feelings of any home or business owner is seeing a water stain popping up on a ceiling within their property.

Water stains and where they actually come from are seldom thought of until they are noticed, and a queasy feeling can often set in from there...

Where is it coming from?

Do I need a new roof?

Is mold forming up there???

These are all VERY natural reactions once this phenomenon is observed. So then, what are some possibilities

Assuming you have eliminated an interior cause (leaky pipe spilling bath/toilet water from the bathroom above, etc.), there certainly are a number of potential exterior candidates for the cause. Here are several:

The Chimney Flashing:
Either where the flashing meets the chimney, how it is tied into the roof, or how it is layered in altogether.

Flashing of Roof Penetrations:
Roof penetrations could be sewer venting pipes, exhaust pipes, etc. If the flanges or flashing along any of these penetrations are compromised, this is a prime candidate area for allowing moisture to seep in.

Flashing along Dormers or Built-out areas:
The flashing in these areas can often not be installed correctly, or perhaps it does not extend far enough on either end of it to properly protect the area.

The Roof Itself:

Although not as often the culprit as you might think (most often, water stains stem from some type of flashing issue), if the roof has just worn beyond its useful life, then water staining could absolutely be coming through "nail pops" in the roof shingles, shingles whose grip or grit has worn away, etc.

The Flashing along the edges:

The drip edge, ice and water shield under the roof underlayments in these areas. A specific main purpose of these types of safeguards is to help keep water coming in from the edges of the roof; if they do not exist or are not properly installed, one definitely could have a challenge of moisture infiltrating from these points and causing some type of water staining underneath them.

As disheartening as discovering a water stain on ceiling areas can be, the source of the water stain is most often one of the items that were reviewed above.

Moisture leaks that lead to water staining can be extremely tricky to pinpoint.

Hopefully, this list may be able to shed some light on identifying potential causes of these frustratingly common annoyances!

The Challenges with Skylights!

Skylights can be an awesome feature of someone's home.

Skylights allow natural light to warm and brighten interiors in ways that artificial lights (think lightbulbs—incandescent, fluorescent, or LED) just cannot do.

If you have a vented skylight, you also have another way to increase airflow in the home and allow fresh air into your home on days when the inside may be a little stuffy, and the outside air may be a bit cooler and more refreshing.

These days, skylights (as with many things) are sleeker and fancier and have more "bells and whistles" than ever before.

Skylights can have shades associated with them (both inside and outside of the glass).

Skylights can have their features (open, closing, etc.) dictated by remote controls—and EVEN off your smartphone.

Some skylights interact with the elements as they can be solar-powered and reactive to rain (knowing when to open or close through rain-sensing technology).

As wonderful as skylights can be, they definitely have their own set of challenges.

Older skylights often present huge issues as they can leak, and the glass on them could be out of code and actually magnify sunlight to unsafe levels.

Besides the skylights themselves, the flashing around them may give way and leak.

If you are in the process of re-roofing, I always recommend that if you have older skylights, they are changed out (or covered over if, for some reason, you would like to see them removed) at that time as it is a whole bunch easier to address skylights in this manner when the old roof is off than trying to install them when they are within a roof system that is not being changed out.

Sometimes, you don't have a choice. Whatever the reason may be, the existing roof is not at the point where it needs to be changed out, and the skylights you have may be experiencing significant problems.

In these situations finding someone who truly knows how to properly change out skylights within an existing roof system can be particularly difficult.

This is where you have to be REALLY careful (if you are not, the results could be disastrous)!!

Another challenge with skylights is ongoing maintenance.

Cleaning the glass (both inside and out) is a bit different than cleaning a normal window because you often have to do it from a precarious ladder situation on the interior, and the exterior glass usually can only be cleaned from the roof.

If the skylight is vinyl on the outside and vinyl on the inside, maintaining its finish is normally not something that you have to be concerned about.

Although skylights may have a weather-resistant finish on their exterior, their interior finish can often be wood and will need to have its paint or stain kept up with.

These areas are super easy to forget about maintaining because they are so high up, and people don't really think about paying attention to them.

The sun's powerful rays, however, are brutal to skylight interior wood finishes and grossly influence an accelerated wearing process that, if you are not careful, can creep up on you and cause more work to keep up with vs. if one is actively able to remember to check their finishes every so often and address problems as necessary.

Skylights can unquestionably be a tremendous feature of one's home.

If you are able to accept and work with the challenges skylights present, then you absolutely will have an aspect to your home that greatly livens whatever room they may be located.

Painting Glossy Interior Trim…and Getting the Paint to Stick!

With all of the excitement in the residential real estate market these days, there are many folks moving into new homes.

One of the first things that people often do when they get that new set of keys is to paint the inside of the new home prior to moving in so that the paint job is knocked out before the house is filled with their belongings.

Sometimes, a professional is hired, and sometimes, people paint on their own!

For some reason, a relatively simple thing to do regarding interior trim painting is often not done, and potential problems may arise down the line as a result. The interior trim on the home can often be painted with an old oil glossy paint or an acrylic product with quite the sheen to it.

If this trim is not prepped properly, there is a good chance the top coat will not properly bond.

Perhaps you may have seen the after-effects of not properly prepping the trim?

If the trim in this particular type of situation gets nicked in any way, the small bit of peeling paint that results can easily peel off in sheets when going to fuss with it afterward.

This is often an extraordinarily frustrating situation and one that is highly avoidable.

If the trim is properly prepped when it is painted, this problem should NEVER occur.

Prepping the trim is really simple.

- The existing coating should be lightly sanded, cleaned of any dust, and then primed with an alcohol-based shellac.

That's it. Literally.

- After this, you are ready for the top coat (assuming any gaps/holes are filled to your satisfaction).

Now, there are a few different ways to approach this issue.

The above-mentioned method happens to be the one that we typically utilize.

Our company has no choice.

We have to back up our work for five years after the job is done; in every situation, we have to use what we believe will maximize the lifetime of whatever we are doing for the client.

While certainly not the only way to assure that your interior trim paint found in the conditions described will not peel, the prescribed method is one that we can guarantee will NOT introduce you to the annoyance of chasing peeling trim paint in this situation should your door frame, window frame, or baseboard be accidentally disturbed at some point in the future.

The Benefit of a Properly Flashed Chimney

There are many roofing companies out there that do a phenomenal job at roofing a home or business.

They are hardworking and knowledgeable professionals who do an absolutely fantastic job of putting a new roof on any given structure.

They do a nice job of stripping the old roof off, disposing of the corresponding debris appropriately, prepping for the new roof, installing the new roof underlayment, flashing components, and laying off the new roof itself.

However, there is one item that, as well-intentioned as many of these roofers are, often becomes the source of a head-scratching issue for the client and an unbeknownst negative knock that scars what otherwise would be pretty perfect roof jobs everywhere.

Chimneys can often rise up in the middle of one's roof, met by the roofing material around it, and if it does not have flashing correctly staggered and cut and pointed into the actual chimney itself and woven into the roof shingles or material around it the correct way, mysterious leaks may gradually make themselves known at the bewilderment of unsuspecting property owners who cannot figure out why their new roof is leaking.

The roofer is often called back in, and they themselves cannot figure things out (the important note of this being that if they knew what to look for, they most likely would have made sure things were done right the first time).

Appropriately flashing a chimney is an enormously important construction item that combines two trades (masonry and roofing) to ensure that moisture does not come in through the penetration of the chimney through the roof.

As common sense as this may seem, we run into situations all the time where much damage is caused below because of inappropriately flashed or tied-in chimneys.

If you have a mysterious leak that seems like it may be stemming from the general vicinity of where your chimney goes through your building and out of your roof, an improperly flashed chimney may be the culprit.

If you are having a challenge determining if your chimney was flashed the way it should have been or not, whether recently or from years ago, feel free to reach out to us to have a conversation about the situation, and we will be happy to provide some guidance.

Dealing with leaks and where they start from is the bane of the existence of many property owners.

Making sure that chimneys are flashed appropriately, however, is one checklist item that should not be forgotten!

What does "Cleaning out my Gutters" REALLY look like?

_____

Since I started out in the painting and repair business, I have frequently been asked, "How much does it cost to clean out my gutters?"

To me, this has always been sort of the contracting version of a loaded question.

To have someone simply scoop the loose debris from the inside of the gutters around your home should be relatively cost-efficient.

I have always been well-aware that a wide variety of hard-working, local handymen do things of this nature quite frequently for $50-$100.

I have always thought that if this is all that someone is looking to do, then the handyman route would most likely make the most sense for them.

My idea of cleaning out someone's gutters has always been quite a bit different, though.

I believe that when cleaning the gutters out, not only should they be cleaned of any loose debris, but the inside of the gutters should be thoroughly flushed with running water.

In fact, here is how my whole protocol for cleaning out someone's gutters is typically set up:

- Remove and bag any loose debris.

- Clean and flush the gutter system with running water from a hose.

- Go to each downspout connection and flush each one so that all water is properly flowing out of the gutter system, down the downspout, and emptying out of wherever it should be emptying, too.

- Check all gutter and downspout connections and seams.

- Tighten up and seal as necessary.

- Ensure the gutters are not leaking from anywhere.

- Clean the exterior of the gutter system as necessary with a Simple Green or comparable product.

Once this is all done, I would consider a gutter system "clean." As you can see, this is all VERY involved. For this, our company typically charges a flat rate of $578.

As fall quickly approaches, cleaning out gutter systems is something many people will be looking to do for fear of gutters backing water up into their soffits/the inside of their homes, etc. (Or perhaps being a catalyst for an ice dam!).

Depending on your expectations of what a "clean" gutter system means to you, it would be ENORMOUSLY helpful for whoever is undertaking the task.

The Biggest Mistake Homeowners Make When Remodeling

The biggest mistake I see homeowners make when embarking on a remodeling project is the failure to properly plan.

This failure may be due to their inexperience in taking on whatever project they are doing (as the majority of people do not remodel that often), it may be due to their desire to hurry up and just "get it done," or it may be due to a number of other reasons. Whatever the case may be, proper planning is critical.

Obviously, the larger the project, the more planning will most likely be involved (i.e., in theory, it should take a whole lot less planning to redo your roof than it would if you were adding an entire second floor to your home).

Any viable, successful business, sports team, military operation, etc., will tell you that the vast majority of the battle is won before the actual action begins.

Remodeling is no different.

When doing something beyond "simple" remodeling (with examples of "simple" remodeling being painting, changing out windows or doors, or putting on a new roof), it is critical to have sets of drawings to work off as a map"of where you want to go.

If the average person were driving from Providence, RI to Los Angeles, CA, your chances of getting there MOST efficiently are certainly MUCH better with some type of map than simply relying on the sun and the stars to guide you.

Remodeling is a similar concept.

Whether you are doing it yourself or hiring a professional, having the proper plans in place is critical.

Even for seemingly easier projects (for example, moving a wall, rearranging the first floor of a home to make it an easier living space for an older relative, etc.), having the appropriate plans in place will make things run MUCH more smoothly.

Adjustments should absolutely be able to be made as you get the actual project underway; however, having the initial plan for the project is VITALLY significant.

If hiring a professional for a more in-depth project, you most likely will be hiring either a design-build firm (where they conduct the design work in-house) or a contractor who works hand-in-hand with an architect or designer to ensure project success.

The relationship between the contractor and the architect/designer is RE-ALLY important!

I recently pulled our company out of the running for a project because I could tell (based on experience) that the architect the client had chosen was most likely going to present what I thought would be unnecessary challenges for us at some point along the course of the project.

Most contractors have at least a few architects or designers that they use regularly and are happy to steer their clients toward.

These professionals are already vetted by the contractor, and if the contractor is the one that you would really like to do the work, my suggestion would be to strongly utilize an architect or designer the contractor is comfortable with. This would most probably give your project the surest chance of things getting completed as well as possible.

Whether changing out a storm door or gutting an existing home entirely and starting completely fresh, having a proper plan in place will not only present you with the best chance of things running as smoothly as possible during the course of the work but will also go a long way toward instilling peace of mind in what is often the most unsettling of undertakings—the home improvement project!!

Painting Ceramic Tile or Glass?—Yes! This Can Be Done!

Once in a while, we get a request to help someone paint (or for advice on painting) ceramic tile or glass.

The most common initial question is often some version of "Can these types of surfaces be painted with readily available paint (paint that can be bought at the local hardware store, paint store, big box store, etc.?)"

The short answer is Yes.

However, the surfaces MUST be prepped properly and primed (with primer being the initial coat) prior to painting.

If one were to just paint regular finish paint on top of tile or glass without proper prep and priming, the finish paint would be able to easily come off.

One would most likely be even able to scratch it off with their fingernail without much effort at all!

Knowing this, what would be the most proper process for prepping and painting surfaces such as these?

The first step would be to clean the surface that is to be painted—utilizing diluted bleach/chlorine with a REALLY thorough rinsing is what I would recommend. Be sure there is no film (soap or other material) whatsoever on the surface after it is dry.

Once you have a clean, dry surface, my recommendation is to prime it with one coat of Stix Primer (made by a company called INSL-X).

A quick search online (or obviously calling local paint suppliers) would be able to tell you where it can be found locally.

We swear by this primer for this type of application.

Other primers may claim they can do the trick, but when it comes to priming ceramic tile or glass, we have found STIX to be the best in terms of promoting adhesion on these types of surfaces.

The final step would be applying the finish coat. Any high-quality finish will do the trick, depending on where the surface is located.

In other words, if you are painting exterior-facing glass, use a premium exterior finish; if you are painting ceramic tile in a bathroom, use premium bathroom paint, etc.

The reasons for painting ceramic tile or glass will vary dramatically.

Though it is not something that is done extensively, there is absolutely a good amount of these types of projects being done regularly.

If the prep and priming process is done correctly, the finish on these surfaces should last for a VERY long time.

However, if the prep and priming process is NOT done correctly, you can potentially have a very challenging peeling dilemma on your hands very soon after the project is completed.

This is another one of those projects where taking the correct steps the first time when attacking it can prevent tons of headaches and frustration if not approached in the proper manner.

Protecting Your Deck!

A feature that many Rhode Islanders enjoy around their homes is their outdoor deck.

As beautiful as they can be, the deck areas of one's home very much need to be maintained in order for them to look their best as well as to have their structure last for as long of a time as possible.

A feature that many Rhode Islanders enjoy around their homes is their outdoor deck.

As beautiful as they can be, the deck areas of one's home very much need to be maintained in order for them to look their best as well as to have their structure last for as long of a time as possible.

Here are some quick deck care tips:

- Appropriately wash the deck when necessary. Over a period of time, decks can be centers for mold and mildew growth. Washing them correctly with the proper solution is critical. There are a number of cleaners available on the market to help with this specific need.

- Inspect and perform any necessary repairs. With the rough winters we are accustomed to, it would not be surprising if your deck has a rotted piece or two that has recently emerged. As one example of accelerated wear, shoveling decks (if you partake in such things) can obviously create areas in need of repair as well. After a thorough review, it should be very apparent as to what specific repairs may be needed.

- Refinish/protect your deck. Although it may seem like an easy task to do, proper deck coating and protection systems can often be a bit involved. Correctly research what coating system should be used on your deck and address it appropriately.

When in question about proper deck care, please reach out to someone who specializes in decks to provide some guidance.

Decks are an awesome and often very relaxing piece of New England outdoor life; the correct care of them is what ensures that they will be enjoyed for years to come!

Possibly the MOST Advanced Flat Roof System YET!

Throughout our part of the country, we have quite a variety of flat roofs that typically need maintenance, minimally, once every 'x' number of years.

Flat roofs can be made from rubber, they can be made out of some type of metal, and they can even be made out of tar and gravel, among other possible building materials.

Regardless of what they are currently made out of, there is a solution that exists nowadays that offers the best protection (that we have found) in terms of protecting these areas on a long-term basis.

That solution is a modified version of the Gaco roof system.

The Gaco roof system is a roof system that I refer to as "liquefied silicone." It is a REALLY thick material that is best applied with a paint roller system and disposable brushes (do not plan on using these items again after applying the system—they will be WRECKED!).

Once properly applied, the Gaco system should last for, literally, at least fifty years before needing to be addressed again. This is not a joke. 50+ years.

One of the biggest keys behind the roof system is the primer system to which the Gaco product itself is attached.

There are specific products that Gaco recommends as a bonding primer, and I would absolutely not steer you away from those.

After a bit of experimentation, however, we have found products that we believe provide even stronger adhesion in line with the substrate to which they are initially applied.

As one example, when converting a tar and gravel roof, we suggest first vacuuming up and properly disposing of all of the gravel.

From there, we apply two coats of an alcohol-based shellac primer (we prefer BIN by Zinsser) and then two finish coats of the Gaco product.

We have found the BIN to do a great job of sealing in and neutralizing the tar on the roof and forming a coating that provides a phenomenal "bite" for the Gaco product to adhere to.

We use the BIN for rubber roofs as well.

With "old-school," rusting, ferrous metal roofs, we use a rust oxide primer as the bonding (and also "rust-neutralizing") coat once the surface has been properly prepped.

Whether using the "Gaco"-recommended primer systems or a bonding system similar to what we have developed for the Gaco product in different situations, if done properly in either case, I believe you are certain to have the most solid flat roof protection system that one will find in place on your roof, one that will not have to be touched for very possibly many decades!

Why does the Paint on Brand New Wood PEEL So Quickly?

We have gotten many calls into our offices over the years stating that the potential client was bewildered by peeling paint on a surface that was fairly brand new.

Most often, they reference a piece of siding or trim that was installed brand new or a replacement piece for another piece that had rotted out.

They are at a total loss of explanation as to why the paint on this surface would have peeled.

After all, it was brand new wood! Not only that, but it may have been brand new wood that already had primer on it from the factory prior to being installed.

Shouldn't paint under these circumstances last for years and years?

Should it? ABSOLUTELY!

Then why do so many of these situations happen?

In our experience, the challenge with these issues comes from the circumstance of the type of wood being used for these applications not being wholly receptive to accepting a paint coating to begin with.

Couple this with the primer that is used in the factories to often pre-prime the wood stock (we have found this primer to be "ok" but certainly not the most ideal, particularly with pre-primed "finger-jointed" trim...).

These two items added together create an environment that has premature paint failure" written all over it.

As one specific example, oftentimes (if one may happen to notice), when the paint peels, it will often peel back to bare wood.

Traditionally, when paint peels to bare wood, many folks, even within the paint industry, assume the issue is moisture related.

Although an easy "out" when offering up an explanation, moisture is NOT always the case.

New lumber is often subject to a phenomenon known as mill glaze.

Mill glaze is a happening that occurs as wood is processed in the mills, and an invisible layer of wax is literally embedded into the fibers of the processed wood.

Mill glaze is not visible to the naked eye and is what ultimately (from our experience) leads to premature peeling paint on new wood surfaces.

The only way to eradicate it is to vigorously abrade the surface until the paint coating that is failing is removed and the grain of the wood is raised to the point that it will be highly receptive to a paint system.

This procedure can be done through sanding (if able to be approached correctly) or by some type of media blasting (most likely best done by a professional).

Once the surface has been properly prepared and can accept a paint/stain system, normal painting/staining methodologies can be applied, and one should not have an issue with the paint/stain lasting for years and years to come.

Although frustrating, all is not lost if you have that trim around your door or that shingle siding on your home that is relatively brand new but just keeps peeling and peeling.

If the challenge is properly recognized and correctly rectified, the coating system on the surface should not peel for years to come—as one would have originally anticipated being the case when the siding or trim was initially installed!!

What to Look for when Buying a Home

Recently, I had a friend reach out to me who was about to embark on the mission of buying a new home.

She wanted to know of some things from a contractor perspective that she should be looking for when searching.

Here is an expanded checklist of what I shared with her:

- Roof condition – Start from the top. If the roof is not fairly new/water-tight, you may be fighting the tide before even moving in. Are there water stains visible on the inside of the home?

- Structural condition – Are there any things that just do not seem right from a structural perspective (weird leaning walls, cracked beam in the attic, or support column in the basement, etc.)? Is there any wood that appears as though it may be rotted?

- Electrical system condition – Has the home's electricity been recently upgraded, or is it still running on fuses in combination with old knob and tube wiring?

- Plumbing – Do all the exterior/interior water outlets seem to be functioning?

- Insulation situation – Is the home correctly insulated or insulated at all, for that matter?

- Heating and Air Conditioning situation – Does the heating system run on oil, gas, propane, etc., and are you okay with whatever the answer is? How old is the system? Would you like a home that already has a central air conditioning system prior to your move-in?

- Exterior/Interior paint condition – Is the paint intact? Do you like the colors?

- Door (including overhead garage door)/Window situations – Are the doors and windows a hundred years old or more modern? Are they more modern but kind of cheap?

- Foundation – Does the foundation seem sound? Is it bowed, warped, or cracked anywhere, and if so, to what degree?

- Driveway situation – Is this OK or in need of repair?

- Condition of exterior features – How is the condition of the garage/deck/patio/shed/landscaping? Would any of these need to be addressed immediately, or are they something that you can "live with" for a bit?

There are so many things to think about from a condition standpoint when purchasing a home.

Although this list is certainly a broad overview, hopefully, these focal points can serve as a helpful guide in your home-buying mission!

Is Vinyl REALLY Final?

A good number of people who own their own home (and/or commercial property, for that matter) would very much prefer absolutely NO maintenance whatsoever to its exterior. They could care less about the potential aesthetic beauty that often comes along with painted surfaces, and they care more about the almost certain hassle of having to keep up with it any time the paint starts to fail.

For these types of individuals, vinyl siding is a solution that is strongly attractive.

The age-old adage, "Vinyl is Final!" had to come from somewhere.

Right??

After all, vinyl will not peel or chip like paint, and there will be no need to spend thousands of dollars every so often to completely re-work the exterior as one has to plan on doing with paint if they truly are going to stay on top of their property.

Vinyl has definitely come a long way in terms of its appearance. In many instances, it has cosmetically grown to look more and more like real wood siding, it is not as susceptible to fading as it has been in the past, and the raw material it is made out of has seemingly grown increasingly durable over time as well.

So is vinyl REALLY "final"?

My stance is that it depends on what one means by "final."

Vinyl will definitely not rot or peel or anything close to these worrisome phenomena. It will "technically" last forever without having to touch it.

However, there are some things to take into consideration if one is on the fence about installing vinyl on their home or commercial property. Here are a few key focus points:

- Vinyl is still prone to mold and mildew growth, particularly as time goes on after it is installed. To remove this growth, it would have to be washed as necessary.

- If the color that is chosen loses the favor of the owner of the property over time, with today's technology, vinyl can be painted, but the question arises: If you are going to possibly want to change the color of your exterior at some point in the future, why vinyl in the first place?

- If the vinyl ever gets damaged (think hockey puck/baseball hitting the siding or perhaps accidentally bumping it with a vehicle, etc.), specifically a long period of time after it is installed, it is very likely going to be impossible (due to incremental fading over time) to get the color of the replacement pieces needed for the repair to match the existing color exactly (even if drawn from a leftover stockpile that may be kicking around the basement or garage).

I would never try to talk someone out of putting vinyl on the exterior of their home or commercial property.

I would, however, ask the individual who is contemplating installing it to think long and hard about the cons of installing the vinyl before going all in on it.

So, is vinyl REALLY final?

My answer is "Sort of..."

Washing Your Windows

Here are some window maintenance items to focus on!

- Condition of window screens – make sure that there are no gaping holes, rips, or tears that could allow unwanted pests in.

- Make sure storm windows freely move up and down, lock where they are supposed to lock, and seem like they stay within their tracking.

- If you have tilt-in windows, test each window to make sure they easily tilt in and then reconnect back into their track without an issue.

- Clean your windows – both sides (including storm windows!)! I recommend doing this twice a year (once in spring and once in fall). Use a squeegee when doing so for maximum effectiveness instead of just pushing the dirt around on the surface of the window with newspaper or paper towels.

- Check the hardware condition of your windows – ensure that all cranks and locking mechanisms are doing their job properly!

If it is found that window maintenance does need to be enacted, many local hardware stores or handymen specialize in these types of types of repairs.

Living in New England, we have a limited time period during the year where we can comfortably have our windows open and enjoy the fresh air from outside if we choose to do so.

To make sure that we make the most of this time period, staying on top of the condition of our windows is an absolute must!

Powerwashing the Exterior of Your Home or Business

Maybe you have heard of the term powerwashing before, or maybe you have not.

Powerwashing is essentially utilizing a machine to wash whatever it is you are attempting to wash (the outside of a building, walkways, etc.), which allows one to use varying degrees of pressure to help accomplish the task.

There are all types of powerwashing machines on the market.

There are hot water and cold water machines. Machines that could literally fit in the trunk of a car and other machines that need to be towed on a trailer. There are super high-pressure machines, super low-pressure machines, and everywhere in between.

There are models available to rent at almost any rental or big box store, and there are other models available only through commercial suppliers.

Utilizing a powerwasher to help in cleaning exterior areas of your home or business, if done properly, can be ENORMOUSLY helpful.

Years and years ago, I realized the value of a powerwasher firsthand when the powerwasher I was using ran out of gas at a home that I was washing, and I decided (for some insane reason!) to wash the rest of the house by hand. Hours and hours later, the job was done, but I sure did make a promise to myself that I would NEVER let my powerwasher run out of gas again!!

Often, proper powerwashing is best left up to a professional, but if you decide to powerwash an exterior area of your home or business, extraordinary care MUST be taken.

Powerwashers often incorporate chemical solutions to aid in the washing process.

Knowing the correct amount of pressure and chemicals necessary to achieve the washing job you are working to get done is critical.

Washing surfaces on the outside of one's property is obviously a necessary maintenance requirement to keep things looking nice and, possibly, even safe.

Artillery Fungus

Do you have small, black, hard spots that look like specks of tar over certain portions of the exterior of your home?

If you answered yes, chances are you have something that is called artillery fungus affecting your home.

Artillery fungus is a wood-decay fungus that likes to live in moist landscapes such as mulch. It is important to note that this fungus is aligned with all different grades of mulch and is not just limited to growth in and around "cheaper" grades.

Many times, when artillery fungus is present, it tends to end up in areas around the mulch. These areas could be the exterior of your home—including the glass on your windows—and your car if it is parked close to an affected area of mulch.

Unfortunately, because artillery fungus is so arbitrary in where it appears, there is no way to really prevent it other than utilizing alternative forms of ground cover (stone, etc.).Once it has affected your home, your options to get rid of it are VERY limited. If you have a painted home, you can prep and paint over the affected areas, and you should be ok. Artillery fungus can be scraped and cleaned off of windows with the help of a razor blade or window scraper. If the artillery fungus hits vinyl siding or your car, however, you are in a very challenging scenario. Artillery fungus cannot simply be powerwashed off or cleaned with some type of special cleaner (regardless of what may be read about it!).

Literally, the best that can be done is for the hard portion of the specks to be gently picked off. An annoying stain will be left behind that will not be able to be washed off. The stain left behind *might* be removed with an ink eraser, but this is certainly *not* guaranteed and should be tested in a small area first to make sure the finish of the substrate you are attempting to remove the stain from is *not* affected! Artillery fungus is a phenomenon that has made homeowners scratch their heads for years as they have tried to figure out what exactly it is and how they should get rid of it. Although there may not be a perfect solution for your situation if you have been affected by this, at least you will hopefully now know somewhat of what you are up against and how to possibly maneuver through this type of nuisance situation.

What is the BEST way to Maintain the Gutters in my Home?

Gutter systems are great tools for funneling away water as it is shed off the roofs of our homes and businesses.

If they are not properly maintained, however, havoc can be wreaked with water backing up into soffits, etc., and potentially causing a lot of damage.

Here are a few tips to help make sure your gutters continue to maximize what they were meant to do:

- Above all else, make sure your gutter systems are free of debris and functioning effectively. All debris should be cleaned out of them, and a water flow test should be done by running water through the system with the aid of a garden hose.

- Check to make sure that all downspout joints are connected properly (with the upper part always being connected *inside* of the lower part). Also, check to make sure that the downspouts are appropriately fastened to the building they were meant to be attached to, with downspout straps in place wherever necessary.

- Make sure all permanent joints (seams on corners or in the actual gutter runs) are sealed and do not allow water to drip. If you do have a leak, there is a product called Geocel (available through a number of local hardware and lumber retailers) that works great when painted on the inside of the gutter system at the seams with a throwaway paintbrush.

- If possible, install a gutter debris protection system for your particular gutter needs. There are quite a number of these on the market (my personal favorite is the Gutterbrush system—see www.Gutterbrush.com for more information). If you decide to go down this route, I encourage you to do your research and pick the system that seems best suited for your particular circumstances.

Gutter systems are tremendously helpful in terms of guiding water away from where it is not supposed to be.

If they are not properly maintained, however, it is quite possible to realize damaging consequences.

Take a little time to make sure that your gutter systems are properly set up and in the position to do what they were meant to do, and it will go a long way!

Recognizing Winter Damage to the Exterior of Your Home

Now that the snow has melted away, it is time to walk around our homes and assess the impact this dreary winter has incurred.

As we venture around our properties, there are certain things we should key in on with regard to our homes' exteriors; here are some suggested focus points:

- Gutters and Downspouts – Does everything seem properly connected? Is there any visible damage from ice, snow, etc.? Is there any leaking from any gutter seams when it rains?

- Roofs – Do there appear to be any missing shingles? Are there any lifting shingles? How does the overall appearance of the roof seem to be (worn? 100% intact? etc.)

- Siding and Trim – Is there any visible water staining? Is there any paint peeling/bubbling greater than what you remember? Is there any evidence of needed repairs or rotted areas?

These are just a few quick examples.

As impactful a winter that we have just experienced, it is best to jump on and take care of any damage right away rather than letting things linger into more costly repairs down the road.

Avoiding a Cabinet Painting Debacle

Recently, I heard a story of a newlywed couple who wanted to freshen up the look of their kitchen.

They thought an easy way to do this would be to paint their kitchen cabinets.

What sounded like a good idea at the time quickly developed into a nightmare.

The couple went down to the big box store, bought some 'trim' paint, went back to their home, and "went to town" on the cabinets.

Everything looked really nice when all the paint was first applied...

But then, after everything was dry, one could see paintbrush strokes and paint roller marks everywhere. On top of that, the cabinets were not prepped correctly, and the paint did not properly bond to the cabinet surfaces.

Now, every time something happens to nick the cabinetry, the paint peels, and if someone goes to pick at it, the paint keeps peeling and peeling and peeling...

My heart dropped in my stomach when I heard this.

To paint cabinetry correctly requires certain systems, products, and techniques to have things come out the way one most often would desire them to look and last.

Painting cabinetry is a rising new trend as the cost of even professionally having them done pales in comparison to what replacing them may be.

If this is a project that you are thinking about doing to your own cabinets, please make sure that the proper planning is done so that you do not end up in the same unenviable predicament as this couple in the story described above.

The two most essential pieces (along with "normal" prep) of the cabinet painting puzzle are using the correct products (bonding primer and finish) and the technique that is used in the product application process.

Usually, if one has disastrous results with their cabinet painting project, it is due to the lack of proper implementation of one of these two pieces.

Painting cabinetry can be a relatively cost-efficient way (when compared to cabinetry replacement) of livening up areas where the cabinetry is located and providing a clean, new look to the cabinetry.

However, if cabinetry painting is conducted but not done in the correct manner, the exact opposite result of what one originally set out to accomplish can easily be realized instead.

How Do Storm Doors Benefit Me?

In this day and age when central air and heating systems are all the rage, there are many who still prefer to "air out" the house as weather permits, and there are quite a few who have not delved into a central air system for their home, and pretty much the entire population aims to keep cold air out and warm air in as doors are opened and closed during colder times of the year.

For all of these circumstances, a discussion of storm door theory would probably be great to have!

As with anything else these days, there are a tremendous amount of manufacturer options to choose from when it comes to storm doors.

There are also a number of things to think about when choosing a storm door: color, style, how much glass/screening, what type of glass/screening, budget, etc.

One of the most important things one should concentrate on is how their particular storm door model will help promote energy efficiency.

Most storm doors are made to keep the heat out in the summer and the cold out in the winter.

The multiple glass panels on many modern-day storm doors assist in reducing the flow of heat into your home during the warmer months.

Having interchangeable glass and screen panels or some variation thereof is a particularly sought-after and discussed option when choosing a storm door.

Something that is often less of a focus in storm door conversations but a GREAT benefit is that storm doors aid in keeping insects (and other critters!!) out of the home!

Storm doors protect the exterior entry door that they lay in front of from accelerated wear-and-tear from the elements.

Security is another benefit of storm doors, as the majority of models certainly make it more challenging to break in.

When evaluating whether to add or upgrade a storm door, there are quite a number of items to think about!

In the end, there should not be a question as to whether a storm door can benefit you or not—only which storm door is the best fit for your specific situation?!?!

Ceiling Water Stains

Ask any experienced realtor how they feel about water stains that are found on ceilings in homes that they are trying to sell, and you will almost feel the realtor's blood pressure rise and see the look of someone who is experiencing electric shockwaves running through their heart.

Whether someone is buying a home, visiting a friend, or perhaps just inspecting their own home, coming across a water-stained ceiling often leads to speculation of greater issues than may actually exist.

- The water stain may be from an ice dam from the previous winter.

- The water stain might be from a leaky roof that has long since been fixed.

The water stain might also be coming from an unknown area that has yet to be determined and is only affected during rainstorms of certain volumes coming from certain angles!

Whatever the root cause of the water stain, it is most often preferable to neutralize the water stain and repaint the ceiling that the water stain is found on as quickly as possible.

There are a number of different remedies on the market for getting rid of water stains.

The one that I have personally found to be most effective is to first seal the water stain (assuming the source of the water stain has been corrected, and the ceiling area around it is dry and mold-free).

Our "go-to" sealant is an alcohol-based, white-pigmented shellac. If this is applied to an inactive water stain, you will NEVER have a challenge of it leaking through your ceiling finish. With other sealants, the long-term effect of them working or not can be a roll of the dice.

After the water stain is sealed, the ceiling can be painted with one or two coats (depending upon what is deemed necessary) of a finish that one may find suitable for the ceiling that is being painted.

The coming months are a great time to address water stain issues because as the weather warms, windows can often be comfortably left open, and the home/building aired out as the process is being done.

When one sees a water stain, the mind can certainly wonder as to what types of problems the home/building they are in have that are causing these stains.

The best way to avoid what can be an uncomfortable conversation down the road is to neutralize the causes of water stains and correct the water stain itself as soon as one is possibly able to do so.

If you have any questions on the water stain phenomena, feel free to reach out to us!!

Drip! Drip! Drip! How do I Know if I Need a New Roof?

Perhaps the most unsettling sound one can hear as a homeowner!

You are lying in bed, well into the night, when the peaceful patter of rain against your window or on the ground outside in the late winter is interrupted by a dripping sound that you just cannot ignore.

You pop up and discover a drip. Possibly stemming from a piece of top window trim. Possibly coming from a light fixture in the living room. Possibly leeching out a seam in the drywall of the bathroom ceiling.

Wherever the dripping is occurring, it is certainly not something fun to endure.

After the rain stops and things are cleaned up, the next obvious step is figuring out where the dripping leak is starting from.

Assuming that things are narrowed down to the roof being the point of origin, is it time to replace the roof entirely, or could it possibly be an issue that can be patched and the roof replacement being kicked down the road a little bit?

In answering this question, certain things should be investigated before ultimately answering it.

Are all penetrations properly flashed? This includes chimneys, your sewer ventilation piping, and other venting that may be coming through your roof.

Are any existing dormers properly flashed?

Inadequately installed and worn flashing is most often at the heart of the issue for the majority of these apparent leaky roof situations.

Are there any really visible areas that need to be patched? If so, this could be the issue and should be addressed as soon as possible.

Even when roofs look really worn, it may actually be a flashing issue or an area that needs minor patching, rather than an entire roof system needing to be replaced, in order to stop the dripping.

If all the flashing in the entire roof area is tight and there are no blatant areas that seem like they need patching, it may be time to look into installing a new roof.

If it appears that the roof indeed needs to be replaced, we ALWAYS recommend stripping the roof back to its sheathing, making sure the sheathing is solid, and installing a roof system in line with modern building code and the manufacturer's guidelines on the roof product that will ultimately be put into place.

"Drip...Drip...Drip..." during a rainstorm in the middle of the night is often not a pleasant sound.

Knowing the difference between a roof repair and replacement, however, will potentially save you thousands of dollars should this disturbing situation ever arise and present itself.

Do You Really Know When the Right Time Is to Paint the Exterior of Your Home?

The answer may sometimes be obvious. If the exterior of your home has widespread peeling and has not been painted for ten years or more, it is surely a good bet to seriously consider addressing the painting of the exterior as soon as possible.

Other times, the answer is not as obvious. Sometimes your home may not have been painted for close to ten years (or more!), and there is not a lick of peeling, but the color is not what it once was—now the answer becomes centered around cosmetics as one really has to decide if they would like to freshen things up and address things with a new coat of paint.

Certain things that one can look for signs that it may be time to consider properly addressing the coating on your home's exterior:

- Excessive mildew (black speckly stuff!!!) – perhaps the mildew resistance of the previous coating has worn off, and it is time to address this.

- Beyond-sporadic peeling – if your home is only peeling here and there, maybe it could be just 'touched-up' or painted where needed; :f not, perhaps a total overhaul is needed.

- Color fading – each side of your home "weathers" differently than the other sides. If it seems that the color has weathered to the point where it is inconsistent from one side to another, it could very well need to be freshened up.

- Checking or cracking of its coating – your home may not look like it is peeling upon first glance, but if you walk up to it and really inspect the paint coating on each side of the home and it appears to have tiny cracks in it, I would certainly suggest addressing things right away. This is where things start to go bad, and if you can catch it in time, you may save yourself a boatload of time and/or money by addressing things at this point.

The answer as to when to repaint one's home can sometimes be apparent and sometimes not so much.

The key is to inspect it at least once each year, and when something seems out of whack, jump on it right away!

When is the Best Time to Hire a Home Improvement Contractor?

There may be home improvement items that need to be addressed on your agenda.

You may be aiming to take them on yourself, hire a contractor for some help with them, or perhaps a combination of both.

If hiring a home improvement contractor is something you are looking to do, whether it is for painting, electric work, installing cabinetry, etc., I really do believe that spring is the very BEST time to hire someone to assist with these needs.

The biggest reason for this is, regardless of the trade, once the weather appears to turn more consistently "nice," it may be next to impossible to find someone who is most capable of executing your project in the time period that is ideal for you.

As spring hits, there is an annual rush in the industry, where the phone of everybody who is looked at as a viable option for whatever it is they do begins to ring nonstop.

At that point, it may be challenging to get the most adept people to even have a conversation about whatever project it is that you would like to talk about, never mind actually scheduling the work.

The dirty little secret in the home improvement industry is that the very best contractors pretty much have a good portion of their year already booked up by the time the weather starts to improve.

If one were to stop and think about it, there is a reason that the most sought-after contractors (those with the best reputations, guarantees, and so on…) are hard to nail down, and those that are not held in such high regard are not.

Your very best chance of catching lightning in a bottle—an awesome contractor with the time to chat about your project—is going to be during the time of year when, traditionally, the phones just aren't as busy.

Home improvement projects are really exciting endeavors!

When tackling home improvement projects on your own, scheduling can certainly be very challenging.

When tackling home improvement projects with the assistance of a hired contractor, planning can be even more intense.

Working with Insurance Companies when Your Property Has Been Damaged

No one ever expects to have to file an insurance claim for damage caused to their property.

I believe the vast majority of home and business owners alike simply consider insurance a necessary evil, paying the bill as it comes in but never really giving it much thought beyond that.

Until a tree falls on your home, a hot water tank gives out, an ice dam backs up, pipes burst, or a wide variety of the other potential culprits of property damage occur, many individuals simply do not have a clue as to the quality of their coverage or what it actually consists of.

In fact, many go through the motions, seduced by the promise of the "lowest priced insurance one will find. . .", etc., as they know they "have to" have it but don't really know much about it.

When an incident of damage does occur, that is when people REALLY find out (if they did not know already) what their coverage consists of.

Over the years, we have been very fortunate (or unfortunate, depending upon how you look at things!) to have had a good amount of experience working with insurance companies.

In my opinion, there are certainly some companies that are very good, some that are "ok," some that are not really that great, and everywhere in between.

To me, what really makes a good insurance company is the way in which they take care of their insured when a claim is filed.

When we are called to help a client put things back together after something has happened, we know that the process is going to go one of two ways.

The first (and most ideal) path the claim could take is that the adjuster assigned the claim is of a reasonable mindset and is very fair throughout the entire ordeal.

The other path is the exact opposite. The adjuster assigned the claim makes it their entire mission to try to ensure that the insurance company is able to settle the claim for as little amount of money out of their pockets as possible.

From what I have experienced, there is no middle ground or gray area, and each path has a 50/50 chance of happening.

If you are lucky enough to be connected with a 'good' adjuster, count your blessings.

If you get dealt the hand of the adjuster trying to nickel and dime and help as little as possible, all is not lost.

There are people out there known as independent adjusters who can be hired to help out with what can seem like a VERY daunting situation. They serve as advocates for the insured, will make sure your claim is maximized to its correct coverage, and typically take a modest fee of 10% of what the claim is settled for.

Even if you are in what you feel to be a fair situation, it still may not be a bad idea to get a reputable independent adjuster involved to make sure all t's are crossed and all i's are dotted.

Going through a situation where a claim has to be filed can be intimidating enough; having the feeling of your insurance company working against you can leave one feeling frustratingly hopeless.

If you would like to talk more in-depth about this topic, feel free to reach out to us.

Although we sincerely hope you never have to navigate through a property insurance claim, we also hope that you have at least a brief understanding of how to approach things if ever needed.

If you are lucky enough to be connected with a 'good' adjuster, count your blessings.

Curing the Contractor Quandary

Are you having a challenge finding a Contractor that you can trust and are confident that can help get the job done correctly?

Let's face it, finding a qualified Contractor is not easy these days.

Finding someone to replace the roof, paint the house, or change out rotted wood is challenging enough.

What happens if you are REALLY in a pinch with something that is much more specialized in nature, such as replacing an old bulkhead or diagnosing and repairing a leak? Then the challenge can often become even greater.

Taking it to another level, what happens if you are in an area that is not the easiest to get to, or in an area where there just do not happen to be that many Contractors in general, and the ones that are even "decent" are booked out for months, if not years?

This can be wholly problematic.

Not only is this an issue because of the way that something may look on the surface from a cosmetic standpoint, but home repair problems beget more problems beget even greater costs to correct things as time goes by.

As an example, an unaddressed leaking roof leads to rotting wood, leads to potential mold challenges, leads to large interior repair problems.

Something as simple as peeling exterior paint could lead to rotten siding or trim areas, which could lead to rotted structural areas underneath them.

And what often happens when we find ourselves in a predicament such as this?

We settle.

We give any breathing soul that says they are a "Contractor" the chance to help out in a desperate effort to "stop the bleeding."

When this occurs, even greater problems can come about and you have folks that may be a very good 'carpenter' fixing chimneys, and you soon find out the hard way that just because someone is a very good 'carpenter', does not mean that same someone is a very good 'mason'.

Many times, family or friends are reeled in to help because you heard that "Cousin Joe" runs his own contracting business.

One thing leads to another, and Cousin Joe is hired to repair a rotted area on the deck and the next Summer the deck caves in.

All of a sudden, Cousin Joe is nowhere to be found and if he is found, the family dynamic certainly will shift a bit (ya think?).

With this all being said, what is one to do?

The folks at LOPCO Contracting may be your answer.

LOPCO Contracting has been in business since 1995, has quite a number of crews in the field across varying trades, guarantees their work for 5 years, and services RI, MA, and CT (RI REG # 21331, MA HIC # 145887, & CT REG #HIC.0610184) – even ALL of the islands!

Whether it is replacing a roof, painting the exterior or interior of your home, replacing doors & windows, replacing rotted wood or an old deck, or pretty much any home improvement item that you can think of, reaching out to LOPCO Contracting may be the answer to the dilemma that has been keeping you up at night for as long as you can remember.

If this may be the right path for you, it is encouraged to call quickly as the early bird gets the worm and there is just so much time for things to be done in a given season.

You do not want to be one of the ones on the outside looking in, perhaps literally, as the walls are all coming down around you.

It is important to note that a call to LOPCO Contracting does not mean that a company representative is going to drop everything they are doing to rush and see you at your home, dance around the yard with you, and figure out a plan to price your project from there.

Instead, if you reach out to LOPCO Contracting, the first thing that will happen is that a phone conversation will be set up so that you can discuss your project in depth with Tom Lopatosky, the owner of the company.

Tom is a highly decorated home improvement industry veteran who has a weekly home improvement radio show (PROTALK Home Improvement Radio) which can be heard every Saturday afternoon at 2pm on 99.7FM or 630AM in the RI and nearby MA & CT area (or via the PROTALK Home Improvement Radio Podcast).

Tom has even written this book that you have just read - 'The Care And Maintenance Of A New England Home'!

If you find yourself in the middle of one of these unfortunate home improvement situations described above, literally, Tom and his company are most likely the perfect resource to turn to.

On the initial phone conversation, Tom will guide you through a process of not only reviewing your project with you, but also providing you with an idea of what it may cost to tackle properly repairing, replacing, or renovating the area(s) of concern.

Depending on how the conversation goes, both you and Tom may decide what makes the most sense to proceed from there.

Perhaps the call will purely be an informational call, or it may end up leading to you FINALLY finding someone that is able to help you out with something that has been eating away at your insides for seemingly the longest time period.

Feel free to check out their website at: LopcoContracting.com

If you think scheduling a conversation makes sense (even if only for informational purposes), reach out to LOPCO Contracting at 401-270-2664, info@LopcoContracting.com, or book a conversation right from their website (LopcoContracting.com).

Who knows, after what feels like eons of not knowing where to turn, by simply reaching out to LOPCO Contracting, you may now be on the path of certainty that leads to the cure for 'The Contractor Quandary.'

Tom Lopatosky has owned LOPCO Contracting (lopcocontracting.com), a painting & repair company located in East Providence, RI, since he broke into the home improvement industry in January of 1995.

Tom also owns Cheer UP Athletics (cheerupathletics.com), an All Star Cheerleading Gym, located in East Providence, RI, which has been in business since April of 2016, as well as The Smithfield Times (smithfieldtimesri.net) since March of 2020.

Tom has two daughters (Tamara and Ivelisse), is an avid New York Yankees and Providence College Basketball fan, and enjoys traveling.

Tom currently lists his favorite cities to travel to (in order of preference) as New Orleans, LA, San Antonio, TX, and Las Vegas, NV.

Tom is a parishioner of St. Adalbert's Church in Providence, RI, and enjoys helping out in the community wherever and whenever he is able to.

Tom has a weekly home improvement radio show (*PROTALK Home Improvement Radio* on 630AM and 99.7FM WPRO, broadcasting from East Providence, RI) which airs every Saturday at 2 p.m. and contributes monthly written home improvement pieces to a variety of publications.

Tom attended Classical High School in Providence, RI, earned his undergraduate degrees (majoring in Marketing & Finance while minoring in Computer Information Systems) at Bryant University in Smithfield, RI, and is in the process of pursuing his MBA (Master of Business Administration) at the University of South Carolina in Columbia, SC.

www.ingramcontent.com/pod-product-compliance
Lightning Source LLC
Chambersburg PA
CBHW041932260326
41914CB00010B/1270